# Blood Relative

# Blood Relative

## MICHAEL GRAY

VICTOR GOLLANCZ

LONDON

*To my wife and children*

First published in Great Britain 1998
by Victor Gollancz
An imprint of the Cassell Group
Wellington House, 125 Strand, London WC2R 0BB

© Michael Gray 1998

A catalogue record for this book is
available from the British Library.

ISBN 0 575 06608 3

Printed in Great Britain by
St Edmundsbury Press Ltd, Bury St Edmunds, Suffolk

98 99   5 4 3 2 1

# Contents

# Dramatis personae

**Countess Dr Martha Apraxine** Born in Simferopol, Russia, in 1913; daughter of Count Peter Apraxine, the Tsarina's secretary. Pictured with Prince Alexander Lieven in the concealed baby photographs with Michael Gray found in 1995.

**Count Peter Apraxine** Secretary to the Tsarina. Lived in Brussels. A regular visitor to Nikolai Couriss at Collon.

**Joseph (Joe) Boyle** Lieutenant-colonel in the Canadian militia and lover of Queen Marie of Romania. Friend of King George V and the British royal family, he was made a duke in Romania and a DSO in Britain for services rendered.

**Grigori Chebotarev** Son of Sister Valentina Chebotarev and schoolfriend of Nikolai Couriss in Tsarskoe Selo; staying with Couriss in Constantinople when the Dowager Empress and her retinue passed through. Later visited Couriss in Ireland.

**Valentina Chebotarev** Sister-in-charge of the Tsarina's annexe of the military hospital in Tsarskoe Selo. A close friend of the Tsarina and her daughters, she continued to correspond with them during their captivity in Tobolsk. Neighbour and friend of the Couriss family in Tsarskoe Selo. Died in 1919 at Novocherkassk while organizing nursing for her friend General Peter Krasnov.

**Natalie Karaulov Cooke** Born 1897, daughter of Mikhail Karaulov, a minister in Kerensky's government. A nurse in the Tsarina's annexe of the military hospital at Tsarskoe Selo. Married Ulster businessman Frank Cooke in 1915. From 1942 to 1946 she sheltered Nikolai Chebotarev and Baroness Hoyingen-Huene in her home, Croft House, in Northern Ireland. In the post-war years her house was the scene of meetings between Nikolai Chebotarev and Princess Marina. Mother of Zoe Cooke.

**Zoe Cooke** Natalie's daughter, born in 1918; a major informant for this book. Lived under the same roof as Chebotarev during the Second World War. In 1946 married an intelligence officer with Mountbatten connections. Served in the WRNS.

**Nikolai Couriss** Childhood friend of Grigori Chebotarev in Tsarskoe Selo. His father was Colonel of the Life Guards. During the Revolution, fought in the White Volunteer Army; was in the Caucasus in 1918–19. Worked in the British Consulate in Salonika and operated as a gun-runner before Alizon Fox brought him to Ireland. Married to Sana Bibikov from Ekaterinburg, he ran a Russian language school at Collon. Couriss saw Michael Gray regularly as a child and was probably responsible for the creation of both his identity in 1948 and that of Nikolai Chebotarev back in 1920.

**Sana Couriss** Born Sana Bibikov, daughter of General Bibikov, in Warsaw. An illegitimate descendant of Tsar Paul I and a cousin of Prince Paul Lieven. Her family was from Ekaterinburg. Her brother's wife was the sister of Mrs Preston, wife of the British Consul in Ekaterinburg when the imperial family disappeared.

**Maureen, Marchioness of Dufferin and Ava** One of the 'golden Guinness girls', a lifelong friend of the present Queen Mother and a friend of Princess Marina. Her son, Sheridan, was taught French by Nikolai Chebotarev in Bangor during the Second World War.

**Alizon 'Zonny' Fox** Quaker and first cousin of Neville Chamberlain. Brought Nikolai Couriss to Ireland, initially setting him up in a chicken farm.

**Alix Hill** Daughter of Alexander Hill and Olga von Berg. Her father was the cousin of the British agents George Hill and Freddie Hill, and of Dame Elizabeth Hill. Her mother was in love with Paul Stepanov, one of Rasputin's murderers, and was present in Yusupov's house on the night of the murder. Her grandfathers were both friends of the Tsar. Alix was a close friend of Nikolai Chebotarev and a major source of information for this book. She was related to Prince Alexander Lieven and worked with him in the 1940s.

**Dame Elizabeth Hill** Sister of Freddie Hill, cousin of George Hill and Natalie Cooke; Professor of Slavonic Studies at Cambridge. Sent students to Couriss' language school at Collon and visited frequently. Befriended Nikolai Chebotarev towards the end of his life and informed the author of rumours that Chebotarev was the Tsarevich.

**Freddie Hill** Cousin of George Hill and Natalie Cooke, and best man at Natalie's wedding; brother of Dame Elizabeth Hill. Cousin of Joe Boyle's deputy, George Hill.

**George Hill** Colonel Joe Boyle's deputy and one of the most active British agents in Russia during the Revolution. Recruited into the Secret Intelligence Service from the Royal Flying Corps in Salonika in 1916. Trotsky appointed him Inspector of Aviation in March 1918. Adviser on the establishment of the Cheka.

**Maureen Hill** Born Maureen Uprichard; her parents' estate adjoined that of Hilda Richardson at Moyallon, where she rode with Nikolai Chebotarev in the early 1930s. Later married another of the Hill cousins who became naval attaché in Moscow in the Stalin era. Nikolai Chebotarev told her, 'I am also Alexei.'

**Baroness Lydia von Hoyingen-Huene** Nikolai Chebotarev referred to her as his aunt and lived with her in Paris, Moyallon and Bangor. Aged about seventy in the early 1940s. Archbishop Theophan referred to her in his letters.

**General Peter Krasnov** Personal friend of Sister Chebotarev's family. His wife lived with the Chebotarevs in their house in Tsarskoe Selo while he commanded troops against the Bolsheviks. Asked Sister Chebotarev to organize White Russian nursing services in southern Russia. Pro-German, he later became General in the Cossack Division of Hitler's SS.

**Prince Alexander Lieven** Son of Prince Paul, half-brother of Prince Leonid and grandson of Tsar Alexander II's imperial chamberlain, the elder Prince Paul. Born at Rostock in 1919. A close friend of Nikolai Chebotarev in the 1940s. Appears with Dr Martha Apraxine in the hidden baby photographs of Michael Gray. Initially under surveillance by Irish military intelligence. Joined British intelligence. Employed in 1947 to bring Princess Marina back to London after her attempt at running away in Belfast. Later worked in the Foreign Language Service of the BBC as Controller of European Services.

**Sir Percy Loraine** British High Commissioner for Egypt and the Sudan; later British ambassador to Mussolini's Italy. In Egypt, Nikolai Chebotarev served as his private secretary. In 1920, as British *chargé d'affaires*, signed Chebotarev's Nansen passport. In 1946 found Chebotarev a job at the United Nations.

**Hilda Richardson** The wealthy Quaker widow whose country home in Ireland, Moyallon House, was frequently visited by Nikolai Chebotarev throughout the 1930s and became his home between 1939 and her death in 1942. She had extensive Russian and aristocratic connections.

**Princess Vera Constantinova Romanov** The oldest living Romanov, a daughter of Grand Duke Constantine. Childhood playmate of the Tsarevich Alexei.

**Archbishop Theophan** Confessor to Grand Duchesses Militsa and Stana and then to the Tsarina. Introduced the imperial family to Rasputin. Throughout the 1920s carried on a regular correspondence with Nikolai Chebotarev.

**'Count' Mikhail Tolstoy** Illegitimate descendant of Tsar Nikolai I. Soviet spy, responsible for the death of Raoul Wallenberg. Had been at school with Nikolai Couriss and was his best man. Lived at Collon but on poor terms with Couriss.

**Margaret Alicia Waring** Lady of the manor of Waringstown, the village where Michael Gray grew up. Related to Dr Martha Apraxine through her Bariatinsky relatives; her sister, Lady Roden, was a friend of Prince Alexander Lieven. Gray's surrogate parents had connections with Mrs Waring going back to the 1920s.

*See also page 270 for a family tree showing the relationships between the Tsarevich Alexei and Princess Marina, King George V and Tsar Nikolai II, the Tsarina Alexandra and Prince Philip, and the Russian imperial family and the British royal family.*

# Acknowledgements

I would like to record my thanks to those who helped me in the preparation of this book.

Special gratitude is due to Alix Hill, who was close to my father, and has been an inspiration throughout difficult times, not sparing herself in the process; to Iya and John Hulbert, whose kindness and helpfulness was evident from the outset; to Stella Tardrew, who knew my father many years ago and was able to bring me closer to him.

Ireland has shown me great kindness, notably at Collon, in the Republic. Kathleen McCarthy in particular has not only been a mine of information but has become a dear and valued friend. I also extend my thanks to Yodie and Peter Tormey, and to Kevin Loughran.

Further north, Mervyn and Helen Kinkead have proved true and reliable friends throughout. Robin and Tatiana Breen have coped admirably with the many demands I put on their translation skills, often under difficult circumstances.

Some friends, sadly, died before the book's completion. Zoe Cooke desperately wanted to live long enough to see publication; indeed, I believe her involvement gave her a new lease on life in her final years. I miss her a great deal. Peter Thornton-Pett, husband of Alix Hill, died in August 1997, and I shall always remember his sage advice and his kindness. Dr William Maples' early death was a tragedy for the scientific community; I valued his encouragement and advice, and was grateful that he took the trouble, shortly before he died, to record a last interview with me even though his time was so precious. It was Bill Maples who ensured that the world knew that two bodies were missing from the Ekaterinburg grave. Though ninety-six at the time of her death, Dame Elizabeth Hill's passing seemed untimely, so alert and perceptive was she. HSH Prince Leonid Lieven, brother of Prince Alexander, was a mine of information given with courtesy and charm. Finally, I regret very much the sudden passing of Meg Potts, the wife of Professor Bill Potts.

For their expert medical guidance I thank Professor Michael Farrell

FRCPI, FRCPC, Professor of Clinical and Neurological Science, Beaumont Hospital, Dublin and the Royal College of Surgeons in Ireland; Dr Rory O'Donnell FRCPI, FRCPG, Consultant Haematologist, Beaumont Hospital, Dublin; and Dr Colin Graham of the City Hospital in Belfast. The forensic expertise of Professor V. L. Popov, of the St Petersburg Military-Medical Academy, contributed greatly. I should also mention the help given by Dr Willi Korte and Professors William and Malcolm Potts, all of whom contributed to my understanding of the issues concerned.

I also thank the following individuals for their assistance: Nicholas and Gale Baratov, Jim and Ella Barrett, Natalie Basilievsky (*née* Wrangel), Alexandra Benckendorff, John Bidlake, Stephen Bird and Melanie Cooper of Labour Party HQ, Andrew Bond, James A. Boyle, Roy Bradford, Alan Burnside, Michael Carbyn, Alicia Chawner, Thomas and Mary Clarke, Wilfred Cooper, Dr Joan Cree, Marianne Cross, Fred Crowe, Frank Crummey (Central Services Agency, Belfast), Norman Edwards, Helene Frankel (*née* Aitov), May Friars, Rosa Frost, Douglas Gageby, Fr Alexander Garclough, Kitty Geddis, Mara Gorbadovsky, Bridie Gorman, Tim Gotts, Colin Griffiths, Baron Otto von Grottus, Corinne Hallenbeck, Baroness Jutta von Heyking, Bishop (now Metropolitan) Hilarion, Harry Haydock Hill, Maureen Hill (*née* Uprichard), Fr Patrick Hodgson, Baron Dietmar von Hoyingen-Huene, Baron Heiner von Hoyingen-Huene, Dr P. D. Hutchinson, Alistair Jackson, David Keogh, Alexandra Kishkovsky, Natasha Kosulina, Revd Dr Una Kroll, Ruairi Mac Eioghan, Jim McCammick, Joe McDonald, William McDonald, Hilda McDowell (QUB), Christopher McMullan, Jack Maginnis, Dr William Martin, Fr Michael (Brooklyn), Peggy Milburn-Fryar (*née* Sinton), Irene Millichap (Birmingham Family Health), Captain R. J. and Mrs Ruby Mitchell, Dee-Ann Moorhouse, Dr Richard Neave (University of Manchester), Sigrid Neuland, Audrey Nightingale, Dr Conor Cruise O'Brien, Michael Occleshaw, Mrs J. Pearson (Office of Population Censuses and Surveys), William A. Pinkney, Sir Ronald Preston, Sonya Bill Robertson (niece of Grigori Chebotarev), HH Princess Vera Romanov, Claire Selerie, Elena Semenlyska, Mother Seraphima, Dr Bill Shields, May Southgate, Hester and Nettie Sterritt, Don Stevenson, Pat Taffe, Stella Tardrew (*née* Dalziel), Albert Uprichard, Fr Viacheslav (Brooklyn), Princess Sophie Wachnadze, Jerry Webb, Professor Marcus Wheeler, Stephen Wright and Professor Dietmar Wulff. To anyone whose name I have inadvertently failed to mention, I extend my sincere apologies.

My thanks also to the Public Record Offices of Northern Ireland and at Kew; Irish Military Intelligence in Dublin; the Trinity College, Dublin, alumni office; the Queen's University, Belfast, records office; Carleton Atkinson Sloan Solicitors, Portadown; Lloyd Birch and Inskip Solicitors, Bristol; the Central Services Agency, Belfast; the General Medical Council; the Irish Medical Council; the *Mairie* of the 16ᵉ Arondissement, Paris; the *Mairie* of Asnières, Paris; the Linenhall Library, Belfast; the Central Library, Belfast; the British Library; the Queen's University Library; the National Newspaper Library, Colindale; the Hill family papers; *The Times*; the *Daily Mail*; the *Belfast Telegraph*; the *Belfast Newsletter*, *Paris-Soir*, *Nezavisimaya gazeta* and *Komsomolskaya pravda*.

Finally, a special word of thanks to the team who made sure that this book saw the light of day. First, to Jonathan Lloyd, my agent, who first believed and then set about translating that belief into results, keeping both the project and its author steady as we progressed; to Mike Petty, my editor, who on his 'secret' visits to Ireland has become almost part of the family and has steered the book with a sure professional hand; to Jane Blackstock, for her faith in the project from the outset and her wholehearted support, which has meant so much to me when it really counted; to Gillian Bromley, ever calm under fire, who has been a pleasure to work with and whose capacity for work never ceases to amaze; to Elizabeth Dobson, Camilla Stoddart and all the Gollancz 'family'.

Michael Gray
*August 1998*

*Northern Ireland and part of the Republic*

KEY:

**A** **Bangor**, home of Natalie Cooke from 1948, and of Michael Gray as a child

**B** **Holywood**, home of Natalie Cooke and Nikolai Chebotarev prior to 1948

**C** **Waringstown**, where Gray was brought up by surrogate parents from 1949

**D** **Moyallon**, home of Hilda Richardson and of Chebotarev prior to 1942

**E** **Ravensdale Forest**, where Gray was brought for picnics by surrogate parents

**F** **Castlebellingham**, site of garage with horseshoe-shaped doorway

**G** **Collon**, home of Nicholas Couriss and the Lievens

*See page 226 for a more detailed sketchmap of Bangor.*

## ～ I ～

# The Fuse is Lit

It was going to be an easy day. After a hectic spell at work I'd awarded myself some breathing space, and my diary for 27 April 1993 had only one engagement pencilled in: a lunchtime appointment with Bill Phillips, the local museum curator. As I drove to work through the cool, misty spring sunshine, the news from the car radio drifted over me. A bomb in the City of London; the first body identified from the Waco massacre in Texas; the Prince and Princess of Wales actually attending a function together; an Irish climber on top of Everest. Everything was happening far away. A calm day, I thought. A day for routine. How wrong I was.

Lunch over, I invited Phillips back to my office for coffee. That way, I thought, I could politely end my lobbying for a new museum to be sited in our town and round off our meeting with a few minutes of incon-sequential talk. But Phillips was not minded to continue our previous conversation – or to indulge in small talk. Suddenly, like a man anxious to get something off his chest, he launched into a new topic. Did I know about a Russian prince who had lived during the last war at Moyallon House – a country mansion about three miles away? It appeared, he went on, that this prince had been a haemophiliac. I couldn't have missed the point. Phillips knew I was an historian by training, and that even if that training had long been submerged in the systematic mayhem of being a college principal, it would not be buried so deeply that I would not string the words Russian, prince and haemophiliac together and come up with the name of the Tsarevich Alexei, son of Russia's last Tsar, Nikolai II.

Outwardly, I responded with polite interest; we parted agreeing to see if we could find out more, but – I thought – with little real intention of actually doing anything. Inwardly, I wondered why he had raised it out of the blue, why he had told me. 'You're an expert on Russia,' he had said to me unconvincingly. 'Not really,' I replied, hoping it sounded modest but knowing it was true. I had last had anything serious to do with Russia as a sixth-former, when I wrote a review of Prince

Yusupov's book on Rasputin for a literary review. Like everyone else, I had heard of the bones, allegedly those of the imperial family, which had been unearthed near Ekaterinburg in 1992. I recalled that while the first news had the entire family in the burial pit, it soon emerged that not all were there – that the bodies of the Tsarevich and one of his sisters were missing.

That evening, as my wife Muriel and I mulled over the day in the kitchen, I mentioned the conversation. She thought it was odd – interesting, but odd. While we were talking, the phone rang. It was Phillips. He had found the visitors' book of Moyallon House,[1] lent him by the current occupant, a great-nephew of the Quaker lady, Hilda Wakefield Richardson, who had been there in the Russian's time. The Russian's name, Phillips said, was Chebotarev, Nikolai Chebotarev. How do you pronounce that, he wondered? Che-bot-aref, Chay-book-aref? One current resident at Moyallon had given him the first pronunciation, another the latter. I wasn't terribly interested; I was more interested in my dinner, which by this point was waiting on the table. But he went on. There were lots of foreign names in the book, he said, many Russians among them – Countess Natalie Kleinmichel for one, Serge Poklevsky, Yuri Besonov, Serge Aitov, Natalie Grushenkov, Zachariah Rychum . . . and there was Neville Chamberlain. I asked him to drop the book over the next time he was passing so I could take a look at it. It struck me that Phillips had been very busy, very quickly. Muriel, wiser than I, said he might not have been quite as busy as I thought. Maybe he knew all this already.

Over the next few weeks, Phillips continued to proffer intriguing tit-bits which engaged me further in the story: a photograph of King Peter II of Yugoslavia found in the Moyallon basement; May Friars, daughter of Hilda Richardson's chauffeur, who not only referred to the Russian as a prince but told of a visit to Moyallon before 'the prince' arrived by Mme Olga Kerensky, a fact she backed up with a photograph and a book – *The Imperial Royal Pronouncing Dictionary*, published in 1896 – given to her by the estranged wife of the former Russian Prime Minister;[2] and the visitors' book of another Richardson mansion, Small Downs House near Deal in Kent, the home of Hilda Richardson's sister-in-law, Gertrude Leverton-Harris. It was crammed with society figures, from the novelist Henry James to the Prince of Wales himself – later King Edward VIII. Lady Louise Mountbatten, the future Queen of Sweden, was there; so was Queen Victoria's grand-daughter, Princess

Marie-Louise.[3] It was a name-dropper's paradise; but my historian's instinct hinted to me that it was more than that. Louise Mountbatten was the Tsarina Alexandra's niece and the Tsarevich's cousin. George Hill was there; and he, I knew, was a top British agent in Russia at the time of the Revolution.[4] My reading on the period had also told me that a Major Jarko Misitch was arrested in Ekaterinburg by the Bolsheviks on 4 July 1918, just twelve days before the disappearance of the Romanovs; and a Voislav Misitch appeared frequently in the Small Downs House visitors' book.[5] By now, I had begun to wonder in exactly what kind of circles this woman Hilda Richardson had moved.

I was also wondering why Phillips had suddenly latched on to me in this way. I had known him for years: we had first met in the 1960s and then, after a long gap, had had some intermittent professional contacts since the late 1980s, but these had never ripened beyond a fairly distant amiability. So why was he now seeking me out so determinedly? I had no objection – he was an agreeable man – but it was, as my wife had said on that first evening, odd. Interesting, but odd.

As the story unfolded, I took a trip with Phillips to Portrush, a bracing seaside town perched on the north Antrim coast, buffeted by the Atlantic. We called on someone I had known back in the 1960s who, Phillips had discovered, had been a friend and a kind of employer of the Russian Chebotarev during the Second World War. Captain Robert J. Mitchell, a former MP and a genial and likeable man, had known Chebotarev well; and with a background of public service, he was also a credible witness.[6] 'Bertie' Mitchell had taken over the running of the farm at Moyallon after Hilda Richardson's death in 1942 and had in effect inherited the Russian Chebotarev with it. The Russian had carried out light work, he said – collecting eggs, delivering milk, that sort of thing; the kind of tasks that could be considered agricultural 'war work'. He recounted how the Russian had worn pigskin gloves to protect his hands from the chickens. Mitchell was emphatic. 'Oh yes, he was a bleeder. They were all bleeders, weren't they, the Russian royal family?' Struck by this comment, I asked him why he mentioned the Russian royal family. Mitchell responded: 'He told me he was a cousin of the Tsar.' Mitchell was equally emphatic that the Russian had been a prince.[7] It was nothing if not intriguing, this story of a mysterious Russian prince. Imperceptibly at first, for the most part still swept along by the normal preoccupations of everyday life, I was gradually becoming hooked on this story. That visit turned out to be the first of several hundred in a quest that took me thousands of miles; a quest that, beginning so casually, was later to engulf my family and change our lives beyond all recognition.

Soon after our visit to Portrush, Phillips announced that he had to go to London on business. While he was there, he said, he would see if there were any files on the Romanovs in the Public Record Office in Kew, and he would see if he could trace Nikolai Chebotarev in the Registrar-General's records. Again, his response came quickly. Phillips telephoned me and, after an over-elaborate description of the supposed pressures and discomforts of working in the General Registry, which I later found more accurately described Dublin's register office than the reasonably comfortable conditions in London, he told me that he had found Chebotarev's death certificate. The Russian had died on 2 January 1987. At the time I didn't stop to wonder how Phillips had known where or when to look for his death; we had not known – or rather, I had not known – that the Russian 'prince' had died in England. Nor did I pause to think that without knowledge of the date of death it would have taken quite some time to search through all the volumes in the General Registry.

Over the following months the visits and phone calls from the museum curator multiplied until I was hearing from him almost daily. In June 1993, not long after his return from this trip, Phillips called in at my college office. I was busy: frantically busy, in a rush to finish Department of Education returns that were already, inevitably and as always, overdue. The pressure was compounded by the presence of my eight-year-old son, off school because of a non-teaching day when teachers attend meetings they don't want to go to. The secretaries had kept him amused on the word processor for as long as they could, but by midday that entertainment was wearing thin and Simon was firmly ensconced, drawing intently, at the end of the great Victorian mahogany board-room table which dominated my room, occasionally dashing out to my secretary's office for more paper. It was into this scene of muted panic that Phillips arrived, his entry into my secretary's outer office coinciding with one of Simon's forays in search of paper. I cannot pretend that I was exactly pleased to see him; but once he had been shown in I could not easily get rid of him. Then, in a bizarre gesture – he was not normally a demonstrative person – he slumped theatrically into the chair on the other side of my desk. I looked up, momentarily wondering what was wrong with him, before returning to the dancing page of statistics under my eyes.

'Have you seen your son?' he exclaimed, exhaling loudly.

'Yes,' I replied tersely, 'rather too much of him, today. I'm afraid I'm frightfully busy.'

'No, not that,' Phillips retorted. 'It's his appearance, don't you see? It's like seeing the Tsarevich in 3D.' Startled into attention, I glanced up, looking at both of them – the preoccupied boy and the apparently shocked curator – pondering what he had just said for the briefest of instants, but still too preoccupied with my work to do more than answer inanely, 'Oh, yes, I see what you mean. He does, rather, doesn't he?' Phillips went on, saying I should speak to my mother and find out if she had anything to do with this mysterious Russian prince. 'Bounce his name off her,' he said. My answer was meaninglessly polite.

He was not to know that I had been racked with doubts about my own parentage for years.

## ᗐ 2 ᗏ

## Questions of Upbringing

I cannot remember exactly when I first began to wonder about my parentage, but it was certainly early on in my childhood. At times it was nothing more definite than an inchoate feeling of not belonging, of being different. I can recall, as a very young child, once trying to run away – of a gathering sense of freedom as my feet pounded along the beach. But there was a lot more to it than that. I had early memories which I could not explain. One of the most persistent of these was of an extremely unusual building whose walls sloped outwards towards the roof. Another was of a car – an old car, a very long time ago – with doors which opened in a different way from modern cars, a mirror at the bottom, not the top, of the windscreen, wipers which worked from the top, not the bottom, of the windscreen, the smell of leather upholstery; pounding rain, and people, and the words: 'He's tired, get him home quickly.' For some reason – I could not explain why – I associated this scene and the strange building with another life, an earlier life, with different people from those I thought were my parents. I seemed to recall seeing one of these people years later and trying to get to her, but failing. Soon after my marriage, I told my wife about these early memories and realized that they, and the sense of not belonging, were not common to everyone.

Living as an only child in a house in the country just outside a village in Northern Ireland, itself a backwater in the 1950s, my childhood was quiet, even placid. Perhaps that is why I remembered anything remotely out of the ordinary. When I was about nine or ten, a man arrived in a Mark II Jaguar and parked at the gate of the house. Like any boy at the time, I was drawn to the car and ran down to the road from the garden where I had been playing – a part of the garden from which the gate could be seen but which could not itself be seen from the road. Later, I recalled the strangeness of the visitor's accent and, for some reason, his brown brogue shoes. He walked with a slight limp. There was nothing strange or undesirable about the encounter – he seemed an ordinary enough man, and if foreign might have been in need of directions – but my mother suddenly appeared and sent me into the house. Unusually, she was quite worked up and her tone was harsh. She began to talk to the visitor herself, in what appeared to be a friendly enough way at first, but then – as I could see from the window – became animated. I couldn't hear what was being said as the gate was too far away, but her manner, her way of talking, all spelled trouble. The explanation she gave me, that he was a tarmac man, carried no conviction at all, even with a child brought up in the Irish countryside. Tarmac men did not drive Jaguars, speak with unusual accents, dress well. Invariably they were from the Irish Republic, drove clapped-out vans, had a squad of men with them and were archetypally shady. In any case, the driveway had only recently been surfaced with tarmac. I knew at the time there was something wrong about the incident. But I kept quiet.

It wasn't the only time I was aware of interest from outside my normal childhood world. We lived about a mile outside Waringstown, from where I walked back after school every afternoon. One day, a year or two after the 'tarmac man's' visit, I was given a lift in a large Wolseley – small boys always know the make of a car – driven by an old gentleman, of decidedly Colonel Blimpish appearance, and full of polite old ladies who appeared to take an unusual interest in me. A year later, when I had gone up to the local grammar school in the nearby town of Lurgan, I saw the man again. He was Chairman of the Board of Governors, a local 'linen lord' called George McCaw. That, and the old ladies whose faces I clearly remembered, stuck in my mind.

Another oddity of my upbringing had to do with my parents' choice of holiday destinations. Even today, there are Ulster Protestants who have never set foot in the Irish Republic in their entire lives, so deep is the alienation; in the 1950s, to visit the South was unusual. But my parents frequently went there, taking me with them: in the main to County Louth, sometimes to Dublin. Often they would visit Omeath, Greenore, Carlingford – even Ravensdale Forest, where the IRA was known to train. These were strange places indeed for Ulster Protestants. Even as a child I could see the enormous difference between Omeath, with its Calvary and holy images for sale in huckster shops along the sea-front, and the fresh-faced, Sunday-closing Protestant Portrush, my parents' other haunt on the north coast, where my mother's sister lived. As a child of about eight, I recall visiting Monasterboice, an Irish monastic ruin near the small town of Collon in County Louth. On another occasion, I remembered a petrol filling station with a bizarre, horseshoe-shaped door – presumably a former forge. Years later, when my own children began to attend music lessons at the Royal Irish Academy of Music in Dublin, I passed this same filling station weekly at Castle-bellingham, a small village about eight miles from Collon.

Even at home pitfalls were laid. Among the stories my mother told me was one about my grandfather who, she said, had been a market gardener. It was a story she reiterated many times; in one of the versions, he had been from Peterborough. As a child, I had rationalized this, assuming his market garden was one I actually knew, located near my mother's child-hood home just outside Banbridge in County Down. It seemed logical. These words and images remained with me, resurfacing at a Christmas gathering at my parents' house years later, when I was grown up and married. My mother-in-law was there, as were my wife and my own children. It was one of those stultifying occasions when an extended family is unhappily confined in a single room for far too long. In conver-sation I recalled, innocently, how my mother had told me years before that my grandfather had been a market gardener. I wanted to know more. It seemed a safe enough subject; but my father's reaction was out of all proportion. He jumped up and began to pace about. 'What have you been telling him?' he growled at my mother, in a gruff and agitated voice. Everyone was shocked. A frosty silence followed. My grandfather, it seemed, had definitely not been a market gardener.

This was not the first time there had been an awkward moment between myself and my parents. There were no photographs of me as a young baby – bar one which was professionally taken – and no photo-graphs of me under the age of two with my parents. Over the years I had tried, with not much success, to get them to tell me more about my early life – to talk about what I remembered and about the incon-sistencies in the stories they had told me. I had married in 1975, and after the birth of my own children I became increasingly determined to find out more. In 1987 I began the quest in earnest; but somehow it was always swamped by the normal routines of bringing up a family and the demands of a successful career. In any case, these efforts had always been met with either a stonewall reaction or yet another incon-sistent story, depending on whether I raised the subject with both my parents together or with my mother alone. Disturbingly, they some-times shifted their ground. On one occasion in 1994, my father asked my mother outright whether my real father was a Jew – 'Was there any money in it?' he asked. Unknown to me, my wife's mother had several times tactfully raised with them the matter of whether I was adopted. My mother-in-law was a lady of some considerable talent in extracting information, but in the end she too admitted defeat. Referring to my mother, she told Muriel: 'You'll never crack that one. I've tried, but I got nowhere.'

Perhaps the most glaring instance of this familial unease over the years was a public one: at my wedding. When my father gave his speech at the reception, he announced: 'You will never know a *real* Gray.' The words jarred. It seemed as if he was telling everyone something. The guests seated around the tables exchanged glances, some nervous, some knowing. It was one of those occasions when you are uncomfortably aware of everyone's reaction at the same time, even in a room full of people. Unsurprisingly, I learned later, there was talk in my wife's family afterwards.

A year on, in 1976, we moved house and I had to change my doctor. I sent my medical card to the health authority to register with the new surgery. It did not come back. Eventually a new card appeared – with a new medical number, MQ FX 258 instead of MR FX 258. I explained this away at the time by suggesting to myself that a letter changed each time you changed doctor, though I knew this was not really the case, since nothing of the kind had happened when I had changed doctor while at university. I thought all trace of the old number had gone until, years later, I turned up an old spectacles prescription from 1973 bearing the old number. I wondered whether the change of letter was simply due to a mis-transcription by some clerk. I telephoned the Office of Population Censuses and Surveys at Smedley Hydro in Southport, to be told that MQ was the prefix for Birmingham, where my birth certificate stated that I was born, but that MR was Peterborough.[1] My mother's words echoed in my mind: 'Your grandfather was a market gardener – from Peterborough.'

That telephone call to Smedley Hydro came about because of something else which happened in 1993. My doctor, to whom I had gone for treatment of a routine throat infection – the inevitable consequence of returning to work in September and talking too much to too many people – offered to let me see my medical record, this now being permissible. Most of it was missing. There was nothing before my time at Queen's University, Belfast, in the late 1960s save for a small sleeve which had been used to contain the earlier and now missing documents.

The sleeve, though, was original and bore all the details of doctors, medical numbers and so on for that earlier period.[2]

It presented a strange picture. First of all, it had been stamped one month before I was born. The stamp read quite clearly: 'Birmingham Executive Council 5 July 1948'. My birth certificate said 5 August, and that date had been entered later by hand on another part of this cardboard sleeve. Secondly, a single word was stamped, twice, unmissably, across the sleeve: 'Cancelled'. When I later asked the Birmingham Health Authority and Smedley Hydro what this meant, the answer was not reassuring. It meant 'dead'. Thirdly, one part of the sleeve resembled a ploughed field. Closer inspection revealed that my childhood doctor, John Paton, had stamped his details over the name of an earlier doctor, and over the word 'cancelled' – with some force. Why on earth had he done it? There was ample space beneath for him to write and stamp his name. Once again Phillips was at my elbow to nudge me along. He just managed to decipher the name of the earlier doctor, along with his number. Northern Ireland had always been small, efficient and over-bureaucratized and each doctor, unlike in England, was assigned a number prefixed with his health authority code. Dr Paton's was D138 – D for 'Down'. The earlier doctor's was D135. When I rang the Central Services Agency in Belfast to confirm the details, they told me that D135 was a Dr J. McL. Bowman of Bangor, in County Down; and, sure enough, the name that I had made out underneath that of Dr Paton was 'Dr J. McL. Bowman, 44 Hamilton Road, Bangor, County Down'.[3]

I recalled that my mother, for some reason she did not reveal, would never set foot in Bangor. My grandmother, my father's mother, went there every year on holiday – a vacation she arranged to coincide with the Bangor Missionary Convention – but my mother would never go. There was always a scene. Bangor was undeniably off limits. I decided to visit Dr Bowman's surgery.

Hamilton Road is not in the part of Bangor which most people visit. Most, myself included, only ever visit the sea-front. Even through traffic would not pass via Hamilton Road. Dr Bowman's former surgery turned out to be a nondescript, grey, end-of-terrace Victorian house overlooking a public park on one side. Opposite it, however, was something which brought me up short. There, right in front of me, was the building from those early childhood memories – the building with walls that sloped outwards to the roof. I remembered it as a mix of battleship grey and green; now it was painted an unengaging shade of pink. In my mind, though, the door had been in a different place. My wife and I walked around to what is now the back of the building and there it was, sure enough, just where I remembered it – just where it had been in 1948. And traces of the earlier green and grey were visible under the pink. Now it is a social centre; but back in the late forties, I later learned, when it was built to cope with the post-war baby boom, it had been a child clinic.

These discoveries, of course, did nothing to quell the doubts I had about my origins. Quite the reverse. That I had been in Bangor was now a matter of record. That my medical record had been tampered with to remove all trace of Bangor was equally clear. What I discovered next disturbed me still further.

In January 1994, Bill Phillips had homed in on a name out of the Moyallon House visitors' book. Not only had this person been at Moyallon at the same time as Chebotarev, but the Russian had apparently left Moyallon for long periods to stay at her home. This was Zoe Lytle, the daughter of Natalie Cooke, an expatriate Russian married to an Ulster businessman.[4] The Cookes' home was at Croft House in Holywood, County Down, which is a few miles from Bangor, and in September 1948 they had moved to Princeton Road in Bangor – the continuation of Hamilton Road, where Dr Bowman had his surgery, and less than half a mile away from the doctor.

For the first time, the uneasy thought began to creep into my mind that Phillips might be right; maybe there really was something in what he had said about my son's appearance. But I kept this thought firmly at the back of my mind and did not allow it to interfere with my enquiries into Chebotarev. Once again, as so many times in the past, I put my quest into my own past into abeyance, and got on with the task in hand. Just who was Nikolai Chebotarev?

## ⁓ 3 ⁓
## Searching for the Key

Asked what I would remember most about the early stages of this quest, during those first few months after Phillips' initial visit, I would, without hesitation, answer: the sheer momentum of the discoveries. All of them seemed to point in one direction – they all suggested that Nikolai Chebotarev might well be the Tsarevich.

Within eight weeks of Phillips' first visit, an impressive array of contacts had been amassed. Not only Bertie Mitchell but John Bidlake, son of Hilda Richardson's land agent and relative Christopher Bidlake, who was actually living in Moyallon House at the same time as Chebotarev, was quite clear on the subject: Chebotarev was a prince, he said, and was related to the Tsar.[1] John Bidlake described a world long gone, a world of house parties and dressing for dinner, to which he said Chebotarev patently belonged with his fastidious, aristocratic bearing; the Russian, he said, spoke good English with a slight accent. Then there was the chauffeur's daughter May Friars, who had been given a book and photograph by Mme Kerensky. And there were more, not only in Ireland but in England too. My initial stirrings of disquiet about the reason for Phillips' sudden interest in me as a research partner dissipated in the excitement of the voyage of discovery on which we were jointly embarked.

Phillips' production of Chebotarev's death certificate led me to the undertakers in Norfolk; they in turn led me to Chebotarev's niece, Iya Zmeova, who had paid for the funeral.[2] She lived in Holt, a small Georgian market town in Norfolk – and, in another of the many perplexing coincidences which littered this business, the base for our last two family holidays. For years I had wanted to go to Norfolk; eventually, in 1990, my wife was persuaded and we took the children over in the summer. We loved the place and felt so much at ease that we used to talk wistfully about retiring there eventually. In 1991 and 1992 we went back, and in 1993 we were to make our fourth visit. How strange it was that the place where we had spent time on our summer holidays for the past couple of years was now the focus of my attention for quite other reasons. Musing that I must have walked past Chebotarev's grave in the churchyard there dozens of times without knowing it, I reckoned that our holiday plans could be adjusted to pick up some of the threads that led out from Moyallon. When the college closed in late June we could cross to England and take the investigation with us. It would be a better diversion, after all, than the usual novel or detective story – a sort of 'living book' that we were writing as we went along. My wife, though warier than I at the beginning, had by now become intrigued by the unfolding story, and the children, Antonia and Simon, were remarkably good-humoured about putting up with 'Daddy's research' on their holidays – though they got plenty of other entertainment with their mother while I was ferreting about. Later on, as the import of my discoveries became clearer and they were a little older, I was glad I had taken them along on my trips from the beginning; they had, after all, a right to know this history.

Peggy Sinton was the daughter of the owners of Banford House, an estate adjacent to the Richardsons'. Now Mrs Milburn-Fryar, she was living near Dorking. Peggy's schoolfriend, Stella Tardrew, or Stella Dalziel as she was back then in the 1930s, had been a former girlfriend of Nikolai Chebotarev. Most interesting of all was Maureen Uprichard, whose parents' estate also abutted that of Hilda Richardson at Moyallon. Just two days before we set out for Norfolk in June 1993, Phillips had tracked down her brother Albert, who, with his sister, had gone riding with Chebotarev back in the early thirties. He told me that the Russian, according to Albert, had told Maureen that his real name was not Nikolai but Alexei.[3] Maureen was now Mrs Hill, having married a Captain Hill, a former British naval attaché in Moscow in Stalin's time. I simply had to speak to her.

Maureen Hill lives in the small village of Loxley near Stratford-upon-Avon. I have never encountered such steep driveways and managed to remove a mud-flap reversing up to her house. It was worth the damage and the diversion. Mrs Hill was a very credible witness. She explained how she had lived in Moscow when her husband had been naval attaché there: how she had watched Stalin's car go past her apartment in the Arbat, how she had dodged the secret police – her flat had two doors – and how her son had been born there. Her husband's family, the Hills, she said were related through several marriages to the family of Prince Paul Lieven, the Tsar's Grand Master of Ceremonies, and to their cousins the Sayn-Wittgensteins. They used to see their relatives' portraits up in official buildings but kept quiet about the connection. Impressively crisp and clear-minded, Maureen Hill was quite definite about what Nikolai Chebotarev had said to her. She had first met him in 1928 when, as a schoolgirl, she had been recruited by Hilda Richardson as a riding companion for the Russian. 'I don't know if he was a cousin of the Tsar, but he was a prince.' They spoke in French; she described him as an enigmatic figure, shy and not keen to talk, reticent about his past. 'Haemophilia', she said, 'rings a distant bell. Mrs Richardson told us we must be careful with him. "I entrust him to you. He must not sustain a fall," she said.' Then came the information which really had an impact on me. Maureen told how one day, when out riding, he had said to her, 'You may call me Nicky but I'm also Alexei.' I took her over this several times but she was clear and unshakeable.[4] I felt a slight chill. I think it was then that I began to believe our 'research hypothesis' might be true.

From Warwickshire we went straight on to Norfolk. Standing by Nikolai Chebotarev's grave in Holt churchyard, all sorts of feelings jostled through my mind. There was a Russian cross on the tombstone bearing his name, in the spelling customary at the turn of the century: 'Nicholas Tchebotareff'. Was this where it had all ended, the final resting place of that little boy in those photographs from so long ago, from that privileged and gilded past? I looked at my own son standing by that grave with me, so like Alexei in appearance, just as Phillips had said. Surely it was impossible? Dismissing these distracting thoughts, I pulled myself back to the task in hand and set off up the walkway from St Andrew's Church back to the road. My destination was a pleasant Georgian building, very much like the squared house a child would draw. The pale green double front door was shielded by a curtain against the sun. The window-blinds were down. Formidable gates at the side were firmly shut. Barriers, I thought. This was his niece. What if she knew who he really was – if he really was? Would she put up barriers? Gingerly, I rang the bell. After a few moments that seemed like an eternity, a lady came to the door. What could I say? I stammered one word: 'Moyallon.'

'You'd better come in,' she said.

Once inside, the first thing that struck me was a photograph of the imperial family prominently displayed on the mantelpiece. It did not increase my composure. Nor did Iya's first answer. I asked, had Nikolai been a prince? 'He might have been,' she said (a response she later revised to 'not to my knowledge').[5] Nearby was another photograph in a silver frame. It was of a young man in white uniform: 'Uncle Nicky', taken when he was an officer cadet at Bela Cirkva in Yugoslavia in 1923.

Iya herself was small of stature with luminous blue-grey eyes, an engaging smile and the hint of a Russian accent. 'Was Iya short for something?' I ventured: 'Anastasia?'

'No, just Iya, that's all.'

Her husband, John Hulbert, was a slightly stooped, well-built, bluff Englishman. Both were friendly – much more so than I had allowed myself to expect. I had tried to contact her through the rector of her church before visiting, only to be told that she was very reserved and had never recovered from the deaths of her mother and uncle. So I was hugely relieved and encouraged to be made so welcome.

Like a bridge through time, Moyallon led us into conversation. On the wall hung a painting of one of the garden walkways at the Irish country house. Iya had fond memories of it back in 1937, of 'Aunt Hilda' and rides in her chauffeur-driven white, open-top Alvis Silver Eagle. She recalled how Hilda had thrown sweets to the village children as they had driven along. I was able to show her a copy of the page from the visitors' book, dated 31 August 1927, on which her own signature appeared alongside that of her uncle, Nikolai Chebotarev, and those of Countess Natalie Kleinmichel, Catherine Takronzov, Helene Aitov, Serge Aitov, Marguerite Aitov, Carlotta Block – and Isaura Loraine, who, it turned out, had been Iya's guardian when, in 1932, her uncle had brought the fourteen-year-old girl to England from Yugoslavia. Why, I wondered, had she needed a guardian when her mother was still alive? Her mother, Lydia Zmeova, remained behind – Iya did not see her for twenty years, until after the war. Isaura was 'a funny woman'; she had gone to see Iya's mother in Yugoslavia without telling her. Isaura's brother Sir Percy Loraine, it emerged, appointed British High Commissioner to Egypt and the Sudan in 1929, had taken Chebotarev with him to Egypt as his private secretary. An Egyptian official had refused to accept her uncle's Nansen passport, Iya said; but Sir Percy soon fixed him, he 'got in the boot'. Feeling my ignorance, I asked what a Nansen passport was and discovered that it was a document issued by the office of the League of Nations High Commissioner for Refugees, the explorer Nansen, to persons left stateless after the First World War. 'You just went along to the consulate to get it.' This apparently rather dubious piece of paper seemed to carry very little clout – much less, clearly, than the authority of a British High Commissioner. Sir Percy had also, it emerged, found a job for Chebotarev some years later, at the United

Nations in New York after the Second World War. Slowly, the pattern of the Russian's life was emerging.

'Uncle Nicky,' she said, 'was up there. He moved in very exalted circles. We were the poor relations. I never really knew him as a person until he moved back to England after retiring from the UN – in the 1970s. He danced with Princess Marina and knew the Duke of Edinburgh when he was a little boy in Paris. He knew the pretender to the Russian throne, whom he visited often. He knew the Grabbes.'

I stopped her there. 'Do you know who the Grabbes were?' I interjected.

'No-o,' came the hesitant reply.

'Count Grabbe was commander of the Tsar's bodyguard, the Cossack Konvoy,' I replied. She seemed taken aback for a moment. Taking the opportunity, the opening in the conversation, I told her some of the things I had been hearing about her uncle – that he was a prince, that he was a relative of the Tsar. Already, Iya had asked me a couple of times if I thought the imperial family had survived. My answers had been non-committal, a suppose-so with reference to the two bodies the press said were missing from the Ekaterinburg burial pit. Now I asked: Was that her mother's name inscribed on the gravestone with that of Chebotarev? Yes, came the reply, but her dates are wrong. Had there ever been a Chebotarev family reunion? No. So no one ever saw any relatives? No. Her uncle was said to have brought her out of Russia but she didn't actually recall seeing him before they travelled together from Yugoslavia in 1933. After the 1930s, she didn't see him again until 1953, when her mother, having finally got out of the eastern bloc, came to live with her in Northern Ireland, where her husband John was stationed with the RAF. The thought crossed my mind: there were two bodies buried in Holt and there were two bodies missing in Ekaterinburg. Had I stumbled on Alexei and one of his sisters?

Iya and John got Uncle Nicky's photograph album out for me – a Pandora's box of a lifetime. One photograph, in particular, caught my eye. It showed Chebotarev sitting with three others round a table (see plates). On the back, it had been neatly labelled in his own hand: 'Davos, 2.2.1938 – Frances and Thom, Lasco Bradley, A and Olga Knoop', referring to himself not as 'N' for Nikolai, but as 'A' – for Alexei? In another photograph I recognized Princess Xenia of Russia (see plates), who had lived on Long Island and had been for many years the sponsor of 'Anna Anderson', who claimed to be the Tsar's daughter Anastasia. Another photograph was produced from upstairs. It was of the Tsarina's sister, Grand Duchess Elizabeth. In an original ebonized rectangular frame, with a brass surround to the oval picture within it surmounted by a gilded imperial crown, it exuded quality (see plates). It had never been opened at the back, but had its original seal. Nikolai kept this by his bedside, his niece explained – always.

Evening had passed and our conversation had rambled on towards midnight. I took my leave but arranged to come back, leaving with them the recently published coffee-table book compiled by Prince Michael of Greece, made up of photographs newly released from the Russian archives. I couldn't help noticing the impact that photographs of the Tsarevich's sister Grand Duchess Maria had on them. For myself, I came away armed with a clutch of Chebotarev's own photographs for copying – and with Chebotarev's own favourite saying, repeated to me by Iya, reverberating in my mind: 'Just because you are born in a stable, it doesn't make you a horse.' He was interesting, this Chebotarev: dancing with Princess Marina and fraternizing with the self-proclaimed Tsar-in-exile, Grand Duke Vladimir, in Madrid. Going over the evening, I was struck above all by Iya's remarkable lack of curiosity about her own family.

Subsequent visits to the Hulbert household during that holiday told me more about Chebotarev's habits and character. Iya and John said his visits were 'quite a production'. He expected to be met by vodka and bortsch, followed by a hot bath and a two-hour rest. Iya said he spoke with a heavy accent. John said he created 'quite a stir' walking through the streets of Holt, immaculate in dress and demeanour. Iya told me he had married – about 1954 – a lady older than himself, too old to have children (a point which seemed to need emphasis). Fanny Tate had been her name; she was a widow and had a daughter by her first marriage. Iya did not appear to know her maiden name. Fanny, like Chebotarev, had worked in the language section of the UN. They had married, said Iya, at Sea Cliff on Long Island; Nikolai was a leading light of the church there. His wedding, she said, had been blessed by General Wrangel's widow, who was present.[6] I filed away this information about a marriage. I could check all that, I thought.

And so I did, when I got back home in August – only to find that nothing was quite that simple. Telephoning the Kazan Orthodox Church at Sea Cliff, I found that Nikolai Chebotarev's wedding had definitely not taken place there. I spoke to Alexandra Kishkovsky, the daughter

of the priest, about Baroness Wrangel's having blessed the wedding; she
suggested I phone the Baroness's daughter, Mrs Natalie Basilievsky.
Natalie Basilievsky remembered Chebotarev all right, but she said her
mother had not attended his wedding, let alone blessed it – adding, how
could she do that, she was not a priest?[7] So much for Iya's story, I
thought. No, Chebotarev had simply appeared presenting Fanny as his
wife, said Natalie. Maybe they married in Brooklyn? They went to
church on 93rd Street. They had no children, she added – Fanny was too
old. Again, that piece of information seemed to loom large. Natalie also
testified to Nikolai's continuing association with the Grabbes, confirming that Chebotarev had attended the Kazan Church and lived before his
marriage in Locust Grove, Sea Cliff, with Dmitri Grabbe – the nephew
of the Count Grabbe who had been commander of the Tsar's bodyguard.
There had been a photograph in his album of the same Dmitri as a boy,
dated Nice, 1924.

I checked a seemingly endless list of Orthodox churches in and around
New York – the Church of the Transfiguration on 228 North 12th
Street, Brooklyn; the Russian Orthodox Cathedral on 93rd Street; Holy
Trinity in Glenmore Avenue, Brooklyn; Holy Trinity in East Meadow
. . . Eventually I contacted Bishop Hilarion, the deputy to the Metropolitan, the head of the Orthodox Church in America, and head of the
Jordanville Monastery. Obligingly, he checked all his parishes: there was
no record of such a marriage.[8] Temporarily stumped, I reported all this
back to Bill Phillips, who had started me out on the trail in the first place
– and he came back with an intriguing suggestion. Apparently second
marriages are 'blessed' by the Russian Orthodox Church. For example,
he said, the first marriage of Prince George Bagration-Mukhransky – the
nephew of Princess Vera Constantinova Romanov – ended in divorce;
but his second, and the christening of his child, were both 'blessed' by
the Orthodox Church. I wondered if Chebotarev could have had an
earlier marriage which had ended in divorce.

That July, on a further visit to her home, Iya had given me a fuller
account of her own background, and of Chebotarev's: how he had
attended cadet school in Bela Cirkva, Yugoslavia, in the early 1920s; how
he had then moved to Paris, attended the Sorbonne, visited 'Aunt Hilda'
in Ireland; how in the early stages of the Second World War he had had
the singular misfortune to have a flat in Paris bombed in the single raid
the Germans mounted on what became an open city. During the 1920s
and 1930s he had shared a flat in the rue Marois with an elderly lady,

Baroness de Huene – a name I had already encountered in the Moyallon visitors' book. Everyone at Moyallon had known her as Nikolai's aunt. Iya was less sure of the connection. 'Something on my mother's side,' was her assessment; 'a great-great aunt, maybe.' That would have made her about a hundred years old in 1940, I thought. I had not imagined her that age. It didn't accord with what they said at Moyallon, according to which she would have been about seventy in the early 1940s. At Moyallon, they believed her husband had been Governor-General of Poland. 'He probably was,' said Iya. Her own father, Colonel Michael Zmeov, had been twenty years older than her mother. For him, the First World War had started at Harbin in northern China, and after the Revolution he had been in charge of transportation for the White government on the Trans-Siberian railway. He had died in 1943 and was buried at Sprikovitse, a small village near Zagreb. Iya herself had grown up in Yugoslavia until that move to England in 1933. These details, while interesting in themselves, did not bring me any nearer to Nikolai Chebotarev. I realized that uncle and niece had not been particularly close and had not seen each other all that often, certainly not until the 1970s, after his retirement. It was time, I felt, to move on and see our other contacts. Taking our leave, I scrawled Nikolai Chebotarev's old address in my notebook, promised to return and headed south.

My first port of call was Dorking, where I had arranged to meet Chebotarev's former girlfriend, Stella Dalziel, and her friend Peggy Sinton, now Mrs Milburn-Fryar. The two women had kept up their friendship since schooldays, and I arranged dinner for everyone at our hotel, The White Horse. Stella was a delight. It was not hard to see why Chebotarev had been captivated by her. Despite her eighty years, she still had that sparkle, that compelling vivacity, a sort of bubbly, champagne quality, which must have entranced him back in the 1930s. Peggy was more reserved but, just as Chebotarev had described her to the servants at Moyallon, 'very sweet'. In a remarkable coincidence we found that Peggy and my wife are related, my wife's great-great-grandfather being Peggy's great-grandfather, Adam Woods – the 'Irish Cadbury', a Quaker chocolate manufacturer from Dublin.

Stella's forthrightness is part of her charm. It is also very helpful when one is trying to piece together details of the past out of a thicket of memories. When I mentioned that his niece had said Chebotarev spoke English with a heavy accent, the riposte was immediate: 'Anyone who says that is talking tosh. Nikolai spoke quickly in perfect English.' That much seemed clear. It confirmed what Bertie Mitchell had told me. But why, then, had he assumed a thick accent with some people? I imagined it must have been to curtail what he had to say to them. As the conversation wore on, I realized Stella and Nikolai had at one time been seriously in love with each other. I had enough sensibility to realize quite early on that we were talking a kind of shorthand. Gradually, I learned that the couple planned a meeting on Russian New Year, 1939, at which Nikolai was to take Stella to the Russian church – for New Year celebrations, for a pledge of some kind, even for a wedding? – but, in a scene redolent of *Brief Encounter*, with both waiting under the wrong clock (there really are two in Victoria Station), the romance ended.

Stella never saw where Nikolai arrived from. She would arrange to be up in London, staying at her mother's club at Hyde Park Gate. She and Chebotarev would arrange to meet and he would simply turn up. He took her to the then fashionable gypsy restaurants – no shortage of money there. He also visited her family home, Shootlands, on Leith Hill near Dorking. Dinner here, as at Moyallon, was invariably a black-tie affair. Monogrammed shirts, Stella added; he wore monogrammed shirts. There was no doubting his aristocratic origin and manners. Peggy, who had known Chebotarev before Stella and had, in fact, introduced them, went further. She recalled hearing that he was a prince and a relative of the Tsar, and that the Baroness de Huene, who was also a visitor at Moyallon, was his aunt; he certainly referred to her as such. She remembered how she and Chebotarev fell into fits of giggles at Hilda Richardson's mandatory hymn-singing sessions in the garden room of the mansion on Sunday evenings.[9]

Notwithstanding their estrangement in 1939, Chebotarev and Stella became friends again in the 1950s, when they would meet in London. On one such occasion, Stella recalled, as they passed Buckingham Palace he remarked in a matter-of-fact way how small it appeared, and told her that his home in Russia had been much larger, with its own Turkish baths. This perfectly describes the Romanov residence at Tsarskoe Selo, which was indeed much larger than Buckingham Palace and had its own Turkish bath-house.[10] Stella insisted that Nikolai never boasted or bragged about anything – quite the opposite: he was good at saying nothing about his past, very tight-lipped; practised, she thought. Again I thought of the intermittent heavy accent, the deterrent to questions and conversation.

As for his marriage, both Stella and Peggy said there was something wrong about it. You could hardly describe him as effervescent about her, they added in an obvious understatement. 'He mentioned her once,' said Stella, 'then never again. I felt it was not a real marriage.'

Chebotarev had told Stella the story of his departure from Russia on horseback, carrying his young niece who had been smuggled out by faithful servants in a pile of dirty washing. It was a variation, with additions, on the tale he had told Iya herself. Going through his books later, I noticed he had a preoccupation with the supposed escape of the French Dauphin, son of the ill-starred Queen Marie Antoinette – whose portrait, incidentally, had dominated the Tsarina's drawing room at Tsarskoe Selo – and that the story he told bore remarkable similarities with some of the stories about the Dauphin. An account of his escape with Iya was also given to the Russian-language newspaper in New York, *Rossiya* – no doubt to get them off his back – and was printed as 'The Cadet's Story' in 1968.[11] It was full of holes. It dated the White Russian evacuation of the Crimea not when it actually happened, in 1920, but in 1921. It said that the baby Iya was reunited with her mother in a hospital in Yugoslavia after the nurses recognized her by her eye colour, even though this was different from her mother's. It seemed a somewhat obvious *non sequitur*. There were, however, also intriguing references in the document, such as one to 'granny's dacha' in the Crimea. I knew that the Tsarevich's grandmother, the Dowager Empress, had just such a dacha, at Harax – but then, many top-class court aristocrats had dachas there, to be near the imperial family.[12] I came to the conclusion that 'The Cadet's Story' was an unreliable mixture of fact and fiction – a judgement later borne out when I found that it had been largely lifted from an account written by a French diplomat, Louis de Robien, and translated into English by Camilla Russell, a friend of Chebotarev and Hilda Richardson. Iya had the Russian version translated for me. I thought she had done it herself, but in fact, as I later learned, it was the work of the next person I was to see after Stella and Peggy.

From Dorking I headed for Edgware, to the address Iya had given me where Chebotarev had lived from about 1971 until 1985, a past considerably closer than the inter-war and post-war years we had been talking over in Surrey. Making my way towards London past Elstree, I discovered the road I was looking for just off the A41 dual carriageway. Semi-detached villas, typical of Edgware, with occasional variations to assert the occupants' individuality in an otherwise completely ordered vista. Number 27 was crisp and clean, now a church retreat house. I rang the bell and was told to wander round at leisure. It seemed empty, my footsteps echoing on the woodblock floors. This had been his space, but there was little of him left in it. I decided to try my luck next door, at Number 25, where I met a Jewish family who suggested I try the other half of the semi. Number 29 had an overgrown front garden, through which I picked my way up a strip of crazy paving. My knock on the door was answered by a tall, lean lady. My eyes instantly fastened on a Russian baptismal cross hanging round her neck; and there was something familiar about her face. It was only later that I realized she looked like the Duke of Edinburgh. She even sounded like him.

I had not expected to find any friends of Nikolai Chebotarev still alive. Iya had given me to understand that his next-door neighbour and friend, Olga Hill, was dead and that was that. Olga Hill had been a formidable lady, not liked by Iya; 'bossy', she said. Chebotarev's wife Fanny had moved from New York to live beside her old friend Olga and had dragged Chebotarev with her. Iya had mentioned no daughter, and I had not asked. Now I mentioned the name Olga Hill, and the tall lady said that was her late mother. I realized at once that Iya had deliberately kept the knowledge of this lady's existence from me. Later I discovered that she had telephoned and told her not to talk to me, to say nothing and 'put him off'. But Alix Hill was too polite for that and invited me in. It was an opportunity I took without hesitating, though afterwards I felt somewhat guilty at having left my long-suffering children in the car for more than two hours. 'Daddy's research', I reflected afterwards, wasn't much of an excuse.

Inside Alix Hill's house, where she introduced me to her husband Peter Thornton-Pett, a retired academic, I breathed the atmosphere of old Russia. There was an icon corner with a candle burning almost imperceptibly, pictures of Russian and German ancestors on the wall, a Russian officer's dress sabre by the door, a portrait of her maternal grandfather Count von Berg over the fireplace, tsarist silver sitting about in a disordered, typically Russian fashion. On both sides of her family, Alix Hill's connections are formidable and go straight to the heart of the Russian imperial court. Both of her grandfathers had been personal friends of the Tsar. Count von Berg was a business partner of Jonas Lied, the Norwegian businessman recruited by King George V to rescue his Romanov relatives.[13] Alix's mother, Olga von Berg, had been in love with Paul Stepanov, the conspirator who helped murder Rasputin. The yachting trophies Alix later showed me had been given by the Tsar to Count von Berg, who had sailed with the Tsar to Ireland. Alix lived for the first seven years of her life at her maternal grandfather's home in Estonia, where the Tsarina's companion, Lili Dehn, read to the ageing lady. Alix's Hill grandfather had been offered the title of Count by the Tsar, but had refused to change his name. And it was to Alix Hill that Sidney Gibbes, tutor to the Tsarevich, turned when he wanted his papers sorted prior to presenting them to Luton Hoo. Gibbes confided to Alix that he knew for certain that the Tsarevich and other members of the imperial family had survived.

The Hills, said Alix, had been involved in the Baltic trade and there had been seven sons, all married off to local girls. Though domiciled in Russia for many generations, they stayed British. She did not tell me on this occasion that her father was the cousin of George Hill, one of the most prominent British agents in Russia at the time of the Revolution, and also of Freddie Hill, sidekick to Robert Bruce Lockhart, Britain's most senior diplomat there in 1917. Nor did she say that she began her own career in Churchill's Cabinet War Rooms as a naval rating, or that both she and her husband had maintained her family tradition by working for GCHQ – the Government Communications Headquarters. She spoke politely, and listened to me; but, on that first visit, she kept her promise to Iya to say nothing of any import. It was obvious, however, that she had known Chebotarev very well. She confirmed that he spoke excellent English, so I assumed he had wanted to talk to her. She named a friend of his, Marianne Cross, already mentioned by Iya and John. She also confirmed that he visited Grand Duke Vladimir in Madrid, adding a funny story about Fanny being awkward and falling over when she curtsied.[14]

Most of what was said confirmed what I had already been told – that Chebotarev went to Egypt, Spain, Morocco; that he was a snappy dresser, never without a hat; that he knew how everybody was related to everybody else. Alix Hill thought she had told me nothing, but in fact she mentioned something which was to give me one of my biggest breaks. This was Chebotarev's close friendship with Alexander Lieven. 'He called himself a prince too,' Alix laughed. 'Nikolai used to go and visit him when he was at Trinity College in Dublin.'

'There's only one thing,' she added, 'he's dead.'

It didn't seem very much, but it proved to be the key to everything.

# ⌢ 4 ⌣

## A Court in Exile

Back in Ireland that August, I was conscious of having both a limited amount of free time to pursue my new-found interest before work began to encroach once more, and a tantalizing number of inviting possibilities to follow up. The weeks in England had paid dividends: my knowledge of Chebotarev had advanced considerably since June. He had described himself as 'A' on the back of a photograph in his own album, which in normal circumstances no one would have seen – certainly not in his lifetime. He had told Maureen Hill he was 'also Alexei'. His circle of friends included Princess Marina, with whom he had danced, and the pretender to the Russian throne, Grand Duke Vladimir. There was no evidence that his childless marriage was ever actually a marriage at all. His home in Russia had apparently dwarfed Buckingham Palace. Evidence suggesting that he could be the Tsarevich was becoming too plentiful to ignore. And there were more leads.

One of these was a friend of Chebotarev whom I had been trying to contact since early July. This was Marianne Cross, who had known him in Paris in the 1930s (although the connection then had been with her sister Musa rather than herself; Marianne had only got to know him well when he had come to live in England in 1971). John and Iya had said that at his funeral she had offered to have them to stay in her London home – though they had thought it a pleasantry rather than a serious proposition. Marianne had married well: her husband was the son of the self-made millionaire George Cross who had made his money developing Edgware. Eventually I tracked her down through her solicitor, who was a trustee of the Cross estate, and in August I telephoned her at her new home in Asnières, Paris. Soon after the introductory pleasantries, she embarked unprompted on a train of thought of her own. I did not interrupt with questions straight away; that would have been impolite and the result much less interesting. Her ruminations are best given verbatim.

'Maybe it was only a rumour,' she began, 'he never told me or my husband. Really, the rumours started in Yugoslavia. Two old ladies. We were very good friends. I can't believe he wouldn't say to us. Any Romanov wouldn't accept it. Was he related? It was a strange time – so much was invented . . . I heard the rumours only recently. It is nonsense. It is not true. I can't remember where I heard it. He carried Iya out of Russia. Personally, I don't think it is so. We were friendly enough. He would have mentioned anything. Don't touch it. Somebody told me. I didn't believe it. Nikolai would have said. Most Russians didn't accept it. The Tsarevich was ill, a haemophiliac. Nikolai was not a haemophiliac – was he?'[1]

By any standards, this was an extraordinary monologue – delivered, I felt, by someone who seemed to be trying hard to convince herself that the rumours were not true. Eventually, I ventured a question. 'When,' I asked, 'did these rumours begin?'

The answer came back staccato. 'A long time ago. In the South of France. In the 1920s. I heard about it from my mother. They invented it. A joke perhaps. In bad taste. The Romanovs have suffered enough already. Don't touch it. It is dangerous. I don't want to talk about it more.'

Despite this avowal, later in the conversation she started up again. 'It was Russians who lived in the South of France. Most are dead who made these rumours. I heard vaguely. Only when he was dead somebody said about it who used to live in the South of France then. I don't believe. We were close friends. He didn't tell me. He never pretended to be the Tsarevich. I heard it from someone who heard it in the 1920s. Soon all these people in the South of France – they are my age – they will be dead.' On Chebotarev, she added, 'Russians didn't want to know who they were. The name Tsarevich was best forgotten then. You'll never be able to prove it.'

The call left me feeling exhausted. Simultaneously rattled and curious, doubting but troubled; there was no doubt about the strength of Mrs Cross's emotional reaction to the subject. Moreover, having spoken to her, I could understand precisely why, if Chebotarev really had been the Tsarevich, he had not told her anything. It was borne in on me with new force that this man had made no extravagant claims for himself; on the contrary, he had been extremely tight-lipped about his Russian past. It had been other people who had spread these rumours. His behaviour patterns seemed more and more like those of the genuine article.

Fortified with this new knowledge of the rumours current in France and Yugoslavia in the 1920s and again at the time of Chebotarev's death in 1987, I decided to trace the man Alix Hill had said had been his friend, but who was now dead. It seemed an easy option, in any case, now that I was back in Ireland. Trinity College, a foundation dating from the late sixteenth century with links to Oxford and Cambridge, nestles snugly in the heart of Dublin. It was here that Prince Alexander Lieven had entertained his friend Chebotarev; and here, in the dusty records of the alumni office, I learned that Prince Alexander Lieven had arrived in Trinity in 1938, had been the leading scholar of his year and had graduated as a prizeman with a double first in 1941.[2] This was a start. One obvious way to a fuller picture was through his contemporaries, and among these three names stood out – those of Douglas Gageby, former Editor of the *Irish Times*; Roy Bradford, a former Stormont Cabinet minister whom I happened to know; and the eminent historian Conor Cruise O'Brien.

Nothing could have been more amusingly at variance than Gageby's and Bradford's descriptions of Alexander Lieven. Bradford spoke of his 'fine, craggy, skeletal head', while Gageby described him as 'a poor, miserable, half-starved sepulchral-looking creature'.[3] Bradford told me of his slight limp and tubercular appearance, his nasally deep voice and his straitened circumstances; at Trinity he had lived in Botany Bay, in free rooms for indigent students. Gageby told me that Lieven's home was in a colony of White Russians living at Collon near Dundalk – a fact confirmed to me by Conor Cruise O'Brien, who had actually studied Russian at a language school run in the Old Courthouse in Collon by one of the Russians, a Captain Nikolai Couriss. O'Brien, with the sure prose of a wordsmith, began to sketch in outline the wonderfully eccentric and singular collection of people in that small Irish town. He mentioned Couriss' wife, who was, he said, 'out of the top drawer' of Russian court nobility, attracting others of that circle; and a Count Apraxine, who had a Muscovite accent while the others had a marked St Petersburg pronunciation. 'Few contemporary things impinged on old Prince Paul Lieven, Prince Alexander's father,' he went on. 'When Khrushchev took off his shoe and banged it on the table at the United Nations, Prince Paul was horrified. Imagine the representative of Russia behaving like that! Awful! The Tsar should besmit him! Immediately!'[4] Alexander himself had apparently arrived in 1932 after his mother and father had separated: it was deemed more suitable that he live with his impecunious father in Ireland than with his bohemian mother in Brussels. He arrived with shoulder-length hair, and Couriss told him to have it cut – 'If you go out with hair like that the peasants will hang you.'

This was all fine stuff, but it wasn't getting me any closer to

Chebotarev. I decided that the only way to do this was, to use an Irish expression, to 'walk the ground'; so, one Saturday afternoon, with my wife and children in tow, I made the hour's drive to Collon. Remembering what Conor Cruise O'Brien had told me about the language school in the Old Courthouse, I decided to make it my first port of call. Today's occupants, Alicia Chawner and her husband Alain, supplied me with the names of some people who had known Couriss or worked for him.

First among these was Henry St George Smith. His home, Piperstown House, was a great grey foursquare Georgian mansion with a stunning fan-lit door, an imposing sweeping driveway and its own swimming pool. Henry himself cut an equally impressive figure, every inch an Anglo-Irishman of the Protestant Ascendancy: bedecked in country garb, complete with tweed hat and body warmer, he looked and sounded like an English colonel. Briskly, he embarked on a review of the Collon Russians. 'First,' he said, 'there was Madame Bibikov, Mrs Couriss' mother and the widow of General Bibikov, a former Governor-General of Poland. Mrs Couriss herself was known as Sana and had been a maid of honour to the Tsarina Alexandra.'[5] I found out later that someone at the imperial court, a young officer known as 'Bibi', had acted as a go-between in a love affair between Grand Duchess Olga, the Tsar's eldest daughter, and another junior officer simply referred to as 'Mitya'. Bibi was, of course, the diminutive of Bibikov. Captain Couriss' father had been a big landowner on the River Don, but he was not quite out of the same drawer as his wife's family. There were no roads, apparently, on the Couriss estate – 'you just drove over the steppes and navigated by the stars.' Governor-General of Poland certainly rang a bell with me; Bertie Mitchell had told me that Baroness de Huene's husband had been Governor-General of Poland, a fact later confirmed by Peggy Sinton. How many Governor-Generals of Poland were there among the Russians in Ireland, I thought? It was an odd coincidence; perhaps a story used once too often by one too many people.

Henry St George Smith then expanded on the Lievens. 'There was Prince Paul Lieven and his two sons, Prince Alexander and Prince Leonid. Prince Paul was Mrs Couriss' uncle and a qualified engineer who had worked on the Omsk–Tomsk section of the Trans-Siberian railway.' It seemed an odd job for a prince. Recalling from a recent re-reading of Anthony Summers' and Tom Mangold's book The File on the Tsar that it was on the Omsk section of the line that an attempt had been made to

rescue the Tsar in 1918, I asked Henry what else he had known about
Couriss and his circle. 'Couriss came to Ireland', he explained, 'because
of a Quaker lady, Miss Zonny Fox, a very large, portly lady of about
eighteen to twenty stone. She found him gun-running in Salonika with
the British navy on his tail and set him up in a chicken farm.' Another
Quaker lady: in the North of Ireland Hilda Richardson had harboured
Chebotarev and here, in the South, Zonny – Alizon – Fox had looked
after Couriss. Was there a connection? The Moyallon visitors' book
revealed that Hilda Richardson had frequently had the Foxes as house
guests. Alizon Fox's mother was the niece of Queen Victoria's physician,
Professor Wilson Fox.[6] Professor Fox was also physician to Alfred, Duke
of Edinburgh and Saxe-Coburg and his wife, Grand Duchess Maria
Alexandrovna of Russia, the daughter of Tsar Alexander II. One of their
daughters was Queen Marie of Romania, who was to appear later in my
investigation; the other, Victoria Melita, was married to the Tsarina's
brother, Grand Duke Ernst of Hesse. Professor Fox would have been
privy to the medical secrets of both the British and Russian royal families. Zonny Fox's stepmother was Lilo Sarrell, daughter of a doctor from
Constantinople; hence her links to the area where she met Couriss.
Henry then told me about another Russian who had come to the village
in 1952, a man who had been in the same class at school as Couriss – he
recalled seeing a class photograph of them together – and who had been
best man at Couriss' wedding; a man who bore a famous name: Count
Michael Tolstoy. Couriss, he said, had disliked and deeply mistrusted
Tolstoy. It emerged that Couriss was an adherent of the Russian Orthodox Church-in-exile, while Tolstoy was a member of the state church,
which compromised with the communists. They differed in politics too,
Couriss being right-wing and Tolstoy a liberal. As I was leaving, having
thanked Henry for his help, he added, almost as an afterthought: 'The
woman you really want to speak to, though, is Kathleen McCarthy,
Couriss' housekeeper. She knew everything.'

I returned to Collon the following Sunday, 15 August. I should have
known better: it was Ascension Sunday, and there were cars and people
everywhere. Deciding to persevere nonetheless, I made for the fountain-
head of all information in any Irish village: the pub. From there I was
directed to Yodie Tormey's. Yodie, who had known the Russians as a
child, had been given her name by old Prince Paul Lieven and it had
stuck. Her house, on Priest Hill, was full of people in somewhat sombre
mood, gathered to bid farewell to her husband Peter, who was leaving

for Saudi Arabia the next day. My arrival provided a distraction that seemed to lighten the atmosphere. They sat me down, I spun my yarn and then the talking started. Kevin Loughran, a family friend, was the most interesting. Deadpan, he proceeded to tell me how he had walked to school with the spies Philby, Burgess and Maclean, who had been studying at Couriss' language school – the 'Russian Academy'. They weren't supposed to speak anything but Russian, or to fraternize with the natives; but they would chatter with the local children as they walked through the village, and the natives were comprehensively shocked when the story of their treachery broke. Collon, he explained, was not the sort of place where famous people came. By this time Yodie had found some old postcards Prince Paul Lieven had given her for the stamps, which to a small girl in rural Ireland seemed to be from all sorts of exotic locations. They all agreed with Henry St George Smith – the person I really should talk to was Kathleen McCarthy. Kevin was sent in the car to fetch her. Nowhere in the world is hospitality quite so well meant or so far-reaching as in the Irish Republic. While I waited, I tried to absorb what had been said. Philby, Burgess and Maclean. What next, I thought? These were nice people; but could it really be true?

Kathleen arrived and was seated next to me at the table. She was aged, certainly, her face wrinkled, yet her expression and bearing were sprightly; she was polite and surprisingly cultured in her speech, and extremely clear and precise in what she said. She had started working for Nikolai Couriss in 1940 and remained with him until Mrs Couriss' death in 1967. Mrs Couriss, she said, was related to the Tsar. Hoping to coax the conversation on to Chebotarev, for while these other Russians were interesting – more than interesting – he was still the main purpose of my enquiry, I produced what I called my 'box of tricks': the collection of photographs I had amassed over the summer from Iya, Stella and Peggy. Kathleen scrutinized the photograph of Nikolai Chebotarev I showed her. A moment passed. 'Yes,' she said, 'he came. It was in the early 1940s, in a white open-top car. But they didn't call him Nikolai – no, it was Alexis.'

I was dumbstruck. There it was again. The Davos photograph with 'A' written on the back; his admission to Maureen Hill, 'I'm also Alexei'; now this. I recalled Hilda Richardson's white, open-top Alvis which I had heard of from the Moyallon servants, Bertie Mitchell and Iya. Preserving my composure, wishing to give nothing away, I said, 'Are you sure?'

'Quite sure,' came the reply.

The subject of another photograph, labelled 'Marsha', Kathleen identified as one of Prince Paul Lieven's sisters. 'His other sister was Alexandra,' she said. 'She became Lady Studd.' Later I checked this obscure
piece of information and, sure enough, Burke's *Peerage, Baronetage and
Knightage* of 1959 yielded confirmation of what the old lady had said. In
1923 Sir Kynaston Studd, brother of the famous cricketer and evangelist
C. T. Studd, had married as his second wife Her Serene Highness Princess Alexandra Lieven, daughter of Prince Paul Lieven, Grand Master
of Ceremonies at the Russian imperial court. Among other regular guests
at Couriss' home in Collon mentioned by Kathleen was Dr Martha
Apraxine, who practised medicine in Dublin and died of cancer, and her
father, Count Apraxine, who was very fond of cooking. I checked up
on these names too when I got home, and found that a Count P. N.
Apraxine, with an estate at Simferopol in the Crimea, had been the Tsarina's secretary.[7] Could it be the same man? Some nine months later I had
my question answered in Cathal Brugha Barracks in Dublin, where I was
allowed to see Irish military intelligence files. In Martha Apraxine's file
were the words: 'born 23 March 1913 Simferopol, Russia. Russian by
birth and parentage.'[8]

The more checks I made on what Kathleen had told me, the more her
reliability as a witness was confirmed. If she did not recognize someone
– George Cross, for example – she said so. That made her positive identifications worth taking notice of. As we went through the photographs
in the box, including some from Chebotarev's own album, she recognized one of his friends, Serge Aitov, and said he was also a friend of
Alexander Lieven; another she recognized as a friend of Louba Couriss,
who was Nikolai's sister and had been secretary to the Secretary-General
of the United Nations – where Chebotarev had worked. I heard about
Couriss' charcoal-powered car, how he had established a charcoal works
at the beginning of the Second World War and had employed twenty-
two people; how Zonny Fox, Couriss' patron, was from Somerset and
when she visited hid money between books on the shelves for Couriss to
find later. So overpowered, though, was I by her words, 'they didn't call
him Nikolai – no, it was Alexis' that I was no longer listening properly.
I did not know then just how much more information Kathleen was yet
to give me.

Alexander Lieven's brother Prince Leonid was easily found in the
London telephone directory, and just as easy to talk to. Prince Leonid,

steeped in the lore of old Russia, confirmed that his grandfather Prince Paul Lieven had been imperial chamberlain to Tsar Alexander II, and said that his father, also Prince Paul, whom he described as a brilliant engineer, had left the country with the assistance of none other than Leonid Krasin, Lenin's henchman and first Bolshevik ambassador in London. Krasin, who before 1917 had led a clandestine life as a Bolshevik revolutionary and fund-raiser, was the representative in Russia of the German Siemens Corporation, whose operation in the country had been closed down by Kerensky's government on the grounds that it was a front for German spying. Krasin, like Lenin himself, was suspected by many of being a German agent.[9] Prince Leonid then went to great lengths to explain that though his family, along with many other courtiers – he called them 'Baltic barons' – had German names, they were thoroughly Russian. Imperial decrees ensured that marriage to a Russian always meant that the children were brought up in the Orthodox Church. This had, of course, been an area of great sensitivity during the First World War; and for Leonid Lieven it clearly remained so. He laboured the point further by telling how, when he was returning to Collon through Wales during the Second World War, a censorship officer saw the name 'Countess Kleinmichel' on one of his letters and seized it, assuming the Countess was a German, when she had in fact been Russian.[10] With one short story, he not only made it plain that he was sensitive about his Germanic roots, but also reminded me that Countess Natalie Kleinmichel's name figured prominently in the Moyallon visitors' book beside Chebotarev's. Moreover, Hilda Richardson had left the Countess money in her will.[11] Later I discovered that Countess Kleinmichel was not only Russian but of royal descent: her father was the illegitimate son of Tsar Nikolai I.[12]

I asked Prince Leonid if it were true that Mrs Couriss was related to the imperial family. Yes, he said; they were related through Emperor Paul, who had an illegitimate daughter, Countess Rosenschild-Paulin. 'Child' on the end of a name always denoted a child of royal blood, he added; 'Paulin' denoted Tsar Paul. Yes, Sana Couriss was the Countess' descendant. This piece of information was corroborated by an obscure book entitled *Descendances naturelles des souverains et grand-ducs de Russie de 1762 à 1910*, written by Jacques Ferrand and published in Paris in 1995, which confirmed that the Bibikovs were indeed descendants of Tsar Paul. Further checks revealed that the family connection continued: on 19 February 1952 Mrs Couriss' nephew George, son of her brother Valerian, had married Countess Xenia Nieroth, the great-great-granddaughter of

Tsar Nikolai I through his mistress Princess Vera Shakovskoya.[13]

'Our own title', Prince Leonid went on, 'derived from Princess Lieven. She was governess to the imperial children, the Children of Russia.' I wondered why a mere governess had been honoured so highly, and drew the conclusion I think I was meant to draw. Almost imperceptibly at first, an idea was taking root in my mind: that these Russians in Collon were no ordinary émigré Russians, but imperial Russians; and not merely aristocrats with links to the imperial court, but blood relatives of the imperial family itself. And among them, mixing with them as friends, was Chebotarev, or, as they called him, Alexis.

My next chat with Kathleen McCarthy, on my October half-term break, deepened this perception still further. Before leaving on my previous visit, I had asked Kathleen to try to remember as much as she could about Couriss and his circle. That day, the bombshells came thick and fast. The first concerned Count Apraxine. 'The Bariatinskys were there,' she began, 'Count Apraxine's nieces. They were about sixteen or seventeen years old and used to make model animals out of pipe cleaners.'[14] With this apparently casual observation, Kathleen had effectively fixed the identity of Count Apraxine as the Tsarina's secretary, for his wife had been Princess Bariatinsky before her marriage. But the significance of the name Bariatinsky went further than that. Countess Apraxine's father, Prince Vladimir Bariatinsky, had not only accompanied the Tsarevich Nikolai on his Far Eastern tour in 1891, but had been the Dowager Empress's lover after Alexander III's death in 1894 – an affair quashed by the new Tsar, Nikolai II.[15] Moreover, the Countess' brother was married to Princess Catherine Yurevsky, the morganatic daughter of Tsar Alexander II.[16] This meant that Count Apraxine's daughter, Martha – the Dublin doctor – shared an aunt with Tsar Nikolai II. Couriss' clique were certainly very close to the imperial family.

Kathleen's second bombshell of the day was delivered in a similarly downbeat manner. 'An Englishman called Preston came in the early 1950s,' she said. 'He was about thirty to forty and Mrs Couriss called him her cousin.' At the time I was reading Michael Occleshaw's book, The Romanov Conspiracies, which included an account of how Lady Preston, widow of Thomas Preston, the British Consul in Ekaterinburg at the time the imperial family disappeared, and her sister Mme Bibikov gave an interview in which they claimed that two of the Tsar's daughters survived.[17] It was not this piece of information which struck me, however, startling enough though it was, but the name Bibikov. It was

Mrs Couriss' maiden name. At that moment it all became clear: Mrs Couriss' brother must have been married to Lady Preston's sister. The tall, blond man called Preston who visited Mrs Couriss in the early fifties must have been the man I had met when I visited his stately home not far from Holt on my trip to Norfolk the previous summer: Sir Ronald Preston, Thomas's son, who had been born in Ekaterinburg.[18] By way of confirmation, I asked Kathleen where Mrs Couriss had come from. 'Ekaterinburg,' came the instant reply. 'She was born in Warsaw, where her father, General Bibikov, was stationed, but the family were from Ekaterinburg.' Not only had the Couriss circle remarkable links with the imperial family; they also had links with Ekaterinburg at the time the imperial family disappeared.

Kathleen had other things to tell me that day. A man called Blunt had come – very cultivated, well-spoken. It sounded like Anthony Blunt, especially as I already knew that Philby, Burgess and Maclean had been there. Kathleen then produced a scruffy A5 size cash ledger which Nikolai Couriss had used as a visitors' book for his Russian language school. She had found it in the chicken house. 'You can have this,' she said, dusting it off. Gingerly, I opened it, fearing it might fall apart, and carefully turned the pages. I was amazed. Not only had Couriss' students recorded their names and addresses, but photographs of many had been inserted as well. Two pages had been carefully cut out. 'What's the story of the missing pages?' I asked.

'Oh, that was when the scandal about Philby broke. Captain Couriss asked me to take out the pages with Philby, Burgess and Maclean on them. I hoped to keep them but he made me burn them in front of him. The rest of the book went into the bin, but I came back and retrieved it later.' Clearly, Kathleen had been aware of the potential importance of such a record.

'He didn't know you had it?' I ventured.

'No,' came the reply.

Further searching uncovered the page for May 1948 (see plates). On it was the signature of George Blake, his address – Bywood, Chalfont St Peter, Bucks – and two photographs. I showed them to Kathleen. 'Is this the spy?'

'Yes, he forgot about that one, he was in such a panic to destroy the others.'

'Did Couriss take many photographs?' I asked.

'Yes, he called them his insurance policies.'

I wondered why he needed insurance policies; and, if Blake had been at Collon as well as Philby, Burgess and Maclean, who else might have been there. Later, in George Blake's book, *No Other Choice*, I read that after leaving Cambridge Blake went 'with a naval friend to a house of Russian émigrés in a small village north of Dublin'. There his host was 'a prince who earned a living growing mushrooms. His wife was a tall, stately woman, the daughter of the last Russian Viceroy of Poland. Old Cossack generals with thick grey whiskers called on our hosts.'[19] There was a history here just as strange as that of the mysterious Russian prince at Moyallon, and both stories beckoned me – but then, perhaps they were not two stories but different aspects of one complex, untold tale.

When I telephoned Alix Hill to tell her how much progress I had made because of her throwaway comment about Prince Alexander Lieven, I learned of another connection in this strange, overlapping set of histories. Alix Hill, Chebotarev's friend and neighbour in later life, turned out to be related to Maureen Hill, the riding companion to whom he had confessed his identity as Alexei. 'Oh yes, she is on the family tree,' said Alix. 'Uprichard. Married John Hill, I think. He was in the navy.' Then she said something that made me more determined than ever to continue my researches. 'Iya is worried about this,' she said. 'The less you say, the better in that way. The past is past. Let sleeping dogs lie.'[20] If there was nothing to be found, why the silence? The warning recalled Marianne Cross's admonition: 'Don't touch it. It is dangerous.'

I turned next to the Russian at Collon whose presence there after 1952 was resented by Couriss: Count Michael Tolstoy. 'Couriss called him a bloody communist,' Kathleen began, confirming the impression of political antipathy already given by Henry St George Smith; and she went on to explain how Couriss had accused Tolstoy of keeping a brothel in Brussels, home of his third wife Myriam. Countess Tolstoy strongly denied this. 'Couriss didn't trust Tolstoy, or Bishop Anthony Bloom who came to see him. He knew they were there to find out what he was up to. Reds, he would say. He laughed at them behind their backs.'[21] Kathleen confirmed what I had learned from Henry St George Smith: that Tolstoy had been at school with Couriss and had been best man at his wedding; and she added that, before the Revolution, Couriss had lent Tolstoy large sums of money – money that was never repaid.

My checks on Tolstoy revealed that he was no count. Returning to Jacques Ferrand and the *Descendances naturelles des souverains et grands-ducs de Russie de 1762 à 1910*, I found him named as Michael Pavlovich

Golenishchev-Kutuzov-Tolstoy – a direct descendant of Marshal Kutu-zov, the one-eyed military commander who had driven Napoleon out of Russia.[22] What was even more interesting was that he appeared to be related to Sana Couriss: first through Marshal Kutuzov's wife, a Bibikov, but also, and more significantly, in that Tolstoy was the illegitimate great-grandson of Tsar Nikolai I, from whose father, Tsar Paul I, Sana Couriss traced her descent. Yet another Romanov connection had sur-faced in that small Irish village.

According to Ferrand, Tolstoy attended the Imperial Lycée Alexander in St Petersburg, so this must have been Couriss' school. Subsequent further checks on Tolstoy confirmed Couriss' assessment of his political leanings. In 1982, two years after his death, the Swedish foreign ministry 'outed' him as a Soviet agent, placing on him the blame for betraying an allied agent, Raoul Wallenberg – the Swede who saved so many Jews in Hungary during the war – to the Red Army.[23] According to Henry St George Smith, Tolstoy claimed to have seen Wallenberg dead.

That same day in October, Kathleen poured out yet more informa-tion tying Chebotarev into the Collon circle. Serge Aitov, Chebotarev's friend who featured in many of the photographs Stella and Peggy had shown me that summer, had been to Collon. This was corroborated by Henry St George Smith, who recalled seeing the photograph Stella had given me on Prince Paul Lieven's wall; it had been taken, he said, at Clogherhead, on the coast not far from Collon. Hilda Richardson was recognized from a photograph of her in Chebotarev's own album; and a 'Carlotta' came, Kathleen said. This must have been Carlotta Block-Schock, who arrived in Moyallon on the same day as Chebotarev, 6 May 1939. Increasingly, it seemed clear to me that Collon was a place where blood relatives of the imperial family lived in the obscurity and anonymity of rural republican Ireland, where titles and degrees of nobil-ity counted for nothing and no one asked questions. If Chebotarev really were the Tsarevich, had it been members of the imperial family who had helped shelter him? I began to suspect that some obligation of blood, some debt of honour was involved. Certainly, the Tsar, when in power, had provided lavishly for his blood relatives. Were they mindful of this when they were with the man they knew as Alexis? I realized that if I was going to pursue this investigation further, I would have to know more about the forces which shaped the Romanovs as a family and about the loyalties and treacheries which surrounded them.

## ~ 5 ~

# The Throne of Blood

Romanov . . . to me, as perhaps to most people, the name conjured up an inchoate impression of lost splendour, almost Byzantine magnificence, and the peculiar poignancy of the early years of this century before war and revolution tore the old world apart. More than eighty years later, the system that superseded the imperial regime had itself been toppled, and I was leafing through the handful of photographic books on the imperial family that had been published since material began to be released from the Russian State Archives in 1991. It was now that I began to see the Romanovs as a family for the first time, their humanity and individuality speaking to me from these long-hidden words and images.

Alexei Nikolaevich Romanov was born to privilege and rank, the child of promise, his imperial father's son and heir, Tsarevich of all the Russias; yet his birth horoscope for 12 August 1904, which spoke of a life of upheaval and disruption, was darkly prophetic. For he was born into a troubled world, seething with the pressures which led ultimately to cataclysm. Nowhere were these pressures more evident, I found, than within the wider Romanov family itself. As I read about them, I was struck by the similarities between them and another lost dynasty: the Bourbons. This was not just a matter of superficial and self-conscious echoes, such as the Tsarina having a huge tapestry portrait of the doomed Queen Marie Antoinette in her drawing room, or her quirky behaviour in sleeping in that Queen's bed while on a state visit to France in 1896. The resonance was far deeper, the scheming and betrayal within the Romanov family recalling the betrayal of Louis XVI by his cousin the Duke of Orléans, the self-styled 'Philippe Egalité'. Such tensions, of course, are part of the territory; for royal families throughout time have regarded themselves as 'family firms', organized in a hierarchy in which everyone is graded by the number of heartbeats which separate them from the throne. It is not a system conducive to loyalty between family members.

In Russia the propensity for plotting among branches of the imperial family was, I found, greatly enhanced by the dynastic rules which governed the succession to the crown, namely the Pauline succession law of 1797 and the imperial decree which modified it in 1855. What they amounted to was the operation of the Salic law, by which males alone can succeed to the throne, and a prohibition on marriage to women of any rank below that of Serene Highness. These restrictions were relatively new. Peter the Great was succeeded by his wife, and Russia had been ruled by women for two-thirds of the eighteenth century, until Tsar Paul changed the rules in 1797 so that this would never happen again, in reaction to the mother he hated – Catherine the Great, arguably the greatest woman ruler in history. Having once been introduced, for however wayward a reason, these rules were unlikely to be changed. For one thing, the Tsarist regime of the nineteenth century was deeply conservative; for another, there would have been instant resistance from the junior branches of the Romanov family to any changes in the rules which would diminish their chances of succession – for example, by allowing a female to succeed.

Nikolai II's reign lay under the shadow of the Pauline succession law, for although he produced four children in the first ten years of his reign, none of them could fill the role of heir. Girl succeeded girl – Olga in 1895, Tatiana in 1897, Maria in 1899 and finally Anastasia in 1901. His wife's reaction when Tatiana was born illustrates how near to panic the imperial couple were. 'My God,' said the Tsarina, 'another girl. What will the country think?'[1] The Tsar's reign lacked the sense of security which an heir would have given it, and the junior branches of the extensive family tree saw their opportunities loom larger with each successive daughter's birth. Until the birth of Alexei in 1904, Nikolai's immediate heirs were first his brother Grand Duke George, who died of TB in 1898, and then his sole remaining brother, Grand Duke Mikhail, known in the immediate family as 'Floppy' from his tendency to fall asleep at the wheel of any car he was driving. Mikhail, I found, had considerably weakened his own credibility by the pursuit of unsuitable women. In 1901 he had tried to elope in Sorrento with Dina Kosikovsky, his sister Olga's lady in waiting;[2] and when that crisis had blown over, he transferred his attentions to a twice-divorced woman, Madame Wulfert, later created Countess Brasova, whom he ultimately married. In doing this, he disqualified any sons he might have from the succession, for this marriage, to a woman below the permitted station in life, was morganatic: that is, any children would have no inheritance rights through their father. When he was actually presented with the throne on a plate in 1917, following his brother's abdication, he refused to accept it. The problem was not simply that for ten years Nikolai II lacked a male heir, but that for six of them his immediate successor was widely regarded as unfit. In 1900, moreover, the Tsar succumbed to a serious bout of typhus which nearly killed him; the episode was marked by unseemly family disputes, with his mother, the Dowager Empress, insisting that her remaining son Mikhail be officially declared Tsarevich,[3] and his wife, the young Tsarina, refusing to allow anyone but herself to tend her husband lest his departure be hastened. The prospect of Nikolai II's sudden death stirred the ambitions of the junior branches of the Romanov family; the throne for a time had come tantalizingly close, and in the continuing climate of uncertainty they nurtured hopes that the crown might after all fall into their hands.

Other resentments also festered within the wider Romanov family. One of the principal causes of dissatisfaction was the restriction placed by the Tsar's father, Alexander III, on the award of the title of Grand Duke. Quite simply, there were too many Romanovs, and their genetic success was expensive. A Grand Duke on marriage received a patrimony from the imperial crown lands and an income for life. By confining the use of the title to the sovereign's children and, in the second generation, to the immediate heirs only, the Tsar had slashed the incomes of many of his relatives; and they did not love him for it.[4] These and other grievances, coupled with the perception of Nikolai II as a weak Tsar in the after-math of the 1905 revolution, with the concession of some rights of consultation to the parliament, the Duma, bred a climate of disloyalty.

Within the family, two main groups of contenders emerged. Next in line, after the Tsar and his brothers, were the Vladimirovichi, the family of Nikolai's uncle Grand Duke Vladimir. Grand Duchess Olga, the Tsar's sister, spoke of Vladimir's 'anglophobia' and of how he 'opposed to the last' Nikolai's marriage to Alix of Hesse, with her English relatives and upbringing.[5] Vladimir's wife, Grand Duchess Maria Pavlovna, was the presiding genius of this clan, and her animosity towards the young Tsarina was legendary. In her palace in St Petersburg, Maria Pavlovna ran an alternative court which was everything the Tsarina's stodgy, dull, official court was not. Unlike her sovereign, who was a home-bird more at ease in 'Cosy Corners' with her young family and 'huzy', Maria Pavlovna, the queen of St Petersburg high society, thrived on the scin-tillating, wicked wit and gossip that was the life-blood of an aristocratic system. Before the French Revolution, Louis XVI's traitor cousin Orléans had alleged that the King's heir, the Dauphin, was not his father's son; Maria Pavlovna tried exactly the same ploy before the Russian Revolution. In indignation, the Tsarina denied this unfounded slur.[6] It was all so predictable. By 1916, Maria Pavlovna's opposition to Alexandra had reached such a pitch that she openly demanded the Tsarina's 'annihilation' of Mikhail Rodzianko, the Speaker of the Duma.[7] It made no difference that Maria Pavlovna had two brothers who were German generals,[8] or that Tsar Alexander III had routinely steamed open her letters because he knew she was betraying national secrets to Germany; unperturbed by her hypocrisy, she still stigmatized the Tsarina as *nemka*, the German woman. Nothing could stem the flow of vituperation from Maria Pavlovna's tongue and her lacerating attacks on the Tsarina, whose reputation suffered grievously under the onslaught. The hostility between the two branches of the family has been maintained irreconcilably ever since. In 1917 Maria's son, Cyril, marched his naval detachment under a red flag and offered his services to a bemused and unresponsive revolutionary Duma. In 1924, despite howls of protest from the Dowager Empress, Cyril proclaimed himself Tsar-in-exile, splitting Russian monarchists into two bitterly opposed camps. Today, despite universal opposition from all the other Romanovs, Maria Pavlovna's great-granddaughter, Maria Vladimirovna, and her son, George von Hohenzollern, claim to be the rightful sovereigns of Russia.[9] What Maria Pavlovna would like to have happened was clear enough; but were she and her brood a serious threat to the Tsar in the early years of the century?

In many respects the Vladimirovichi were more of a perceived than a real threat. Grand Duke Vladimir himself died in 1909, seriously weakening their position. That left the Vladimirovichi fortunes in the hands of his son Cyril – the 'marble man', as his cousin, Queen Marie of Romania, called him; he was, she said, 'extraordinarily cold and selfish . . . he seems to freeze you up and has such a disdainful way of treating people'.[10] Cyril had seriously blotted his copybook by marrying the divorced and non-Orthodox wife of the Tsarina's brother, Grand Duke Ernst of Hesse. Spurred on by his vengeful consort, the Tsar stripped Cyril of his titles, rank, Imperial Highness status and income. Cyril was eventually rehabilitated in 1915 during the heat of the Great War, but even then he was in no position to present a serious challenge to the Tsar. His brothers were no more capable than Nikolai's. Boris was a noted lecher with a string of young mistresses; Andrei was happily living with the Tsar's cast-off lover, the ballerina Matilda Kshesinsky, with whom he later contracted a morganatic marriage.

The real challenge to the Tsar, I found, came from a more unexpected quarter. Nikolai's great-grandfather, Tsar Nikolai I, had four sons, a superfluity of heirs which itself usually presages trouble in royal ranks. The third of these, also Nikolai, had eked out his existence as Governor-General of the Caucasus and had left two sons, Grand Dukes Nikolai and Piotr Nikolaevich. Grand Duke Nikolai, or 'Nikolasha' as he was known in the family, twelve years older than the Tsar, was a tall, strong man who reminded many of the Tsar's own father, the physically massive and politically reactionary Alexander III. Once, when the Austrian ambassador had talked at the dinner table of sending two divisions into a Balkan trouble-spot, Alexander III had picked up a fork, bent it with his two hands and thrown it in front of the ambassador. 'That', he said, 'is what I will do with your two divisions.'[11] Such stories appealed to the simplistic vision of the far right. Beside Nikolasha, the diminutive five-foot-seven-inch Tsar seemed uncomfortable. Grand Duke Nikolai looked like an emperor; he did not. The Tsar owed his lack of height to his mother, the sister of Britain's Queen Alexandra who, rather unfeelingly, described her own son, the Tsar's cousin and look-alike King George V, as a 'dwarf'. Nor was Nikolasha's power simply a matter of personal presence; in 1914–15 he was supreme commander of the Russian military forces. And while he might be a very junior Romanov, he had important connections.

Nikolasha and his brother Peter had married two sisters, the Montenegrin princesses Anastasia (called 'Stana') and Militsa. Their father was the parvenu and impecunious King Nikolai of Montenegro, a poverty-stricken Balkan mountain principality; his palace at Cetinje was little more than a two-storey villa. Militsa and Stana, however, had grown up in Russia and had been educated at the prestigious Smolny Institute – which, incidentally, ended up as Bolshevik party headquarters during the Revolution. Nikolai of Montenegro may have inhabited the bargain basement of European monarchy, but he did well for his daughters: two became Russian Grand Duchesses, another became Queen of Italy and another married a Battenberg.[12] Later in my researches this set of family connections was to become significant. These statuesque women – both over six feet tall – were not popular in the wider Romanov family. They came from an alien, unruly Balkan background where political intrigue frequently spilled over into bloody violence. As recently as 1903 the

King and Queen of Serbia, which adjoined Montenegro, had been dragged from their beds and butchered in a palace coup. Regarded as pushy and obsessed by their own station and place in the order of precedence, Militsa and Stana were also known devotees of the occult, an enthusiasm that earned them the nickname 'the black peril', and were as a result thoroughly disapproved of by the Dowager Empress. Perhaps it was the fact that her mother-in-law disliked them, or their willingness – unlike the rest of the family – to grovel to her, that first attracted the Tsarina to them; whatever the root of the attachment, it is certain that they built up a formidable influence over her.

That influence began in 1901 when the young Empress, panic-stricken at her failure to produce a male heir, turned for help to the occult practices of Militsa and Stana. Proffering the services of a Monsieur Philippe, a 'spirit doctor' who among other things claimed to be able to determine and influence the sex of unborn children, the Grand Duchesses took their first major step towards controlling the Tsarina's thinking. Alexandra was already predisposed to favour occultism; she had seen her grandmother Queen Victoria dabble in spiritualism after her beloved Albert's premature death, and, as the young chatelaine of her widowed father's court in Darmstadt after she came of age,[13] had gathered a numerous retinue of occultists around her. It is interesting to note how Militsa and Stana found their 'spirit doctor'. Philippe Vachot, a former butcher's assistant from Lyons, was picked out of the Calve occultist circle in France by Piotr Ivanov, the Paris head of the tsarist secret police, the Okhrana; and Okhrana connections kept on reappearing in the Militsa and Stana circle.[14] Despite an initial failure of staggering proportions – Vachot said Anastasia would be a boy – the desperate and therefore gullible Tsarina believed his obviously fraudulent explanation that he had been called in too late. Within a short time he had established a pattern of control over the Empress involving the administration of hallucinogenic and other drugs which he obtained from a Buddhist herbalist then all the rage in St Petersburg high society, 'Dr' Piotr Badmaev. Significantly for our story, Badmaev also supplied the infamous holy man, Grigori Rasputin, with drugs for the imperial family.[15] Rasputin was another protégé of the Montenegrin princesses, having first met the imperial couple at Stana's home. It was the similarity of the methods used by Vachot and Rasputin that first drew my attention to their common sponsors, Militsa and Stana. When I examined the actual mechanism by which Rasputin met the imperial family, I found it opened a very interesting can of worms.

In 1905, faced with imminent departure from court and country under a cloud after a negative secret police report on his background, Philippe Vachot had told the gullible Tsarina that 'another friend' would come. Militsa and Stana then had a lean time parading before the imperial couple a procession of religious freaks, including such unappealing candidates as the 'holy fool' Mitya Koliba, whose inarticulate gruntings even the susceptible Tsarina found 'irksome'.[16] More prestigious influences were also brought to bear, like Father John of Kronstadt, made a saint after his death; but Vachot's true successor, and the crowning glory of Militsa and Stana's deceit, was Grigori Efimovich Novykh, better known as 'Rasputin', a name which means 'the dissolute'. It was Rasputin who performed simultaneously the twin tasks of convincing the Tsarina that only he could keep her son alive and discrediting her by association with his notoriously licentious ways. His principal advocate with the imperial family in the first instance was Archimandrite Theophan, then rector of the prestigious St Petersburg Theological Seminary, later to be Bishop of Yamburg and Archbishop of Poltava and Pereslavl – and formerly confessor to Grand Duchesses Militsa and Stana, who passed him on to the Tsarina to be her confessor. Theophan was thus in an unrivalled position to influence the Tsarina.

Archimandrite Theophan, contrary to the saintly image promulgated by the Church-in-exile, was a very political bishop. Part of a clique of extreme right-wing nationalists around Nikolasha with connections to the Okhrana, he had secret links with the 'Union of True Russian Men' or SRN (Soiuz Russkogo Naroda), a pan-Slavic, anti-Semitic and anti-Western group that was involved in the 'Black Hundreds', the disgraceful pogroms against the Jews which followed the 1905 revolution. This clique, with its powerful court connections, even persuaded the Tsar to wear its insignia on his uniform.[17] Nor was Theophan's later life in France, after the Revolution, that of the self-denying ascetic his flock was encouraged to admire. Though the Church describes him as a holy hermit and cave dweller, the truth is somewhat less dramatic. Theophan's 'cave' in France can still be seen. Situated near the village of Limeray on the north bank of the Loire, close to the town and château of Amboise, it is not, as might be imagined, a literal cave. Rather, it is one of the well-known Loire Valley troglodyte dwellings which are built into the limestone bluffs that run parallel to the great river and are predominantly used for wine storage. Theophan's 'cave' has no open mouth but looks rather like an ordinary house with doors and windows, simply built into the cliff

face. Two ladies attended him, one of whom, Marie Strekalov Fedchenko
from St Petersburg, owned the group of caves. In the other caves lived
Theophan's twelve fierce Dobermann Pinschers – capable, it was said, of
tearing a man apart – as well as goats, geese and ducks. According to the
*mairie*'s registration certificate Theophan moved here on 1 September
1939, five months before he died; previously he had lived for two years
in Tours and, prior to that, in Clamart in the suburbs of Paris from 1933.
The picture is one not of a simple saint but of a sophisticated individual
well used to taking care of his physical and social protection.

Similarly Badmaev, who supplied both Vachot and Rasputin with
drugs for the imperial family, was far more than a mere Buddhist herbalist. Born Piotr Alexandrovich Zhamsarain, an hereditary noble and a
godson of Tsar Alexander III, he had operated as an imperial secret agent
in the Trans-Baikal or Buryat region, a Buddhist enclave north of Tibet,
and from 1875 had also worked in the Asiatic department of the Russian
foreign ministry.[18] Now a doctor of Tibetan medicine, his associates included Agvan Dorzhiev, the emissary of the Dalai Lama. In fact, in 1907
Badmaev engineered a meeting between Dorzhiev and Nikolai II at
Tsarskoe Selo – a meeting which caused fears in the British imperial establishment that the Tsar was about to establish a protectorate over Tibet,
thus threatening the north of India, the jewel in Britain's imperial crown.
Dorzhiev, for his part, openly spoke of his vision of the Tsar as head of
a massive Buddhist empire, seeing Nikolai II as the rather unlikely re-
incarnation of the mythical King of Shalambala – a messianic Buddhist
kingdom better known to us as 'Shangri-La'.[19] Badmaev was part of the
Far Eastern lobby at court, headed by men like Prince Esper Ukhtomsky,
the Tsar's adviser on Far Eastern affairs, and finance minister Count
Witte, whose objective was Russian hegemony in Asia. It was they, for
instance, who had pushed the Tsar into the disastrous Russo-Japanese
War of 1904–5 which led directly to the revolution of the latter year and
fatally damaged belief in Russian military prowess. Badmaev himself even
possessed timber concessions on the Yalu River in northern China – an
area which was being successfully penetrated and developed by the Russians at this time, with Harbin in northern China becoming more of a
Russian city than a Chinese one. Russia was an expansionist imperial
power and Britain was its deadly enemy in what was euphemistically
called 'the Great Game'. But Nikolai II had a wife with strong English
connections, and an English alliance which ultimately took him into the
war which destroyed his empire. As Tsarevich he once wrote to his father,

'India will be ours one day'; as Tsar, he might share the aspirations of the expansionists – but would he actually do anything about it?[20] More characteristic of his temperament, perhaps, was his role as sponsor of world peace: the idea of the International Court of Justice at the Hague, to settle disputes between nations in a peaceful manner, was his.

Nikolasha, though, was another matter. Darling of the far right, he was perceived as a strong man who would not bend to accommodate the creeping parliamentarianism and political change which Nikolai II's allegedly weak rule permitted. Yet he turned out to be a man of straw, considerably less impressive in action than his image would lead one to expect. Extreme, unstable, excitable and inconsistent, he was said by Count Fredericks, a minister of the imperial court, to suffer from 'the hereditary hysteria of the Oldenburgs' (his mother's family);[21] during the 1905 crisis, after advising the Tsar to grant a constitution and refusing himself to become dictator, 'he went out like a madman'. Ironically, the instability of this supposed strong man of the right would probably have rendered him more open to the influence of the far right and the Okhrana than the supposedly 'weak' Nikolai II. The Tsar, like his father before him, had to be fed a diet of police misinformation which fanned his dislike and mistrust of the forces of change in the attempt to convince him that his throne was in danger from subversion and that the only way to deal with this was by repression.[22] He was, however, well aware of the threat posed by Nikolasha as a focus of disaffection on the part of those Romanovs who believed that the Tsar was making a mess of the 'family business', damaging their collective interest and the status of the crown, and eventually dismissed the older man from his post as commander-in-chief of the imperial forces on the grounds of complicity in plots against himself. This was not over-reaction to routine family feuding: these plotting dynasts still thought in terms appropriate to a different age – an age in which thrones belonged to the strong, and palace coups were still the norm. As the Tsarina reminded her friend Lili Dehn, Russia was not England. Probably, in the time-honoured fashion, Nikolasha kept himself at arm's length from these conspiracies, making it possible to deny involvement while being ready to benefit if they should succeed – though in December 1916 the Tsarina told Lili Dehn that she had documentary evidence of Nikolasha's intention to oust Nikolai and take his place on the throne.[23] In any event, I believe it was Militsa and Stana, rather than their intellectually limited husbands, who were playing the deadlier and more insidious game.

In 1902 the Tsarina had a pregnancy which has never been written about. Her 1903 phantom or hysterical pregnancy is well recorded in the history books, but that of the previous year has remained a closely guarded secret. In brief, after a pregnancy lasting more than nine months during which she had consulted none of her regular doctors – only Vachot – she gave birth to a fertilized embryo which had died at the fourth week. This startling episode was documented in a set of imperial medical records found in Tsarskoe Selo and sent to me by Willi Korte. (Korte, in his capacity as Europe's leading expert on stolen works of art, had received them as part of an information trade.)[24] This remarkable archive, never before seen in the West, proves not only that medical records of the imperial family do exist, but that the information contained in them will significantly alter our understanding of events. This is what the medical record says of the 1902 affair:

Her Imperial Highness, Alexandra Feodorovna, had no monthly bleeding and expected the birth to take place in early August, in the normal term of pregnancy . . . She seems to have felt well and had no pains or unpleasantness. Her Highness felt that the pregnancy was proceeding normally and did not therefore think it necessary to ask for medical help . . . The term had passed, as far as 16 August, when in the morning some bleeding appeared. It was of the same character as her monthly period. There was not much blood loss. In view of the above circumstances we advised her to turn to further specialist medical advice from Professor Otti who was invited to visit Her Highness at about 10 a.m. on 16 August for a gynaeco-logical inspection. He excluded all idea of pregnancy – herbs were given. On the evening of 18 August, Her Highness felt pains similar to birth pains which ceased by the following day. During her morning toilette on 20 August, she expelled from her vagina a fleshy substance which, on inspection, proved to be a dead, fertilized egg at a stage of development of about four weeks. The expelled embryo was dissected by Professor Otti and was found to have suffered from a lack of blood in the early stages. Peterhof, 26 August 1902. Signed Dr Hirsch, Professor Otti.[25]

The record is corroborated by a letter from the Tsar's sister Grand Duchess Xenia to her friend Princess Obolensky on 20 August 1902 in which she writes: 'This morning Alexandra Feodorovna had a minor miscarriage – if it could be called a miscarriage at all! That is to say a tiny ovule came out! Mama [the Dowager Empress] and I talked to them [the Tsar and Tsarina] about Philippe.'[26]

Given that during this pregnancy the Tsarina refused to see her normal doctors and consulted only Vachot, who administered to her drugs supplied by Badmaev, and that in the following year, 1903, the Tsarina had a false or hysterical pregnancy which is a matter of record, I wondered if Militsa and Stana could have been using Vachot to prevent the Tsarina giving birth. It was a sinister and unpleasant thought; but it is certain that Vachot was administering drugs to the Empress, who had already given birth to four healthy daughters, after normal pregnancies, in a regular pattern between 1896 and 1901 – the year she was introduced to Vachot. Since the Tsar's near-demise in 1900 the prospect of the imperial throne had appeared tantalizingly close to other branches of the family; another birth now might bring forth a boy – the long-expected heir – and with him the prospect of a long line of descendants of Tsar Nikolai II inheriting the throne. For Militsa and Stana, this was the nightmare scenario.

In 1904, when Alexandra actually succeeded in giving birth to a male child, the nightmare became reality. The disappointment, even shock, to the junior members of the Romanov family must have been severe. These people, though, were playing for high stakes, and their plotting and scheming were now transferred from the Tsarina to the new Tsarevich. They had not wanted him born in the first place; now he was an obstacle that had, if possible, to be removed.

Stories began to emerge that the Tsarevich had an incurable bleeding disorder and was not likely to live long. Bleeding disorders do not inevitably mean early death; but such an outcome would obviously suit the plotters within the Romanov family, providing the desired end result without implicating them in its cause. Militsa and Stana were well placed to foment such an idea. They had the Tsarina's confidence, she was constantly in and out of their homes, and they certainly would have had access to any information about bleeding disorders in the Tsarina's family through their sister, who like Alexandra's eldest sister was married to a Battenberg.[27] They could easily have implanted in the highly suggestible Tsarina's mind the idea that her son had a bleeding disorder following a trivial bleeding from the navel shortly after his birth. Almost certainly this was hypoprothrombinemia, a phenomenon both common and normal in infants; but it gave Militsa and Stana a perfect opening. Now they could foster the notion that the Tsarevich would not survive.

What I had found was a family whose members were the victims of their own elevated circumstances and a young heir whose very existence was anathema to powerful factions among his relations. There was enough evidence to justify wondering if the rumours of his illness, like the rumours of Mark Twain's death, had been 'greatly exaggerated'. I mentally reviewed all the people who would have preferred Alexei dead; and as that list lengthened, I realized that if Chebotarev really were the Tsarevich, as I was increasingly coming to believe, then he had good reason to remain in obscurity, under a false name, a man with no past. This might have remained mere speculation, reflections about possibilities for ever irresolvable, events whose prints had been lost in the shifting sands of time – had it not been for the bones.

## ∽ 6 ∽

# Bones and Blood

On 10 May 1992 the *Sunday Times* carried the front-page banner head-line: REMAINS OF TSAR AND FAMILY FOUND IN FOREST. What a scoop! Even in the Irish edition, it drove CATHOLIC BISHOP'S LOVE-CHILD off the front page. The Romanovs were in the news once more. What had seemed like a played-out story, too often reworked, now leaped sensationally back into the public gaze. Of course, I did not imagine then, a year before the beginnings of a quest that was to turn my life upside-down, that this could have any relevance to me personally; it was a good read, a good conversation piece, that was all. My wife, with the magpie instincts of a good history teacher, cut out the article and filed it away with all the other stories that might be useful some day. Even at the time, though, I soon realized – like many others – that the story had to be far less straightforward than that first over-confident account would have had us believe.

It was immediately apparent to a disinterested observer, as I was then, that something was badly wrong with the *Sunday Times* account. While the text stated authoritatively that there were eleven corpses, the plan-view diagram used to illustrate the piece showed only nine. There was no mention of the Tsarevich's body, and the diagram showed three, not four, Grand Duchesses. Nevertheless, the article stated confidently that 'none of the family' had escaped assassination and that 'overwhelming' forensic evidence showed that 'Nikolai II, his wife and all five children' were present at the site of discovery. There were a lot of absolutes here, I thought, for the normally cautious voice of the British Establishment. Within nine paragraphs the article, which ranged across the front and back pages of the paper, speculated on the likelihood of the remains being accorded a state burial, with the British royal family being present.

Puzzled as I was at the time by the lack of two bodies, like everyone else I assumed from the magisterial and authoritative tone of the article and the apparent conclusiveness of the discovery it chronicled that the Romanov mystery was finally at an end. By September 1992 Grand

Duchess Maria Vladimirovna, the Vladimirovichi clan's pretender to the Russian throne, and her 'Renaissance for Russia' Foundation were indeed demanding a state funeral for these remains. A head of steam seemed to be building for a line to be drawn under this business, for it to be 'put to bed', as Prince Rostislav Romanov said at the time. Soon, however, the cracks began to appear. The *Sunday Express* of 24 January 1993 flaunted a somewhat different banner headline: GREAT TSAR'S BONES HOAX. Along with many others I watched with a certain bemusement as a totally contradictory version of events was uncovered. Drawing together the many discordant voices within Russia itself who felt that a massive fraud was being perpetrated, it was in stark contrast to the perhaps over-neat account rendered by the *Sunday Times*.

Some of the new information was disquieting. Vladimir Bolshakov, a local historian, spoke of residents in the area who saw a group of people tampering with the grave area one month before Geli Ryabov, the 'discoverer' of the site in 1979, dug up the bones.[1] Ryabov himself, it emerged, was a graduate of the Moscow State Institute of Law, a holder of the USSR State Prize for criminal investigation, a former employee of the interior ministry department better known to us as the KGB, and an assistant to Soviet interior minister Shchelokov – hardly the credentials of a paragon of disinterest.[2] Ryabov and his associate Alexander Avdonin had special permission to work in the Central State Archive; this alone, at the height of the Soviet era, points strongly to state involvement in, or at least knowledge of, their enterprise. Similarly, it is difficult to believe that Boris Yeltsin, at that time the autocratic Communist Party boss in Ekaterinburg, then known as Sverdlovsk, would not have been aware of Ryabov's and Avdonin's excavations on the Koptiaki Road. Accounts of the official discovery of the bones in 1991 – twelve years later – by Lyudmilla Koryakova, an Ekaterinburg archaeologist, savoured of heavy continuing official involvement. When she was asked to leave her flat during the night of 11 July, she found she was accompanied by 'two of everything just like Noah's Ark – two police colonels, two detectives laden with cameras and video equipment, two forensic experts, two epidemiologists, the town procurator, his secretary and two policemen with sub-machine guns'. All this happened on the day after Boris Yeltsin's inauguration as post-Soviet Russia's first President. Koryakova's response to the nocturnal visit from this forbidding squad was telling. Though told only that this involved a secret burial 'from the Soviet period', she responded immediately, 'Oh, you mean the grave of Nikolai II.' In

Ekaterinburg what had been going on in the Koptiaki Road appeared to be an open secret; in fact, the area was the haunt of souvenir hunters every Sunday.[3]

Nikolai Sokolov, who had produced the most authoritative contemporary investigation of the fate of the Tsar's family for the White government in 1918, had apparently made a minutely detailed search of this very same site in that year without finding anything; yet no one has ever questioned the thoroughness of his methods. The Russian government's initial refusal to release imperial dental records and the later refusal to examine part of a bandage soaked in the Tsar's blood from an attempt on his life in Japan in 1892 rode uneasily with Boris Yeltsin's denial that 'the President or his administration took part in any forgery related to the Tsar family remains'. Despite contemporary Bolshevik accounts that the Romanovs were finished off by bayoneting, there were no scars on the bones. Professor Alec Jefferies of Leicester University, the founding father of DNA testing in Britain, went on the record as saying that if bones had been switched with those of close relatives, it would be very difficult to tell them apart. Taking all these factors together, it became obvious that the truth about the bones was neither pure nor simple.[4]

The authors of the *Sunday Express* article, Vitaly Kozlikin and Cathy Scott-Clark, interestingly revealed that 'the British monarchy is so interested in the fate of the Tsar that Prince Philip recently donated a blood sample to Aldermaston'. Once the focus of anti-nuclear protest, this forbidding military establishment in Berkshire was then the site of the British Home Office Forensic Science Service Laboratory. Bone samples from Ekaterinburg had apparently been undergoing tests there since September 1992. But it was not until August 1993, nearly one year later, that the Ekaterinburg bones were formally identified as the Romanovs' by the Aldermaston team led by Dr Peter Gill, practitioners of the relatively new science of DNA testing. Once again the pendulum seemed to swing away from the sceptics towards the believers, weighted by the new wisdom of state-of-the-art scientific practice. Now, verification seemed a foregone conclusion. The world eagerly awaited Gill's learned paper on the subject; but it was February 1994 before this was published in the journal *Nature Genetics*.[5]

Two types of DNA exist within the human body – nuclear or genomic DNA and mitochondrial DNA. Nuclear DNA is inherited from both father and mother, whereas mitochondrial DNA is inherited from the mother alone, passing unchanged through the female line down the succeeding generations. Dr Gill called it a 'time machine', and indeed, cases of mitochondrial DNA from bodies four thousand years old matching that of living individuals have occurred. Mitochondrial DNA, said Gill, gives a more reliable result than nuclear DNA precisely because it remains unchanged. Prince Philip's mitochondrial DNA, inherited from his mother and ultimately – like that of his maternal great-aunt, the Tsarina – from Queen Victoria, had apparently matched the Tsarina skeleton perfectly. Since five of the skeletons appeared to be a family group comprising a mother, father and three children, and could be shown to be so by their nuclear DNA, it seemed reasonable to assume that these bones were those of the imperial family.

Nuclear and mitochondrial DNA had been extracted from these seventy-five-year-old bones using the latest PCB technique, developed by the American firm Perkin-Elmer. In this method an old, degraded sample is taken and the DNA within it multiplied to yield sufficient quantities for testing. It all seemed very high-tech and convincing. Only one cloud hovered on Gill's horizon. Apparently, mitochondrial DNA from the Tsar skeleton did not match donations from two living relatives, Irina Sfiris and the Duke of Fife. Gill explained this away as a mutation or heteroplasmy, claiming that the Tsar had two kinds of mitochondrial DNA in his blood. Because of this supposed mutation, Gill identified the bones as those of the imperial family with only a 98.5 per cent degree of certainty.[6] Such a mutation, however, occurs only once in every 120 generations – a period of 3,700 years[7] – which makes it very long odds against its happening in the Tsar's case. It was the more unlikely since the two relatives with whom the bones were being compared, who after all belonged to later generations than the Tsar, had still not mutated. The mutation argument did not seem to carry a great deal of conviction; but the alternative would have been to announce that the 'Tsar' did not match his own relatives. In any event, 98.5 per cent certainty was not good enough for the Russians, particularly the Orthodox Church which, declining to be blinded by science, demanded further testing.[8]

Other facts suggesting caution in respect of the Gill results soon began to emerge. Apparently, the PCB technique used to multiply the DNA had shortcomings: as well as multiplying the material for analysis, it also multiplied any contamination that might be present in the sample.[9] Reporting, meanwhile, continually played down the inconvenient absence of the missing Tsarevich and Grand Duchess as if it were of no consequence that their bodies were not there. Sloppily, it kept repeating that the whole imperial family had been found. But they hadn't.

In 1993 the Ekaterinburg authorities, working independently from Moscow, had called in the anthropologist Professor William Maples, head of the C. D. Pound Human Identification Laboratory in the University of Florida at Gainesville. Maples was a forensic warrior with some important historical identifications behind him, including those of the Nazi war criminal Josef Mengele and the Spanish conquistador Pizarro. Maples made a huge difference to the case by being the first to declare publicly that two bodies were missing from the burial pit – those of Alexei and one of his sisters. Having swept away the existing ambiguity on this point, Maples showed every sign of being equally ruthless with other aspects of the case. Among the team he gathered around him were Dr Lowell Levine, a dental expert, and Dr Michael Baden, the forensic pathologist who had openly condemned the Gill result as 'nonsense': 'With DNA it's either 100 per cent or it isn't,' he said.[10]

I had been dimly aware of this escalating controversy, which had all the makings of a scientific showdown, throughout 1993; but after Phillips' approach to me over Chebotarev and my discovery soon thereafter that he and his sister were buried together in Holt, I became quietly excited. Two bodies were missing; and we had two bodies. Knowing what I already knew about Chebotarev, I really did wonder if we possessed the solution to the Ekaterinburg mystery. Summers and Mangold, using the expert evidence of Professor Francis Camps, had shown conclusively in The File on the Tsar that it was impossible to dispose of bodies entirely – a finding reiterated by the Russian playwright and historian Edvard Radzinsky in his book, The Last Tsar.[11] Even the Nazis with their massive crematoria and ovens had failed to obliterate completely the remains of all their victims. Finding it increasingly difficult to accept that the two missing bodies had been totally destroyed, I began to interest myself thoroughly in the whole question of these Russian bones. The story I uncovered was riddled with inconsistencies and unanswered questions, all of which cast increasing doubt on the authenticity of the 'imperial' remains.

I decided to contact William Maples directly. Not only was he the man who had first made public the fact that two bodies were missing from the burial pit; he had actually handled these remains and identified them. We first spoke in early February 1994; I found him engaging and open, with a dry Texan accent and wry humour, and we soon developed a telephone friendship. Bill Maples was married to an Irish American whose family were from Armagh, about an hour's drive from where I

Nikolai Chebotarev in 1985

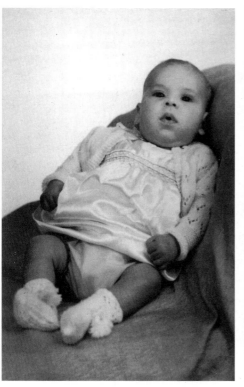

*Above left* The only picture of 'Michael Gray' as a young baby in the Gray family album

*Above right* Gray with his surrogate parents, c.1954

*Left* The medical record, showing the inconsistencies referred to on p. 10

Christian Names

National Registration Identity Number

MQFX | 258: —

Doctor's Name

Coalditt Cipher and Stamp

.M. Robertson

138.

W. B. PATON,
MAIN STREET,
WARINGSTOWN,

138

CO. DOWN.

5 JUL 1948

EXECUTIVE COUNCIL

NI

2/8/49

*Above* The Old Courthouse, Collon, Co. Louth, where Nikolai Couriss
lived from 1932 to 1977

*Below* Left to right: 'Mr White', Count Peter Apraxine, Kathleen McCarthy,
Maire McEntee, Mrs Sana Couriss, Nikolai Couriss, Dr Martha Apraxine,
Conor Cruise O'Brien; seated at front, Prince Paul Lieven. Collon, 1959

*Below* Kathleen McCarthy today

*Above* From the Collon visitors' book: George Blake (right), the spy, May 1948

*Below* Blake with the Courisses and Paul Lieven

*Above* Prince Paul Lieven's modest house at Collon
*Below right* Sana Couriss, *née* Bibikov from Ekaterinburg, on the day of her presentation at the imperial court
*Below left* Mme Bibikov, Mrs Couriss' mother

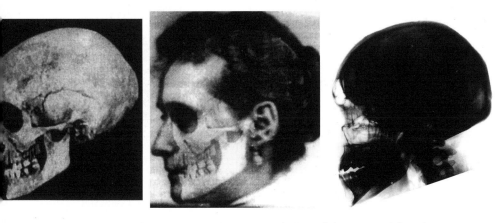

Comparison of author's skull (far right) with that of the 'Tsarina' found
near Ekaterinburg

*Below* The alleged Romanov bones

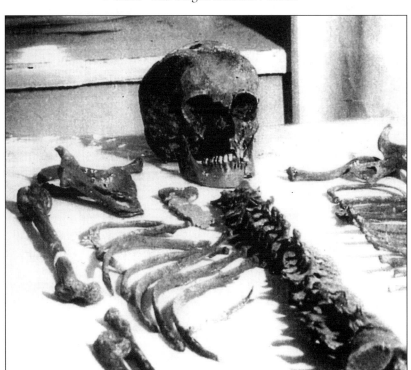

*Facing page:* *Top left* Grand Duchess Militsa    *Top right* Grand Duchess Stana
*Centre left* Grand Duke Vladimir    *Centre right* Grand Duchess Maria Pavlovna
*Bottom left* Grand Duke Nikolai (Nikolasha)    *Bottom right* Rasputin

Петербургъ

Правительственный Вѣстникъ копіи Освѣдомительному Бюро Телеграфному Агентству и Князю Гагарину Фонтанка 20 для свѣдѣнія

Напечатайте нижеслѣдующее сдѣлавъ заголовокъ: "Сообщеніе Министра ИМПЕРАТОРСКАГО Двора": Острый и тяжелый періодъ болѣзни ЕГО ИМПЕРАТОРСКАГО ВЫСОЧЕСТВА НАСЛѢДНИКА ЦЕСАРЕВИЧА и Великаго Князя АЛЕКСѢЯ НИКОЛАЕВИЧА миновалъ и нынѣ является возможнымъ дать общую картину заболѣванія ЕГО ИМПЕРАТОРСКАГО ВЫСОЧЕСТВА по нижеслѣдующимъ даннымъ пользующихъ АВГУСТѢЙШАГО Больного врачей точка За время этого періода со всѣхъ концовъ Россіи поступали и продолжаютъ поступать на ВЫСОЧАЙШЕЕ Имя ИХЪ ВЕЛИЧЕСТВЪ обращенія, въ которыхъ различные слои общества въ самыхъ сердечныхъ выраженіяхъ сообщаютъ о молитвахъ, возносимыхъ ими о выздоровленіи НАСЛѢДНИКА ЦЕСАРЕВИЧА точка Это всеобщее проявленіе вѣрноподданническихъ чувствъ любви и преданности глубоко тронуло ИХЪ ВЕЛИЧЕСТВА точка ГОСУДАРЮ ИМПЕРАТОРУ и ГОСУДАРЫНѢ ИМПЕРАТРИЦѢ АЛЕКСАНДРѢ ѲЕОДОРОВНѢ благоугодно было соизволить выразить отъ Имени ИХЪ ВЕЛИЧЕСТВЪ сердечную ИХЪ благодарность всѣмъ, выказавшимъ душевное свое участіе по случаю болѣзни ЕГО ИМПЕРАТОРСКАГО ВЫСОЧЕСТВА НАСЛѢДНИКА ЦЕСАРЕВИЧА точка Министръ ИМПЕРАТОРСКАГО Двора, Генералъ-Адъютантъ Баронъ Фредериксъ 21-го Октября 1912 года Спала.

Непосредственно за симъ напечатайте двѣ-точки:

Въ первыхъ числахъ истекшаго Сентября мѣсяца, на первыхъ дняхъ пребыванія въ Бѣловѣжѣ, ЕГО ИМПЕРАТОРСКОЕ ВЫСОЧЕСТВО НАСЛѢДНИКЪ ЦЕСАРЕВИЧЪ, прыгая въ лодку, сдѣлалъ очень широкій шагъ. Первое время послѣ этого не набл... сколько нибудь улов... СТВА. Этому случаю, писать появившуюся... тября - въ лѣвой по... тотчасъ-же опредѣл...

димомъ покоѣ и соовѣтствующемъ леченіи кровоизліяніе это стало черезъ три недѣли настолько незначительнымъ, что почти вовсе не прощупывалось, и больной уже началъ дѣлать попытки становиться на ноги. 28-го Сентября, желая сдѣлать нѣсколько самостоятельныхъ шаговъ, НАСЛѢДНИКЪ ЦЕСАРЕВИЧЪ, не смотря на самый бдительный надзоръ, вслѣдствіе неловкаго движенія, упалъ, чѣмъ, нужно думать, и объясняется новое кровоизліяніе въ ту-же область, проявившееся въ ночь на 2-е Октября. На этотъ разъ оно заняло гораздо большее пространство, а именно: всю лѣвую подвздошную область и всю поясничную той-же стороны, причемъ внутренняя граница его заходила нѣсколько за среднюю линію живота. Подобныя забрюшинныя кровоизліянія въ видѣ послѣдствія даже не очень сильной травмы встрѣчаются, какъ видно изъ спеціальной литературы, чрезвычайно рѣдко и представляютъ собою совершенно опредѣленную, - крайне тяжелую, клиническую форму / haematoma retroperitoneale /. Частью подъ вліяніемъ всасыванія излившейся крови, частью вслѣдствіе развивающагося вокругъ нея реактивнаго воспалительнаго процесса, такія гематомы могутъ сопровождаться- т.е. кровяныя опухоли могутъ сопровождаться очень возвышенной температурой, каковая и наблюдалась у ЕГО ВЫСОЧЕСТВА. Естественнымъ послѣдствіемъ такихъ обширныхъ кровоизліяній является значительное малокровіе, требующее иногда не малаго времени для полнаго его излеченія, а также могутъ быть весьма длительное затрудненіе въ свободномъ пользованіи той ногой, со стороны которой была гематома, какъ вслѣдствіе бывшаго пропитыванія кровью сгибающей бедро мышцы / musculus ileopsoas / и окружающей клѣтчатки, такъ и отъ продолжительнаго давленія опухоли на соотвѣтствующій нервъ. Подписали Лейбъ-Педіатръ Раухфусъ, Почетный Лейбъ-Хирургъ Профессоръ Ѳедоровъ, Лейбъ-Медикъ ЕГО ВЕЛИЧЕСТВА Ев. Боткинъ, Почетный Лейбъ-Медикъ С. Острогорскій. Октября 20 дня 1912 года Спала.

Мосоловъ

*Above* The Tsarevich's medical record

*Left* The Tsarevich in obvious good health, June 1917

was living, and we made repeated (though, sadly, unfulfilled) plans to meet on one of their annual forays to London. In the meantime, we talked freely with one another: I told him about my discoveries relating to the mysterious Russian prince; he confided in me his serious concerns about what was happening over the Ekaterinburg bones.

His concerns were many, and began with the procedure surrounding the uncovering of the remains. For one thing, he never actually saw the bones in the ground; when he arrived they were laid out, washed, on mortuary tables in the morgue in Ekaterinburg. Twenty tons of earth had been sifted through, he said, and there was not a single trace of Alexei or the missing Grand Duchess.[12] As for the remains that had been found, the impression that nine complete individuals were present in the burial pit was entirely misleading. More than half the total number of bones nine bodies would possess were missing – over a thousand bones in all. Half of the backbone of the skeleton Maples presumed to be Grand Duchess Tatiana, for instance, was absent. Also, though adipocere or 'grave grease' – a fatty substance generated by decomposing bodies – had been present in the ground around the remains, no bioforensic tests by enterologists had been carried out at the site.[13]

To my layman's mind it seemed that if large bones like vertebrae were missing, this probably indicated that the skeletons had, at some time in their history, been moved. Bill Maples admitted to me that the bodies might well have been buried not in 1918 but at some time after that. He even conceded that, if these individuals had been killed and buried only two years later, the skeleton identified as that of Anastasia would have exhibited more signs of maturity, with bones in the skull fusing, for example, and that this would go some way towards bridging the gap between his interpretation of the discovery and that of the Russian scientist Sergei Abramov. Abramov, who had developed the technique of computerized imaging of skulls, had claimed that the missing girl was Maria, while Maples maintained it was Anastasia because all of the girls' skeletons were mature, whereas in 1918 Anastasia had still been only seventeen and not all of her cranial bones would have fused. But if the burials had taken place even a couple of years later, Anastasia would have exhibited the same maturity as her sisters and so it would have been impossible to say which was the missing Grand Duchess.[14]

Nevertheless, Maples continued vehemently to dismiss Abramov's computerized facial reconstruction technique, which superimposed a photograph on top of the image of the skull, and which, because of its undoubted visual impact, was widely used on television. 'The faces were so badly smashed up,' Maples said, 'and putting them together was really a matter of guesswork . . . I could have created George Bush or Bill Clinton from the same skull.'[15] The much-vaunted Russian technique, was, he believed, producing a kind of 'Piltdown man', a spurious image designed to fit the photographs. The Russian forensics expert and criminologist Professor Viacheslav Popov of the St Petersburg Military Medical Academy, a member of Maples' team, pointed out that all the cardinal points – the points from which facial measurements are taken – are missing from all of the smashed-up skulls, and that it is these cardinal points, at the nose and mouth in particular, that determine facial appearance.[16]

Maples' reservations about the treatment of the grave and the putative identification of its occupants by dubious means were just the beginning. He was also concerned that the authentication of the bones by Dr Peter Gill and the British Home Office laboratory rested entirely on a solitary blood sample from Prince Philip, Duke of Edinburgh. To Maples, this reliance on a single sample was bad scientific technique. He wanted more blood samples from other living relatives of the imperial family with which to compare the bone samples and teeth he had taken back to America from Ekaterinburg; and he had sent a researcher, Dr Willi Korte, to Germany to try to obtain them. He suggested that I speak to Korte who, he said, worked on the fringes of the intelligence community and knew more about what was going on than anyone else.

Shortly after this conversation, in February 1994, I contacted Willi Korte at his home at Silver Spring in Maryland, just down the road from CIA headquarters at Langley near Washington.[17] Several important pointers emerged from that contact. Korte, who had been working on this project since the spring of 1992, spoke of the wall of secrecy which surrounded Gill's operation at Aldermaston. Like Maples, he found Gill's unwillingness to discuss his work hard to understand. Why did he need to protect his work, and from whom? Willi Korte believed that the process of identifying the Ekaterinburg remains should have been an international co-operative effort, properly structured and internationally supervised. 'That is what everyone hoped,' he said, 'when US Secretary of State Baker visited Ekaterinburg back in 1992.' Gill's laboratory may now have been a 'Next Steps agency', working at 'arm's length' from the Home Office, but it seemed to have lost none of its old culture of secrecy from the days before the public service reorganization when it was an integral part of the department. Indeed, how could it when the same people worked there? Korte, again like Maples, voiced his discomfort about the direct involvement of the British government in the whole affair.[18]

What Maples and Korte said seemed eminently sensible and fairminded; and there was at least one precedent for a different way of going about such a sensitive investigation. Work on the authentication of the Turin Shroud – alleged to be the winding-sheet that had covered Jesus' body after the crucifixion – had been carried out by three independent teams, each of which took samples under supervision which passed down a clear chain of custody from that point to each laboratory where they were tested. Why were such methods not employed with the Ekaterinburg bones? Pavel Ivanov, Gill's Russian associate, had arrived at Heathrow airport with the bone samples he had brought for testing in a blue Aeroflot flight bag which also contained his sandwiches.[19] Scientific detachment is one thing, but this appeared slipshod and slapdash, not to mention disrespectful.

So much of what was being done surrounding these bones seemed to be cloaked in secrecy. Metropolitan Ioann of St Petersburg, one of Russia's leading churchmen whose cathedral was the last resting place of Russia's Tsars, stated publicly that the Church would not be burying the Ekaterinburg remains and spoke darkly of the 'secret means' of their discovery. 'I think', he added, 'that there has been an attempt to fool the public with these bones.'[20] His distrust was widely shared. As recently as February 1998 the Holy Synod of the Russian Orthodox Church criticized First Deputy Prime Minister Boris Nemtsov for the secrecy which has surrounded and still surrounds the work of the state commission on the bones.[21] In 1993 Tikhon Kulikovsky, son of the Tsar's younger sister, Grand Duchess Olga, said he believed the whole thing was a tourist stunt to make money, refused to give a blood sample and denounced the bones as false.

In Germany, Korte succeeded in obtaining an additional blood sample from Prince Philip's only surviving sister, Princess Sophie of Hanover. Maples had lined up the laboratory of Dr Marie-Claire King in the Berkeley campus of the University of California to carry out the testing. The Berkeley DNA database was universally recognized to be the best available anywhere in the world, containing DNA from over one thousand individuals whereas Gill's had fewer than three hundred.[22] The testing was actually carried out by Dr Charles 'Chuck' Ginther. Everyone waited anxiously for the result. And waited. Nothing happened. Maples became quietly desperate, and then more noisily desperate. On these results depended not only the completion of his report – a report the Ekaterinburg authorities were now demanding – but the whole credibility of his team.[23] Up to this point, the Berkeley lab had appeared keen to co-operate in what was, after all, a headline-grabbing enterprise. Now silence had fallen. Clearly, something had gone badly wrong after the blood sample from Princess Sophie arrived for testing. Things came to a head during a meeting with Sir Brian McGrath, Prince Philip's private secretary, at Buckingham Palace on 8 May 1994, at which Willi Korte was accused of tampering with or 'manipulating' Princess Sophie's blood. In exasperation, Willi blurted out to me: 'What can you do to a blood sample? Nothing. What did they think I did to it? Did they think I peed on it?'[24]

Maples could get nothing in writing from Berkeley but he did get some kind of verbal comment. At first he spoke openly about it: Princess Sophie's mitochondrial DNA, it appeared, did not match that of her brother Prince Philip. Later, he was more coy. 'Berkeley wanted to do everything. Then they got Princess Sophie's blood sample. Then nothing. I could get nothing out of them. Draw your own conclusions.'[25] To me it seemed surprising that one scientist would fail to respond to another in this way. It emerged that there had been considerable friction between Dr King and Dr Ginther which, according to Willi Korte, resulted in Dr Ginther's dismissal early that summer.[26] Dr King, holder of two professorships in Berkeley, one of America's most prestigious seats of learning, has since moved to Washington State University in Seattle.

Nothing that has been written about this controversy to date, by the two authors who have touched on the subject – John Klier and Robert Massie – amounts to an adequate explanation of what really happened. Massie, basing his account on Dr Maples' court deposition at the time of the Anna Anderson tissue sample case in November 1993, points out that Dr King, unlike Gill, found no heteroplasmy at position 16169 in the mitochondrial DNA of the Ekaterinburg Tsar skeleton. That, put simply, would mean that the Tsar skeleton was not the Tsar. It was a non-match. Massie asserts that Maples' position had changed by June 1994, when he said that Dr King had difficulty in the same region but was unsure whether to attribute it to heteroplasmy or simply, and more probably, to contamination. Contamination would certainly have been exaggerated by the PCB techniques Gill used, which multiply the degraded DNA in old bones using chemical gels; and it could have occurred at many points.[27] The bones had been piled into the shallow grave one on top of another; somebody had washed them before displaying them in Ekaterinburg; Maples found them lying uncovered in the morgue where anyone could have touched them; and they were known to have been handled by many people, including US Secretary of State James Baker. Yet I found it hard to accept that Dr King would fail to respond to Bill Maples over this matter, especially if he knew the information sufficiently well already to have made a statement and court deposition. It seemed more likely to me that Princess Sophie's sample had not matched that of Prince Philip. Maples told me of a case where two sisters he knew with certainty to be the children of the same mother had different mitochondrial DNA readings; there was no doubt that the issue of two siblings not having matching mitochondrial DNA was preying on his mind.[28] He appeared to be rationalizing the non-match of Prince Philip and Princess Sophie by saying that mitochondrial DNA was not as reliable as people thought and that it varied far more often, by a set of rules not yet understood, than people imagined. Bill Maples was a troubled man.

It was only as recently as 17 February 1998 that the shortcomings of mitochondrial DNA came into the public domain. Speaking in Philadelphia, at the one hundred and fiftieth annual meeting of the American Association for the Advancement of Science, Dr Bill Shields of New York State University cited studies which showed that 'up to 30 per cent of individuals in a DNA database produced mitochondrial matches where there was no family link'. Dr Shield's paper to the AAAS demonstrated that out of a total population of 333 Caucasians, 123 could expect to have mitochondrial DNA sequences identical with at least one other individual in that population. Put simply, this means that about one in three people shared the same mitochondrial DNA with another individual to whom they were not related. This feature is peculiar to Caucasian populations – the group to which the Tsar and his family belonged. It does not happen to anything like the same extent in Hispanic, African American, Afro-Caribbean or African populations. Studies on these groups produced much lower ratios: one in nine in Hispanics and zero in Africans.[29] Calling for a moratorium on the application of mitochondrial DNA evidence until the technology was more advanced, Shields effectively demolished the main basis for the identification of the Ekaterinburg bones as the Russian imperial family.

Both the Tsarina and Tsar skeletons had been identified using mitochondrial DNA, and only mitochondrial DNA: it was the single thing
linking those skeletons to Romanov relatives, living and dead. What Bill
Shields now characterized as the far more reliable nuclear DNA could
establish only the existence of a family group in that burial pit – a
mother, father and three daughters. His findings also clarified the concerns Bill Maples had expressed back in 1994 about non-matches in
siblings. What Peter Gill had claimed to be the most reliable form of
DNA appears, in the present state of research, simply not to be so. With
a one in three chance of unrelated individuals having matching mitochondrial DNA, the identification of the Ekaterinburg bones now began
to look distinctly shaky. Put bluntly, if mitochondrial DNA was all we
had to go on, the bones might be anybody's.

Dr Shields' findings had further implications for the tests already conducted. Mitochondrial DNA, he said, was unpredictable: two samples
from the same individual, for example one from the bone and one from
the saliva, or one from hair and one from blood, could be different. He
added that when cell-multiplication techniques were used – as they had
been by Dr Gill – 'tiny mutations in mitochondrial DNA could multiply
confusingly.'[30] If mitochondrial DNA can vary within one individual,
this could be another reason why a sample from Prince Philip might not
have matched one from his sister Princess Sophie; by the same token, it
further weakens any identification of the Ekaterinburg bones on the basis
of mitochondrial DNA. It could also throw light on something Bill
Maples had told me back in summer 1994. Apparently, in another case
Dr Marie-Clare King's Berkeley laboratory had obtained two different
mitochondrial DNA readings from the same bone. Contamination with
other human remains was unlikely to have taken place, since the remains
were from a lone-pilot American spy plane shot down over Armenia
during the Cold War. At the time Maples had confided to me his grave
anxieties about the implications of this result for the use of mitochondrial
DNA to establish identity.[31]

Nor were the problems with DNA testing confined to the purely biological elements of the process. Another paper presented to the same
meeting at which Bill Shields dropped his bombshell revealed serious
problems in the way DNA evidence is presented to courts. Dr Jonathan
Koehler of the University of Texas, who was a consultant on the O. J.
Simpson team, explained to the AAAS that surveys had shown that if the
probability of a coincidental blood sample match were presented to a

jury as 0.1 per cent, they would convict on the basis of a match, whereas if the same information were presented in a different way, as a one in a thousand chance of a coincidental match, they would not.[32] David Foskett QC, a leading counsel working in this field who has questioned the use of DNA evidence, pointed out that in a typical DNA sample only one thirty-thousandth of an individual's DNA is used.[33] Potential problems were also identified in the way tests are conducted. Many scientists conducting tests in crime laboratories know enough about the cases under investigation to make it impossible for them to carry out truly 'blind' tests. This cannot but increase the danger of biasing the findings where there is an element of ambiguity in the result. In the USA, thousands of legal convictions have been based solely on DNA evidence, and disclosures such as those made by Drs Shields and Koehler could be expected to produce unprecedented upheaval in the court system.

Four years earlier, though, we were still putting our trust in Dr Gill's 'time machine', and mitochondrial DNA was still being widely presented as utterly reliable, a 'tool of justice' as an editorial in Nature Genetics described it.[34] No one back in 1994, when Gill was already saying the Tsar skeleton did not match his relatives because he had mutated, would have accepted that Prince Philip's DNA might have mutated too – that would have been straining public credulity too far – and at that point no other scientifically valid explanation was available. Covering up the results was probably the only feasible option, which may well explain the silence over Princess Sophie's mitochondrial DNA reading. If a non-match between Prince Philip and his sister had been announced then, before our more recent knowledge about the unreliability and random unpredictability of mitochondrial DNA could be brought to bear to explain the discrepancy, the question was bound to have been asked: who was not his or her mother's child? Rightly or wrongly, people would have speculated on Prince Philip's parentage, and that would have had serious implications for the identification of the Ekaterinburg bones. As far as the bones were concerned, the obvious next step at that time had to be to see if there were any other people against whom the bones could be tested in order to clear up the lingering doubts and ambiguities.

Tsarina Alexandra had shared the mitochondrial DNA of her maternal grandmother Queen Victoria, whose relatives, as well as those of Victoria's maternal half-sister Princess Feodora of Leiningen, can be readily traced in the pages of Burke's Royal Families of the World, volume I. Eventually, after some grinding work in this compendium, I arrived at a list of eighty-four living individuals, apart from Prince Philip and his sister, who should share the Tsarina's mitochondrial DNA, all being descended in the various female lines of descent from Queen Victoria and her half-sister. On the basis of the assumptions about the reliability of mitochondrial DNA tests current in 1994, if samples from two or more of these individuals from different lines of descent had been tested and matched each other, that would have given a clear and unambiguous picture of the real Tsarina's mitochondrial DNA profile. Such a result, if it failed to match the Ekaterinburg bones, would plainly show that the female bones were not those of Alexandra and her daughters. Tests carried out along these lines back in 1994 would have gone a long way towards answering Maples' doubts about reliance on one blood sample from Prince Philip. It was an obvious solution and logistically straight-forward; yet at no time between 1994 and the announcement in early 1998 suggesting that mitochondrial DNA might not be the 'tool of justice' it had hitherto been considered did anyone attempt it. On the contrary, Prince Philip's sample has become the 'gold standard' against which everything is measured. The claim of Anna Anderson to be Grand Duchess Anastasia was dismissed out of hand: she was declared not to be a Romanov because she did not match Prince Philip's blood. End of story. Of course, if the results of tests on descendants of Queen Victoria through the female line did not tally with Prince Philip, then this would not only have cast major doubt on the Ekaterinburg remains, raising the disquieting possibility of a hoax; it would also – given the then existing assumptions about mitochondrial DNA – have cast a certain doubt on his own maternity. Skeletons can be found in cupboards just as often as in burial pits. Russia's leading forensic scientist Vladislav Plaksin, speaking of the Ekaterinburg bones, said: 'If this is not the Tsarist family, then all the British royals are not who they say they are.'[35]

Prince Philip had certainly evidenced a very keen interest in Rom-anov affairs, an interest that went well beyond the simple donation of a blood sample. Sir Brian McGrath, the Duke's private secretary, seems to have been actively involved in the campaign to discredit Anna Ander-son, who claimed to be Anastasia – a campaign waged lifelong by Lord Louis Mountbatten, who appeared to have passed the baton on to his nephew. 'Game, set and match' was McGrath's satisfied and hardly im-partial comment following the apparent debunking of Anna Anderson, again by Dr Gill, in 1995 – over ten years after her death.[36] What Dr Gill actually did was to show that Anna Anderson's mitochondrial DNA did not match that of Prince Philip. He went on to 'prove' that Anna Anderson could not be Anastasia because she was someone else – Fransiska Schwankowska, a deranged Polish factory worker. This was achieved by matching Anna Anderson's mitochondrial DNA to that of Karl Maucher, Schwankowska's great-nephew. Dr Richard Schweitzer and his wife Marina Botkin, grand-daughter of the doctor supposedly slain with the imperial family – both Anna Anderson supporters – were confronted with the news on film. Good television it may have been; but it was surely ethically questionable, since the Schweitzers had never given permission for this further comparative test against the Maucher sample. In their shock and disbelief the Schweitzers began to question whether something might be wrong with the sample block of tissue, purportedly from Anna Anderson, that had been retrieved by Gill from the Martha Jefferson Hospital in Charlottesville, Virginia. The hospital, which had conducted a bowel operation on Anna Anderson in 1979, had initially denied that it had any material, admitting only later to possessing this sample. Another sample of Anna Anderson's blood, taken in 1951 in Germany by Professor Stefan Sandkuhler and tested by Professor Bernd Hermann of Göttingen University, did not match the Virginia sample; and Gill himself has admitted that one of these samples – Charlottesville or Göttingen – has to be false.[37] Schweitzer believes the Charlottesville sample must have been switched or contaminated, and the hospital has conceded that the area where it was kept is far from secure. Whatever the rights or wrongs of the case, the intensity with which it was pursued is in no doubt, and testifies to Prince Philip's relentless continuation of Lord Mountbatten's preoccupation.

In respect of his family's relationship with the Romanovs, as in many other areas of his life, Louis Mountbatten promulgated a carefully crafted image. At his Hampshire home, Broadlands, he kept a photograph of Grand Duchess Maria by his bedside. In fact, Mountbatten relations with the Romanovs were not so cordial. In 1886 Tsar Alexander III had deposed Prince Alexander of Battenberg – Louis Mountbatten's uncle – as the sovereign prince of Bulgaria. Prince Alexander, who owed his position as ruler of this Slav country in the Balkans to the Tsar, had been acting more independently than was tolerable to Russia, in whose sphere of influence Bulgaria fell at the time. His unceremonious removal at the hands of the Tsar began a feud between the imperial Romanovs and the Battenbergs which festered and never really healed. It was a feud of the worst kind – a feud within a family: for Tsar Alexander III's mother was Prince Alexander of Battenberg's aunt, and in the next generation the Tsarina Alexandra's sister was married to Louis Mountbatten's father. Clearly, then, the Mountbattens had deep-seated reasons for disliking the Romanovs.[38]

Buckingham Palace itself is not so far removed from active political involvement as constitutional protocol would have us believe. Andrew Morton, better known for his exposé of the Princess of Wales's marital problems, made this clear when he wrote of the existence of a 'shadowy royal club', with its own formal and informal networks, and a cryptic language used in messages between its member sovereigns.[39] Morton went on to allege that the Queen, the Prince of Wales and King Juan Carlos of Spain had been 'active in co-ordinating moves to restore monarchies in newly democratic eastern bloc countries'. Enquiries conducted in the course of researching this book support Morton's claim of interest on the part of the British royal family in the fate of the former royal houses of Europe. A researcher was informed by a source close to the Palace that Prince Michael of Kent is intensely interested in the Romanov affair and has discussed the Romanovs in meetings with other members of the royal family, and was warned not to probe too deeply since the royal family still wields great power.

Recently it has been disclosed by the Ekaterinburg authorities that one of the vertebrae from the 'Tsar' skeleton went missing during filming by a television crew from Granite Films accompanied by Prince Michael of Kent. The filming was taking place at night. The same crew was also present, again with Prince Michael, on a separate, later occasion when the corpse of the Tsar's brother, Grand Duke George, was removed from the Romanov crypt in the Cathedral of St Peter and St Paul in St Petersburg.[40] Resulting in the removal of bone samples from the Tsar's brother, again for testing by Gill, that visit occurred when both Metropolitan Ioann – who would never have given his approval for the operation – and his representative, the Eptarchal Bishop, were absent from the city. It seems a less than regular way to proceed.[41]

Gill's associate Pavel Ivanov staged another publicity-grabbing coup with mitochondrial DNA analysis of Grand Duke George's femur. This time testing was carried out at the American Armed Forces Institute in Maryland, USA. Like Aldermaston, this was not regarded as a neutral venue by many Russians.[42] Apparently Grand Duke George's mitochondrial DNA exhibited exactly the same polymorphism as the Tsar's. Closer examination of the test results shows, however, that this is not exactly true. Certainly, at position 16169 in hypervariable region one Grand Duke George, like the Tsar, appears to have a heteroplasmy – but it is not the same heteroplasmy. There are two chemicals involved, cytosine and thymine. At position 16169, the Tsar skeleton's mitochondrial DNA was a mix of 72 per cent cytosine and 28 per cent thymine, whereas Grand Duke George's was almost the reverse of this with 70 per cent thymine and less than 30 per cent cytosine.[43] Grand Duke George's DNA, in other words, was predominantly thymine, like that of the Tsar's known relatives Irina Sfiris and the Duke of Fife – neither of whom matched the Tsar skeleton – whereas the Tsar skeleton was predominantly cytosine. Yet this has been trumpeted to the world as an 'exact' match. It is nothing of the kind.

In view of his presence on the two occasions noted above and his declared interest in Romanov affairs, the connections of Prince Michael of Kent merit some scrutiny. In January 1995 it emerged that Prince Michael's secretary, John Kennedy, had been arrested by Scotland Yard, having been followed by MI5 for two years.[44] Though this arrest appears to have been connected with alleged involvement in an attempt to embezzle money from a member of the Libyan royal family (a charge vigorously and successfully denied), some of Kennedy's links, to Bosnian Serb leader Radovan Karadzic for example, excited much comment at the time. Born to a Serb father and an English mother (his real name is Gvozdenovic), Kennedy's claim to be connected to the Montenegrin royal family had earned him the nickname 'Prince of Suburbo-Croatia' among his university friends. Among his associates were the acknowledged MI6 operative and Tory MP Harold Elletson, at that time parliamentary private secretary to the Northern Ireland education minister Michael Ancram. Kennedy and Elletson were both directors of the public relations company Thunderbolt and another company, Responsive Recycling, whose chairman was Henry Bellingham, Conservative MP for Norfolk North West and parliamentary private secretary to the then Foreign Secretary, Malcolm Rifkind. Kennedy's name has been persistently linked to Serb donations to the Conservative party.[45]

At the time of his arrest, Kennedy said MI5 were running a dirty tricks campaign against him personally and that the whole business was an attempt by 'a foreign intelligence agency to undermine Prince Michael of Kent'. Precisely in what way this would 'undermine' Prince Michael was never spelled out, since Prince Michael receives no money from the Civil List and has no official status in Britain. Later, it emerged that

Kennedy was 'paid off' by Prince Michael with two substantial amounts, one of £50,000 in 1995 and one of £105,000 in 1996, after serving writs on the prince containing what Prince Michael's aides described as 'shoddy and unsubstantiated claims'.[46] Prince Michael's spokesman spoke of Kennedy's 'extraordinarily aggressive behaviour in demanding payment', and on 19 May 1996 *The Times* revealed that Kennedy would have considered using information 'to bring down the whole bloody lot of them' if his case had gone ahead. *The Times* had alleged in January 1995 that Queen Elizabeth had been present at Kennedy's questioning by police[47] – though the Palace later denied this – and that, following his private secretary's arrest, Prince Michael of Kent had canvassed support for his trusted aide among members of the royal family. Prince Michael's payments to Kennedy were said to come from 'private royal resources', which presumably means the Queen since Prince Michael is known to have sustained heavy losses as a member of a Lloyd's insurance syndicate and is believed to be over £1.5 million in debt, with even his home at Nether Lypiatt Manor at risk.[48]

In 1996 Kennedy/Gvozdenovic became engaged to Princess Lavinia of Yugoslavia, the adopted daughter of Prince Andrew of Yugoslavia.[49] Prince Andrew's first wife was the daughter of Princess Sophie of Hanover, Prince Philip's sister and donor of the blood sample; his second wife was Princess Kyra of Leiningen, niece of Grand Duke Cyril of Russia, the self-styled 'Tsar-in-exile' and grandfather of the present claimant, Princess Maria Vladimirovna.[50] Princess Maria Vladimirovna has been in the forefront of those demanding that the Ekaterinburg bones receive a state funeral as those of the imperial Romanovs. Mr Gvozdenovic/Kennedy certainly has some interesting in-laws. There may be a split in the ranks, however, for in September 1996 Frederick Forsyth spoke to the *Daily Express* of the possibility of Prince Michael of Kent being a future Tsar of Russia; he even wrote a novel on the subject, entitled *Icon*.[51]

Claims that hidden connections exist between all of these people, and Morton's statements about a royal club, are buttressed by the similarities in much of what they have said. Princess Lavinia's uncle, Crown Prince Alexander of Yugoslavia, spoke of King Juan Carlos of Spain's achievement as the provider of unity for Spain. 'Grand Duchess' Maria Vladimirovna similarly spoke of the Spanish template for a new Russian monarchy. Ex-King Michael of Romania, an old schoolfriend of Prince Philip from his days in St Cloud near Paris,[52] is actively sponsored by Buckingham Palace for restoration in his former kingdom. So, according to Morton, is Crown Prince Alexander of Yugoslavia (now mainly Serbia). The Duke of Kent, the Queen's cousin and head of Britain's freemasons, has been openly spoken of as a future King of Poland. While he denies active interest, he is nonetheless learning Polish – by all accounts a difficult language and hardly a leisure activity to occupy idle moments.[53] During the Second World War the head of the Polish government-in-exile, Marshal Sikorski, offered the crown of Poland to the present Duke's father in an effort to bind Britain more closely to his beleaguered country, lying in the shadow of the overweening power of Soviet Russia to its east. At the time, since Russia was Britain's ally, the offer was wisely declined; Sikorski, like the then Duke of Kent himself, met his end in an air crash. Prince Edward, the Queen's third son, has been offered the crown of Estonia, another former part of the old Russian Empire, by that country's monarchists, who command 10 per cent of the electorate.[54]

What is important in all this for present purposes is not that Buckingham Palace may be acting unconstitutionally and outside Britain's national interests – that is a matter for others – but the implication that the royal family is not entirely detached from Russian affairs. Queen Elizabeth not only made a state visit to Russia in 1994 but on several occasions expressed a desire to attend a state funeral of the Ekaterinburg bones. In the event, she did not attend the burial of these bones on 17 July 1998, surrounded as it was by massive controversy and the active opposition of the Russian Orthodox Church. Prince Michael of Kent did, however, attend, supposedly with the Queen's blessing. He used the occasion to criticize the Russian Orthodox Church for its decision to boycott the ceremony and its refusal to declare the bones genuine. 'I have studied the results of the DNA testing carried out in England,' he said; 'I am quite convinced the remains are of the Tsar and his family.'[55]

What emerges is a picture of royal engagement, ranging from the donation of Prince Philip's blood sample, through Prince Michael of Kent's involvement with John Gvozdenovic/Kennedy and his presence with a camera team when one of the 'Tsar' vertebrae went missing, to Prince Philip's pursuit of the dead Anastasia claimant and the British royal support for a state funeral for the remains. All of this suggests the possibility of a conspiracy around these Ekaterinburg bones. Otherwise, we must believe life is just full of coincidences.

## ~ 7 ~

## Burying the Evidence

At the same time as these doubts about the reliability of the Prince Philip 'gold standard' in the identification of the Ekaterinburg bones emerged, increasingly numerous and serious inconsistencies in the evidence relating to the bones themselves were becoming apparent. As we have already seen, Nikolai Sokolov, the magistrate appointed by General Dietricks of the White government in 1918 to investigate the presumed deaths of the imperial family, had searched the area of the Koptiaki Road and did not find these bones, yet no one disputed his thoroughness as an investigator; local historian Vladimir Bolshakov remarked that people in the area had seen a group tampering with the grave site in 1979, a month before Ryabov and Avdonin found the bones; and Professor Alec Jefferies, the inventor of the mini-satellite DNA tests which Gill uses, said that 'if the bones had been switched with close relatives, particularly the Tsar's brother, it would be very difficult to tell them apart.'

The possibility that a substitution had taken place could not be discounted. The body of the Tsar's younger brother is still officially missing. Grand Duke Mikhail was taller than the Tsar by five inches – by the same variation, in fact, as that between the height of the 'Tsar' skeleton as measured by the Russians on exhumation and its height as measured later by Dr Maples. Maples complained that the femur and arm bones had been sawn through and cut into sections, which made determining height very difficult.[1] Everyone denied all knowledge as to when and why this had happened, or who had done it. His concerns dismissed with a shrug, Maples had to be content with measuring what lay in front of him – complete or not. He was convinced that the Tsar skeleton had been given the arms of the servant Trupp, who was six feet tall: he said it made the Tsar look like an orang-utan. But if the original Russian estimate of the Tsar skeleton's height was correct, perhaps these were not Trupp's arms after all but those of a six-foot man. If that were the case, it patently could not be Nikolai, who, like his cousin George V, was only five feet seven inches tall. As the forensic scientist and criminologist Viacheslav Popov said on

Russian television news on 20 February 1998, 'Skeletons, if anything, shrink after death, they do not grow.'

Ryabov and Avdonin's story of their discovering the bones in 1979 is well known. They removed three skulls: Ryabov took two of these to Moscow while Avdonin, somewhat bizarrely, kept the third under his bed. One year later, in 1980, they reburied all three. In 1991 the grave was opened and the bodies exhumed. That much is admitted by the key participants.[2] What appears to have been overlooked in the official presentation of the bones story is that there may have been other exhumations. In 1993, writing in Britain's *Royalty* magazine, historian Alexander Bokhanov illustrated his article entitled 'A Quest for Truth' with a photograph of 'the findings of a Judicial Medical Investigation'. It was dated in Russian 'IX. 89 r.', with instructions to circulate to 'Abramov'. In other words, the bones – or at least the skulls – had been exhumed in September 1989.[3] Though the document attributed the three skulls incorrectly, identifying one as the Tsar, one as Anastasia and one as Alexei, whereas all three were apparently female, its dating is explicit. Abramov, who performed the computer imaging work on the skulls, was not supposed to have seen them – or, indeed, to have been involved in the case at all – until July 1991; yet according to Professor Popov, who carried out the ballistics tests on the Ekaterinburg bones, Ryabov 'privately' showed a cast of one of these skulls to Professor Abramov in Moscow in 1979.[4] What was he doing with this report in 1989? What sort of official collusion does this imply?

Olga Kulikovsky, widow of the Tsar's nephew Tikhon Kulikovsky, writing in the *Imperial Russian Journal* in the autumn of 1995, spoke of yet another exhumation, this time in 1991.[5] The findings of the subsequent forensic examination were that the grave site was only between fifty and sixty years old, placing it firmly in the Stalinist terror period of the 1930s. In October 1995, in Moscow, Olga Kulikovsky also asserted that some parts of the alleged Tsar skeleton showed that it belonged to a bulky man who lived a sedentary life – hardly a description of Nikolai II.[6] None of these inconvenient suggestions tallies with the commonly presented official version of the story. Edvard Radzinsky, in his 1992 book *The Last Tsar*, even cites two visits paid to the grave site by the poet Mayakovsky, one of which was in 1928.[7] So, far from the bones being 'discovered' in 1991, they appear to have been wholly or partially exhumed or interfered with in 1979, 1980, 1989 and 1991 (twice) – and these are only the occasions we know about.

The names of some of those involved with the Ekaterinburg bones offer some suggestive coincidences. Ryabov, who discovered the graves, shares his name with one of the six assassins who, the day after the supposed murder of the imperial family, killed seven of their relatives and two others in Alapaevsk.[8] Abramov, the forensic scientist who did the imaging work on the Ekaterinburg skulls, shares his name with the head of the Cheka in Alapaevsk at the time of those killings.[9] Nemtsov, First Deputy Prime Minister and chairman of the state commission on the bones, shares his name with the Bolshevik Commissar for Tiumen province and chairman of the Perm Guberniya Central Executive Committee of the Communist Party in 1918.[10] Medveev, the historian who sits on the state commission on the bones, shares his name with the man who claimed to have shot the Tsar in Ekaterinburg. In this last case there is a known connection, for Medveev the historian is Medveev the assassin's son.[11]

Information which may have a direct bearing on the case appears to have been suppressed or, at the very least, ignored. In April 1991, soon after the first official exhumation of the bones, the sonorously named 'Group for the Investigation into the Circumstances of the Death of the Family of the Imperial House of Romanov', based in Ekaterinburg and led by Vadim Viner, released a diary, purporting to be that of Stepan Vaganov, named by Sokolov as one of the imperial family's assassins back in 1918. Intriguingly, that diary spoke of the family of a rich local manufacturer – a family said to be similar in number, age and sex to the Romanovs – being executed at the same time as the Romanovs disappeared, with the clear implication that they might have been executed instead of the imperial family.[12] In an article in *Komsomolskaya pravda* in January 1998 entitled 'Don't Rush to Bury Us', Alexander Murzin revealed that KGB archives contained a ten-volume report of an investigation relating to 'the burial near the village of Koptiaki of a group of persons nine in number outwardly resembling the family of the Emperor Nikolai II'.[13] Taken alongside the Vaganov diary, this suggests the real possibility of substitutes – perhaps related to the imperial family, perhaps not – having been murdered in the place of the Romanovs.

This ten-volume KGB archive was also cited in the dissenting report issued by three expert members of the state commission on the burial of the bones, in which they spoke of the 'documented disgrace' of the commission.[14] Most of the commission members are state servants, dependent on salaries paid by the government and therefore potentially vulnerable to pressure, but these three are independent experts – two academics and a churchman – and their dissent is therefore of great importance. S. A. Belaiev, V. V. Alexiev and Metropolitan Yuvenali of Krutiski and Kolomna sent their report to President Yeltsin following the publication of the commission's findings by its chairman Boris Nemtsov on 28 January 1998. In article 2 on page 3, the minority report quotes the KGB archive as mentioning the interment of bodies by the NKVD at Koptiaki in 1946. According to this minority report, evidence such as this has not even been considered by the commission.

Not all of the tests which could have been carried out on the Ekaterinburg remains have been performed. Comparing the putative Tsar with himself, or for that matter all of the skeletons with themselves, would have been perfectly possible. There would have been no need to compare them to relatives. Dress uniforms belonging to various members of the imperial family exist and are on display in the Ekaterinsky Palace at Tsarskoe Selo.[15] The Tsarevich's sweat-stained waistcoat is available at Peterhof, and his Cossack dress uniform is on display at Gatchina. Other items like boots are in the Kremlin Palace in Moscow. Dress uniforms are heavy and notoriously sweat-inducing, so it should have been possible, as indeed Willi Korte suggested back in 1994, to slough some sweat or flaked skin from the lining at the armpits or similar regions.

The story of the Otsu bandage, too, leaves more questions unanswered than resolved. In 1892, at Otsu in Japan during his tour of the Far East as Tsarevich, Nikolai was attacked by a fanatical policeman. Apparently, the Tsarevich needed desperately to answer a call of nature and proceeded to relieve himself against a stone by the roadside, unaware that it was a sacred object. The affronted policeman, appalled at this sacrilege, drew his sword and aimed a hail of blows at Nikolai's head. The Tsarevich was saved by the quick action of his companion, Prince George of Greece, who deflected the worst of the assault with his cane. But there was a lot of blood, and a piece of bone was dislodged from the Tsarevich's skull. The scar from this wound, the 'Otsu mark' as it came to be known, was clearly visible on the Tsar's right forehead for the rest of his life, and the wound left him with a tendency to headaches.[16]

Professor Popov said on 11 February 1998 that 'while there is much evidence to support the position that the remains are the Romanovs, Nemtsov's commission still has not shown its scientific data to the public. The commission's work has been done amid great secrecy. Seeds of doubt are caused by the fact that Nikolai II should have a sword scar on the right side of his head that was inflicted by a would-be assassin when the then Tsarevich visited Japan. But that scar is missing from the skull the government says is Nikolai II's.'[17]

Immediately after the attack the Japanese wrapped the wound in a cloth, which naturally became saturated with the Tsar's blood. This cloth was kept carefully in a box in the local museum until 1993, when the Japanese Emperor, prompted by his friend the Russian cellist Rostropovich, persuaded the local authorities in Otsu to give up a sliver of cloth, measuring three inches by one-eighth of an inch, for testing. Offered this undoubtedly important artefact, Dr Gill dismissed it curtly. 'The handkerchief had been handled by too many fingers. Cells slough off from fingers. There was a lot of blood on the handkerchief, but who knows how much of it was Nikolai's? And there was a lot of dust and dirt. It would be impossible to say that any result you got from that handkerchief was reliable. There were too many other possible contaminants.'[18] Gill seemed to be more scrupulous in respect of this cloth than he had been when it came to the bones themselves, which might well have been contaminated by contact with each other and by handling. What blood other than the Tsar's could have been on the bandage? Surely, in such a case, it is important to sift all the available evidence. Professor Popov believed that Gill's Russian associate, Pavel Ivanov, did in fact test a piece of the Otsu bandage in Moscow and obtained a negative result, failing to match the 'Tsar' skeleton – or, as Popov calls it with studied detachment, 'skeleton number four'.[19]

On 28 November 1997 the Otsu bandage made a reappearance in the controversy when Vladimir Malevianny, writing in *Nezavisimaya gazeta*, a middle-brow, non-tabloid and non-sensational newspaper with a large circulation, said the results of a DNA test comparing the bones both to the Otsu bandage and to a lock of the Tsar's hair, preserved by his mother when he was a child, were negative.[20] That such important evidence has been ignored by the state commission on the bones clearly calls its objectivity into question. Malevianny raised other points, too: for example, he suggested that full-length X-rays of the Tsar and Tsarina might exist in an English museum. This echoed information given to me by Korte in 1995 that X-rays of the imperial couple's chests existed in Boston, Massachusetts. X-rays that could be compared with the bones would be a powerful forensic tool; yet the commission seems not to have made any attempt to find them. Malevianny also mentioned the alleged departure of the Tsarina and her daughters under a secret protocol of the Treaty of

Brest-Litovsk, and the failure to conduct a proper search for information in the state and KGB archives, where much material still awaits discovery. 'If the official investigation is renewed,' the article continued, 'we can expect real sensations opposing all earlier well-known versions – there is also some evidence of the secret transportation of the Romanovs out of Russia where they became commoners with the help of the English secret service, living under assumed names.' To anyone reading this, it was obvious that the commission had ignored rather more evidence than could be explained away by mere inefficiency. Nor was the charge that enquiries were being officially masterminded levelled at the Russian authorities alone: Malevianny went on to assert explicitly that both Aldermaston and the Maryland laboratory of the American Armed Forces Institute, which have carried out tests on the bones, are under the control respectively of the secret services of Britain and America, MI6 and the CIA.[21]

Even more forms of testing are possible. At the back of the skull, in the lamboid suture, there was a fusion of bones producing a protrusion known as the 'Wormian' feature in four of the skeletons – those of the 'Tsarina' and her three daughters. This feature, according to Dr Maples, appears in only 5 per cent of the population, and could be present in living relatives of the Tsarina.[22] This is easily checkable, but it has never been done. Professor Popov said that the four female skulls supposed to be those of the Tsarina and three of her daughters, as well as that of the 'Tsar', were all elongated with a protruding rear. This is rare, occurring in less than one in ten of the population. Another unusual feature pinpointed by Popov in the same skeletons is the horseshoe-shaped lower jaw, which crowds the teeth in the front of the mouth; again, this occurs in only one in ten of the population. On the left and right lower jaw of the same skeletons tooth number six sits at an angle to tooth number five, so that the two partially overlap. All these features are rare and represent powerful forensic markers. The presence of any or all of them in another individual would link them strongly with these skeletons.[23]

Another forensic test which might yield interesting results would be tooth layering. This was suggested by Professor William Potts, co-author of *Queen Victoria's Gene* – the book that, perhaps more than any other, popularized a basic understanding of DNA.[24] In the same way as tree trunks grow outwards, leaving rings in the wood, human teeth lay down a thin layer of enamel each year. The thickness of each layer depends on the health of the individual at that time. By counting these layers, it would be possible to arrive at an accurate age for each skeleton at the time of death. Since the age of each member of the imperial family believed to be in the burial pit is known, it should be possible to determine which skeleton is which. None of the Grand Duchesses, for instance, should be over twenty-three years old; and since the ratio between their ages is known, this should be exactly replicated in the remains. The Tsar's tooth layers should establish his age at time of death and therefore when he was killed. If, for instance, it showed an age of fifty-three for the Tsar, that would point to their having been killed in 1921; but if one of the daughters was more than twenty-six at this time, then this could not be the imperial family. Such findings would be a very significant forensic tool. They could confirm the identification, or they could cast serious doubt on it. Yet again, these tests have never been carried out. Financial constraints within Russia cannot be the reason, for many of these teeth were taken by the Maples team back to the United States. On its own such a test would not be decisive; but it should be part of a barrage of tests, whose results taken as a whole could generate a persuasive conclusion. Maples always insisted that DNA tests should never be treated as conclusive in themselves, but only set within the context of other forensic findings. DNA testing is too young a science, he maintained, to be relied on exclusively; we are still at the cutting edge. In retrospect, now that doubts have been cast by the scientific community on the reliability of mitochondrial DNA itself – the main instrument used by Gill to identify these remains – his caution is entirely vindicated.

Disputes also rage over the two missing bodies. This remains the unfinished business of the burial commission. Among the lore surrounding these supposedly missing remains is the story of the box concealed in the wall of St Job's Cathedral in Brussels. Brought out of Russia by Sokolov in 1920, this material was supposed to comprise the assorted debris from the mineshaft. Sokolov offered the box to Grand Duke Nikolai, who curtly refused it, and then to King George V, who did likewise. Perhaps they knew better than to take it at face value; possibly they even knew the truth of what had happened to the imperial family. Whatever the reason, they declined to accept the box; and it is surely inconceivable that King George V would have turned away the remains of his near, and dear, relatives. But what is in the box? There are two versions, one of which has had some coverage again recently. Prince Alexei Scherbatov of the Russian Nobility Association said that it contained 'little pieces of bone, a lot of earth full of blood, two little bottles of congealed fat from the bodies and several bullets'.[25] Prince Alexei is the first cousin of Dr Martha Apraxine and doubly related to her father Count Apraxine, the Tsarina's secretary who was a friend and associate of Couriss and Chebotarev at Collon. Father Nikolai Semyonov of St Job's Cathedral in Brussels, part of the Russian Orthodox Church-in-exile which has canonized the entire imperial family as martyrs and therefore requires them to be dead, has restated this position again recently. He claims that the box is concealed within the walls of the cathedral – no one knows exactly where – so that the Communists would never find it. There is a monument to the Tsar and his family at the door, so the Sokolov box is probably there.

The second version concerns Grand Duchess Olga and Grand Duchess Xenia, the Tsar's two sisters, who actually saw inside this box when Sokolov brought it to their mother, the Dowager Empress. Grand Duchess Olga was totally open with her biographer, Ian Vorres, about what it contained – 'Half burnt bits of clothing, a few buttons, bits of broken jewellery and suchlike' was how she described it; no bits of bodies, no bottles of fat, no bones.[26] It would seem that these rumours are as persistent and as wrong as the rumours about the difficulty experienced in killing Rasputin. Professor Richard Pipes has shown that the autopsy on Rasputin was quite clear – he died from three gunshot wounds. Yet, though this was published at the time, fantastical stories about his strange vitality and how he eventually drowned persisted for eighty years. The story of the box in St Job's, which appears to have been buried earlier in Clamart in Paris before being transferred there, is of the same order as these inventions. It contains no bodily remains. Not surprisingly, the Church-in-exile refuses to produce these alleged remains. Dr Bill Maples' comment rings with more truth than the walls of St Job's: 'They sifted twenty tons of earth and there was nothing there which could represent either Alexei or the missing Grand Duchess.'[27]

It is no exaggeration to say that Russia is awash with bodies from the revolutionary and civil war period, Ekaterinburg having a particularly bloody reputation. Among the dead of this time are other members of the wider Romanov family whose bodies have unaccountably gone missing. About eighty miles north-east of Ekaterinburg on 17 July 1918 a Romanov massacre did take place. Though it did not involve the imperial family itself, it did involve their relatives, seven of whom, along with a secretary, Feodor Remez, and a nun named Barbara, died there. These included the Tsarina's strikingly beautiful sister, Grand Duchess

Elizabeth, known as Ella in the family, whose husband Grand Duke Sergei, Governor of Moscow, had been killed by a terrorist bomb in 1905. The other bodies thrown down a mineshaft with a grenade to follow were those of Prince Ioann Constantinovich Romanov, Prince Igor Constantinovich Romanov, Prince Constantine Constantinovich Romanov, Grand Duke Sergei Mikhailovich, and Prince Vladimir Paley, the morganatic son of Grand Duke Paul. After the White liberation of Alapaevsk the bodies were moved to the Russian Orthodox Cathedral of St Seraphim of Sarov in Beijing. Soon after this, in 1921, Grand Duchess Ella and Nun Barbara were moved to the Martha and Mary Convent in Jerusalem when the saintly Grand Duchess's body was found to be uncorrupted. The others remained in Beijing until 1945, when the victorious Russian Red Army swept through that city.[28] Though the cathedral was left intact, the six remaining Romanov bodies were moved to a destination that remains unknown. No logical explanation of this strange obsession with Romanov corpses exists – unless it is that someone thought they would come in useful one day. Genetically many of these individuals were close to the Tsar – the Constantinovichi Romanovs were all his second cousins, Grand Duke Sergei was the cousin of Alexander III and Vladimir Paley's father was the Tsar's cousin Paul.[29]

Similarly, as we have already seen, the whereabouts of the body of Grand Duke Mikhail, the Tsar's brother, has never been established. Two totally different accounts exist of his death: one has him shot near Perm with his English secretary Johnston; the other has him surviving for a while in Omsk and then being killed in a cavalry charge against Reds in the Atlai region.[30] Whichever is true, there is no body. Grand Duke Mikhail had only two interests – cars and women. Until 1901, when he nearly eloped in Sorrento with Dina Kosikovsky, the annals are silent on the subject of Mikhail's paramours. It is possible that he sired children before this, but nothing definite is known. On the illegitimate side of the family, Count Alexei Belewsky-Jukovsky, the natural son of Nikolai's uncle Grand Duke Alexei, was the Tsar's first cousin, and so genetically very close to the Emperor. He was shot in 1932 by the Communists in Tbilisi, Georgia, and the whereabouts of his body is unknown. One thing is certain – Russia has no shortage of Romanov bodies. Whether they could have been cobbled together into a credible 'imperial family' of corpses is another matter.

Of course, that job may have been done by the Tsar himself. Employment of doubles is a well-established means of protecting prominent individuals perceived to be vulnerable: during the Second World War, for example, both Winston Churchill and Field Marshal Montgomery had doubles, both of whom have been the subjects of films. In his biography of Anastasia, James Blair-Lovell tells the story of how, following an assassination attempt in Berlin in 1913, Nikolai II had recruited imperial look-alikes and built a second imperial 'blue' train.[31] Though the expatriate Russian community was wary of any of the Anna Anderson stories, this one did chime with other things they talked about in the 1930s, according to Alix Hill.[32] Apparently the assassination attempt in Berlin occurred while the Tsar was attending a royal wedding; and such a wedding did indeed take place on 24 May 1913 – that of the Kaiser's daughter Princess Victoria to Prince Ernst August of Hanover. Presumably these look-alikes the Tsar had recruited were substituted for members of the real imperial family in situations of perceived danger before the Revolution. Nor was Nikolai the first of his dynasty to have recourse to this ploy: Professor Popov recounts how Tsar Alexander III, his father, asked the interior ministry to recruit three teams of doubles after the near-fatal bombing of the imperial train at Borka in 1888 when only the Tsar's massive strength – he held up the roof of the railway carriage while his family escaped – saved the imperial family.[33] It is possible that the use of doubles persisted under his son. It is also possible that some of these were illegitimate relatives of the imperial family. This would have been a logical source for the secret police to tap for doubles, since they monitored these people in any case, along with all other Romanov indiscretions. Such look-alikes may well have been substituted for the real imperial family in Ekaterinburg; and this may explain the ten-volume report in the KGB archive which speaks of a family 'very like the Romanovs' being executed near Ekaterinburg in 1918. Speaking of the talk in the White Russian community in the 1930s – talk they kept strictly within the confines of their homes – Alix Hill explained that her parents' Russian friends believed Anna Anderson was one of these doubles and that was why she was so well schooled in the details of Romanov court and family life. 'She was, yet wasn't, Anastasia,' said Alix.[34] Certainly, this would explain a great deal. It also raises the questions of exactly when a substitution of the fake for the real Romanovs might have taken place and whether some of these substitutes were killed while others escaped. These matters are more fully discussed in chapters 10 and 11.

Intrigued by indications that Chebotarev and his sister, now lying interred together in that quiet churchyard in Holt, might be the missing

Tsarevich and Grand Duchess, I decided in 1994 to try what I then regarded as a 'long shot'. I had only half-seriously listened to Phillips when, in the summer of 1993, he suggested that I should find out if I were related to the mysterious Russian prince of Moyallon. But as the evidence mounted, piece by piece, that Chebotarev might really have been the Tsarevich, I decided to contact Dr Peter Gill myself. Though I had many reservations about the Ekaterinburg bones – since, as this chapter has already made plain, so much that cast doubt on their authenticity was coming out of Russia – I decided that it might just be worth comparing my own DNA to that of the remains. I knew that if the bones were a hoax, this might not produce any meaningful answers. Indeed, one of the possibilities was that the bones might well have been chosen *not* to match the real Romanovs: if such bones could be officially authenticated and buried, this would pre-empt any subsequent claimants to the lineage, who would inevitably fail to match the standard thus falsely established. Alternatively, as we have just seen, the bones might be those of people close to, but not of, the immediate imperial family – perhaps those of Romanov relatives, as many émigré groups were now asserting. But with even the hint of a personal connection, however distant and uncertain, hovering in the back of my mind, I felt it was worth some cautious investigation.

I was careful to keep this at one remove. I explained to Dr Gill that we had been finding out disquieting things about the Russian émigré at Moyallon and would like to have a blood test done on a sample from a living person. Gill suggested that the subject simply prick his or her finger and put a drop of blood on a tissue, and that I send this to him in an envelope. This seemed very casual and hardly consonant with his later comments about the inadmissibility of the Otsu bandage due to contamination. Indeed, I wondered about the risks of contamination at the time; but he was the expert, so I went along with what he said. What Gill would do was compare the nuclear DNA of this sample at five short tandem repeat positions with that of the Tsar and Tsarina skeletons. I kept reminding him that, if there were a relationship, it was no more than grandpaternity. After two months I received a phone call at work: there appeared to be three or four matches out of five positions. This result was later revised when I received written confirmation from Dr Gill, which presented the outcome as two double matches and one single match, while at the other two positions my nuclear DNA was only one position away from that of the putative Tsar and Tsarina.

When I told Dr Bill Maples, his reaction was immediate. 'I think you have a serious proposition here,' he said. Double matches, he added, indicated that one's parents were closely related. He also asked me my blood group.

'A Positive,' I replied.

'The same as the Ekaterinburg skeletons,' he retorted.[35] I had never heard this before, but Maples told me how it had leaked out at a group conference at which the Russian forensic experts and dental experts had been present with his team. 'At first,' he said, 'they would not tell us the blood group. "We must keep some secrets, you know," was their argument. But later one of the dental experts just blurted it out,' he added. '"It's A Positive," they said.' A Positive is a comparatively rare blood group – as I already knew from repeated requests that I give blood – shared by only 15 per cent of the population.

Concerns over the result of my DNA test first arose when I showed Dr Gill's letter to Dr Colin Graham, a DNA and genetics expert at Queen's University, Belfast. Dr Graham saw at once that what Gill was presenting to me as a difference at one short tandem repeat position was not as great as Gill was making out. At position SE33, which for some reason Gill characterized differently in his *Nature Genetics* article as HUM ACTB P2, he had presented the result as showing a difference of four points between me and the 'Tsar' and 'Tsarina', whereas Dr Graham explained that that particular calibration went up in fours, and that the actual difference was less than one.

At position THO1 the 'Tsar's' reading was 7, 10 and the 'Tsarina's' 8, 8. Any offspring would be 7, 8 or 8, 10, according to Gill, and my reading was 8, 10. If these bones were genuine in the first place, if Chebotarev were the Tsarevich, and if I were his son, then I would only be a grandson and could therefore only be expected to have one of these number matches – a 7, 8 or 10. That I had two of these was a double match – which is what occasioned Bill Maples' remark that my parents must be closely related. According to Gill there was a 62 per cent chance of this happening by chance in paternity – but he gave no percentage likelihood of it happening in grandpaternity.

At position F13A1 the Tsar's reading was 7, 7 and the Tsarina's 3, 5. According to Dr Gill, any offspring would be 3, 7 or 5, 7. My reading was 5, 7 – another double match. Again, Gill said there was a 58 per cent chance of this happening by chance in paternity, but gave no corresponding percentage for grandpaternity. It would seem obvious that the chances of this happening would be significantly less.

At another position, designated FES/FPS, the Tsar reading was 12, 12 and the Tsarina's 12, 13. Mine was 11, 12 and therefore a single match, consistent with grandpaternity. There was, he said, a 27 per cent probability of this happening by chance. At the position he called VWA, my reading was 12, 14, the Tsar's 15, 16 and the Tsarina's 15, 16. Gill said this was an exclusion; but, as at position SE33, it was only one position away – a 14 rather than a 15. So there it was – two double matches, one single match and two others at one position away. What did it mean?

Dr Graham ghosted a letter to me for Gill, requesting some clarification.[36] Not much clarification came in the reply. Gill admitted that he had ignored 'flanking sequences' but did not say what any of these were, save for VWA where he claimed that they were 12, 14 in my case. All the figures, he said, were based on a nomenclature no longer used by them. He added curtly at the end of the letter that any further work by him would incur additional expense.[37] Dr Graham suspected that all the extractions had not been carried out on the same day and wanted to compare the actual length of the alleles of DNA, not just the mathematical figures given by Dr Gill. Seeking further clarification, we asked for the chromatograph traces for the 'Tsar', 'Tsarina' and my own sample at the VWA position and at the ACTB P2 locus. No reply from Dr Gill was ever received to this letter. When I showed the exchange of letters later to Professor Bill Potts, he summed up his impressions in one word: 'obfuscation'.

Maples probed further. He told me of the special feature present in four of the skulls, the Wormian feature mentioned above. 'It appears', he said, 'as a small protrusion at the back of the base of the skull.' Gingerly, I felt the back of my head. It seemed to be there. X-rays confirmed the presence not only of this feature, but also of the three others noted by Popov as common to the skulls purporting to belong to the Tsarina and her daughters – the protruding rear, the horseshoe-shaped lower jaw and the overlapping teeth in the lower jaw.[38] In April 1998 Popov carried out extensive tests in St Petersburg, comparing detailed X-rays of my skull with X-rays of the skulls of the four female individuals from the Ekaterinburg grave. The results recorded a degree of correlation between my skull and those retrieved from the grave comparable to that established among the four individuals already shown by nuclear DNA tests to be blood relatives.[39] Popov concluded that the possibility of a blood relationship between me and the four Ekaterinburg skeletons could not be ruled out. Since most of the problems with the identification of the remains lay with the supposed 'Tsar' skeleton rather than the females, the possibility existed that only that skeleton was 'wrong', and that the other bones were indeed those of the Tsarina and three of her daughters – albeit in a grave cobbled together long after 1918. The diagram below shows schematically how the body of the Tsar's brother Grand Duke Mikhail (which has never been found) could, if placed in such a grave, appear to be that of the father of the three young women present, with whom his DNA would match; but it would not match the other daughter or the Tsarevich – who are, of course, missing from the grave.

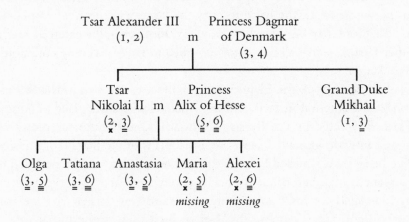

x  an allele which could only be passed by the Tsar
≡  an allele which could be passed by the Tsarina
—  an allele which could be passed by either Grand Duke Mikhail or the Tsar

*How Grand Duke Mikhail could appear, erroneously, to be the father of a family group in the Ekaterinburg burial pit*

My attitude to the DNA findings on the bones remains sceptical. As for the bones themselves, I believe that DNA tests, along with other forensic findings, point to their being either relatives of the Romanovs who could have acted as doubles or – more likely – some, but not all, of the imperial family themselves. The absence of the Otsu mark on the 'Tsar's' skull is difficult to explain away. A more conclusive finding would require new tests on the Otsu bandage, on the actual uniforms of the various members of the imperial family, for both nuclear and mitochondrial DNA – testing the imperial family against themselves – and on the mitochondrial DNA of some of the eighty-four mitochondrial relatives of the

Tsarina known to be alive today. And even then, the doubts recently cast on the reliability of mitochondrial DNA could undermine the whole process.

Given the problems with blood samples, postulated mutations, skeletons growing after death, the absence of an Otsu mark on the 'Tsar's' skull, the debunking of mitochondrial DNA's reliability as a 'tool of justice', the Russian government's 1996 reclassification of documents relating to the discovery of the bones as 'secret', and so much relating to the discovery of the bones themselves involving the 'secret means' of which Metropolitan Ioann spoke, let alone the numerous inconsistencies in the whole affair, the haste to bury the bones may amount in practice to little more than burying the evidence. Once again, the carefully crafted official 'truth' – that all the Romanovs died in 1918 – is being consciously repackaged.

On 17 July 1998 the Ekaterinburg bones were buried in the St Peter and Paul Cathedral in St Petersburg, traditional resting place of Russia's Tsars. Boycotted by the Russian Orthodox Church, the ceremony was significantly downgraded from the initial plans of the State Commission. The bodies were buried beyond the iconostasis in a side chapel used for morganatic members of the Romanov family and not in the crypt reserved by Nikolai II for his family. Only one priest was present, and he conspicuously omitted naming the Tsar or his family in the burial service, referring to them only as nameless victims of the Revolution. Fearful of alienating the church, 'Grand Duchess Maria', her son and her mother, who had been calling for a state funeral since 1991, and actually issued invitations to the event, refused to attend, going instead to a rival ceremony in memory of all the victims of the Revolution, organized by the Russian Orthodox Church. President Yeltsin, unpredictable as ever, decided at the last moment to attend the lacklustre ceremony, watched by Romanov relatives from the United States and elsewhere. To the end, the skeletons remained bones of contention, with many refusing to accept that some or any of them were genuine.

Whatever the truth, one thing is certain: the Tsarevich Alexei's bones have not been found.

# The Inheritance of Blood

Throughout the disputes which have raged around the Ekaterinburg bones there has been a persistent tendency to ignore the fact of the two missing bodies. Whenever the subject has been raised the retort has always been that these two bodies must have been destroyed – a very big and totally unsubstantiated assumption. Any suggestion that the Tsarevich might have survived is met with incredulity: how could he have? He had haemophilia; surely he was bound to have died in any case? If asked what they know of the Tsarevich, it is this which still comes first to most people's minds: haemophilia, the disorder of the blood in which clotting is impaired, and which Alexei is said to have inherited through his mother who, like her grandmother Queen Victoria, is believed to have been a carrier of the disease. Equally ingrained in the public consciousness is the image of Grigori Rasputin, the unkempt Siberian *starets* or 'holy man' and mystic whose debauched habits did irreparable damage to the reputation of the Tsarina and fatally tarnished the image of the whole imperial family, significantly contributing to their downfall – and who apparently possessed a unique ability to restore the ailing Tsarevich to health. In fact, just as the enduring legends about Rasputin's mystical powers and superhuman strength crumble in the face of the evidence, so too assumptions about the nature of Alexei's illness, his inheritance of blood, turn out on closer examination to be unwarranted.

Rasputin's perceived ability to heal the Tsarevich lies at the heart of this issue. If we can work out how he brought about the dramatic improvement in the boy's condition with which he is credited, we are well on the way to finding out what it actually was that afflicted the young prince. Certainly, Rasputin's apparent healing powers were attested to by several contemporary witnesses, most notably the Tsarevich's aunt, the Tsar's younger sister Grand Duchess Olga. Speaking to her biographer, Ian Vorres, she said: 'There is no doubt about that. I saw those miraculous effects with my own eyes and that more than once. I also know that the most prominent doctors of the day had to admit it. Professor

Fedorov, who stood at the very peak of the profession and whose patient
Alexis was, told me on more than one occasion; but all the doctors dis-
liked Rasputin intensely.' Fedorov told Olga that the recovery of the
Tsarevich from a severe bleeding incident at Spala in Poland in autumn
1912 was 'wholly inexplicable from a medical point of view'.[1] Speaking
of an earlier attack in March 1912, the Tsar's other sister, Grand Duchess
Xenia, commented: 'Everything stopped when he [Rasputin] arrived.'[2]
Those within the imperial family appeared to be in no doubt about
Rasputin's role.

Over the years, there have been many attempts to explain the strange
healing power exercised by Rasputin. Robert Massie, biographer of the
Tsar and Tsarina, suggests that he may have used hypnotism, inducing an
emotional change in Alexei's body and thereby slowing down and eventually stopping the bleeding. Massie himself admits, though, that this
theory falls down on two counts. First, Rasputin was not actually present
at his most celebrated healing of Alexei, at Spala in 1912: the boy's
recovery occurred after Rasputin, who was twelve hundred miles away
in Siberia, sent the Tsarina a message down the telegraph wire: 'God has
seen your tears and heard your prayers. Do not grieve. The Little One
will not die. Only do not allow the doctors to bother him too much.'
Secondly, Massie admits that Rasputin did not actually learn about hypnotism until 1913, a year after the Spala episode. In the end, Massie
admits that he does not really understand what it was that Rasputin did.[3]

In considering this account, moreover, it should be recalled that
Robert Massie is himself the father of a Factor VIII haemophiliac son;
indeed, he and his wife have written an important book, *Journey*, about
their experience as the parents of a haemophiliac.[4] As the principal expo-
nent today of the most widely accepted version of Alexei's illness, Massie
may have extrapolated, even unconsciously, from his own experience in
presenting the story of the ailing Tsarevich. We are left with an official
version of events which asks us to believe that a sickly and ultimately
doomed haemophiliac Tsarevich was kept alive by the mysterious ministrations of the 'holy man' Rasputin, using a mixture of hypnotism and
mysticism. This is hardly a credible or scientifically defensible viewpoint;
the truth, surely, must lie elsewhere.

Contemporary evidence exists which provides a perfectly rational explanation of Rasputin's apparent healings of the Tsarevich. Prince Felix
Yusupov, husband of the Tsar's niece Irina and one of the conspirators
who murdered Rasputin, states it clearly and unequivocally: Rasputin

admitted to him that he was administering 'roots and herbs' to the Tsarevich to 'stop and aggravate haemorrhages'. According to Yusupov, Rasputin obtained these drugs from Piotr Badmaev, the Buddhist herbalist whose 'alternative medicine' practice was all the rage among the court aristocracy of St Petersburg. In his book about Rasputin, published in 1927, Yusupov reports one revealing conversation the two men had in which the 'holy man' spoke of Badmaev: 'He's got every remedy you could wish for. He's a real doctor, he is. Botkin and Derevenko [the imperial physicians] are no good at all. They just write down some rubbish or other on bits of paper. Badmaev's medicines are nature's own. They come from the forests and mountains, and they're planted by God himself – and God's blessing is in them.' When Yusupov asked Rasputin why the Tsar and Tsarevich were not being treated with these medicines, the answer was equally revealing. 'What do you mean,' Rasputin answered, 'not treated with them? Of course they are. She [the Tsarina] and Annushka [Anna Vyrubova, the Tsarina's confidante] see to that. They're all afraid Botkin will find out – but I tell them – if one of your doctors finds out about my medicines, the patient won't get better but very much worse. So they're on their guard and they do everything on the sly.'[5] Within these few sentences the reality of what Rasputin was actually doing is clearly stated. Using a gullible Empress and her trusted friend Anna Vyrubova, Rasputin's own disciple, the 'holy man' was administering drugs supplied to him by Badmaev both to aggravate and to stop haemorrhages in the Tsarevich. As explanations go, this is infinitely more acceptable and credible than the existence of strange mystical healing powers that could be exercised by their possessor even down a telegraph line.

The comments of Prince Yusupov, moreover, make a great deal of sense in the context of the court intrigues dedicated to undermining the Tsar and his heir, as described in chapter 5. The Grand Duchesses Militsa and Stana, who were at the forefront of these schemes, were Rasputin's sponsors: it was they, and their confessor Archbishop Theophan, who had introduced him to the imperial family. The birth of an heir in 1904 had been a major setback for those Romanov family members with claims on the succession, and his very status placed the Tsarevich's life under threat from the beginning. It is a very small step from acknowledging this to seeing Rasputin's administration to Alexei of Badmaev's 'drugs and herbs' to 'stop and aggravate haemorrhages' as the means of preparing the ground for the boy's demise.

The picture becomes more complicated, however, with the split in the ranks of the plotters that occurred in 1910. Seeing the potential of his position as guarantor of the Tsarevich's health, Rasputin broke with his erstwhile sponsors Grand Duchesses Militsa and Stana and set about exploiting his position of dominance over the imperial couple for his own advantage.

Drug-taking reached epidemic proportions among the upper classes in those last decadent years of the tsarist regime, and in this milieu the administration of all sorts of substances with supposed beneficial effects seemed perfectly acceptable. In court circles especially, experimentation was rife. Modern censoriousness about, and disapproval of, drug-taking dates from 1930s America, where it first became a widespread public health problem. But in the rarefied atmosphere of the untouchable upper reaches of the pre-revolutionary Russian aristocracy, no opprobrium whatsoever attached to drug use. Drugs were regarded in the same way as tobacco and alcohol, and almost everybody dabbled. Like many others of her class, Natalie Karaulov Cooke, Chebotarev's hostess at Croft House – and also the great-niece of Prince Esper Ukhtomsky,[6] Badmaev's protector and the Tsar's adviser on Far Eastern affairs – left Russia with a serious drug habit which, her daughter Zoe told me, led to her nearly being prosecuted during the Second World War.[7]

Nikolai II himself routinely took cocaine for a head cold. While he was at the front during the First World War, the Tsarina sent him 'powders' supplied by Badmaev which he kept in a drawer in his desk at the Stavka or military headquarters in Mogilev. By 1916 the Emperor was frequently stoned on a mixture of henbane and hashish, the effects of which the Tsar himself described as 'marvellous'.[8] Count Kokovstev, the former Prime Minister, gives a revealing picture of the Tsar's condition in his account of his final interview with Nikolai in December 1916.

His eyes . . . seemed faded and wandered listlessly from one object to the next, instead of remaining as in the past on the person with whom he was talking. The whites of his eyes had yellowed, the black pupil had lost its lustre and become grey and lifeless. There was a lost expression on His Majesty's features. And his lips preserved a sad, forced smile. He heard me to the end with this new desolate smile and with his glance wandering in every direction. Then I asked him for immediate instructions about the task he had given me, which question – for it was a simple one for it never crossed my mind that the Tsar with his marvellous memory could have forgotten what he said to me two or three days before – threw him into a state of confusion, to me inexplicable. That strange, forced expressionless smile was still there as he looked at me as if begging for my help to call back something that had completely slipped his mind.[9]

Eight days after this incident the French ambassador, Maurice Paléologue, spoke of the Tsar's 'vague, unseeing eyes', of 'long intervals of silence', of his 'wandering thoughts' and of 'his strange overwrought appearance'.[10] Certainly the Tsar's symptoms – loss of insight, short-term memory loss, difficulty in completing thought processes – accord with the known side-effects of hashish, which affects both the central nervous and cardiovascular systems. Black henbane grows naturally in Russia, and had been used as a relaxant, anaesthetic and sedative since the middle ages.[11]

The Tsarina's drug-taking has been traced by Blair Lovell, Alexandrov, Snelling and others to the early years of the century, to the period when, as described in chapter 5, she employed the 'spirit doctor' Philippe Vachot, the early protégé of Grand Duchesses Militsa and Stana – before they found Rasputin. Not only may this habit be linked to the gynaecological misfortunes which befell the Tsarina in 1902 and 1903, it may have permanently undermined her health. And yet, given their own reliance on drugs, it would have seemed perfectly natural to the Tsarevich's parents that such substances should be administered to their ailing son.

Yusupov was not alone in alleging that the Tsarevich's bleeding was being artificially induced or aggravated. In 1911 Sergei Trufanov, also known by his monastic name Illidor, said much the same thing – and at that time he was still a leading and respected member of the Russian Orthodox Church, an associate of Bishop Hermogen and Archbishop Theophan. Illidor alleged that Rasputin was giving Alexei mysterious 'yellow powders' supplied by Badmaev.[12] It was only later that Illidor's exclusion from affairs of Church and state led him to make still stronger claims; but when he first spoke out on the subject he could certainly not be dismissed as a crank. His breach with Rasputin, the allegations about his former friend's treatment of the Tsarevich, and the end of his own career followed his discovery of embarrassing and intimate letters written by the Tsarina to the *starets* in Rasputin's home in Pokrovskoe in Siberia.

Incensed at this proof of his friend's lewd behaviour, Illidor began to publish the letters, though the Tsar managed to have the publication suppressed. (Nikolai is known to have kept the originals of the letters locked in his desk.) Illidor's statements about Rasputin's use of drugs were taken up in a sensational book published in 1917, in the wake of the Revolution, by William Le Queux, allegedly a British agent. In this book, *Rasputin, the Rascal Monk*, Le Queux claimed that Rasputin induced haemorrhages in the Tsarevich using a powder supplied to him by Badmaev and produced from the new horns of stags mixed with ginseng (which he renders 'jen-shen').[13] Deer horn is composed of keratin, a fibrous protein produced in the outer layers of skin, while Chinese or Indian ginseng (*Panax pseudoginseng*) is a stimulant. The book is undoubtedly sensational, but, written soon after the events it describes, probably drew on widespread contemporary gossip.

This interpretation of events is reinforced by the correlation which emerges between the various efforts the Tsar made to rid himself of the Rasputin incubus and the bleeding bouts suffered by his son. Examination of the circumstances surrounding the best-known of these attacks, at Spala in 1912, demonstrates this correlation very clearly. In 1911 the scandal surrounding the Tsarina's letters to Rasputin had provoked the Tsar into imposing internal exile on Rasputin in his home village of Pokrovskoe. By March 1912, however, the Tsarina and Anna Vyrubova were making plans to reinstate the *starets* in their entourage and smuggled him on board the imperial train for its journey south to Livadia in the Crimea.[14] The Tsar discovered the deception and had Rasputin ejected from the train. Almost immediately after this incident, on 10 March, the Tsarevich had a kidney haemorrhage.[15] Predictably, Rasputin was sent for – and, as we have seen, according to the Tsar's sister Grand Duchess Xenia, 'everything stopped when he arrived.' Rasputin was not reinstated by the Tsar for his efforts, however, but advised to leave the Crimea at once and go back to Siberia. Six months later, in September 1912, Alexei suffered an injury to his groin while boarding a rowing boat at the royal hunting lodge at Bielowesa in Poland.

Of key importance in following the story from this point are the imperial family's medical records referred to in Chapter 5. These records offer some very interesting insights into the medical issues surrounding Alexei. In carefully chosen language, the record says that the Tsarevich's groin injury 'was attributed to him taking a wide step while jumping into a boat at Bielowesa'. Why 'attributed to'? Does this suggest some reservation, some hint that there might be another possible interpretation? In any event, by all accounts Alexei recovered quickly from this injury – Massie says in one week, though the medical record puts it at three weeks, saying that by then the haemorrhage was 'so insignificant as to be undetectable'.[16]

A few weeks later, at the beginning of October, the Tsarevich went for a carriage ride with his mother and Anna Vyrubova, newly arrived from St Petersburg. He returned from this trip in agony. Our source for this information is Vyrubova herself. No mention is made of it in the imperial family's medical records – perhaps because it would point too clearly to the truth and because the doctors were trying to protect themselves and their reputations. Speaking of Alexei's sudden turn for the worse, the imperial medical record suggests it was caused by a fall, saying coyly: 'This, one must assume, explains the new haemorrhage.' Again, the choice of words – 'one must assume' – is curious in its indefiniteness; is there here a suggestion that the real explanation lay elsewhere – an explanation so explosive that it could not be written down? Could this be what Dr Fedorov was hinting at when he later told Count Mosolov, the head of the imperial chancellery, who had enquired about the real reasons for the Tsarevich's cure: 'You can see for yourself what is going on here'?[17] What exactly did this cryptic comment mean?

Massie says Alexei was treated by the paediatrician Ostrogorsky and Rauchfuss, the surgeon. Actually Rauchfuss was the paediatrician and Ostrogorsky the surgeon, according to the medical record. But that is a point of detail. Where the imperial medical record departs significantly from Massie's account of this illness is in specifying the site of the haemorrhage. Massie locates it in the thigh and groin.[18] The imperial family's medical record locates it in the abdomen.[19] Describing it as spreading from the 'entire Illiac region', the record speaks of the haemorrhage, which it calls a *haematoma retroperitanale*, affecting 'the whole lumbar region' and, most interestingly, 'overlapping the central line of the stomach'. Dr Botkin, the imperial physician, warned the Tsar that bleeding from the stomach, if unchecked, might well kill the Tsarevich at any time. There is no mention of the leg whatsoever. Nor, for that matter, is there any mention of haemophilia – either here or anywhere else.

Alexei's condition deteriorated rapidly; his temperature soared and he became anaemic due to blood loss. Soon his life was perceived to be in imminent danger and he received the last offices of the Russian Orthodox

Church. Then, in response to Alexandra's appeal, came the Rasputin telegram: 'God has seen your tears and heard your prayers. Do not grieve. The Little One will not die. Only do not allow the doctors to trouble him too much.'[20] By the next day, the boy was on the mend and Rasputin was reinstated in the royal favour. Thus the eleven-day crisis came to an end with an incident that might be construed as a simple case of cause and effect – if one were disposed to believe in miracles, that is; and if history had not repeated itself almost exactly in 1915.

In April 1915 there was an incident in the 'Yar' night-club in Moscow.[21] Apart from exposing himself, Rasputin publicly claimed that he could do whatever he liked with the 'old girl', as he called the Tsarina – implying what all of society suspected: that there was a sexual side to their relationship. Again, the 'holy man' was exiled internally on the Tsar's orders, and this time a commission of inquiry was set up under General Junkovsky; but when the Tsarina found out about the inquiry and its very damaging findings, she insisted on Junkovsky's dismissal.[22] On these occasions the Empress invariably got her way by an outburst of shouting and hysteria. Admiral Nilov, the predecessor of Lili Dehn's husband as captain of the imperial yacht, the *Standart*, recounted that when he raised the subject of adverse public comment about Rasputin with the Tsar, the Emperor's reply was very telling: 'Better one Rasputin than ten hysterics!' Though he may have recognized them for what they were, the Tsar was powerless before his wife's tantrums. Even the Tsarina's own brother, Grand Duke Ernst of Hesse, said, 'The Emperor is a saint and an angel but he does not know how to deal with her.'[23] These events surrounding Junkovsky's report occurred in August and September 1915. On 24 August, in what may have been a reminder of what could be expected if Rasputin were crossed, the Tsarina wrote to the Tsar that Alexei's arm hurt and was swollen.[24] In October, the Tsar responded by taking his son away with him to the front – an unusual, even foolhardy move if Alexei were a haemophiliac. The heir slept in a camp bed at the foot of his father's bed and rarely left Nikolai's side.[25] Perhaps the Tsar calculated that this was the only way to protect the boy from Rasputin's ministrations – by taking him away from both his mother and Vyrubova, the two named by Yusupov as Rasputin's (possibly unwitting) accomplices.

Within six weeks of his departure with the Tsar, in December 1915, Alexei had a sudden nosebleed. Evidence conflicts as to its immediate cause: some sources ascribe it to violent sneezing during a head cold,

THE INHERITANCE OF BLOOD 89

others to striking his nose on the window pane of a railway carriage.[26] The treatment appears to have involved cauterization, a normal medical procedure which seems to have worked – although again, reports vary. As usual, the Tsarina made a melodrama out of the crisis and got her way: Alexei was returned to Tsarskoe Selo and Rasputin was recalled. Once again, the pattern repeated itself: Rasputin was sent away because of an indiscretion (to put it no more strongly); the Tsarevich sustained an injury; Rasputin was recalled and the situation returned to what passed for normal. The course of events points inexorably to Yusupov's assertion being substantially correct.

In 1917, in the months after the first 'democratic' revolution but before Lenin's October coup, the unnamed aristocratic author of an earlier book entitled *Russian Court Memoirs* produced a new volume, *The Fall of the Romanovs*, which made this very point about Rasputin:

> Each time the Tsar was prevailed upon to send Rasputine [sic] into exile, something happened to the Tzessarevitch [sic]. It has since been proved that the staretz was hand in glove with an oriental quack doctor of some renown, who treated his patients with infusions of herbs brought from Tibet. It was insistently rumoured, especially during the last two years that Grigori frequently brought the Empress philtres to give to the Tsar, to make him more amenable to her wishes. It may likewise have happened that a few drops of some cordial might have been added by a devoted hand to the food of the Tzessarevitch, making him temporarily ill, confirming thus the Empress in her superstitious dread of the saint's removal from her vicinity.[27]

By May 1916, the Tsar had managed to get his son back to the front with him; and the boy was never allowed out of his sight thereafter until after Rasputin's murder in December that year.

Rasputin's death produced a conventional public response from the Tsar. 'Murder is murder' was his uncompromising message to those in his extended family who pleaded for clemency for the assassins.[28] Yet, though the Tsarina was baying for their blood, Nikolai II was strangely inactive when it came to punishing Rasputin's murderers. Yusupov was exiled to one of his many estates, at Kursk, and Grand Duke Dmitri, the Tsar's young cousin, was sent to the Persian front – a decision which saved his life, since he was well out of harm's way when revolution erupted. When the Tsar was first told, in private, the news of Rasputin's death, his reaction was to walk away carefree and whistling. General Voyiekov, the Tsar's military aide, said that 'from the very first report, about Rasputin's mysterious disappearance, to the last, about the placement of his body in the chapel, I did not observe once signs of sorrow in His Majesty but rather gathered the impression that he experienced a sense of relief.'[29] Nikolai II was close to his mother, the Dowager Empress, and she, in turn, was a close friend of Princess Zinaida Yusupov, Felix Yusupov's mother.[30] The Tsar himself was particularly fond of Grand Duke Dmitri, whom he had brought up as his own son since 1905;[31] there was even talk of his marrying one of the Tsar's daughters. Perhaps, in the time-honoured fashion, the Tsar 'knew but did not know' about Rasputin's impending fate, just as his own predecessor Tsar Alexander I had 'known but not known' about his father Tsar Paul's murder in 1801. Perhaps it was another case of King Henry II, Becket and a 'meddling priest'. Grand Duchess Olga, the Tsar's eldest daughter, who was particularly close to her father, spoke of Rasputin's murder to Valentina Chebotarev, the sister in charge of the Tsarina's annexe of the military hospital at Tsarskoe Selo, saying, 'Maybe it was necessary to kill him [Rasputin], but not so terribly – we are a family, one is ashamed to admit they are relatives.'[32] This admission, 'maybe it was necessary to kill him,' probably comes close to the Tsar's attitude.

Nikolai II's reaction to Rasputin's death, as noted by Voyiekov, would be even more understandable if he was not only fearful for his son's safety, but a cuckolded husband as well. William A. Pinkney, a close friend of the Tsar's sister Grand Duchess Olga in Hamilton, Ontario – his uncle was the Grand Duchess's veterinary surgeon when she set up a farm in Canada – said that Olga had told him that the Tsarina was 'spellbound' by Rasputin and had a 'close physical relationship' with him. She used Alexei's illness, Olga said, as an excuse for having Rasputin 'about the palace' – as the cover to provide the reason for Rasputin's presence at court.[33] Alexandra had a precedent for this attachment. Only six when her mother died, she had been brought up during her formative years by her grandmother, Queen Victoria, at Osborne on the Isle of Wight. There she had witnessed at first hand Queen Victoria's relationship with her 'Highland servant' John Brown at its height in the late 1870s and early 1880s. The satirical magazine *Punch* referred to the Queen as 'Mrs Brown' and produced an irreverent parody of the official Court Circular featuring Brown's exploits. Victoria's relationship with her Scottish attendant was complex. She was emotionally dependent on him after Prince

Albert's death, and he may well have been a medium to whom she turned for contact with her dead husband. She is alleged to have had a child by him in 1866, going to Geneva to give birth.[34] Unkempt, drunken and over-familiar, Brown was the template for Rasputin. Like Brown, Rasputin met a religious need in his mistress. Little wonder, then, that the Tsar repeatedly tried to get rid of Rasputin, or that, each time, the Tsarina created a scene. And there were the 1911 letters found by the monk Illidor, which the Tsar kept locked in his desk.

Alexei's first bleeding problem occurred in 1907, soon after Rasputin's first appearance in the imperial circle. (Though he had met the imperial couple in 1906, the *starets* did not become a regular feature of life at Tsarskoe Selo until the following year.) True, in 1904, just after he was born, Alexei had bled from the navel; but this had lasted for less than one day,[35] and may have been nothing more than hypoprothrombinemia, a common phenomenon in infants now associated with Vitamin K deficiency and jaundice. Nevertheless, it may well have given Grand Duchesses Militsa and Stana the idea of fostering the notion that the young prince suffered from a bleeding disorder, for at that time the Tsarina confided everything in the Montenegrin sisters. Thereafter, there was no sign of anything seriously wrong with the boy until Rasputin's appearance.

Indeed, it is a striking feature of Alexei's health problems that he was ill on comparatively few occasions. There were only three, or at most four incidents during his entire childhood which might be called in any way major. These were the two in 1912 described above, the nose-bleed in 1915, also mentioned above, a leg injury in 1913 and another leg injury in 1914. Other than that, there was a minor leg injury in 1907 of one evening's duration, a minor leg injury of fifteen minutes' duration in 1916 and a stomach upset in 1916. The acute incidents, then, were bunched up in the years 1912–15. Up to 1912, when Alexei was eight, there was nothing much; and in the three years after 1915 until he was lost from sight it was the same. Thus summarized, the picture is not one of a child lurching constantly from one crisis to another, always on the brink of catastrophe throughout his short life.

With the release of archive material following the demise of the Soviet Union, another Alexei emerged. No weakling here: the photographs and clips of film show a healthy, one might even say strapping lad, well-built and full of life and energy. Rolling in the snow, on horseback, riding sleds and toboggans, tumbling with playmates on the grass – these were not the activities of a sickly haemophiliac. Nor can they all be explained away as the risk-taking tendency remarked on in those so afflicted. For years, the only film of the Tsarevich seen in the West was a short piece erroneously presented as having been taken at the Romanov tercentenary celebrations in 1913, in which Alexei appears being carried. On the basis of this one occasion, the rival junior branches of the Romanov family have portrayed Alexei as always having to be carried. That was simply not the case. In fact, the film in question was taken on the declaration of war on 5 August 1914, the day after Alexei had injured his leg. Tsar Nikolai II was anxious since he did not want his heir iconized as an invalid in his public appearance next day – which is exactly what happened.[36] But this propaganda is roundly demolished by the films and photographs showing a highly mobile and active Alexei, including one snap of him naked after a swim.[37]

The further we look into the evidence on the Tsarevich's ill-health, the more fragile the accepted version becomes. Take the 1913 incident. Our only source for this episode is Pierre Gilliard, the imperial children's French tutor.[38] But Gilliard's version seems at odds with what Anna Vyrubova wrote in a letter to Rasputin at the time. Gilliard dates the incident at June 1913. Though Massie asserts that Alexei could not walk for a year after the Spala crisis, here he is less than nine months later balancing on top of a chair, on top of a desk in his schoolroom. Gilliard speaks of injury to the leg; yet Vyrubova wrote to Rasputin that 'an inner vessel has burst because of high fever and cough, there is haemorrhaging, swelling on the side, pain and fever'.[39] Not only does this sound very different from Gilliard's account, but it reveals that Vyrubova was in touch with Rasputin over the boy's health. Massie dismisses the theory put forward – oddly enough, by Gilliard – that Vyrubova was in league with Rasputin and kept him in detailed touch with the boy's symptoms, advising him when the symptoms suggested recovery; he claims that she was simply too ignorant and stupid to do this. This letter, however, shows Vyrubova providing the *starets* with detailed clinical descriptions. Though it does not prove collusion, or that she was advising Rasputin when recovery was on the way so that he might stage a healing, it is disquieting. At the very least, it shows she was working hand in glove with the Tsarina's 'holy man'. Nor has Massie's estimate of Vyrubova's capabilities gone unchallenged. The Russian writer Edvard Radzinsky, working on a new study of Rasputin, maintains that her image as a primitive individual 'as commonplace as a bubble in biscuit dough' is erroneous, and that she was in fact a clever woman.[40]

THE INHERITANCE OF BLOOD

The myths surrounding Rasputin himself, too, crumble under scrutiny. Tales of how hard Rasputin was to kill are intimately bound up with the presentation of the *starets* as a miracle-working mystic; and yet he was no superman, endowed with strange powers, but simply an ordinary human being. Rasputin's daughter Maria was understandably exercised by her father's murder, and set herself the task of discovering exactly what had happened on that December night in 1916. At the heart of the legend lay Rasputin's failure to die after eating cakes laced with potassium cyanide. This apparent indestructibility is said to have panicked his already on-edge assassins. Maria Rasputin, speaking in 1977, said: 'I know he had a superb physique but my father was not a fictional character, not some superman that inhabits today's comic books. When Chionya Guseva stabbed him, he bled and nearly died – I have to come to the conclusion that it was more likely Dr Lazovert substituted some opiate for the potassium cyanide he was supposed to have used.'[41] She was right. In 1995 Professor Richard Pipes of Harvard University demonstrated that 'the autopsy on Rasputin revealed he had been dead from three bullet wounds by the time he struck the water, which did not stop the legends that his lungs filled with water. No traces of poison were found. The absence of poison in Rasputin's remains must mean that in fact it had not been inserted into the wine and pastries.'[42] In other words, Lazovert – the conspirator charged with this task – had got cold feet. Historian Brian Moynahan has since found more corroboration for this conclusion in the newly opened police archives, which show that Lazovert himself said that 'the legend of invincibility was false' and that Rasputin, far from taking four hours to die, was taken out of the River Neva, dead, by masked men after only two hours, to be dumped back in the water once they had affirmed his identity.[43] Despite all this, books on Rasputin – like Greg King's, published as recently as 1996 – still perpetuate the old myth of his virtual indestructibility, showing, if nothing else, how persistent such legends, once established, can be.[44] Rasputin was a mere man, and a corrupt and sinister one at that; and his ability to cure the Tsarevich lay not in the realms of science fiction, but in those of science fact. If he aggravated the bleeding in the first place, clearly he could also stop it. How?

Inevitably, the further question arises: what exactly were the 'roots and herbs' supplied by Badmaev which could 'stop and aggravate haemorrhages'? Badmaev was one of the losers of the Revolution; the Communists who replaced the Romanovs had no use for his nostrums (though subsequently his lucrative medical practice was revived by his nephew

N. N. Badmaev, whose patients included the writer Alexei Tolstoy and the Communist leaders N. I. Bukharin, A. I. Rykov and even Josef Stalin himself; another Badmaev continued to practise in Warsaw, and descendants of the family still live in St Petersburg today).[45] No recipe book of his potions has ever been found, if indeed one ever existed. Nevertheless it is possible to make some intelligent guesses at the basis for the drugs he supplied to Rasputin to manage the Tsarevich's symptoms.

Top of the list must be aspirin or acetylsalicyclic acid. Though first synthesized as a drug and produced in powder form as recently as 1899, just five years before the birth of the Tsarevich, aspirin in its natural form had been known since the days of the ancient Greeks. It was derived from the bark of the willow tree, which was plentiful in Russia – a source which fits easily with Rasputin's own description of medicines which were 'nature's own', coming from 'the forests and mountains'. Aspirin irritates the lining of the stomach, producing bleeding; also, when taken even in low doses it impairs platelet formation and thus the function of coagulation in the blood. Aspirin inhibits the formation of an enzyme known as cyclooxygenase which is involved in the production of a substance called thromboxane A2 in blood platelets. It also stops another substance, protacyclin, forming in the endothelial cells which line the walls of blood vessels. Taken in large doses, aspirin can cause inflammation of the kidneys (nephritis) and damage the organs.[46] We have already seen that on 10 March 1912 the Tsarevich suffered from bleeding from the kidneys – which could well have been caused by aspirin – and that Grand Duchess Xenia, the Tsar's sister, said that 'everything stopped when he [Rasputin] arrived'. We have also seen how Dr Botkin warned the Tsar in the autumn of the same year, during the crisis at Spala, that bleeding from the stomach could kill Alexei at any time. This sounds exactly like aspirin poisoning.

Bleeding can be caused by impairment of platelet function just as readily as it can be the result of haemophilia; the effect is just the same. Platelets are the small plugs which seal breaks in the blood vessels, and bleeding occurs spontaneously when the platelet count in the blood falls below a certain critical level. Normal platelet counts are between 150,000 and 400,000 per cubic millimetre. Spontaneous bleeding may occur when that count drops to between 50,000 and 75,000, and will almost inevitably do so if it reaches a level as low as 10,000–20,000.[47] Blood simply oozes into the tissues. This is exactly what happened to Alexei at Spala in 1912 after his mysterious carriage ride with his mother and Anna Vyrubova. Up to that point the Tsarevich had recovered well from his groin injury the previous month, and had been given a clean bill of health by Dr Botkin. Did the two women use their opportunity alone with the boy, out of reach of his doctors and away from prying eyes, to give him a Badmaev potion, made from aspirin in its natural form, sent by Rasputin ostensibly to benefit the boy?

There are other possibilities, too. Another drug which Rasputin may have used is quinidine, an alkaloid drug derived from the roots and bark of the chinchona tree. Again, this accords with Rasputin's description of Badmaev's drugs as deriving from 'roots and herbs'. Chinchona trees, moreover, were found in India, from where Badmaev is known to have obtained medicines. Formerly known as 'Jesuit's bark' or 'sacred bark,' today quinidine is used to treat heart disease.[48] Illidor's 'yellow powders' suggest sulphur and sulphate drugs, later developed for use in antibiotics; these substances can have harmful side-effects, again causing blood abnormalities and kidney damage. Benzine is another candidate; it too triggers bleeding by reducing platelet production. Other, more bizarre agents which have similar effects are dead foetus cells and snake venom.

So much for initiating bleeding; how might haemorrhaging be stopped? One substance which Badmaev might have used was *Claviceps*, a fungus which today has been developed into the anti-uterine bleeding drug ergotoxine. *Claviceps* is the fungus which produces the cereal disease ergot, known in the middle ages in its human form as St Anthony's Fire.[49] Of course, to stop the bleeding Rasputin may simply have desisted from giving the Tsarevich the drug he had administered to him in the first place.

Behind all these questions and possibilities lurks the larger, and hugely significant question: if Alexei's haemorrhaging could be initiated and staunched at will by medicinal means, did he in fact suffer from haemophilia at all?

# ᯓ 9 ᯓ

## 'This disease is not in our family'

Written history has a cyclical character. Contemporary accounts of events are often later dismissed as partial or biased, and superseded by the first supposedly objective histories – which, it must be noted, are usually written by the winners; certainly not by the losers. These are in turn revised, and these revisions or further revisions often revert in content to something approximating to the original contemporary sources, which in many cases turn out to be not so far from the truth after all.

In a perverse variant of this pattern, early and straightforward accounts of events are displaced by partial interpretations which, so far from being objective, gain a hold on popular consciousness by their appeal to mysterious and inexplicable forces. Only when these persistent legends are challenged and the unfounded assumptions beneath them laid bare can the truth once again be approached.

Such was the case with tales of Rasputin's death. The published autopsy report was widely read in St Petersburg, and its conclusions were clear: the *starets* had died from three gunshot wounds. Yet for upwards of eighty years people preferred to believe that Rasputin had been hard to kill and had, in the end, only drowned in the icy waters of the River Neva. It was not true, but it became the commonly accepted version.

Such was also the case with the Tsarevich's illness. For eighty years people have believed a preposterous account of a near-superhuman figure – Rasputin – delivering from repeated crises the heir who, afflicted with an incurable illness, was doomed eventually to a premature death. But when we peel off the layers of myth and assumption, we find an entirely different picture emerging. We have already seen that Rasputin was no miracle healer. Furthermore, an incurable disease is not necessarily synonymous with a certain early death: many incurable conditions are consistent with survival, haemophilia among them. Further still, it is by no means certain that Alexei was a haemophiliac.

Even before the advent of modern techniques of treatment and transfusion, haemophilia was not an inevitable death sentence. Bleeding disorders of whatever kind vary widely in intensity, and it is perfectly possible to have a mild form of any such condition that is not life-threatening. Prince Valdemar of Prussia, the son of the Tsarina's sister Princess Irene of Prussia, was the first cousin and near-contemporary of the Tsarevich and was believed to suffer from the same blood disorder. Born in 1889, some fifteen years before Alexei, Prince Valdemar lived to be fifty-six, married, and died only in 1945. Prince Leopold, Duke of Albany, fourth son of Queen Victoria, the Tsarina's uncle and allegedly the first haemophiliac in the family, married and had a son who was to become the infamous Nazi Duke of Coburg. His descendants are still alive today.[1]

The question of how grave an affliction haemophilia was in the early years of this century is complicated by the loose application of the term. Haemophilia itself is a generalized term used to describe a bleeding disorder caused by the blood's inability to clot properly; there are, in fact, no fewer than thirteen different types of haemophilia.[2] Even if we knew – and we do not – that the Tsarevich definitely suffered from haemophilia, we would not know from which type. As William and Malcolm Potts pointed out in their 1995 book, *Queen Victoria's Gene*, pathology has never established which clotting factor was absent from the Tsarevich's blood – or from the blood of any of the descendants of Queen Victoria to whom she is said to have transmitted this destructive gene.[3]

Nor are all 'bleeders' haemophiliacs. As the *Encyclopaedia Britannica* states succinctly: 'The term bleeder once was considered to be more or less synonymous with haemophilia. Now that many other causes of abnormal bleeding besides deficiency of anti-haemophilic globulin have been discovered, the term bleeder has no specific meaning.'[4] Thrombocytopenia is another bleeding disorder which is caused not by the lack of, or deficiency in, a clotting factor in the blood but by a failure to produce enough platelets, the small plugs which seal cell walls after damage or rupture. Aspirin, as noted in the previous chapter, has a major impact on platelet production. If the Tsarevich already had a predisposition to a low platelet count because of a disorder like thrombocytopenia, aspirin would have a devastating effect – particularly if administered in its raw, natural form. Abdominal bleeding, from which the Tsarevich suffered at Spala in October 1912, is more typical of thrombocytopenia than of haemophilia. So is bleeding from the nose, as in the incident of December 1915.

It is clear, then, that the Tsarevich's 'haemophilia' may not be quite so

simple and straightforward a diagnosis as is usually assumed. Given that
Rasputin was administering drugs obtained from Badmaev to 'stop and
aggravate haemorrhages' in the Tsarevich; given that those drugs may
well have included the natural form of aspirin; given that Rasputin was
no mystic superman but a calculating opportunist whose advent was
linked to the plotting of the imperial family's relatives; given that the
Tsarevich had comparatively few bouts of illness; given that a correlation
exists between these episodes and Rasputin's periods of disgrace; given
that the imperial medical record does not actually mention haemophilia;
given that some of the Tsarevich's symptoms indicate blood disorders
other than haemophilia – given all of this, we have to ask: did Alexei
have haemophilia at all?

In pursuit of the answer to this question, it becomes important to
uncover the sources of the rumours about the Tsarevich's medical condition. Suggestions that the young heir was frail in health were first made
public through the vitriolic pen of Princess Catherine Radziwill. The
princess, who wrote a book published in 1913 entitled *Behind the Veil at
the Russian Court* under the assumed name of Count Paul Vassili, appears
to have had what her biographer Brian Roberts called an 'almost pathological detestation' of Tsar Nikolai II and his wife, a hostility towards the
imperial couple that he describes as 'excessive, by any standards'.
Radziwill set off speculation throughout the courts of Europe when she
wrote: 'The child, who has been very delicate ever since his birth, suf-
fers from an organic disease of the arteries which are liable to rupture
upon the slightest provocation and even without cause.'[5] Once such a
statement had become common currency, it is hardly surprising that the
concept of a sick Tsarevich entered the popular consciousness. But how
reliable was Radziwill as a witness? The answer must be: not at all. Not
only was her prejudice against the imperial couple a matter of record, but
her own credibility bore no scrutiny. She had previously served a prison
sentence in South Africa for fraudulently writing cheques in the name of
the Prime Minister of the Cape, Cecil Rhodes; and on a more mundane
level, there are many assertions in her books which are demonstrably
untrue – such as the claim that by 1912 the Tsarevich had no tutors. In
fact, he had five.

Those close to the imperial family have a very different story to tell.
The Tsarina's close friend Lili Dehn was among those to whom the
Empress gave her confidence; her son was a playmate of Alexei. Lili
Dehn published her memoirs, entitled *The Real Tsaritsa*, in 1922. What

she had to say about Alexei's health is very interesting and does not con-
form to the traditional picture.

> The Tsarevich . . . was born in 1904, and he was a healthy boy
> weighing eleven pounds at the time of his birth; many of the
> stories about the delicacy of his constitution which have been given
> to the world are very exaggerated . . . the Tsarevich certainly suf-
> fered from the hereditary trouble of thin blood-vessels which first
> became apparent after a fall at Spala but he was otherwise a nor-
> mally healthy boy and at the time of the Revolution he was really
> getting much freer from this complaint.[6]

The suggestion that the boy's illness was 'very exaggerated' is borne out
by the new evidence from the photographic and film archive which
shows a healthy Alexei. By 1918 the Tsarevich, even if he did have
haemophilia, had already passed out of that critical childhood phase
when sufferers are most susceptible to injury. But what if Alexei had
never suffered from haemophilia in the first place?

In 1995 Professors William and Malcolm Potts, two brothers – one
holding a chair at the University of Lancaster and the other at the
Berkeley campus of the University of California – produced a book
which caused something of a sensation. *Queen Victoria's Gene* put forward the possibility that Queen Victoria was illegitimate. The authors
based this central thesis on the contents of a seven-foot-long scroll which
they had discovered neatly packed away in the library of the Royal
Society of Medicine in London. What they had found was a detailed
study of Queen Victoria's ancestors that was part of the background
research conducted by Professor William Bullock and Sir Paul Fildes
for their definitive work *Haemophilia, a Treasury of Human Inheritance*,
published in 1911 by the Eugenics Society. Bullock and Fildes had not
included the results of this research in their book because, quite simply,
the findings did not fit in with their thesis. Going back over eighteen
generations on both sides of Victoria's family to the early sixteenth century, they did not find a single haemophiliac. So they put the scroll away,
where it remained undisturbed until the 1990s.

The Potts brothers, not unreasonably, argued that the unpublished
research could only mean either that Queen Victoria's haemophilia gene
was a mutation or that the Duke of Kent was not her real father.
Mutation was so very unlikely – the odds were between 1 in 25,000 and
1 in 100,000 – that they came down in favour of illegitimacy, suggesting

further that the Duke of Kent was sterile. However, since publication of the brothers' book, illegitimate descendants of the Duke of Kent have come forward to make themselves known to Bill Potts, and scientists have found the porphyria gene among Queen Victoria's descendants.[7] Since this was the disease which afflicted King George III, the Duke of Kent's father, this suggested that Victoria was legitimate after all. There is also the simple observation that Queen Victoria *looked* like her father, and King George III.

There was, however, a third option which the Potts brothers had not considered: namely, that Queen Victoria was not a haemophilia carrier and that the royal bleeding disorder she had supposedly passed on was actually a different condition. This would be entirely consistent with Bullock's and Fildes' failure to find any trace of haemophilia over eighteen generations of the Queen's ancestors. Quite possibly, the Potts book is a classic case of drawing the wrong conclusions from the right evidence; in any event, it has done a valuable service in opening up this whole subject.

Supposed cases of haemophilia among Queen Victoria's descendants are all explicable in other terms. Sourcing their work from an article by V. McKusick in the *Scientific American* entitled 'The Royal Haemophilia',[8] the Potts brothers ascribed the deaths of several descendants of Queen Victoria to haemophilia; but closer examination of these cases shows that other possibilities cannot be excluded. Prince Leopold, Queen Victoria's fourth son and supposedly the first family member to exhibit the disease, died after falling downstairs and landing on his head; that does not make him a haemophiliac. (Interestingly, Leopold did not bleed after being bitten on the leg by a youthful Kaiser during the future King Edward VII's marriage ceremony in 1864.) Frittie, the Tsarina's little brother, died after running out of a first-floor window of the family palace in Darmstadt and falling to the cobbled courtyard below; that does not make him a haemophiliac. Viscount Trematon died in a car crash in France in 1928 while overtaking at high speed; that does not make him a haemophiliac. In this case, too, the Potts brothers admit that haemophilia was not mentioned in the medical report or obituary; and since it was a well-known disorder, there was no medical or social pressure to keep quiet about it. Nor should Viscount Trematon have been a haemophiliac in any case since his mother, Princess Alice of Athlone, was the daughter of Prince Leopold, and the gene can only be passed on by females. Queen Victoria's grandson, Lord Maurice Mountbatten, died of wounds received during the battle of Ypres during the Great War; this does not make him a haemophiliac – and it must be said that soldiering in the front line in the Great War was a singularly unlikely occupation for a haemophiliac. His brother, Lord Leopold Mountbatten, was described as 'constitutionally delicate' and died after a hip operation; again, that does not make him a haemophiliac. The Pottses themselves admit that yet another descendant in the female line from Queen Victoria through her daughter Princess Beatrice, Paul-Alexandre Weiller (1970–5), whom they initially listed as a haemophiliac, did not, in fact, suffer from the disease. Paul-Alexandre's doctor said that he had '*un problema de sangre*', but his mother was quite clear about this – it was not haemophilia. This is very significant information since it explicitly opens up the possibility that the bleeding disorder in the family was something other than haemophilia.[9]

In any case, the Bourbons, the Spanish royal dynasty into which Princess Beatrice married, may well have had a bleeding disorder of their own. Queen Isabel II of Spain, mother of Princess Beatrice's husband, suffered from chronic eczema which may well have been misdiagnosed lupus – a skin complaint closely linked to the blood disorder thrombocytopenia. Her mother, Queen Marie Christina, suffered from violent nosebleeds (indeed, she met her second husband, the Duke of Riansares, when he came to her aid during one of these attacks). Our source for this is the Infanta Eulalia, her daughter. Certainly the genetic record of the Spanish Bourbons was not a good one. Queen Isabel II's father, King Ferdinand VII, had twelve brothers and sisters, but only three out of the family of thirteen lived beyond the age of nineteen. King Carlos IV of Spain, Ferdinand's father, lost eight out of thirteen siblings by early adulthood. During the eighteenth century the infant mortality rate of the Bourbons was two and a half times higher than among other royal families in Britain and Germany. King George III of Britain had fourteen children of whom only two died young. King Frederick William III of Prussia likewise lost just two children out of nine. Nor was the problem restricted to the Spanish branch of the Bourbon family, but extended to its French and Neapolitan branches as well. King Ferdinand I of Naples – Queen Marie Christina of Spain's father – had eighteen children, of whom only four survived into their thirties. In view of this evidence, it seems a little unfair to ascribe all the blame for the royal genetic disorders of the royal families of Europe on Queen Victoria.[10]

Whatever one thinks of the Potts brothers' conclusions, the work of

Bullock and Fildes stands. There was no trace of haemophilia among Queen Victoria's ancestors over a period of eighteen generations. Furthermore, Princess Feodora of Leiningen, Queen Victoria's maternal half-sister, has left no haemophiliacs among her descendants. Victoria herself was quite explicit on the matter. 'This disease,' she said, 'is *not* in our family.'

There is other evidence tending to reinforce this judgement. Prince Leopold, Victoria's fourth son and the Tsarina's uncle, was long held to have been the first haemophiliac in the family. That only one of the Queen's sons contracted the disease is below expectations, since 50 per cent of a haemophilia carrier's male offspring can expect to have the disease. Statistically, therefore, Queen Victoria should have had two haemophiliac sons. Assuming nonetheless that she improved on the statistics, there remains another unusual feature of the disease as it presented itself in Queen Victoria's family. Writing in her journal, the Queen herself records that Dr Marshall, Prince Leopold's physician, reported that her son had a haemorrhage from the bowels – a symptom which is less typical of haemophilia than of thrombocytopenia, which, as noted in the previous chapter, is caused by a low blood platelet count.[11] Other symptoms include bleeding in the nose, gums and occasionally other sites such as the urinary tract and the intestines. Spontaneous recovery occurs in 80–90 per cent of cases.[12] The complaint can be congenital but can also be caused by other illnesses, for example leukaemia, anaemia, a malfunctioning spleen or congestive heart failure. It can also be the result of the administration of drugs – particularly aspirin.

The similarities between these symptoms and those of Alexei's illness are striking. At Livadia in 1912, the Tsarevich had bleeding from the kidneys, involving the urinary tract; at Spala in October 1912 he suffered from abdominal bleeding; in December 1915 he suffered from a severe nosebleed – all sites commonly associated with thrombocytopenia.[13] His recovery in each case appeared to be spontaneous – again a feature of thrombocytopenia. Thrombocytopenia can be induced by the administration of aspirin, and this, as we have seen, is a distinct possibility, given what we know about Rasputin's activities.

Another piece of evidence which has been ignored since it was first published in 1960 involved an anecdote related by the Tsar's sister, Grand Duchess Olga, to her biographer, Ian Vorres. Apparently, soon after the start of a routine tonsil operation being performed by Dr Seleriov, the

Tsarevich's sister Grand Duchess Maria started to haemorrhage profusely. Seleriov in a blind panic ran from the room, to be met by the formidable Tsarina who insisted that he return to the operating theatre and finish the operation despite the blood. 'He managed to do so successfully,' Grand Duchess Olga said, 'despite the persistent bleeding.' Understandably, this incident impressed itself on Grand Duchess Olga's memory – and recalling it led her to reveal something more: all the Tsar's children, she maintained, were 'bleeders'.[14] But the Tsarevich had four sisters, no brothers. If he suffered from Factor VIII haemophilia, only he would have had the symptoms, since under the genetic rules governing the disease, only boys contract the disorder whereas girls are merely carriers. This is extremely significant. Whatever was wrong with Alexei, therefore, it cannot have been Factor VIII haemophilia. It might have been Factor IX Haemophilia B, better known as 'Christmas disease' and not identified as a separate condition from Factor VIII haemophilia until 1952.[15] Girls can inherit 'Christmas disease', which is not constrained by the same rules as Factor VIII haemophilia. Or it might have been thrombocytopenia. In view of the evidence from the case of Prince Leopold, and the strong correlation between the symptoms of the Tsarevich's disorder and those of thrombocytopenia, it seems likely that the latter was the case. And if this is so, its effects may have been severely exacerbated by the administration of aspirin – if not caused by it in the first place. Such a circumstance may well explain why the Tsarevich was 'much freer from this complaint', as Lili Dehn puts it, in that period from 1915 onwards when the Tsar had his son away with him at the front – and when Rasputin had conveniently predicted that he would be free of the disease;[16] or, for that matter, after 1917 when Rasputin was dead. Lili Dehn read aloud to Alix Hill's grandmother, Countess von Berg, when the latter was an old lady; within this aristocratic Russian community, Alix Hill told me, it was generally accepted that Rasputin had been poisoning the Tsarevich.[17]

Alix Hill also provides an interesting footnote to these reflections. She recalled that Chebotarev had a horror of aspirin and would never take it. She also recalled how, after a party at which the Tsarevich's illness had been mentioned, Chebotarev took her aside and said, with an emphasis and certainty that struck her forcibly: 'Maybe he was not as ill as people supposed. It could have been greatly exaggerated. He could have got better.'[18] If he was the Tsarevich, this information accords with what medical evidence suggests – evidence not widely available and counter to the official propaganda of the day which was still presenting a haemophiliac Tsarevich cured by a mystic's miracles.

In early 1998 I submitted as complete a dossier as could be compiled of the Tsarevich's medical history and symptoms to the haematology department at Beaumont Hospital, Dublin, seeking a modern opinion on the possible nature of his disease. The response in May was uncompromising. Dr J. R. O'Donnell, consultant haematologist at the hospital, stated that in the case of Alexei, 'Factor VIII haemophilia A is extremely unlikely. The hallmark of this condition . . . is serious joint bleeding which was never evident. Epistaxis [bleeding from the nose] and GI [gastrointestinal] bleeding would not be found in haemophilia.' Emphasizing the multiplicity of both congenital and acquired forms of bleeding disease, none of which would have been recognized at the turn of the century, and the impossibility of being definitive about any of them at such a distance of time, he went on to say that 'thrombocytopenia is a possibility'; and though 'it was not possible to measure the platelet count accurately at this time . . . certainly platelet function is adversely affected by aspirin and this or another agent toxically administered could be responsible.'[19] In a subsequent letter Dr O'Donnell said that the available evidence certainly did not rule out the possibility of Alexei living to a great age.

Another fertile source of data on the Tsarevich's condition is provided by the health problems of his immediate family, many of which echo aspects of his own symptoms. Tsar Alexander III, Alexei's grandfather, had died at the early age of forty-nine from the kidney disease nephritis.[20] In 1912, as we have seen, the Tsarevich suffered from haemorraghing from the kidneys, and in 1913 Anna Vyrubova reported to Rasputin that Alexei had pain and swelling in the side: nephritis can cause pain in the flank. At the time of Alexander III's death there were dark rumours that he had been poisoned, probably by the Germans. Could aspirin have played a part in his death? Grand Duke George, whose body was exhumed in 1996 to compare with that of the 'Tsar' skeleton in Ekaterinburg, died from a haemorrhage that occurred while he was riding his motor-bike at Annas Touman in Georgia where he lived after contracting tuberculosis. Grand Duchess Olga said that her brother George suffered from weak lungs and nosebleeds as a child.[21]

Even closer to home, the imperial physician Dr Botkin reportedly told an officer in Siberia that the Tsarina suffered from an 'inherited family weakness of the blood vessels which often led to progressive hysteria'.[22] The phrase 'weakness of the blood vessels' recalls Lili Dehn's description of Alexei's illness as the 'hereditary trouble of thin blood vessels'. 'Progressive hysteria' has even stronger resonances with another malady which was not publicly linked with the British royal family until the mid-1960s – namely, porphyria, often referred to as 'the madness of King George'. Porphyria has been traced in the lineage of the British royal family at least as far back as Mary, Queen of Scots and possibly as far as Henry VII's daughter, Queen Margaret of Scotland. The disease is characterized by the excessive production of porphyrins, from which it takes its name. These are biological molecules which include haemo-globin, the principal constituent of red cells in blood. The symptoms of hepatic porphyria, the most common variety, include intestinal pain, limb weakness and hysteria – as well as the production of purplish urine, through which it has been possible to trace its incidence through the generations.[23] Bill Potts records that Princess Charlotte, George III's grand-daughter and Queen Victoria's cousin, died from what he believes was a fatal attack of porphyria brought on by pregnancy. Exhibiting signs of excitement and difficulty in breathing – symptoms shared by the Tsarina – Princess Charlotte died from a massive haemorrhage in her uterus extending as high as her navel.[24] Recent research involving DNA tests on the remains of Queen Victoria's grand-daughter Charlotte of Prussia and Charlotte's daughter Feodora of Reuss, both of whom ex-hibited mental and physical symptoms similar to those evidenced by present-day sufferers from variegate porphyria, has established a very high degree of probability that the porphyria gene was indeed passed down through the royal line from George III to his grand-daughter, Queen Victoria, and on to her descendants. (Incidentally, in the course of their investigation the researchers found not only that Prince Philip's DNA sample did not match that taken from the bones of Princess Feodora, but also that Princess Feodora's mitochondrial DNA profile was different from that of her own mother, Princess Charlotte of Prussia. This strongly reinforces the doubts expressed about the reliability of mitochondrial DNA as a tool for the establishment of identity, as dis-cussed in chapter 6.)[25] Both the Tsarina and the Tsar were descended from King George II of Great Britain – she through Queen Victoria, he through his mother, the Danish Princess Dagmar. So porphyria could have been transmitted to both family lines.

Grand Duchess Olga, her sister-in-law, said of the Tsarina: 'She was indeed a sick woman. Her breath often came in quick, obviously painful gasps. I often saw her lips turn blue.'[26] Prone to use her wheelchair and to lounge on her day-bed, the Tsarina spoke continually of having 'overtired muscles of the heart' and an 'enlarged heart'. Dr Grotte and Dr Fisher, called in by the Tsar to find out what exactly was wrong with his wife, produced a report in 1908 which was suppressed when the Tsarina found out about it. Fisher himself was dismissed, having insisted on treating not the Empress's heart, which he found to be in good condition, but her nervous system.[27] Madeline Zanotti, the Tsarina's maid, recalled: 'It seemed to me she was suffering from hysteria. What was the cause of the Empress's hysterical condition, I do not know. Perhaps she was suffering from a woman's disease . . . When she found herself among congenial people she was always quite well but the moment anything displeased her she immediately began to complain. Believing her heart was affected, she used to spend the greater part of each day lying on her sofa.'[28] At the very least, the implication was that the Tsarina had a tendency to hypochondria and was highly suggestible. It would have been easy to persuade such a woman that she was ill – or, for that matter, that her son was ill. Such a condition may well have predisposed the Tsarina to listen to Grand Duchesses Militsa and Stana when they fanned fears for her son's health.

The Tsarina's high anxiety levels are attested to by many, not least her cousin, Princess Marie-Louise, who told her: 'Alix, you always play at being sorrowful: one day the Almighty will send you some real crushing sorrows and then what are you going to do?'[29] Alix was only six when her mother died, and the impact of this loss on her was incalculable. She had formerly been known in the family as 'Sunny'; after this traumatic time her nickname began to sound like a cynical joke. But was there more amiss with Alix than the mental and emotional anguish caused by a young child's loss of a parent; and there is a genetically transmitted disorder which may well have been at the root of the Tsarina's problems.

SLE or systemic lupus erythematatosus is an auto-immune disease which causes inflammation of the organs, high fever and joint pain, sometimes accompanied by a blotchy red rash on the face. At times of stress the Tsarina did suffer from a rash. Meriel Buchanan, daughter of Sir George Buchanan, the British ambassador to Russia at the time, described it as 'a dull, unbecoming flush'. Another observer spoke of her 'red arms, red shoulders and a red face which always gave the impression that she was about to burst into tears'.[30] Interestingly, one of Queen Victoria's and the Tsarina's common ancestors in the early sixteenth century was Anne of Bohemia, whose brother, King Louis II of Hungary, was known as 'Ohne Haut' – the skinless one.[31] Did he suffer from a disfiguring case of lupus? Despite the reproductive imperatives in the Jagiellon dynasty to which Anne and Louis belonged – it ruled no fewer than four separate east European kingdoms – the line died out through the failure of either to produce a direct heir. Research shows that both the Spanish Bourbons and the British royal family had a common ancestor in 'Ohne Haut's' sister, Anne, and thus their bleeding problem may have had a common origin.

Along the genetic pathway this tendency may have been enhanced by numerous marriages among first cousins which, geneticists tell us, can lead to the transmission of autosomal recessive disorders – notably blood disorders – caused by a gene mutation.[32] Quite simply, they were inbred. Among Anne's more notorious relatives was Countess Erzbet Bathory, daughter of the Prince of Transylvania, who was accused of vampirism and bathing in the blood of young virgins. Vampirism was probably erythropoietic porphyria, a recessive disorder which has the side-effect of drawing back the cheeks, exposing the teeth while at the same time reddening them – producing the classic Dracula effect. Drinking blood was the treatment used in the sixteenth century.[33]

Lupus can cause shortness of breath, from which the Tsarina periodically suffered, and heart disease, from which the Tsarina herself believed she was suffering and for which she took medication. Many of Alexei's recorded symptoms – haemorrhaging in the kidneys, high fever, joint pain – are associated with lupus. Lupus is also associated with thrombocytopenia, which, as we have seen, has strong claims to be considered the complaint from which Alexei suffered. In his report on the illness of the Tsarevich, Dr O'Donnell mentioned SLE – and also porphyria – as among the possible diagnoses. Interestingly, aspirin, the bleeding agent, is one of the treatments for lupus.[34]

What this raft of disorders among the Tsarevich's close relatives suggests is that Alexei suffered from a disorder other than haemophilia, probably thrombocytopenia, in a relatively mild form which was, however, aggravated by the administration of an aspirin-based drug by Rasputin. Other symptoms, such as joint pain, may well have been caused by a rheumatoid factor associated with thrombocytopenia and latent lupus, from which his mother probably suffered.[35]

It would, of course, be naïve to believe that the Tsarevich suffered from only one complaint which was solely responsible for all his bouts of illness. Several of the examples of joint pain, for instance, may have been

linked to a separate rheumatoid disposition – not all need necessarily
have been connected to the blood disorder. Some, doubtless, amounted
to no more than the Tsar suggested when he recorded on 16 July 1913
that 'Alexei's right elbow hurt from waving his arms about too much
while playing.'[36]

Alexei's inheritance of blood was far from being a straightforward,
cut-and-dried case of haemophilia. Factor VIII haemophilia, the most
common variety, is ruled out by the fact that his sisters, and particularly
Maria, were also bleeders. Any variety of haemophilia is unlikely given
that Queen Victoria did not have a single haemophiliac among eighteen
generations of her ancestors, that her sister Princess Feodora has left no
haemophiliac descendants and that many of Queen Victoria's descendants alleged to have had haemophilia may well not have had the disease.
In an interesting sidelight, the Potts evidence appears to offer the British
royal family a stark choice: either Queen Victoria was illegitimate or, if
she was not, then she did not carry haemophilia. If she did not, then the
Tsarina could not have been a carrier either; and Alexei could not have
been a haemophiliac.

That the royal disorder might have been something other than
haemophilia – possibly thrombocytopenia – is suggested by the symptoms of both Prince Leopold, supposedly the first haemophiliac in the
family, and the Tsarevich. That the Tsarevich's condition was, at the
very least, being aggravated by drugs supplied by Badmaev and administered by Anna Vyrubova acting for Rasputin is strongly suggested by
contemporary evidence. Manufacture a situation where you could create
an injury, induce or simply aggravate a haemorrhage and produce a
healer with the apparent antidote, and you have the control system.
Relationships in that triangle of the Tsar, Tsarina and Rasputin were
more complex than the uncritical picture of the Tsar slavishly obeying
the *starets*. From the Tsar's repeated exiles of the 'holy man' to his reaction to the murder, there is evidence of a man who wanted to be free of
this problem. And what was the nature of that problem? Rasputin held
the Empress 'spellbound – in a close physical relationship': the verdict
not of a scurrilous book but of the Tsar's own sister.[37]

The Tsarina herself may well have had medical problems, associated
with lupus and thrombocytopenia but unconnected to haemophilia,
which contributed to her son's condition. For all the complex of medical disorders that lay among these ruling families, still Queen Victoria's
verdict on haemophilia stands: 'This disease is not in our family.' Too

many of the people who have perpetuated the haemophilia story have had a vested interest in doing so, from Princess Catherine Radziwill, with her pathological hatred of Nikolai II and his wife, to the junior branches of the Romanov dynasty who wished to press their claims to the imperial throne and for whom a sickly and doomed Tsarevich meant a passport to power. Alexei, like his father, was a victim – a victim of the isolation and envy that supreme power attracts and of the extraordinary lengths to which people will go to seize it.

# Windows of Opportunity

With the Tsarevich's body missing from the burial pit in Ekaterinburg, and the growing evidence that his illness was not only exaggerated but misdiagnosed, the possibility of his survival could no longer be dismissed. With the swelling body of evidence suggesting that Alexei Romanov and Nikolai Chebotarev were one and the same person, a tantalizing vision was emerging of what might have happened to him after that escape. I had to find out what really happened to the imperial family in 1917 and 1918.

It has generally been assumed that from the moment Lenin came to power the Romanovs were doomed, nothing but living corpses, and that they could not possibly have survived the ferocity of the Bolshevik Revolution. Yet for a period of nine months, from October 1917 to July 1918, the former imperial family, now just plain Citizen Nikolai Romanov, his wife and five children, did precisely that. And there was no particular or pressing reason why the Bolsheviks should have changed their attitude to their prisoners after that date. Europe remained at war until November 1918. Large tracts of the former Russian Empire were still under the control of the German army or its puppet regime in the Ukraine, headed by Hetman Skoropadsky. In such an uncertain and dangerous situation, ideological considerations could not be allowed to override the imperative of survival. Lenin was above all an intelligent pragmatist, well able to judge the need to take unpalatable actions: the humiliating surrender of 750,000 square miles of territory to Germany at the Treaty of Brest-Litovsk in March 1918 in order to obtain peace with Germany is a case in point,[1] as is the abandonment of war communism in favour of the New Economic Policy in 1921. Lenin's overriding objective was the survival of his fledgling Bolshevik government, and in pursuit of this objective bargains, possibly distasteful ones, would have to be made. The Bolsheviks consequently needed material to bargain with, and in the great game of peace and war the Romanovs were tradable goods. There is sufficient evidence of diplomatic activity to make it clear that the German government at least took a real interest in the fate of the former imperial family.[2] Uncertain as to the outcome of the war, Lenin could afford to take no chances with German monarchist sensibilities. Seen in this light, the choice of 16 July 1918 as an appropriate or opportune time to liquidate the former ruler and his family makes no sense at all. Yet this is what the official version of events would have us believe.

Of course, the official version has been challenged over the years – most robustly perhaps by Anthony Summers and Tom Mangold in *The File on the Tsar*, which posed several major objections to the traditional story. Two points in particular arising from their analysis stuck persistently in my mind.

First, Summers and Mangold had described Bolshevik proposals for the exchange of two Communist activists then in German hands – Karl Liebknecht, the German Spartacist leader, and Leo Jogiches, the Polish Marxist and friend of Rosa Luxemburg – for the imperial family as 'the strongest possible diplomatic evidence that the imperial family were still alive'.[3] Both were, in fact, freed – Liebknecht on 23 October 1918 and Jogiches soon thereafter.[4] Given that all the instincts and inclinations of the Kaiser's government would have been against such a move as the release of two known agitators, and that the fate of the two socialists had been persistently linked to the fate of the Romanovs, it seems reasonable to wonder whether the other side of the deal had been wholly or partly delivered.

Second, it is entirely plausible that some sort of international action at royal level had been concerted to obtain the release of the Romanovs. Queen Victoria had been the 'grandmother of Europe', numbering the Tsarina, the Kaiser, King George V, his sister Princess Victoria, Grand Duke Ernst of Hesse and Queen Marie of Romania among her many grandchildren. These grandchildren were understandably concerned for the fate of their Romanov relatives, cousins they had grown up with, holidayed with, been godparents to, cared for and even, in some cases, loved. Queen Marie, for instance, declared that she would never desert 'poor dear Nicky and his family'.[5] And there is more to this than a generalized supposition of family feeling. Summers and Mangold found a Foreign Office file in the Public Record Office at Kew that was highly significant not for what it contained but for what was scrawled across the outside of the empty cover. Here, in what may be the only physical trace of an entity whose very *raison d'être* was inimical to documented records, someone had penned the words 'The Trust of Kings'.[6] The initial capitals are important; this is a proper noun, not an abstract reflection on the fiduciary relationship of monarchs. The clear implication was that some shadowy royal club had been at work on behalf of their Russian relatives. I had already seen in the course of my own researches – as described in chapter 6 – how a very similar network still operated; how much more likely, then, that an even more formidable organization, something with real teeth, existed back in 1918 when monarchs still operated outside the constraints of national governments and even national interests, and thought nothing of conducting a personal foreign policy in pursuit of their own private concerns. Action across national boundaries, while it posed certain logistical problems, especially in wartime, would have presented Europe's royalty with few if any moral dilemmas – particularly if it were done, as these things were, in secret and beyond the gaze of curious subjects.

For its part, the new Soviet government was no monolith, no uniform expression of a pure doctrinaire stance. At this stage at least, it was rather a coalition of interests united mainly by their common concern with merely staying in power. If the Bolsheviks were to stand a chance of defeating the anti-revolutionary 'White' forces, they needed peace with Germany; and the Romanovs were prime bargaining counters in their pursuit of this end. Various contemporary sources attest to a persistent German interest in the fate of the Romanov women in particular, an interest expressed particularly strongly in May–September 1918. At the time of the imperial family's disappearance from Ekaterinburg, the German Chancellor himself was a former contender for the hand of Alix of Hesse: Prince Max of Baden, whose suit in 1891 had been actively supported by the princess's 'darling grandmama' Queen Victoria.[7] Nor was the question for the Bolsheviks simply one of the ideological survival of their movement; the revolutionary leaders were far from convinced of their own personal survival. Certainly their prospects in 1918 did not look particularly promising. Most of Russia lay under the control of anti-Bolshevik forces, White Russian administrations, the German army or foreign interventionists. This was fertile ground for the Trust of Kings to exploit.

Under constant threat, both as individuals and as a political force, the Bolshevik leadership was in some respects more amenable to a deal on the Romanovs than their democratic predecessors had been. Though the possibility of despatching the imperial family into exile with a friendly foreign power was briefly entertained in the early months of 1917, the evidence on how enthusiastic the Provisional Government was about this solution to the problem is mixed. Kerensky was reluctant to relinquish control over Russia's former rulers and, for all his dislike of capital punishment and revolutionary violence, had planned a show trial for the Tsar and Tsarina in Moscow. That was the whole purpose for which his 'truth commission' had been gathering evidence on the 'dark forces' of pre-revolutionary Russia. In 1966, speaking in his flat on 93rd Street in New York, he admitted this much to author Viktor Alexandrov: 'In the spring and summer of 1917, when we were still engaged in a terrible war, it was impossible to divulge my plan which was to bring the Tsar, and above all the Tsarina, before a revolutionary and democratic court.'[8] It was difficult for allied governments to intercede with Kerensky over the Romanovs; apart from the sensitivity of their position at the head of democratic polities in which popular sympathy for the Russian imperial family was in short supply, keeping Kerensky's Russian government in the war against Germany was a higher priority for Britain and France than the fate of their former loyal ally, the Tsar. But the Bolsheviks were willing to consider even unpalatable options, as was only too apparent from their acceptance of the Treaty of Brest-Litovsk, mentioned above. If peace could only be bought by humiliation and abandonment of principle, so be it. The same considerations could not but influence the Bolsheviks' attitude to the imperial family.

By the time Lenin came to power Nikolai Romanov was in effect a spent force, a leftover from history. Another intervening regime distanced Lenin from the tsarist past. The possibility that the imperial family might at some juncture become a rallying point for monarchist or other anti-Bolshevist forces, however remote, was nevertheless difficult to dismiss with confidence while the revolutionary regime remained insecure and under constant threat. That in itself would ensure that the Bolsheviks kept a close watch on their prisoners; but more important, surely, to a pragmatist like Lenin was the potential usefulness of these individuals as negotiable chess pieces. Prudence alone, therefore, would have dictated careful supervision. Rescue for the Romanovs was never a real option. An arrangement for their departure involving some form of mutual agreement was much more likely. Logically, the Bolsheviks were bound to be in the business of trading Romanovs for whatever their royal relatives were willing to offer.

Logical it may have been, but was it what actually happened? Any evidence for the operation of something as nebulous as the Trust of Kings would inevitably be scant. The royal families and their agents were well practised in the arts of concealment; and, since they operated outside official governmental channels and beyond any legal constraint, they had the means to obliterate all trace of what they had done. They would be aided in this, moreover, by the sheer chaos that was Russia in 1918. Nothing provides a better smokescreen than disorder. History, though, is hard to destroy and while it may be comparatively easy to 'weed' official documents, a record of what actually happened may live on in collateral sources – sources not even guessed at by official authorities and therefore beyond their power to erase. A witness here, a diary there, a disregarded receipt somewhere else – tiny links to tie together previously unconnected information are all it takes to begin to put together a picture of the shadowy operations of the Trust of Kings and a deal with the Bolsheviks over some or all of the Romanovs. The Trust of Kings had to operate through people, and while many of these agents were no doubt careful to cover their tracks, it was a fair bet that someone, somewhere would have left some trace of their activities. And so it proved. A lead turned up in the unlikeliest of places: the Public Record Office of Northern Ireland – not somewhere you would expect to find material relating to Russia in 1918. Yet there it was. Locked away in the papers of a Canadian militia colonel were clues to the shadowy operations of the Trust of Kings.[9]

Lieutenant-Colonel Joseph Whiteside Boyle has already attracted ample notice. Two books have been written about him, and he has featured in another written by a man whose name is synonymous with espionage.[10] Captain (later Brigadier) George Hill was cited by Summers and Mangold as one of the most famous British agents in Russia in 1918.[11] He was also the cousin of three other individuals who feature in the life of Nikolai Chebotarev. One was Alexander Hill – Alix Hill's father. Another was Freddie Hill, sidekick to Robert Bruce Lockhart, the top British diplomat in Russia in 1918.[12] In St Petersburg in 1915, Freddie Hill had been best man at his cousin Natalie Karaulov's wedding to Frank Cooke;[13] it was Natalie Cooke who harboured Chebotarev in the years of the Second World War. And Freddie Hill's sister was Dame Elizabeth Hill, who sent language students from Cambridge, where she was Professor of Slavonic Studies, to Nikolai Couriss at Collon.[14] Of George and Freddie Hill, Alix Hill was protective: 'Don't call them spies. My father said they weren't spies. They were gentlemen agents.'[15]

Whatever we choose to call them, George Hill at least openly admitted to being agent I-K8 in the Secret Intelligence Service, recruited from the Royal Flying Corps and the Manchester Regiment in Salonika in 1917.[16] His service record shows that he was commissioned as a second lieutenant in the Manchester Regiment on 13 May 1915, seconded as an interpreter on 11 January 1916 and appointed a flying officer on 29 May 1917.[17] Though vague, it does show service in Salonika, Russia, Romania and Turkey. His Second World War record is fuller, and shows him working for the intelligence division ME 73.

For George Hill, Colonel Joe Boyle was 'a man whose equal I have encountered neither before or since and to have enjoyed his friendship and to have worked under him and with him will always remain one of the proudest memories of my life'.[18] Dr Una Kroll, George Hill's daughter, told me how her father and mother, then Evelyn Pediani, had spirited the Romanian crown jewels, £25 million in gold and the state archives – which, somewhat ironically, had been stored with the Tsar's government for safe keeping – out of Bolshevik Russia, her mother literally sitting on them in the railway carriage while her father rode shotgun.[19] Such exploits as these told me something of the mettle of the people with whom I was dealing.

Joe Boyle himself had quite a past. He had been a Chicago fireman, amateur heavyweight boxing champion of the USA, manager of the world heavyweight champion Frank Slavin, a Yukon gold miner and founder of a gold-mining company.[20] A millionaire by the start of hostilities in 1914, he had equipped at his own expense a machine-gun company run according to his concept of war. Boyle came from Ulster Irish stock, and regularly visited his family's old homestead at Upper Buckna in County Antrim, from which his grandfather had emigrated in the 1830s. His cousin Jimmy Boyle still lives there – which was how his papers came to be in Northern Ireland, where I found them.[21]

Swashbuckling and intrepid, a hero straight from the pages of *The Boys' Own Paper*, a man who believed in getting the job done – Joe Boyle was all of these things; but he also had one other qualification which suited him uniquely for involvement in an attempt to rescue the Romanovs. He was the lover of Queen Marie of Romania. In stark contrast to the Queen's ineffectual husband, King Ferdinand, or 'Nando' as he was known in the family, Boyle was a man of action, matching Marie's own temperament, and was entrusted by her with the most delicate of family matters, as for instance when she sent him to bring back her son, Crown Prince Carol, who had eloped with a commoner, Zizi Lambrino, in August 1918.[22]

Queen Marie was uniquely placed to operate on behalf of the Trust of Kings in the matter of the Romanovs. As the daughter of Queen Victoria's son Alfred, Duke of Edinburgh, she was cousin at once to King George V, the Tsarina and the Kaiser.[23] Her mother was the daughter of Tsar Alexander II, making her Tsar Nikolai II's cousin. Her sister, Victoria Melita, now married to Grand Duke Cyril, had previously been married to the Tsarina's brother, Grand Duke Ernst of Hesse. The Romanian royal house, into which she had married, was a branch of the Hohenzollerns, the Kaiser's family. Romania shared a border with Russia and, like Russia, was a Black Sea power. It would have been easy to mount operations in Russia from a Romanian base; Odessa, in particular, was easily accessible. In 1914 the possibility of a marriage between Crown Prince Carol and the Tsar's eldest daughter Olga had been raised.[24] Though Olga declined at the time, the discussions were amicable and negotiations had been reopened in 1916. Queen Marie also had a daughter, Princess Ileana, who was a suitable age for the Tsarevich and who had taken a great liking to him in 1914. Queen Marie, then, was the obvious choice to front any Romanov rescue planned by the Trust of Kings, and Boyle would have been her obvious choice of a man of action to carry it out.

In March 1918, Trotsky, newly appointed Commissar for War in Lenin's government, got to hear of Joe Boyle's latest exploit.[25] The Canadian had managed to bribe the Odessa Bolsheviks, some of the most aggressive in Russia, into releasing fifty high-ranking Romanian hostages – members of parliament, generals and the like.[26] Trotsky, though often portrayed as a purist ideologue, was by no means blind to the power of money. Foremost among the Soviet leaders in the acquisition of the trappings of power, he had obtained Arkangelskoye, the former estate of Prince Yusupov and reckoned to be the best in Russia, as his weekend dacha.[27] He of all people would be aware that a struggling revolutionary government could not afford to ignore any possibility of swelling its coffers. The Bolsheviks were a small party, newly and unexpectedly in power, and their appetite for money, in particular to fund propaganda, was voracious. In 1918 the Germans paid them about 50 million gold marks for this purpose.[28] Boyle had £10 million at his disposal and, in addition, 100 million francs from the French – a massive sum in those days, out of which he could offer the Odessa Bolsheviks handsome

*Above left* Lieutenant–Colonel Joseph W. Boyle  *Above right* Boyle with Queen Marie of Romania and Princess Ileana, 1918  *Below left* Boyle (centre) with the Romanian hostages whose freedom he secured with bribes, still under Bolshevik guard at Theodosia  *Below right* A bill from the Army & Navy Stores sent to Boyle at Buckingham Palace, December 1918

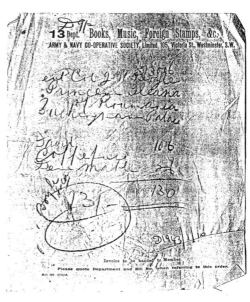

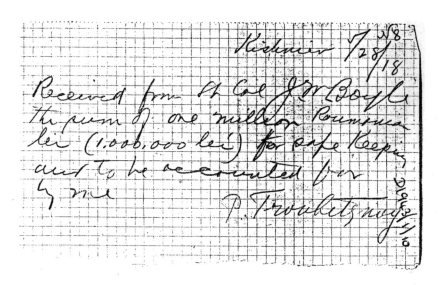

Two receipts, each for one million lei, from Boyle's agent Prince
Trubetskoye. One is dated 28 May 1918, before the Imperial family
disappeared, the other 22 July 1918, immediately after

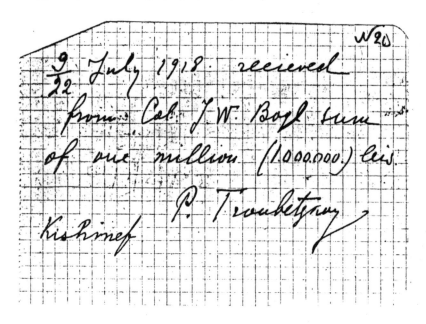

*Above left* Captain George Hill DSO
*Left* Captain 'Freddie' Hill, George's cousin; also cousin to Natalie Cooke and best man at her wedding, and Robert Bruce Lockhart's deputy *Above centre* Dame Elizabeth Hill, Professor of Slavonic Studies at Cambridge, who sent students to Couriss at Collon *Above right* Alix Hill, close friend of Chebotarev and cousin to George, Freddie and Dame Elizabeth

*Below left* Mara Gorbadovsky (right), Helene Aitov (left)
*Below right* Richard Meinertzhagen

*Above* The Dowager Empress disembarks from HMS *Marlborough* in Malta

*Right* Sister Valentina Chebotarev

*Above* The school at Tsarskoe Selo attended by Grigori Chebotarev and Couriss

*Left* Grigori Chebotarev with his mother and sister

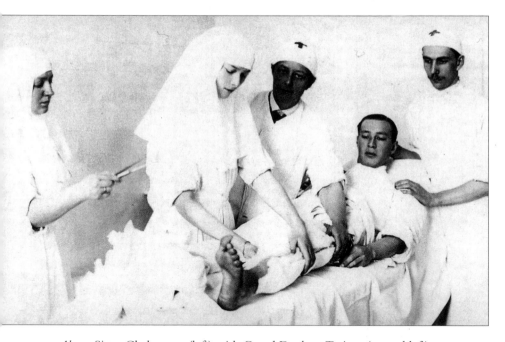

*Above* Sister Chebotarev (left) with Grand Duchess Tatiana (second left)

*Below* Patients and staff at the hospital. Alexei is at the rear to the right

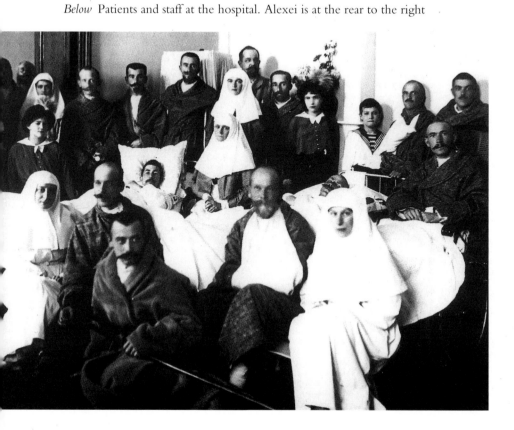

Natalie Cooke, seated (sixth from right) in front of the Tsar and Tsarina
at the hospital, 1914. Her cousin Nina Berberov is to her left

The Crimean Cadet Corps, Bela Cirkva, 1923

A page from Chebotarev's sketchbook at Bela Cirkva, showing his drawings of Imperial Guard uniforms from Tsarskoe Selo

*Above* The children of Count Grabbe, Commander of the Tsar's bodyguard, Nice, 1924

*Right* Chebotarev in Nice, 1925

*Above* Chebotarev with Hilda Richardson in Egypt, 1929

*Below left* Archbishop Theophan, the Tsarina's confessor. He introduced Rasputin to the imperial family   *Below right* One of the ninety-nine letters Theophan sent to Chebotarev between 1921 and 1932

recompense for their hostages. Sensing the opportunity offered by Boyle's bribes for hostages deal, Trotsky let it be known that he urgently wanted to meet the Canadian. Bruce Lockhart, who had taken over the British Embassy after ambassador Sir George Buchanan had left in January 1918, and Captain George Hill conveyed the message. Lockhart wrote to the Foreign Office in London: 'Trotsky has frequently asked about him [Boyle] and would be glad to make use of his services. If there is any chance of coming to an agreement with the Bolshevists, his presence here might be very useful.'[29] At the beginning of April 1918 Lockhart managed to track Boyle down in Sebastopol in the Crimea.

Boyle's dealings with the Soviet leadership went further than Trotsky. Through Nadezhda Krupsky, Lenin's wife, he met the Bolshevik leader and his colleagues immediately after the party's takeover in October 1917, while its headquarters were still based in the Smolny Institute, and took on an official role as adviser to the Russian government on railways. In this capacity he obtained passes from the revolutionary leadership which enabled him to move around freely on the railway system – which he did in style, in the former Dowager Empress's carriage.[30] In itself this was an interesting choice of vehicle. And Boyle was in the business of Romanov rescue even before Trotsky managed to track him down; in March 1918, he had got Grand Duchess Marie, the niece of Queen Marie of Romania, out of Odessa.[31]

Boyle kept detailed lists of expenses incurred by himself and his agents for eventual accounting at the Foreign Office. His papers record two substantial payments made by him following this approach from Trotsky. The first, on Tuesday 28 May 1918, was for one million Romanian lei, a sum equivalent to £1.8 million at today's values.[32] A second payment followed on 22 July 1918, again for one million lei – another £1.8 million. That the payments were for two equal amounts suggests that they were two instalments; and such large amounts point to bribery on a large scale and at a high level. There is no record elsewhere in Boyle's papers of comparably large sums being disbursed – ten thousand lei is a more typical amount.[33] The imperial family disappeared from Ekaterinburg on 16 July: seven weeks after the first payment, and six days before the second.

Other papers show comparatively modest expense claims, but some of these are also suggestive. On 2 July Boyle spent the equivalent of £35 on 'photography'. On 5 July this hard-bitten Canadian ex-gold-digger bought ribbons. He also spent over £500 at the tailors on 6 July, which suggests clothes for more than one individual; and on 10 July he spent the equivalent of £30 in current values on sweets – hardly his normal bill of fare, but very appropriate for children.[34] Yet while he was punctilious in recording such detail, Boyle was less forthcoming about the purposes of his expenditure, a reticence which later drew down on him considerable criticism from the Treasury. 'The money is being very well used,' was all he would say.[35]

Both of the receipts for the two payments of one million lei were signed by 'P. Troubetskoy'. Though he makes no mention of these receipts, Boyle's biographer refers to the Colonel's agent Prince Piotr Trubetskoye, who he says was a former diplomat. Ruvigny's *Titled Nobility of Europe 1914*, however, yields two Prince Trubetskoyes with the initial 'P' – Prince Paul Petrovich Trubetskoye, a former imperial chamberlain who was a justice of the peace for the district of Balti near Mount Kazbek in the Caucasus, and Prince Piotr Sergeevich Trubetskoye, a former civil servant in the ministry of agriculture who lived at the Castle of Baku, again in the Caucasus. The two men were cousins; Prince Paul was also related to the Sayn-Wittgensteins, who were in turn relatives of both the Hills and the Lievens.[36]

Trotsky, meanwhile, in his new role as War Commissar, had obligingly recruited George Hill as inspector of aviation – one of a number of appointments of British and French experts made in blatant disregard of the constraints imposed on him by the punitive Treaty of Brest-Litovsk.[37] In this remarkable move he had given Hill unlimited access to all Russian airfields and the means to transport individuals over long distances with no questions asked. Boyle and Hill had two de Havilland planes at their disposal in southern Russia which they operated mainly out of Kishinev and Odessa.[38] On 2 July, five weeks after the first payment of one million lei was made, the unusual sight of an aeroplane over Ekaterinburg caused great excitement among the guards of the Ipatiev house where the imperial family were held. This was reported to British Foreign Secretary Arthur Balfour on 5 October 1918 by Sir Charles Eliot, the British High Commissioner in Siberia.[39]

Appointed in August 1918, Eliot took up his post in September. Possessed of a diplomatic and linguistic training, a formidable intellect and a reputation for thoroughness and precision, he rapidly made it perfectly clear that the most reliable sources he had encountered dismissed the idea that the Romanovs had been killed. He further contended that the imperial family had been disguised before their removal and that the murder stories were clumsy falsifications. Eliot wrote: 'It is supposed the victims were five, namely the Tsar, Dr Botkin, the Empress' maid and two lackeys. It is the general opinion in Ekaterinburg that the Empress, her son and four daughters were not murdered but dispatched on 17 July to the north or west.'[40]

Investigation of the events in Ekaterinburg has always been surrounded by intrigue, even tragedy. No fewer than five of the early investigators – Khotinsky, Sakovich, Medvedev, Nametkin and Sergeyev – died in suspicious circumstances.[41] Judge Ivan Sergeyev was shot one month after giving a controversial interview to the *New York Tribune*, published on 23 January 1919. In it he said: 'I do not believe that all the people – the Tsar, his family and those with them – were shot there. It is my belief that the Empress, the Tsarevich and the Grand Duchesses were not shot in that house. I do believe, however, that the Tsar, Dr Botkin, the family physician, two lackeys and the maid, Demidova, were shot in the Ipatiev house.'[42]

Early investigations, though they had the benefit of being close in time to the events of July 1918, were clouded by the attitude of the White government. Bluntly, the Romanovs were of more value to the Whites as dead martyrs, iconic witnesses to the brutality of Bolshevism, than as living bearers of the banner of counter-revolution. As the *Times* correspondent Robert Wilton remarked cynically to the French envoy Lasies, 'Even if the Tsar and the imperial family are alive, it is necessary to say that they are dead!' According to George Hill, Wilton was a British agent, and Foreign Office files show that he received payments for political purposes;[43] so he may well have been voicing an official British government line. Certainly it suited British foreign policy that the Romanovs, as the directing intelligence of an empire that menaced Britain's own prized possession in India, were no longer around. But this is not to say that the privately held attitudes of everyone in Britain were in accord with this broader political position; in particular, there is no reason to suppose that the attitude of King George V towards his cousin's family was anything other than benevolent.

Richard Meinertzhagen, another British intelligence agent involved in Russia, committed an account of a Romanov escape by aeroplane to his diary, which he typed up after the event on 18 August 1918. Meinertzhagen claimed that on 1 July he was seen by King George V at Buckingham Palace, where he was commissioned to attempt a rescue of the monarch's imperial cousins, and that Major-General Sir Hugh Trenchard, founding Chief of the Air Staff, was also present at this meeting.[44] Meinertzhagen claimed the mission was only partially success-ful and that Grand Duchess Tatiana alone escaped, being injured in the process.[45] Doubts have been cast on Meinertzhagen's credibility, largely on the basis of allegations of plagiarism in his capacity as a leading ornithologist.[46] Certainly he had an exaggerated personality; but then, so had Boyle and Hill or, for that matter, anyone involved in this highly dangerous kind of activity. It is not a job for clerks. And no one disputes the truth of what George Hill did – the Romanians had their crown jewels to prove it. Nevertheless, Meinertzhagen's account has to be viewed with some caution. It is not clear from his diary whether he was actually personally present at the rescue attempt; he speaks only of talk-ing it over with Trenchard, of making arrangements for a rescue party and of 'being able to try to get some of the children out'.[47] His role may have been that of organizer rather than executor.

It is worth noting in this context that Meinertzhagen had some inter-esting connections with the circles in which Nikolai Chebotarev later moved. His sister Margaret was married to George Macaulay Booth, a director of the Bank of England, and Booth's sister Antonia was the wife of Sir Malcolm Macnaghten, whose sisters were regular visitors at Moyallon House and friends of Chebotarev.[48] The Macnaghtens had been royal fixers for years – ever since Sir Malcolm's cousin Sir Melville Macnaghten had been sent into Scotland Yard in an attempt to sort out the 'Jack the Ripper' mess.[49] Margaret Meinertzhagen, like Chebotarev's hostess Hilda Richardson and Couriss's sponsor Zonny Fox, was a Quaker; the Quakers ran relief camps all over Russia which would have provided perfect cover for refuelling dumps. Meinertzhagen claimed that the plane used in the rescue mission, a de Havilland 4, was flown by a Major J. S. Poole; a Staff Captain Poole is known to have served on the staff of the Dvina River column, a small British force that was part of the RAF contingent at Arkangel under the command of General Poole, who headed a British mission to northern Russia in 1918.[50]

The air route from north Russia to Ekaterinburg would have involved following the Dvina, Vychedga, Pechora and Kama Rivers, overflying Perm and the railway lines as far as Viatka. Meinertzhagen claimed that the rescue mission left Ekaterinburg by the eastern route, ultimately landing at Vladivostok. Since most of this territory was held by the Whites this was perfectly possible, if logistically fraught, involving a total distance of 3,160 miles. Eight fuel dumps would have been required beyond Ekaterinburg as the de Havilland 4 had a range of about four hundred miles and an endurance of four hours. Travelling south from Ekaterinburg to the Caucasus would have presented far less of a problem. Just one hundred miles from Ekaterinburg was a Quaker relief camp at Buzuluk, where a fuel dump and landing strip could have been easily concealed.[51] From Buzuluk to Armavir in the Caucasus was only seven hundred miles, requiring only one dump. After Samara, the route was simply a question of following the River Volga.

Flying at 120 miles per hour, the de Havilland 4 could rise to a maximum height of 15,000 feet. Without a bomb load, the M92 version of the aircraft, produced from April 1917, had a 1,000 lb capacity. Eight M92s were delivered to the British mission in northern Russia in 1918. With a full fuel complement of 240 lb, there would have been spare capacity for about 760 lb of passengers as well as the pilot – enough to carry all the children. Internally, the plane would have had to be modified and the fuel tank moved. (Even in these early days of aviation, aircraft could be quite versatile: only the next year a modified de Havilland 4 provided the first regular passenger air service from London to Paris.)[52] A second plane would have been required if the whole family were to be transported; Joe Boyle and George Hill had two planes at their disposal in southern Russia, while other de Havillands were operational from RAF bases in Baku, Novorossisk, Ekaterinodar and Kotelnikov in the Caucasus.[53] Kotelnikov was closest to Ekaterinburg, so that could have been the fuelling point. After refuelling near Ekaterinburg – the Czech lines were a mere twelve miles from the city – they could return to Buzuluk and from there fly on to the British base at Kotelnikov in the Caucasus. The journey would not have been an easy one – in secrecy, in time of war, it could only have been undertaken by brave, resourceful and technically competent agents – but it was certainly possible.

Given that Boyle and Hill had two planes, that there were operational RAF bases between Ekaterinburg and the Caucasus, that the route south was a simple matter of following the River Volga, that the Prince Trubetskoye who signed both one million lei receipts found in the Boyle papers – whichever of the two it was – had an estate in the Caucasus, and that the connections between Boyle and Hill, whom Trotsky had just appointed inspector of aviation, are well known and a matter of record, whereas the link between Hill and Meinertzhagen is not established, it seems most likely that it was Boyle and Hill, and not Meinertzhagen, who actually carried out the plan, and that they took the southern, rather than the eastern route.

If some or all of the Romanovs were released under an arrangement such as this, conditions would almost certainly have been imposed, either by Trotsky acting alone or by the Bolshevik government as a body. To some extent, by abdicating for himself and his son, Nikolai II had taken them both out of the political arena; but even Kerensky had to admit to Alexei that his father had acted illegally in renouncing the throne on the boy's behalf.[54] And whatever the formal position thus taken, it would be naïve to imagine that the Tsarevich would not have been a credible rallying point for monarchist forces. It is doubtful if the Bolsheviks, in any arrangement for their departure, would have been content to settle for mere guarantees of good conduct on the part of the former imperial family. They would have wanted something more tangible. At most this would have been a hostage. At least it would have entailed knowledge of exactly where members of the former imperial family were living. Dr Willi Korte told me of a conversation he had had with an associate, Dietmar Wolff, in which the latter had alluded to 'strange things in the party archive in Moscow . . . hidden and cryptic . . . with the imperial family mentioned . . . and involving Lenin, Trotsky and Chicherin'.[55] Almost certainly the imperial family would have been split up, not merely for transit out of the country in case they were recognized but after their departure: Alexei might go here, Maria there, Tatiana there. This was, after all, a great state secret. They would all have needed new identities, and their real identities would have been extinguished.

For the Bolsheviks, the pay-off might have been diplomatic recognition at a time expedient for the other powers. It came soon enough. On 18 November 1920, only one week after French warships had evacuated the last White troops from the Crimea, the British Cabinet started negotiations for a trade agreement with Lenin's government.[56] In March 1921 a Russo-German treaty was concluded permitting the manufacture of armaments by German companies on Russian soil – to side-step the restrictions imposed on Germany by the Treaty of Versailles which ended the First World War – and the following year Germany established full diplomatic relations with Soviet Russia at the Treaty of Rapallo.[57] In 1924 a Soviet ambassador was appointed to London. It is perhaps no accident that Britain was one of the first two powers to recognize Soviet Russia.

As for Tsar Nikolai II and his family, they were now missing, presumed dead.

# The Glory is Departed

Given the number of interested parties within Europe's royal families, it is highly likely that any deal to procure the release of the Romanovs was done with multiple partners and through one or more levels of intermediary. Activities of this kind would be undertaken at a deniable distance – for example, in the case of Britain, through states ruled by nominally independent sovereigns, such as Romania, and agents with connections to more than one employer, such as Boyle. It was in the interests of the rescuers, as well as the rescuees and their former gaolers, that the traces of these events should be thoroughly brushed over. Accordingly, such an intelligence operation, albeit eased by bribery, is likely to have involved several operatives, using different methods at different times, bringing out only part of the family on each occasion. A certain amount of evidence exists as to who these other operatives might have been.

One obvious candidate is Major Stephen Alley (known to his secret service friends, for obvious reasons, as 'Sally'). In 1974 Robert Bruce Lockhart confirmed to Anthony Summers that Alley had joined the Secret Intelligence Service in 1914 and was sent to Russia, where he acted as head of the SIS from 1916 until the spring of 1918.[1] He then returned to England and in 1919 joined MI5. Stephen Alley appears in George Hill's book *Go Spy the Land*, published in 1932, as one of Hill's closest associates.[2] Like Hill, Alley was Russian-born; the son of a railway engineer, like Joe Boyle he was involved in the oil business. In a letter to Anthony Summers written on 22 July 1974 his widow Beatrice said that her husband had told her that 'two of the sisters from the imperial family were known to have escaped'; also that 'the Tsarina was much disliked and she and one or two of her daughters may have been sent to Ekaterinburg', but that Tsar Nikolai II had escaped and 'been sheltered by peasants or White Russians. The peasants were religious and very superstitious and would have caused trouble had the Tsar been ill treated.' This suggests that not all of the family were in Ekaterinburg in the first place. Beatrice Alley also referred to strange goings-on at Buckingham Palace. She wrote: 'The royal family had quite a few cousins . . . they often visited the Palace. They were all very fond of dressing up. And even used to go out in their dressed-up clothes. I was wondering whether some wrong identifications may have been made?' Was she alluding to Tsar Nikolai II's striking likeness to his cousin, King George V? Later, she went on to reveal that Stephen Alley knew Rasputin, Prince Yusupov and the Tsarina; and that he was 'quite a friend of Queen Marie of Romania, first going there on a military mission. She seemed to like him and embroidered a glove case and shoe bag for him. I still have these.'³ Given Queen Marie's close relationship with Joe Boyle and the fact that Alley worked with George Hill and was in Romania on a military mission in 1917 and 1918, it is highly likely that he was part of Boyle's team.

In 1972 Commander Michael Peer-Groves, himself an intelligence officer in MI6 during the Second World War, wrote to Summers and Mangold that his father Major William Peer-Groves was involved in a Romanov rescue mission in 1918. Major Peer-Groves, he said, was a member of one of two air force groups 'who went north from Odessa'; one of them, he believed, reached Kiev. Peer-Groves said his father 'returned to Odessa considerably after both groups had arrived back escorting various royalty'.⁴ According to his son, Major Peer-Groves always contended that the story of the murder of the Russian royal family was untrue, and when pressed, he said the family did not die in Ekaterinburg.⁵ Peer-Groves brought two pieces of jewellery out of Russia with him, one of which he presented to the Dowager Empress, the other to another member of the Russian imperial family: it is possible that these were tokens showing that Nikolai and his family had survived. Certainly, Peer-Groves' mention of aircraft involvement in a rescue accords with what we know about the capabilities of Hill and Boyle.

Whatever actually happened, there was no shortage of operatives on the ground – or of varying, even conflicting, motives and agendas. Other relationships which may have played a major part in the fate of the Romanovs were kept well hidden from public view at the time and have remained so ever since. George Chicherin, the Soviet Commissar for Foreign Affairs, was a member of the Russian nobility and the cousin of a Polish countess, Alexandrine Hutten-Czapski.⁶ Of itself, this was not remarkable; many Bolsheviks had noble status and aristocratic links, including Felix Dzerzhinsky, the dreaded head of the Cheka secret police, and even Lenin himself. But Countess Czapski's connections are of particular interest. Her second marriage made her the morganatic wife of Grand Duke Ludwig IV of Hesse, the Tsarina's father – and thus the Tsarina's stepmother.[7] This raised howls of protest from Queen Victoria, the mother of Grand Duke Ludwig's late wife, and the Grand Duke was forced to live apart from his new wife and annul the marriage. When he died, the Countess married again, in 1893; her third husband was Vassili Bacheracht, the Russian minister in Berne, Switzerland, where she henceforth made her home until her death in 1941.[8] Mme Bacheracht, as she now became, remained a prominent figure in Russian diplomatic circles, even after the Revolution. There was, in fact, a remarkable degree of continuity in many government departments, the foreign ministry included; despite an initial strike, many civil servants stayed in post to work for the Bolsheviks. There were unsurprising reasons for this, as Gurovich, an official of the Supreme Economic Council under Lenin, noted in 1922: 'One-time officials of the Tsarist ministries . . . in joining the Soviet service . . . were motivated by material need or, no less often, by longing for the accustomed work to which each had devoted more than a decade of his life . . . These people tried to serve conscientiously; they were the first to come and the last to leave, they stuck to their chairs as if chained.'[9] George Chicherin himself had formerly been a clerk in the Tsarist foreign ministry.

No doubt Chicherin would not have wished to advertise the fact that his cousin was the former Tsarina's stepmother; in the new Soviet state it would have been a distinctly unwise career move. And subsequent research has until now overlooked the significance of the Countess's position, no doubt obscured by her several changes of name. Such a connection would not have been ignored, however, by the Trust of Kings – it was far too valuable. Not only had Mme Bacheracht once been stepmother to Grand Duke Ernst of Hesse and his sister, the Tsarina; through her grandmother, Countess von Hohenstein, she was also related to Queen Mary, the consort of Britain's King George V.[10] These links would have made her a useful channel of communication for both King George V and Grand Duke Ernst. Four years after the disappearance of the imperial family, Chicherin was asked at a press conference about the fate of the Tsar's children. 'The fate of the four young daughters', he replied, 'is, at present, unknown to me. I have read in the press that they are now in America.'[11] A cynical joke, perhaps? Perhaps not.

The Soviet government of which Chicherin was a member contained groups of widely differing backgrounds and sympathies, a diversity which could have been exploited by those working in the interests of the imperial family, notably the Trust of Kings. Trotsky and Chicherin had not always been Bolsheviks; both had previously belonged to the rival Menshevik faction. Trotsky's last-minute conversion to Bolshevism came only in August 1917, a bare two months before Lenin's *coup d'état*.[12] Differences existed in external as well as internal political alignments, with pro-German and pro-allied factions co-existing within the council of ministers. Doubtless these allegiances, and the respective strengths of their adherents, fluctuated according to perceptions of the likely outcome of the war. Since any royal rescue plan was likely to have involved both the German and British relatives of the Romanovs, working outside national constraints irrespective of the fact that their countries were still officially at war with each other, what matters for our present purposes is not so much the existence of pro-German and pro-allied factions within the Soviet government, or who belonged to which, but the fact that these sympathies, whether purely tactical or more deeply rooted, could be separately exploited by the royal families on each side.

Another factor within Russian national politics at this time that had a bearing on the fate of the imperial family was the role of the Social Revolutionary Party. The SRs, as they were known, had initially been more popular than the Bolsheviks but gradually lost support to the latter as Lenin's grip on power tightened. Nonetheless, Lenin and the Bolsheviks owed their tenure of power to the military intervention of General Mouraviev, a noted SR, on their behalf in November 1917. By the summer of 1918 Mouraviev had been appointed by War Commissar Trotsky to command the Ufa and Orenburg front, where fighting with the opposing White forces was brisk. As his deputy Mouraviev was given Vassili Yakovlev, another SR who, immediately prior to this, had been given by the Central Committee the sensitive task of conveying the former imperial family from their relatively comfortable imprisonment at Tobolsk to stricter confinement in the more perilous location of Ekaterinburg.[13]

On 6 July 1918, just ten days before the imperial family disappeared from Ekaterinburg, a general SR uprising against the Bolsheviks erupted, led by none other than Mouraviev. Others have drawn attention to the proximity of these two dates. The uprising itself came to an abrupt end with the murder of Mouraviev on 12 July. Yakovlev's story, though, has no such definite ending. It continues until 1938, when he eventually succumbed in one of Stalin's gulags. Accounts of the intervening twenty years differ so widely that it is hard to believe that they all refer to the same individual. One fact that is not in doubt, however, is that in 1928 he was rehabilitated for some great wrong he had committed in the past.[14] No one has ever specified what this wrong was.

Some maintain that Yakovlev's real name was Myachin. Edvard Radzinsky describes him as a professional revolutionary, whose original occupation was as a turner. Yakovlev/Myachin had been involved in several bank robberies – a traditional method of funding terrorism – including one at Miass, near Ekaterinburg, in 1907, in which seventy-two pounds of gold were stolen. He was allegedly in Kiev in 1911 when Prime Minister Stolypin was murdered there, after which he went to Belgium. Yakovlev supposedly perished when he was shot in his home town of Ufa after he had publicly defected to the Whites, taken over a White command and openly propagandized the Red troops encouraging them, as their former commander, to defect. Radzinsky, however, traced him as a Cheka agent operating in Harbin after this date.[15]

Yakovlev's behaviour towards the imperial family is suspect, to say the least. When he arrived in Tobolsk to take them to Ekaterinburg he seems to have expressed a remarkably detailed and solicitous interest in whether Alexei was fit for travel. Leaving the boy behind with three of his sisters – only Maria initially went with her parents – Yakovlev, according to the Tsarina's diary, then tried to take the Romanovs to Omsk, Tomsk and all points east, with the aim of ending up in Japan. He was prevented only by the concerted last-minute action of the Omsk and Ekaterinburg Bolsheviks. Earlier, he had tried hard to persuade Sverdlov, chairman of the Central Executive Committee back in Moscow, to allow him to take the imperial family to Ufa where they could be held, he argued, until taken to Moscow for trial. Two weeks after this request Ufa fell to the Whites. In the light of Yakovlev's own subsequent desertion to the Whites this looks very suspicious.[16] Taking these events together with the SR uprising on 6 July, it seems likely that the SRs were trying to get their hands on the Bolsheviks' prime bargaining counter – the captive Romanovs. It is possible that the sub-plot of the rescue succeeded while the main political aim, the SR rising itself, failed.

Another, older account of Yakovlev's life exists which might hint at a more complex agenda. According to this version his real name was not Myachin but Zarrin, his father had been a Lithuanian engineer and he had been born in Ufa. He joined the navy and deserted in Finland during the 1905 revolution. Making his way to Canada, he was recruited into British intelligence in Vancouver – which is, incidentally, the home territory of Joe Boyle – and remained in the country for a time, working as a technician in Saskatchewan, before reappearing in Petrograd in March 1917. This accords with an early account by William Le Queux who claimed that a British agent, an SR repatriated from Canada on the eve of the October 1917 Revolution, had been placed by the British among the Tsar's guards. Though the account is somewhat garbled, with claims that this individual was also involved in the assassination of the German ambassador, Count Mirbach, on 6 July, it does tally with what we know of Yakovlev. Among Yakovlev's papers later found in the Hotel Granada in Moscow was the draft of a novel – a love story involving a young revolutionary and a princess, whose description fitted Grand Duchess Maria, the Tsar's third daughter. So Yakovlev may have had a personal as well as a political motive for helping the Romanovs to escape. No man, it is said, should serve two masters; but Yakovlev appears to have been serving the British, Sverdlov, the Whites, the SRs and possibly even his own emotional interests all at the same time.[17]

Peter Voikov, one of the party who is supposed to have assassinated the imperial family in Ekaterinburg, claims in his memoirs that Yakovlev was not only a British agent but in fact a British subject. He adds that according to Cheka rumours, Yakovlev fled to Romania where he was helped by Gibson, Britain's secret service representative in Bucharest.[18] If British intelligence had been able to infiltrate an agent into the centre of Soviet affairs in this way, it says a great deal for the extent and effectiveness of British covert operations at this time.

Relations between the intelligence services of Russia and Britain were certainly close in this period, although it is difficult to pin down precisely what kind of relationship existed between British intelligence and the new Bolshevik secret police, the Cheka, and later the KGB. No doubt there were elements of both mutual dependence and mutual distrust. Captain George Hill was not only appointed inspector of aviation by Trotsky, but was also asked to advise on the organization of the Cheka. His acceptance of this task damned him as something of a black sheep within the Hill family; but it gave him unrivalled access to the operational methods of his opponents. Boyle's papers speak of Hill's regular attendance at Bolshevik meetings, at great personal risk to himself, for which Boyle recommended him for the DSO.[19]

A photograph exists of Boyle purportedly standing in front of a fireplace in the Ipatiev house, where the imperial family was held, in 1918.[20] Boyle is known to have had dealings with Captain Stepanov, the monarchist agent operating out of Odessa who had made his way to Ekaterinburg where he is known to have contacted Dr Vladimir Derevenko, the imperial family's physician and the only outsider who had contact with the Romanovs in the Ipatiev house.[21] Colonel Sidorov, another monarchist from Odessa who was also in Ekaterinburg, is likewise known to have made contact with Derevenko.[22] The physician had loyally followed his employers to Tobolsk, visiting them regularly in the governor's mansion where they were lodged. His son Kolya was the same age as Alexei and looked remarkably like him, just as Dr Derevenko himself bore a passing resemblance to the Tsar.[23] In Tobolsk, the two boys were inseparable. Day after day, the Tsarina's diary is littered with references to Kolya. On 24 December 1917, she wrote, '7½ dined downstairs with all, *Kolia* too'. The emphasis was hers. Again, on Christmas Day, she wrote, '4½ *Kolia* too'; again, the emphasis is hers.[24] Dr Derevenko's arrival in Ekaterinburg with his son on 30 April 1918 can only be described as prescient. After all, the Tsar, Tsarina and Grand Duchess Maria were not told where they were heading until just before they arrived in Ekaterinburg on the same day. How, then, did Dr Derevenko know to set up both a home and a medical practice there on 30 April?[25] Foreknowledge is the only possible explanation – which raises another question: who told him, and why? When Derevenko was sought by the Whites' investigator Nikolai Sokolov, it was found he had left Ekaterinburg and was living in Tomsk under a Red regime.[26] General Dietricks, who had put Sokolov in charge of the inquiry, regarded Derevenko with intense suspicion.

One of the windows of opportunity for escape was the period immediately after Yakovlev's departure from Tobolsk with the Tsar, Tsarina and Grand Duchess Maria, while Alexei and three of his sisters remained behind. For ten days thereafter the guard remained under the command of Colonel Evgeni Stepanovich Koblinsky, who had been appointed by the previous regime and was sympathetic to the Romanovs, before its replacement by a contingent of Bolsheviks. This period, amid the confusion of the Tsar's departure and before the new guard arrived, was the logical time for doubles to be substituted for some members of the imperial family. The incomplete evidence of what went on during these days, and later in Ekaterinburg, offers some tantalizing clues to the family's eventual fate. Diaries, in particular, provide some suggestive pointers. Alexei's diary, for instance, which had been rigorously kept since his mother gave it to him in 1915, ends abruptly on 11 April 1918, eleven days before Yakovlev even appeared in Tobolsk.[27] The date 12 April was written in, but no text followed. His last written entry on 11 April refers to Kolya Derevenko. For some reason Maria and Anastasia burned their diaries on the evening before Yakovlev arrived from Moscow on 22 April.[28] Such drastic action is hard to explain, given that the Tsar and Tsarina did not burn theirs. Even more significantly, the Tsarina's diary shows a major change in the patterns of behaviour of the imperial family at the time of the transfer from Tobolsk to Ekaterinburg. Before this they hardly ever played cards. In the one hundred and twenty days of 1918 before the transfer, they played only once – at kabalah on 3 March. After the transfer, games of bezique, patience and simply 'cards' are recorded almost every day: out of seventy-seven days after the move to Ekaterinburg they played cards, usually bezique, on no fewer than forty-seven occasions. It may seem a small point; but patterns of behaviour are important indicators of identity. Different people behave differently. It was the same with the Scripture readings. Before Alexei's diary ended on 11 April, these were entered by the Empress in her own diary, with details of chapter and verse. After this date they are not. Whole weeks pass without a mention of Scripture; and where reference is made, it is usually in much more general terms, as 'spiritual reading', without details of chapters and verses read. In changing and volatile circumstances, established routines assume exaggerated importance, and help create a sense of normality and continuity; it is thus all the more startling that the family's habits seem to change so markedly at this point.[29] They might literally have been different people. Kolya Derevenko appears repeatedly in the Tsarina's diary before Alexei's diary ends. After 7 April he does not appear again. The two boys are not there together. Could one have replaced the other at some point after 11 April?

Not only the content but the very form of the diaries is also suggestive. The handwriting in the Tsarina's diary before the family's departure from Tobolsk is notably different from that of the final entries in the diary in Ekaterinburg. The earlier entries show a regular, slanted script; the later, a markedly more erratic and upright hand.[30] While the differences are not so extreme as to make it impossible that the same person wrote all the entries, they are certainly compatible with the existence of two writers.

We know, too, that a Tsarina 'look-alike' existed and was in Alexandra's company in early 1918 in Tobolsk. Lili Dehn records among the guests at the family musical evenings a 'Countess Rabinder [actually Rehbinder]', whom she describes as 'a faulty likeness of the Empress'.[31] There were at this period in Russia three women bearing the title Countess Rehbinder; the Tsarina's guest and near-double was most probably Countess Magdalena Rehbinder, née von Kotzebue, a relation of Lili Dehn.

Two other dates from the Ekaterinburg period are worth considering here. The first is 23 June – the day left showing on the calendar, from which the Tsarina habitually tore off a page each day, which hung on the wall in the Ipatiev house.[32] That evening, the Tsar was instructed in an anonymous letter signed by 'an officer' to leave a window open – a letter believed now to have been written by Peter Voikov, the Ekaterinburg Bolshevik, to suggest an escape attempt that would justify a subsequent death sentence.[33] The second is 8 July, the date of Dr Derevenko's last visit. What actually transpired during that visit is open to doubt, since it depends on third-party evidence, but the fact that it took place is not in dispute. It seems strange that the doctor refused – as he did – to return thereafter to a patient he had treated faithfully since 1912.[34] On 14 July the priest Storozhev and deacon Buimirov came to the house to say divine service, as they had done previously on 2 June. Buimirov's words on leaving, 'They are all some other people, truly,' are so remarkable that it might have been expected that Sokolov would have followed them up.[35] Yet, though both men were available when he conducted his investigation, he interviewed neither. Both these abrupt cut-offs – the cessation of the regular updating of the calendar and of Derevenko's previously regular visits – add to the impression that a substitution may have taken place. Nothing is heard of Kolya Derevenko in Ekaterinburg, though he was supposed to be living there with his father. If Kolya Derevenko had been substituted for the real Tsarevich on or around 11 April in Tobolsk, that would explain the doctor's alacrity in reaching Ekaterinburg, concerned as he would naturally be to be near to his son. Derevenko's absence after 8 July may mean that his own son had also departed, leaving a substitute in place. By this time the real Tsarevich may have been long gone.

While on their way to Alapaevsk, eighty miles north-east of Ekaterinburg, on 2 May 1918, Princess Helen, the wife of Prince Ioann Constantinovich Romanov, and Grand Duchess Ella, the Tsarina's sister, had passed through Ekaterinburg and had tried to make contact with the imperial family through Dr Derevenko while they were staying at a hotel in the town run by a Cossack couple, the Atamanovs. Derevenko, strangely, had proved less than co-operative.[36] At that time the Tsar, Tsarina and Maria had only been in Ekaterinburg for three days, and the other children would not arrive until 23 May. Why should Derevenko have wanted to avoid direct contact between the Empress and her sister, unless to avoid Ella's discovering that the real Tsarina was not actually in Ekaterinburg?

The various cut-off points noted above begin to make sense if we consider that the Romanovs would not all have left together, but would have been taken away in groups or even individually. To have moved the whole family at once would have been very risky, as the number of family members was well known, and also logistically difficult. Some sort of rolling programme of release and substitution, with those remaining behind acting as hostages or guarantors for each stage of the process, would have been most likely. Alexei, as Tsarevich and heir and thus politically the most important individual, would have been the obvious choice to move first. One – or more – may never have been released, acting as the ultimate hostage to ensure silence from the others.

We know of two payments, each of one million lei, made by Joe Boyle, because we have two receipts. It is possible that there were other payments, for which the receipts did not survive. Perhaps the price was £1.8 million for each Romanov – a total of 7 million lei or £12.6 million in today's money. Boyle first heard of Trotsky's urgent desire to meet him immediately after his success in securing the release of the Odessa hostages on 4 April 1918 – one week before the abrupt end of Alexei's diary. One week is a lot of time for action if you have an aeroplane at your disposal.

Captain Stepanov is known to have attended a meeting of an underground monarchist group in Simbirsk on 6 July 1918, learning there that the Czechs, who already surrounded Ekaterinburg, were planning to begin their offensive to take the town on 15 July. Captain Schveits of the First Regiment of Hussars, the source of this information, was the monarchist liaison officer with the Czech forces of General Gaida.[37] Stepanov was arrested by the Cheka on 13 July. Just nine days earlier, on 4 July 1918, twelve days before the imperial family's disappearance, a Serbian officer had also been arrested, in Ekaterinburg. Major Jarko Misitch had been sent with a small team by King Alexander of Serbia to rescue his sister Princess Helen, who was married to Prince Ioann Constantinovich Romanov. Princess Helen was held in Alapaevsk with other Romanovs – not in Ekaterinburg itself. Misitch's presence in the town where the imperial family was held suggests he may have been engaged in quite another task. Cheka files reveal that a Serbian called 'Magich' was responsible for letters smuggled in to the Tsar, thus tying Misitch directly to the Tsar rather than Princess Helen.[38]

Misitch was a famous name in Serbia. Marshal Misitch was the Serbian general who came up with the plan for disengaging all military forces at the end of the First World War. He lived in Skopje in Yugoslavia and at Salonika in Greece – a hive of espionage activity. It was here that George Hill had been recruited into the secret service, and here too that Couriss later worked as a passport clerk. Marshal Misitch was the father of Voislav Misitch, who appears regularly in the visitors' book of Small Downs House, the residence of Hilda Richardson's sister-in-law, Gertrude Leverton-Harris. The Richardsons appear to have paid for Voislav Misitch's education at Eton, where he was in the same class as Queen Marie's son, Prince Nikolai of Romania.[39] Among the closest friends and regular guests of Gertrude Leverton-Harris at Small Downs House, along with Voislav Misitch, were Earl Beauchamp and his family.[40] Since Lady Mary, the earl's daughter, married Prince Zevelode Romanov,[41] the son of Princess Helen of Serbia, the subject of Major Jarko Misitch's rescue mission, it seems likely that Voislav Misitch was, if not the brother, certainly closely related to Major Misitch. Anne Richardson, the Vice-Principal of Westfield College in the University of London and Hilda's other sister-in-law, appears to have taken a close interest in the boy and brought him to Small Downs with her. If Voislav Misitch was the son of Marshal Misitch and the brother of the Major Jarko Misitch arrested on 4 July 1918 in Ekaterinburg, and if Hilda Richardson's house guest Nikolai Chebotarev was the Tsarevich, the family's interest in the Serb boy may have been by way of paying a debt.

One thing is certain: there was no shortage of activity geared towards rescuing the Romanovs in the months leading up to their final disappearance. Whether some of these activities were diversions, or simply the unsuccessful machinations of dispersed royalist groups, is unclear. In any event, they may well have simply drawn attention away from the real operation, which was no snatched abduction but a high-level arrangement oiled by bribery.

There are indications that there may have been previous unsuccessful attempts to get the imperial family away. Boyle's involvement, for example, may well have begun considerably earlier than Trotsky's approach in 1918. On 9 August 1917 he had arrived by train in Tsarskoe Selo, just five days before Nikolai and his family departed for Tobolsk in Siberia.[42] His appearance here makes no sense in terms of his stated mission – the reinvigoration of the Russian railway system. Tsarskoe Selo had only one focus of interest: it was the place of captivity of the imperial family. The possibility of an escape attempt at this time is supported by events over the preceding months. At the time of the Tsar's abdication in early March all the imperial children suffered an attack of measles. Officially, this is said to explain the shaving of the children's hair; but Alix Hill, whose mother was a Red Cross nurse during the First World War, insisted that this was not, and never had been, a treatment for measles.[43] Rather, the treatment was to leave the patient in a darkened room – as was indeed done with the Romanov children: when the Tsar arrived on 9 March he noted this in his diary. Their heads were not shaved, however, until 9 June.[44] Pierre Gilliard's memoirs, our source for this, gives the reason: 'The Grand Duchesses were all losing their hair as the result of their illness.' But this was three months after they had succumbed to the illness, and hair loss is not a normal outcome of measles. Alix Hill said that in those days hair was normally shaved in preparation for a journey south, to the Crimea or the Caucasus where typhus was endemic. Apparently there were different 'crops' available, measured in centimetres.[45] On 11 July the Tsar noted in his diary: 'I took a walk with Alexei in the morning. When I came back home, I learned of Kerensky's arrival. In our conversation, he mentioned that we would likely go south, given the proximity of Tsarskoe Selo to the uneasy capital.'[46] From this it seems that Kerensky was in broad agreement with the Tsar's own declared wish to retire to his palace at Livadia in the Crimea or some other destination in the south, which would of course include the Caucasus. In this context, the shaven heads are readily intelligible. Cropping hair, of course, has another effect: it depersonalizes and disguises, inducing a remarkable change in appearance. In the context of the Romanovs' plight, then, the shaven heads could have had the innocent purpose of preparing the children for a journey south or the covert purpose of facilitating escape and possibly the substitution of other individuals in their place – or both. What is undeniable is that Joe Boyle appeared in Tsarskoe Selo five days before their departure for Tobolsk in Siberia; and moments of transition like this, with the concomitant change of surroundings and people, are good times for escape attempts. It is known from Princess Elizaveta Naryschine, Mistress of the Robes, that there were complications at the time of the family's departure and that they had to wait about at the station, where Joe Boyle is known to have been, sitting on their suitcases. Kerensky was embarrassed by the long delay.[47]

However many attempts it took, after Boyle visited the Dowager Empress on 24 November 1918 the old lady, known to be hard-headed and a consummate realist, never doubted that her son and his family had survived. She maintained this apparent certainty right down to her death in 1928. Boyle presented himself with the intention of bringing the Dowager Empress out of Russia, for which purpose he had taken a yacht, loaded it with the finest of delicacies and two hundred soldiers, and commandeered the Romanian Prime Minister Margiloman's car; but Empress Maria Feodorovna was not for leaving.[48] At that time the Crimea, where she was living, was still relatively free of Red troops and the White Volunteer Army was there in strength; it was far from clear which side would prevail. In the event, the evacuation did not happen until April 1920, some eighteen months later. In the West there is a common misconception that the Russian Revolution of 1917 marked a clear-cut end of one regime and the beginning of another. This was simply not the case. Large parts of Russia remained under various White governments for some time. Natalie Cooke, who had been living in Ireland since 1918, continued to receive rental income from her Russian estates right up to 1920.[49] In many ways, 1920, not 1917, was the year of transition.

Boyle certainly did something to earn the profound regard of the British royal family. Immediately after this visit to the Dowager Empress, in December 1918 Boyle went on to stay with King George V at Buckingham Palace. Officially, he was staying in the Ritz Hotel; but among his papers there is a bill for thirteen shillings from the Army and Navy Stores addressed to him at the Palace (see plates).[50] Further checks established that the Army and Navy Co-operative Society Limited of 105 Victoria Street, Westminster, SW1 furnished Lt-Col. J. W. Boyle, account number 73006, with a total bill for £105 10s 41/2d, which Boyle settled with a cash payment of £200 on 1 January 1919, keeping himself well in credit. Boyle's bill for £10 18s from the Ritz Hotel for a stay of four days was presented on 27 February 1919 and paid on 7 March, bearing witness to a later residence there.[51] Though he was

accompanying Princess Ileana, Marie of Romania's daughter, this of itself
would not have elicited an invitation to stay at the Palace. At the time
Queen Marie wrote, 'He [Boyle] is great friends with all the British royal
family who have taken up with him and trust him as I do.' When the
Canadian government ordered Boyle to stand down and relinquish his
rank at the end of hostilities in November 1918, King George V issued a
countermanding order requiring Boyle to remain in uniform. Boyle is
known to have carried letters from the Dowager Empress to Queen
Alexandra and from Queen Marie of Romania to George V. He must
have been reporting on family matters. In April 1919 Queen Marie confided to her diary, 'came home to find with joy my old friend Boyle.
He has seen everybody – my sister Beatrice, her husband Ali [Prince
Alfonso of Orléans-Bourbon], George and May [George V and Queen
Mary], Aunt Alix [Queen Alexandra], Minny [the Dowager Empress],
and Xenia [Grand Duchess Xenia, the Tsar's sister] . . . has seen Nicky
[her son who was at Eton] but alas not Mignon [her daughter].'[52]

And then there were the rewards. King George V made Boyle a DSO
in the birthday honours list in 1919, but his cousin Queen Marie of
Romania improved on that, creating him Duke of Jassy in Romania and
awarding him that country's highest decoration, the Star of Romania.
Local Canadian newspapers referred to him as the 'Duke of Dawson', his
home town; British newspapers called him 'the Duke of Bucharest'.[53]
Hill was similarly decorated by Queen Marie. The sheer scale of these
honours suggests great service extending across national frontiers. Nor
was the appreciation all one way. Queen Marie herself was thanked in
the most effusive of terms by General Alexiev, head of the Russian
monarchist Volunteer Army, but also a former ADC to the Tsar. 'The
restored Russia, driven by an unlimited consideration and gratefulness,
will print your name with golden letters on the pages of her future
history.'[54] Even by Russian standards, this was extravagant praise for the
surgical dressings Queen Marie had supplied to the White armies.
General Alexiev died of a heart attack in September 1918, so the services
to which he alluded must have been rendered in the summer of that year.

Boyle's daughter Flora claimed in June 1938 in *Maclean's Magazine*
that her father had met the Tsar in Ekaterinburg but that the Tsar had
resolutely refused to leave Russia. Her source for this story was Prince
Trubetskoye, the man who signed those two one-million lei receipts in
1918.[55] Lili Dehn reports the Tsar taking a similar attitude: 'I'd rather go
to the uttermost end of Siberia', he told her, 'than leave Russia.'[56] That

the Tsar refused to leave Russia, though, does not necessarily mean he refused Boyle's offer of rescue; he may simply have stated the condition of a destination within Russia. Both Prince Trubetskoyes had large estates in the Caucasus – at Balti near Mount Kazbek and at the Castle of Baku – within which escapees could easily be concealed. At that time, the Caucasus region was untouched by the revolutionary war; though persistent inter-ethnic and other conflicts continued irrespective of the Bolshevik takeover, it remained free of Red armies throughout 1919 and was therefore comparatively safe for White sympathizers careful to keep their heads down.

Among Nikolai Couriss' papers is part of the handwritten manuscript of a book he was writing for his American friend, the publisher Alicia Patterson. Though all copies of the book seem to have disappeared from libraries everywhere, including copyright libraries, this fragment is very revealing. Describing his service in General Alexiev's monarchist army in the Caucasus in 1918 and 1919, Couriss wrote:

> I went to Poltava, Kharkoff, Rostoff, some of the Cossack villages along the Don, hence to Sebastopol and finally to Odessa . . . The way that life had reverted to pre-war days was literally astounding. A look of plenty lay over the land. The crops were splendid, prices had fallen to their normal level. The whole countryside looked prosperous and content. It did one good to see railway officials and gendarmes at the stations dressed in their old uniforms, to see timetables, posters and newspapers written in old Russian and not that horrible simplified orthography of the Bolsheviks. At atmosphere of peace and relief breathed over the whole land.[57]

The picture Couriss painted is very different from the traditional image of Russia at this time, one of generalized mayhem. Couriss' housekeeper, Kathleen McCarthy, confirmed that Couriss and his wife had spent a lot of time in the Caucasus and in Georgia, where they saw Mount Ararat. She specifically remembers them having an argument about Yerevan, the town which lies at the foot of Mount Ararat.[58]

Couriss was active in the Caucasus at the same time as Boyle, and serving in the volunteer army of General Alexiev – the man who went to such effusive lengths to thank Queen Marie. One of the guards serving in the Ipatiev house in Ekaterinburg when the Romanovs were held there was Kabanov, a former soldier in the Tsar's own Life Guards regiment. Nikolai II, well known seldom to forget a face, recognized the man and told him so.[59] The commanding officer of the Life Guards had been Colonel John Couriss, the father of Nikolai Couriss. Colonel Couriss was stationed in Warsaw under General Bibikov, the future Mrs Couriss' father.[60] According to Irish military intelligence files, Nikolai Couriss himself was said to have been an officer in that same regiment, called the 'Spot Guards' because of the star on their cuirass. This is unlikely. As we saw in chapter 4, Nikolai Couriss was the same age and in the same year at school in the Imperial Lycée Alexander in St Petersburg as Michael Golenishchev-Kutuzov-Tolstoy. Jacques Ferrand's book *Descendances naturelles des souverains et grand-ducs de Russie de 1762 à 1910* gives Tolstoy's year of graduation from the school as 1917 – in fact, it only says '*promotion anticipée*' in 1917: in other words, his year had not actually left school, making the automatic move into the officer corps, before the Revolution in February 1917.[61] Couriss himself has claimed only that he served as an officer in the ranks of the White armies – specifically in the Volunteer Army – not that he bore arms in the Life Guards at all, certainly not before the Revolution. He was still the commanding officer's son, however, and would have been known by the men in this capacity.

The significance of when exactly Couriss served in the White army lies in an anecdote he related to his friend Henry St George Smith. Couriss recounted how, as a young officer, he had formed part of the guard of honour for the Tsar when the sovereign met a group of Georgian centenarians, famed for their great age. One of the elderly men claimed to have been in Moscow in 1812 and to have seen the Emperor Napoleon as the conqueror entered the city. Couriss told how the Tsar asked the man, who had obviously dined out on the story for years: Was he the man who had seen the Emperor Napoleon? The man replied: 'Little Father, I did indeed see the Emperor.' When the Tsar asked him to describe Napoleon, the reply came back with great assurance: 'Oh! He was a great, big man,' labouring the words 'great' and 'big'. This, of course, did not describe Bonaparte at all. The Tsar politely took his leave.[62] It was a good story. What was important, though, was when it happened. Couriss was not an officer until after the Revolution. No record exists of the Tsar meeting a group of centenarians at any time during the war, before his abdication. No doubt these men, some of whom claimed to be well over a hundred years old, were frail and would not have travelled – certainly not en masse. This meeting must, therefore, have occurred where the men lived, in Georgia. Couriss' presence in the Caucasus in 1919 indicates that the meeting took place then. Less than thirty miles across the Caucasus mountains from where these men lived, in the mountain villages under the shadow of the peak of Mount Kazbek, lay Balti, the Trubetskoye estate.

This curious set of circumstances in Couriss' past prompted me to look for more evidence which might link him to the Romanovs and to those involved in their disappearance from Ekaterinburg. The search uncovered a dense and suggestive web of personal connections. Couriss' wife Sana came from Ekaterinburg,[63] though her father had commanded the Russian army in Warsaw and she had been born in the Polish capital. Nikolai and Sana did not marry until after they had left Russia, but they were there together earlier: Henry St George Smith told me that Couriss had saved his future wife's life by rescuing her from captivity in a Bolshevik compound.[64] We saw in chapter 4 how Sana Couriss was connected to Thomas Preston, the British Consul in Ekaterinburg at the time the Romanovs disappeared, through her sister-in-law Mme Bibikov, whose sister was Thomas Preston's wife. One of Joe Boyle's most active agents in Russia at this time was Count Jean Tolstoy, the uncle of Sophie Bibikov who was married to Mrs Couriss' brother, Valerian Bibikov.[65] Count Jean Tolstoy was the cousin of Count Peter Tolstoy, the ADC to Grand Duchess Marie, the Tsar's cousin who was rescued in Odessa by Joe Boyle.[66] Grand Duchess Marie's brother-in-law, Prince Poutiatine, was the uncle of one of Couriss' greatest friends at Collon, Kitty Hunter-Blair. Her great-uncle, Major-General Sir Walter Hunter-Blair, was charged with making arrangements for the accommodation of the Dowager Empress in Malta immediately after she left Russia in 1920.[67] Alizon Fox, the Quaker who brough Couriss to Ireland, was the cousin of Major Waldo Trench Fox, who served in the Canadian militia – as did Joe Boyle.[68] In 1972 Guy Richards, in his book *The Hunt for the Tsar*, produced two letters, the authenticity of which has never been tested. One is claimed to have been written by the Tsar in 1919 to a 'Fox' who had taken part in his rescue, thanking him for his efforts.[69] Kathleen McCarthy remembers a British officer called Captain Hill visiting Collon in 1940, soon after she entered Couriss' service. She went on to identify George Hill from his photograph.[70] Hill did indeed hold the rank of captain from June to November 1940, when he was promoted major.[71] According to Irish military intelligence files, Couriss claimed to have worked for five years from 1926 to 1931 as a passport and visa clerk in the British consulate in Salonika, where George Hill says he was recruited into the intelligence services.[72]

None of this proves that Couriss worked for Boyle, but it certainly makes his involvement in underground activity in Russia a real possibility. Perhaps the Russians at Collon actively participated in the plans for the rescue of the imperial family. As blood relatives, they would have had a personal motive for helping the beleaguered Romanovs: having been well looked after by Nikolai when he was in power, provided with jobs, public and court offices and pensions, they may now have felt an obligation to repay this support with practical help in his time of trial. If Couriss was involved, what of the others at Collon – particularly the Lievens?

Prince Paul Lieven, Couriss' companion at Collon, was a Latvian; his Irish military intelligence file held the number of his Latvian passport.[73] The Latvians played a particular role in Russian revolutionary politics. Lenin's government always turned to the Latvians when it wanted a sensitive job done, and Lenin himself relied on Latvian guards to protect him from the sullen and restive population when he took up residence behind the walls of the Kremlin in Moscow. Trotsky ensured that Latvians held key positions in the Cheka and also in the Red Army – including the overall command, held by the Latvian Vatesis. Six of the guards at the Ipatiev house were Latvians.[74] The peculiar value of the Latvians to the Bolsheviks lay in their strong national identity as Balts, not Russians; Russia to them was an occupying power. However, this independent spirit was something of a double-edged sword for the Bolshevik government, for it went hand in hand with a natural affinity with the Germans that dated back to the middle ages when the German Teutonic Order of Knights and the Knights of the Sword had held sway over the Baltic. Vatesis himself was a major security risk, since he was in open negotiations with the Germans throughout 1918, for which he was eventually dismissed. Vatesis was quite open about his views and those of his men. He was first and foremost a Latvian nationalist and no Bolshevik.[75]

According to his eldest son, Prince Leonid Lieven, Prince Paul had been the chief engineer on the Omsk–Tomsk sector of the Trans-Siberian railway at the time of the revolution.[76] That was the sector where the mysterious Yakovlev, who had been sent by the Central Committee in Moscow to convey the imperial family from Tobolsk to Ekaterinburg, staged what looked suspiciously like a rescue attempt with the object of taking the Tsar, Tsarina and Grand Duchess Maria east to Japan.[77] When I interviewed Prince Leonid in 1993 I noted that he seemed over-sensitive about his German Baltic roots. When his father, Prince Paul, left Russia in 1918 with the assistance of Leonid Krasin, he lived in Rostock in Germany; his younger son Alexander was born there in 1919. Krasin was not only close to Lenin; he was also the newly appointed Commissar for Transport in the Bolshevik administration, and thus Lieven's superior as chief engineer on the Trans-Siberian railway. According to Prince Leonid, Krasin was a friend of his father, and had appealed to Lieven not to leave Russia. Before the revolution Krasin had been Russian director of the German Siemens Corporation,[78] whose offices in Russia had been closed down under suspicion of acting as a front for German espionage. Krasin, a veteran Bolshevik, was later made the first Soviet ambassador in London. Both Krasin and Lenin were undoubtedly in the pay of the Germans, though whether the relationship reached the point where they could be justly described as German agents remains a moot point. Perhaps the German–Latvian axis was as important in any Romanov departure as the Trotsky–Chicherin–British axis. Alternatively they may have been twin aspects of the same operation, two sides of the one coin.

Certainly Prince Paul Lieven's friendships went to the very top of the Bolshevik government; and there may well have been more to these connections than friendship alone. When his son Prince Alexander Lieven died, the *Times* obituary said that he had been taught Russian by 'a former close companion of Lenin', and went on to describe Victor Serge, 'a notable communist dissident of the 1920s and 1930s', as his 'mentor'.[79] Prince Paul Lieven's relationship with Couriss was of long standing, pre-dating the Revolution. Lieven was related to Couriss' wife, who referred to him as 'cousin Paul'.[80] Again, such evidence as exists links Prince Paul Lieven to the area of the escape, to some leading Bolshevik players and to Couriss. It is far from conclusive; and yet, like so many of the people around Couriss, there is more to him than appears on the surface. Boyle, Couriss, Prince Trubetskoye – all had been in the Caucasus, a likely site for any Romanov evacuation. And Chebotarev, by his own admission, had been there too.

At a higher level, Britain's King George V was almost certainly involved in these rescue operations. Meinertzhagen names him. Boyle stayed with him and was honoured by him. Queen Marie had been close to him since his youth, notwithstanding the contrast between his stuffiness and her free spirit. Princess Victoria, his sister, with whom he had a particularly close bond – a bond Queen Mary, whom Victoria disliked, could never penetrate – had loved the Tsar since they were teenagers together in Denmark.[81] Yet his role could never be admitted, involving as it almost certainly did close liaison with his German relatives while the two countries were at war. This was no light matter. Anti-German feeling was very real, amounting to widespread hysteria. So intense was public suspicion of the royal family's German sympathies that the King was moved to take the unprecedented step of changing his family name from Saxe-Coburg-Gotha to Windsor. Royal relatives with German names, most notably the Battenbergs and the Queen's own immediate family, the Tecks, were obliged to follow suit. By the nice gradations of the day, a German prince was reckoned to be the equivalent of an English marquess, a rank usually reserved for former Viceroys of India: so the Battenbergs became Mountbattens and surrendered princely rank for the title Marquess of Milford Haven, while the Tecks became Marquesses of Cambridge.

The King himself, highly sensitive to this public suspicion of his German roots, was well aware of how such suspicion would be inflamed were it to become known that he was co-operating with his German relatives to obtain the release of the Russian imperial family. Large sections of the press had been conditioned to regard the Tsar as a despot and the February 1917 'democratic' Revolution as a good thing. Nikolai II's loyalty as an ally was quickly forgotten. There was a very real danger of serious domestic disaffection, and this was something the King, his advisers and the British government alike wished to avoid at all costs. And yet there is no doubt that the King was genuinely and strongly attached to both Nikolai and Alexandra and would not lightly have abandoned their cause. These conflicting imperatives made the position of King George an invidious one, and throw some light on the ambiguities of the offer of asylum for the Tsar and his family made to the Provisional Government in Russia in the spring of 1918 and then withdrawn. Opinions differ as to whether it was the King himself or his Private Secretary, Lord Stamfordham, who was responsible for the retraction of the offer. Stamfordham had an acute sensitivity to the delicate nature of his royal master's position, and was determined that his sovereign, who looked so much like his Russian cousin, should not suffer the same fate, swept from his throne by a revolution.[82] By the time the offer was withdrawn in April 1918, the British government was well aware that Kerensky's regime in Russia was under severe pressure from the Soviet to prevent the Tsar's departure for any safe haven. Not wishing to make the position of their embattled ally any more difficult, it would have suited them very well to have the offer of asylum cancelled. It is entirely plausible that the King said what he knew the government wanted to hear – and that he had realized by this point that a public welcome for his distressed relatives was not the right way to approach this difficult personal and political problem.

Certainly, by 1918, King George was thoroughly alarmed by the deteriorating situation in Russia. March that year marked the first anniversary of Nikolai II's abdication. Within his own family, the King would have been under pressure to take action from his German relatives now living in England, whose particular concern was 'Alicky' and the children, from his sister Princess Victoria, who was close to the Tsar, and from his own 'motherdear', Queen Alexandra, the sister of the Dowager Empress, whom George knew as 'Aunt Minnie'. In the circumstances, a highly secret operation, outside the constraints of government, was the only way to proceed. The King had a direct relationship with the secret services outside the official channels of government and could call on personal loyalties to serve his private interests. He is known, for example, to have had a particular connection with Sir Reginald 'Blinker' Hall, Director of Naval Intelligence, because of their shared past in the navy.[83] Hall vetted Norwegian Jonas Lied for a failed expedition in March 1918 to rescue the Tsar by fast motor boat, via the Ob River and Kara Sea. Again, the connections reached into the world that was later to be Chebotarev's. Sir Douglas Brownrigg, Hall's colleague as the chief naval censor at the Admiralty, was a regular guest at Small Downs, coming with Voislav Misitch.[84] Arthur Leverton-Harris, the owner of Small Downs and Hilda Richardson's brother-in-law, had been a minister at the Admiralty during the war with responsibility for running the blockade of Germany.[85]

The charmed circle of royal cousinhood had centuries of experience of cover-up, far more than any twentieth-century secret service. Covert operations are part of the ivy than grows round those intertwined royal family trees. Artificially created history is second nature to them. Removing Nikolai II and his family from Russia to lives of obscurity as commoners living separately from one another was something the royal club would know exactly how to do. Some have argued that the Duke of Clarence, arguably the greatest ever embarrassment to the British royal family, did not die in 1891 but lived on until 1933 in the custodianship of the Earl of Strathmore.[86] Successfully to lose one of the most high-profile families in the world may seem impossible to us, living in the days of the global village. But in those days of deference, of massive royal estates scattered over countries still ruled by crowned heads and peopled by servants who knew not to ask questions, such a proposition was far from impossible. Newspaper images were grained and distant. Children grow up and become men and women. Men and women grow old. Appearances change.

Not all appearances, of course, change out of all recognition, and there are tantalizing hints in the circles around Nikolai Chebotarev as to who, besides Alexei, may have survived – and where. Inevitably, the woman Chebotarev said was his sister, known to her friends simply as 'Babushka', by her very existence poses an interesting question. Could she be a sister of the Tsarevich, and if so, which one? There are certain indications that she may have been the Grand Duchess Maria. Principal among these is a mark on the third finger of the right hand which, she told Alix Hill, was the result of an accident. Alix said that she was self-conscious about it and would sit rubbing gently at it.[87] A photograph of Babushka with Nikolai taken in 1933, when he went to Yugoslavia to bring his niece – her daughter Iya – back to England, shows the mark clearly (see plates). The Tsar's third daughter, Maria, had a mark in exactly the same place on the same finger (see plates), which was caused by an accident in a railway carriage in 1910.[88] Another feature Babushka shared with Maria was her extraordinary physical strength. This was remarked on by Alix Hill as well as by Iya and her husband John. They all told me the story of how Babushka had apprehended a burglar at her home in Singapore, where John Hulbert was serving in the army and she was living with Iya in service quarters. So strong was her grip that although the intruder escaped, she tore the clothes from his back as he fled – and she was already an elderly lady at the time.[89] Grand Duchess Maria, who appears even in official photographs as a girl of ample proportions (see plates), was known in the family as 'Le Bon Gros Toutou' on account of her plumpness, and Count Mosolov remarked that she was 'distinguished by her muscular strength'.[90] She also had a great interest in peasant life. She quizzed the servants, officers and ordinary soldiers about their home life and even in captivity spoke to her guards about their homes, their plots of land and their children. This characteristic too she shared with Babushka, who chose to live the live of a peasant in Bosnia after fleeing revolutionary Russia. Nor did Maria set her sights on a princely marriage; she signed her letters to her father 'Mrs Demenkov', signalling an infatuation she had for Kolya Demenkov, a young regular army officer.[91]

Alix Hill reminisced about a conversation she had with Nikolai Chebotarev after seeing the 1971 film *Nicholas and Alexandra*, based on Robert Massie's book. Nikolai liked the book a great deal – I still have his copy – but did not think much of the film. However, when Olga Hill haughtily dismissed one scene where the Tsar's daughters laughed and played in the snow with their guards as 'impossible', Nikolai contradicted her. 'No, it did happen,' he said, 'they were just natural, healthy girls, with normal appetites.' He spoke with authority – an authority that silenced even Olga Hill – but, as Alix said afterwards, how did he know? The incident reminded Alix of his equally authoritative tone when he had said of the imperial family, 'But they were all so happy, when they were still together.'[92] All of these pointers towards the identity of Nikolai Chebotarev's sister as Grand Duchess Maria are consistent with his own identity as the Tsarevich.

In October 1993 Kathleen McCarthy had given me the visitors' book for Nikolai Couriss' language school at Collon and along with it several photographs, once the property of Couriss. One of the photographs depicted a bearded old man standing with three other individuals (see plates). At the time, Phillips had made a joke about his looking like George Bernard Shaw and I had left it at that. Carelessly, I continued to ignore the photograph for nearly three years. Then, in 1996, I asked Kathleen McCarthy, as a matter of routine, to confirm who was in the picture. Mrs Sana Couriss and Prince Paul Lieven I recognized. But who were the other two – the man with the beard and the other woman? Kathleen told me the lady was Princess Sophie Lieven, Prince Paul's sister from Paris who was involved there with the Salvation Army. The man, she said, was known as 'Nikolai Alexandrovich'.[93] He was a chain-smoker, she said, and he went for long walks. In one short, economical sentence she had described two of the principal characteristics of the Tsar; and this man bore the Tsar's name.

'And she was there,' added Kathleen. The 'she' Kathleen was referring to appeared in another photograph I had brought for her to see. This was of the Baroness de Huene, described by Nikolai Chebotarev as his aunt, who had lived with him in Paris, and in Ireland at Moyallon and Croft House. I asked whether she had often visited Couriss and Kathleen said yes, she had first come with Hilda Richardson in the early 1940s. 'When that photograph was taken,' she added, of the picture including Nikolai Alexandrovich, 'that lady was standing on over, just out of view of the camera.' Describing her as 'a bit of a lost soul', Kathleen also told me that the Baroness spoke English – something the old lady had not revealed to the occupants of Croft House or Moyallon.[94] Realizing that I had never really investigated the Baroness properly, I began to scan all the notes I had made on her in what had now become twenty-five volumes of evidence. It was a revealing exercise. Zoe Cooke had told me that the Baroness de Huene suffered from a heart condition, for which she took digitalis, and insisted on a ground floor room.[95] Servants at Croft House and Moyallon had told me she habitually wore a long black tea gown – indeed, she was dressed in this fashion in most of the photographs of her known to exist. Zoe and the servants had emphasized her deep religious piety, her highly strung nature and her depressive personality.[96] All of these characteristics perfectly described the Tsarina. Alexandra Feodorovna believed she suffered from a heart condition, she always slept in a downstairs bedroom, she favoured a black tea gown, she was religious and she was depressive. Tentatively, I looked at the photographs of the Baroness and compared them to the Tsarina. The face was the same; as with Nikolai Alexandrovich and the Tsar, older, but strikingly similar to the known images. And there was the goitre that appeared to afflict the Baroness. From about 1912 the Tsarina had begun to develop a very similar condition, referring to it in letters to the Tsar in 1916 as a 'gouty jaw' and to Xenia in 1917 as 'neuralgia in the face'.[97] Baroness de Huene's stance was the same as the Tsarina's. Her hands were clasped in exactly the same way as the Tsarina's. In the photograph, apparently taken in North Africa, of Nikolai Chebotarev with the Baroness (see plates), it is unmistakably apparent that there is a powerful chemistry between them. It is well known that the Tsarina and the Tsarevich were inseparable, and Zoe Cooke and the servants at Croft House remarked on the closeness of Nikolai Chebotarev's relationship with the Baroness.

All these correspondences are, of course, circumstantial; and, as we say in chapter 7, it may be that the Tsarina's remains are indeed among those in the Ekaterinburg grave. However, as we have also seen, the evidence for this being the case remains far from conclusive; and the mysterious figure of the Baroness reminds us that, for the present at least, the question of Alexandra Feodorovna's fate remains unresolved.

Evidence suggesting that the Romanovs escaped – evidence of secret intelligence activity, of the effective operations of men like Boyle, Hill, Meinertzhagen, Alley and Peer-Groves, of Trotsky's involvement with Boyle and Hill in particular, of the web of connections, hitherto uncovered, which bound together that shadowy royal club, the Trust of Kings, of elderly Russians with Romanov characteristics living secreted away among royal connections – is simply too plentiful to ignore. Up to now, it has been possible to dismiss claims of rescue bids as the ineffectual and seemingly uncoordinated activities of disparate monarchist groups. Boyle, Hill and their associates do not fit into that category; and events that seem uncoordinated may appear so because we cannot see the real links that operated out of sight. Some attempts at rescue may have been aborted; some may have been deliberate decoy operations. As the story unfolded, it was not the paucity of such attempts, but on the contrary their multiplicity, which impressed. And all of them were connected, one way or another, with royalty.

# ⁓ 12 ⁓

# The Shoemaker

'He left Russia on board the same ship as the Dowager Empress. She found a cabin for him.'[1] With these words spoken by Mara Gorbadovsky across a dinner table in her small flat near the porte d'Auteuil in Paris, a whole new perspective opened on Chebotarev and his departure from Russia. She confirmed that the ship she spoke of was the British warship HMS *Marlborough* and that Chebotarev himself had told her the story. I knew this departure with the Dowager Empress was important; but at the time, I did not realize just how important. HMS *Marlborough*, it turned out, was not crammed with refugees like many of the other ships leaving Russia at this time, but had been sent specifically to evacuate the Dowager Empress and her entourage. No one but members of the imperial family and their retinue were on board that ship; and Nikolai Chebotarev was among them. The ship's manifest listed sixty-one passengers, ten of them – unnamed – children. Cipher 735Z received in Malta, the ultimate destination of HMS *Marlborough*, on 21 April 1920, shortly before her arrival, lists twenty adults, ten children and thirty-one attendants. Again the children and attendants are not named.[2]

At this time, the British navy in the Black Sea and Mediterranean was in the hands of notable royal 'fixers'. Admiral Sir Somerset Gough Calthorpe, the immediate past commander of the Mediterranean fleet and an ADC to King George V, was the British High Commissioner in Constantinople, HMS *Marlborough*'s first port of call after her sad farewell in Yalta to the strains of 'God Save the Tsar', the old imperial national anthem, heard there officially for the last time. Second in command of the British fleet in the Mediterranean was Vice-Admiral Sir Michael Culme-Seymour, who the previous year had commanded the British navy in the Black Sea and Caspian Sea. His family had a particularly close connection with the royal house. His sister, Mary Elizabeth Culme-Seymour, was reputed to have secretly married King George V in Malta in 1890 before he married Mary of Teck; the ensuing speculation ulti-mately ended in a famous court case in 1910 when, anxious to dispel the rumours, George V had forced the government to sue a hapless journalist, Mylius, for criminal libel. Mylius was imprisoned, but the stories never quite went away – especially as Mary Culme-Seymour's father, also an admiral, perjured himself by saying in court that his daughter had not seen George V between 1888 and 1902 when it was recorded she had led the dancing with the then Duke of Cornwall in Portsmouth in 1891.[3] Whatever the rights and wrongs of that case, the Culme-Seymours were definitely close to the British crown. Admiral Sir Michael also held the Order of St Vladimir of Russia Fourth Class – the highest class, since the Russians rank honours in the opposite order from the British. The family was also close to the circles in which Chebotarev moved. Admiral Culme-Seymour's son married Faith Montagu, daughter of the Earl of Sandwich and a regular visitor at Small Downs House, the home of Hilda Richardson's sister-in-law Gertrude Leverton-Harris.[4]

Following the evacuation of the Crimea, HMS *Marlborough* docked over the Orthodox Easter weekend in Constantinople, arriving on 11 April 1920.[5] The event was heavy with irony, for Constantinople, seat of the Ecumenical Patriarch, the head of the Orthodox Church worldwide, had been a war objective of the imperial Russian government, the prize promised by the allies. Tsargrad was what they called it; and now here they were, not as conquerors, but destitute. The city was teeming with Russian émigrés, with the massive overspill of refugees following the forced evacuations of defeated White troops from southern Russia. And it was full of resentments, particularly resentment that the former allies had not done more for their erstwhile comrades.

Overlooking the harbour in which HMS *Marlborough* was anchored was Arnaout Keoy; here, in an old and dilapidated house uninhabitable in winter but enjoying a glorious view over the Bosporus, lived Nikolai Couriss; and here, I believe, the former Tsarevich, Alexei Nikolaevich Romanov, was to obtain his new name and assume a new identity as Nikolai Chebotarev. From 1920 to 1922 Couriss was manager of the American Red Cross warehouse in Constantinople, employing thirty men, both Turkish and Russian, and responsible for $500,000 worth of supplies. He also dabbled in gun running. Prior to his arrival in Constantinople Couriss had acted as an interpreter for Captain Phillimore and Admiral Fremantle in the Black Sea squadron of the British navy. At the very least, this indicates relations with the British at an early stage, some years before becoming a passport and visa clerk at the British consulate in Salonika in 1926. Couriss was a gifted linguist. As

a young boy in Tsarskoe Selo he had had his own English tutor, a Mr
Fry, and according to Irish military intelligence files 'he spoke English
like an Englishman'. He also had a command of Greek, French and
German.[6]

Staying with Couriss at the time the *Marlborough* arrived was an
old schoolfriend from his boyhood days at Tsarskoe Selo, Grigori
Chebotarev, who had arrived from Ismailia in Egypt. Chebotarev was
ostensibly in Constantinople to make contact through the Russian community there with his sister Valentina; but she was still in Batumi,
hundreds of miles to the east, which suggests that Chebotarev must have
had other compelling reasons for joining Couriss in Constantinople.[7] In
any event, at Couriss' house, where the paths of many Russian refugees
crossed, Grigori Chebotarev met Prince Kozlovsky who retrieved his
sister for him.

Grigori Chebotarev had a connection to the imperial family of which
few outside the exclusive world of Tsarskoe Selo would have known.
He was the only son of Valentina Ivanovna Chebotarev, who had been
sister in charge of the Tsarina's annexe of the military hospital at
Tsarskoe Selo. With nursing experience from the Russo-Japanese war of
1904–5, she was the ideal person to head the nursing team in this unit, a
former isolation ward for contagious diseases separated from the main
three-storey hospital by parkland. Here she supervised the work of the
Tsarina and her two eldest daughters, Olga and Tatiana; among the other
nurses were Natalie Karaulov, who as Natalie Cooke was to harbour
Nikolai Chebotarev in Ireland during the Second World War, and her
cousin Nina Berberova.[8] Sister Chebotarev became a close friend of the
Empress and her daughters – indeed, the association aroused comment
from Count A. A. Mosolov, the head of the imperial chancellery, who
believed that Sister Chebotarev exercised 'undue influence' over the
Tsarina. 'Which of the ladies has influence with the Empress, I asked?
Some said Princess Gedroitz, the Head Physician of Her Majesty's
Hospital, an entirely masculine woman. Others said to me, in a tone of
surprise, Why, don't you know? The Head Sister. She dictates to the
Empress who is to have every important post.'[9] Certainly it was a close
community. Princess Dr Vera Gedroitz, by all accounts a formidable
woman, was the principal surgeon and was sufficiently close to the
Empress to try to influence her against Anna Vyrubova, who in this context, like her imperial mistress, was just another nurse.

Both the Tsarina and her daughter Tatiana were particularly close to

Sister Chebotarev. When the Russian Red Cross exchange and inspection team reported to the Tsarina that they had seen Sister Chebotarev's
husband in a German prisoner-of-war camp, the Empress acted at once.
'I think it will be possible to arrange his transfer to a neutral country,' she
told the sister. 'If the doctors won't do it, maybe I will succeed.' Sister
Chebotarev confided to her son that the last comment worried her, since
it seemed to confirm that the Tsarina had direct channels of communication with the Germans.[10] The young Grand Duchesses and their
mother turned to Sister Chebotarev for advice and to share confidences
– including the Tsarina's difficulties with her mother-in-law. On 6
November 1915 she confided to the sister: 'He [the Tsar] has gone to
Petrograd to see his mother – he must talk, they have so much to say to
each other. If I come, she remains silent.'[11] On one occasion Olga and
Tatiana questioned the sister as to how to go about buying something,
having gone incognito into St Petersburg's main shopping arcade, the
Gostinny Dvor, only to realize that not only had they no money but
they had never bought anything in their entire life. When, later, the
imprisoned Romanovs were sent to Siberia, they stayed in the closest of
touch with Sister Chebotarev: the Tsarina (who signed herself affection-
ately 'your old sister') and Grand Duchess Tatiana sent Valentina
Chebotarev ninety-six letters in an eight-month period – an average of
three each week.[12] Tatiana wrote the last letter from Tobolsk on 14 May
1918 as they were preparing to leave for Ekaterinburg. These were not
just short notes; they averaged about eight pages each. Among the
mutual friends about whom the Tsarina enquired in these letters was
Baroness Sophie von Medem, known as Sonya, who was godmother to
Sister Chebotarev's daughter and doubly related to Prince Paul Lieven, a
member of Couriss' circle at Collon. Also mentioned was General Piotr
Krasnov's wife Lydia, who was living with the Chebotarevs while her
husband marshalled anti-revolutionary forces. Food was more plentiful
in Tobolsk than in Tsarskoe Selo, and so in January 1918 the Tsarina was
able to send Sister Chebotarev a hamper. After the imperial family had
left Tsarskoe Selo, Sister Chebotarev even took an interest in the fate of
their pet cats: her friend Mme Geringer went into the palace kitchen
through a secret tunnel from one of the houses at the gates and rescued
the three imperial felines, which otherwise would undoubtedly have
starved to death. It was at this very personal, human, even humdrum
level that these people connected.

There was no doubting that the Chebotarevs were close to the

Romanovs. They also had a close and long-standing relationship with the Couriss family. Tsarskoe Selo, which literally means 'the Tsar's village', was a small town of about two thousand inhabitants which clustered around the gates of the palace complex. This included the massive Ekaterinsky Palace, built by Catherine the Great, by this time used only for public receptions, and the more modest Alexandrovsky Palace where Nikolai II and his family lived. The Chebotarevs lived at 6 Zakharevskaya Street, about two blocks away from Grand Duchess Maria Pavlovna's palace. For the most part, the town was peopled by court functionaries, officials and army officers from the guards regiments like Grigori Chebotarev's father. Also on Zakharevskaya Street, directly opposite the Chebotarevs, had lived their best friends, the Courisses.[13] Colonel John Couriss, who commanded the Life Guards, was of Lithuanian descent. His son Nikolai, or Nika as his friends called him, played as a boy with Sister Chebotarev's only son, Grigori. The closeness of the two families can be gauged by the fact that when Sister Chebotarev left Tsarskoe Selo to organize field hospitals in southern Russia at the request of her friend General Krasnov, now elected Ataman of the Don Cossacks, she left her most valued possessions in Couriss' attic.[14] Sister Chebotarev's granddaughter Sonya, who still lives in Princeton where her uncle Grigori became a professor of soil mechanics, today insists that there was no 'Nikolai' in any part of the Chebotarev family. She did know, however, of her Uncle Grigori's close friendship with Nikolai Couriss, and clearly remembered him visiting Couriss in Ireland. On her uncle's character, she was very clear, describing him as very discreet and a repository of secrets.[15]

The name 'Nikolai Chebotarev', with all its connotations, is a compelling signpost to the true identity of the mysterious refugee who bore it. If Chebotarev was the Tsarevich, as I was increasingly coming to believe, then it was almost certainly in Constantinople on that Easter weekend, sometime about Sunday 11 April 1920, that he began the secret life under another identity which was to last for another sixty-seven years. Given Couriss' known resourcefulness, it was likely to have been his idea, inspired by the name of his old schoolfriend, who was there with him at the time. The Chebotarev identity offered a background in a real family, coming from a real place – precisely what a boy like Alexei Romanov, now with no legal identity, needed. In many ways, it was an ingenious choice. Sister Valentina Chebotarev had perished of typhus, a constant hazard in the Caucasus, while serving under

General Krasnov, and had been buried in Novocherkassk on 6 May 1919. Only a few people in the emigration from Tsarskoe Selo would remember the name. Who would ever guess that a name that meant 'shoemaker' was now borne by the scion of Europe's most glittering dynasty?[16] Of course, it is possible that Couriss may have been involved at a much earlier stage, while he was still serving in the Caucasus and Sister Chebotarev was still alive. Valentina Chebotarev may have been party to the secret; such was the affection she bore the imperial children that it is difficult to imagine that she would not have willingly co-operated in such a plan for the sake of the Tsarevich.

Identity is both a physical and a legal concept. To some extent it depends on having the requisite documentation, but it depends also on other factors, notably, of course, appearance or physical characteristics – and on being where you are expected to be. Without proof, it is extremely difficult to establish identity. No one put this more eloquently than the woman who claimed to be Anastasia, later known as Anna Anderson. 'How shall I tell you who I am?' she said. 'Can you prove to me who you are?' In 1918 the Romanovs' legal identity was terminated. The people they had been were, for all legal purposes, dead. They may have existed *de facto*, but *de jure* they did not. Take individuals out of their normal environment, alter their appearance, break up a traditional and known family unit, provide them with new names and the papers to back this up and you have gone a long way to creating new identities. Combine all of this with the widespread presumption that they are dead, and the deception gains strength. Set all of this against a background of major social and political upheaval, distancing the individuals socially and geographically from their previous environment, and a survival plan for the former imperial family takes shape.

Many of these conditions already existed in embryonic form before the imperial family disappeared from Ekaterinburg. Tsar Nikolai II had become plain Citizen Romanov. In Tobolsk they were far removed from the reality of their former life. There, in the wastes of Siberia, they were not personally known as they were in Tsarskoe Selo. A further move to Ekaterinburg, capital of the Red Urals, distanced them still further from that past reality. By the time they had reached that place, only Dr Derevenko out of all their retinue was still there and had his freedom; only he saw them after 30 April 1918.[17] Initially, too, at Ekaterinburg the family unit was not together: four of the five children remained behind in Tobolsk. As noted in chapter 10, any release plan would have split them up to reduce the chance of identification and facilitate movement. At this point, too, a substitution may have taken place, with Kolya Derevenko, the doctor's son who looked so like the heir, possibly taking Alexei's place. If he did, then Alexei may well have had more than one transitional persona before assuming the identity of 'Nikolai Chebotarev'. Such a tactic would distance the Tsarevich still further from his true identity, making pursuit more difficult.

On 16 July 1918, at 8 p.m., the Tsarina noted in her diary: 'Suddenly Lyonka [Leonid] Sednev was fetched to go and see his Uncle and flew off – wonder whether it's true and we shall see the boy back again!'[18] Sednev was sent by Commandant Yurovsky to the Popov house across the street, which acted as the guardhouse. There Philip Proskuryatov, a young guard, noted: 'He slept on my bed and I spoke to him . . . at the time he complained that Yurovsky had taken away his clothes.'[19] Leonid Sednev was fourteen years old, the same age as Alexei, and had been the Tsarevich's playmate in Ekaterinburg. His clothes can only have been needed for another teenage boy: Alexei – or, if the real Alexei was already gone, perhaps Kolya Derevenko.

There was no shortage of people who believed the Tsar and his family had escaped execution – including the Dowager Empress herself. When HMS *Marlborough* arrived in Malta bearing Chebotarev and the surviving Romanovs, she insisted to Captain Robert Ingham that her son the Tsar and all of his family were still alive and that she knew where they were.[20] She never departed from this conviction. Now, too, the strength of the connection with the British royal family became immediately apparent. Almost the first thing the Tsar's sister Grand Duchess Xenia did in Malta was to send a telegram to Princess Victoria in London, then living with her mother Queen Alexandra at Marlborough House.[21] As noted in chapter 10, it was Princess Victoria who had real influence over her brother. 'Is that you, you old bugger?' she would enquire of the switchboard at Buckingham Palace, eliciting the reply: 'I'm sorry, Your Royal Highness, the King is not on the line yet.' The Dowager Empress travelled from Malta to London, and Chebotarev must have done likewise, for it was there, in 1920, that a Nansen passport was issued in his new name.[22]

Many years later, Chebotarev asked his friend Alix Hill to burn this document. Before doing so, she examined it carefully. What was particularly significant about Chebotarev's Nansen passport was the signatory, who must have vouched for him: Sir Percy Loraine.[23] As noted in chapter 3, Sir Percy found work for Chebotarev in 1929, when he was appointed British High Commissioner for Egypt and the Sudan, and again in 1946, this time with the United Nations; but back in 1920, Sir Percy was British *chargé d'affaires* in Poland – a long way from the Caucasus, Constantinople and Malta.[24] How, then, did he come to vouch for the identity of Nikolai Chebotarev?

Poland in 1919 was associated with a controversial document which came to light in the research undertaken by Summers and Mangold for *The File on the Tsar*. This was the famous Hardinge telegram. Dated 3 or 5 June 1919 and supposedly written by Lord Hardinge, Permanent Under-Secretary of State at the Foreign Office in London, on the basis of information supplied by the *chargé d'affaires* in Vienna, it purported to be an itinerary for the imperial family, moving through Odessa, Constantinople, Sofia, Vienna and Linz and ending at Breslau (now Wroclaw) on 10 May 1919.[25] Breslau, on the River Oder, actually remained a German city, capital of Silesia, until 1945, when it was incorporated into Poland. Summers and Mangold dismissed the telegram on three counts. First was the form of address: Hardinge, an experienced Foreign Office man, would have addressed the King not as 'Your Majesty' but simply as 'Sir'. Second, there was no *chargé d'affaires* in Vienna at the time. Third, the telegram called Vienna by its German name, Wien, which is unlikely in a message from one Englishman to another.

Cogent as their reasoning was, it is not impregnable. The Hon. F. O. Lindley was not the *chargé d'affaires* in Vienna; but he was the British High Commissioner in Vienna in 1919; what is more, immediately prior to this, from June 1918 to 1919, he had been British High Commissioner in Russia and before that Counsellor at the British Embassy in Petrograd (St Petersburg).[26] So though the designation is incorrect, 'our man in Vienna' did exist and he had a relevant Russian past. The title *chargé d'affaires* may have been used to refer to his brief rather than a designated post: after all, he was in charge of His Britannic Majesty's affairs in Vienna, and the only reason he was called High Commissioner was that Austria was one of the defeated central powers, its empire in a state of disintegration and the constitutional status of the new republics uncertain. Lindley's subsequent glittering career suggests notable success in this role, however ill-defined it was: he went on to be minister to Austria and ambassador in Athens, Oslo, Portugal and Japan. Created KCMG in 1929, a member of the order reserved for diplomats, he was given its

Grand Cross in 1931. In 1929 he became a Privy Counsellor, an honour normally conferred only on Cabinet ministers and unusual for a career diplomat.

Another curious footnote to the Polish connection is provided by the entries in the Moyallon House visitors' book for August 1931. Beside Nikolai Chebotarev's signature is that of one Zachariah Rychum, who gives his address as Koslinice, Wotyn, Poland. This same small village was home to Colonel Mical Goleniewsky, the Polish KGB defector who claimed to be Alexei. After crossing to the West on Christmas Day 1960, Goleniewsky became a controversial figure. While there is no doubt that his claim to be the Tsarevich was false – he was at least fifteen years younger than Alexei – he was certainly a KGB operative who was intimately involved in unmasking British MI6 traitor Kim Philby, and Philby had been one of Couriss' pupils at Collon. It is perfectly possible that he had access to KGB files on the former imperial family. Goleniewsky claimed that the Tsar died in Koslinice in 1952, aged eighty-four.[27] Koslinice is six miles from Wotyn and about forty miles from Wroclaw, which is mentioned in the Hardinge telegram as the ultimate destination of the imperial family. It is also close to the German frontier; as noted above, Wroclaw remained a German city, Breslau, until 1945. To find this small village mentioned in the Moyallon visitors' book near to Chebotarev's name is more than strange. Even stranger is the fact that in 1935 the Moyallon visitors' book yields up another Polish name: 'Swanowsky', written in the book by the hostess herself, Hilda Richardson, as was her common practice when guests forgot to sign. Swanowsky is perilously close to Schwankowsky, the name of the family from whom Anna Anderson, who claimed to be Anastasia, was alleged actually to have come – and who lived in that same part of western Poland near the German frontier. Nikolai Chebotarev, as he had become, kept newspaper cuttings from *Paris-Soir* about the Mical Goleniewsky case among his papers. No doubt, if challenged, he could point to this man as the real Tsarevich. But the clues tying him to Poland – Sir Percy Loraine, Zachariah Rychum of Koslinice, Goleniewsky from the same village and 'Swanowsky' – are, like so much else, intriguing and suggestive. If the refugee Tsarevich, freshly endowed with the pseudonym on which his safety depended, had arrived in Poland in 1919 across the border from nearby Breslau, it would have fallen to Sir Percy Loraine, as the British High Commissioner in Poland, to certify his new identity as Nikolai Chebotarev by taking the young man to England under his wing and providing him with a passport – thus establishing a connection that was to endure for at least another quarter-century.

Chebotarev did not remain in England, but by 1921 was in Yugoslavia. This country, created by the Versailles Peace settlement, was in effect an enlarged Serbia – Serbia which, mindful of the assistance of previous Tsars, had remained loyal to the Romanov cause to the end. Countless thousands of Russians found refuge there in an environment which was friendly, Slav and sympathetic. As one more Russian refugee among the crowd, one more man without a country, Chebotarev could reasonably have expected to be able to melt into the background and simply disappear. It was not to be that easy.

## ∽ 13 ∾

## Rumours

I had first heard of the rumours that Chebotarev was the Tsarevich from his friend Marianne Cross on 11 August 1993 – right at the start of my investigation. From her I had learned, as described in chapter 4, that the rumours had started in Yugoslavia, which placed their advent firmly in the early 1920s, very soon after he acquired the name and identity of Nikolai Chebotarev. Apparently, someone was not fooled.

In Yugoslavia, at Bela Cirkva, Chebotarev attended one of the cadet schools set up by King Alexander for the large numbers of Russian refugees flooding into his country. Two were for boys, doubling as gymnasia or grammar schools and military training academies to turn out young officers, and three were gymnasia for girls. Many of the Russians were rapidly assimilated into their new country; many more moved on to France, Germany and America. Those who remained were valuable, indeed necessary additions to the indigenous population: many had official, medical, civil service and military backgrounds in Russia which equipped them to provide the new state of Yugoslavia – or, to give it its full name, the Kingdom of the Serbs, Croats and Slovenes – with the officer corps and public officials it needed. In time, the five separate schools were amalgamated, and ultimately they disappeared, no longer needed.[1]

In 1921, though, when the process of assimilation had hardly begun, it might be supposed that Chebotarev would be invisible among the hordes of young educated Russians. Certainly it may have seemed highly unlikely that anyone would recognize him as the Tsarevich; after all, the imperial family had been intensely private – indeed, that had been one of their problems. Shut away in Tsarskoe Selo, in a privileged enclave on one edge of their vast realm, they were invisible to the vast majority of Russians. Alexei was iconized as a little boy, and that was how the world at large did, and does, remember him. Yet even before the end of his father's reign, the Tsarevich had outgrown this image. In 1918, when the imperial family disappeared, he was fourteen years old – an adolescent undergoing all the changes in appearance which inevitably accompany puberty and approaching adulthood. A photograph of the Tsarevich taken in April 1918 with his sister Tatiana, shortly after their father's abdication, shows a more mature Alexei, more adult in appearance; an Alexei bearing a startling resemblance to Nikolai Chebotarev in his white officer cadet's uniform in a photograph taken at Bela Cirkva in 1923.

Comparing these two photographs (see plates), it is not difficult to understand why there were rumours that he was the Tsarevich; for not all the Russians in Yugoslavia in 1921 remembered Alexei as a small boy in long-ago family photographs. Among the exiles were men who had served in the army in 1916 when the Tsar, accompanied by his son, toured the front. They remembered an Alexei who was beginning to mature. There were women, too, who had served in the Tsarina's annexe of the hospital at Tsarskoe Selo hospital and could remember Alexei's visits – visits which for generations exiled Russians said never happened until, when the archives were opened after the collapse of the Soviet Union, photographs were revealed showing Alexei posing with his sisters in that very hospital.[2] Thousands of Russians had the official portrait of the imperial family, taken in 1913 in the tercentenary year of the Romanov dynasty, sitting in their homes. In it was a childish Alexei, aged nine. But a few could remember the other, older Alexei; and it needs only a few to start a rumour.

Confirmation of the existence of rumours that Chebotarev was the Tsarevich came from other sources. One was Dame Elizabeth Hill, the former Professor of Slavonic studies at Cambridge University. Towards the end of his life, Nikolai Chebotarev had been befriended by this formidable academic. Alix Hill, her cousin and Chebotarev's friend and neighbour, recalls her going to church with him at the Orthodox Brookwood Convent each Sunday and frequently returning to the house for lunch with him. Dame Elizabeth, entered in the Hill family bible simply as 'Bessie', had been born in Russia in 1900. She was the cousin both of Alix Hill's father and also of Natalie Cooke, who provided a home for Chebotarev during the Second World War. Her brother, the spy (or 'gentleman agent') Freddie Hill, had been best man at Natalie Cooke's wedding. Captain George Hill was another cousin. And she was well known at Collon. Kathleen McCarthy, Couriss' housekeeper, recalls Professor Hill coming over regularly to check the accommodation and arrangements for the students she sent from Cambridge – students who, as I had discovered, included double agents George Blake, Kim

Philby, Guy Burgess and Donald Maclean. Born a subject of Tsar
Nikolai II and an old girl of the famous German Realschule in St Petersburg, Dame Elizabeth was avidly interested in all things Romanov, and
at the time of her own death in 1997 was working on a book on the
strange circumstances surrounding the death of Tsar Alexander I in
Taganrog in 1825. Rumoured not to have died at that time but to have
substituted another body in his place, Tsar Alexander I was said to have
lived on as the itinerant holy man Feodor Kusmich, at first in the Holy
Land and then later in Siberia, dying only in 1858. This story was taken
sufficiently seriously by the imperial family for them to set up an internal commission of inquiry under Grand Duke Constantine in the 1880s:
its findings were never made known.

By the time I met Dame Elizabeth for the first time, early in 1996,
Alix Hill was certain that I was Chebotarev's son and she had discussed
the matter in detail with her cousin. Dame Elizabeth's first words to me
were memorable. 'Do you know what they said about your father? That
he was the heir to the throne? Some said he was an impostor. I don't
think so.'[3] Dame Elizabeth went on to confirm she had heard the
rumours in France in the 1930s. In 1997 Tatiana Torporkov, a Russian
living in New York, not only recalled that her brother had heard the
rumours that Chebotarev was the Tsarevich, but also confirmed that
Chebotarev had visited Grand Duke Vladimir, the claimant to the imperial throne, in Spain – as Alix Hill had told us back in 1993.[4]

However, while talk may have spread within the exiled Russian
community, there was a conspiracy of silence as far as the outside, non-
Russian, non-Orthodox world was concerned. It is hardly surprising that
this should have been so. Constantly anxious about Soviet infiltration
and disorientated by their forcible ejection from their homeland, it is
small wonder that the White Russian émigrés did not share their knowledge with outsiders. It was a community characterized by fear at all
levels which expressed itself in both dramatic and commonplace ways.
Bill Pinkney, a close friend in Canada of the Tsar's sister Grand Duchess
Olga, said that she slept with a revolver under her pillow. Alix Hill told
me of Mme Makarova, a friend of her mother, who would never leave
the house after dark.[5] Nor were these fears unfounded: General Miller,
Dame Elizabeth Hill's uncle, was murdered by Red agents in Paris in
1926 while visiting his mistress. To talk outside the closed circle of the
exile community would be to invite trouble. But in my view there was
sufficient talk about Chebotarev within that community itself to justify a

serious investigation. Indeed, so potent were these rumours that they resurfaced at the time of Chebotarev's death in 1987, and they linger today – with, I became convinced, good reason. And they still generate enough fear to elicit the advice: 'Leave this alone.'

A powerful stimulant to the rumours was provided by a remarkable correspondence which came to light only after Chebotarev's death. Ninety-nine letters written to Chebotarev by Archbishop Theophan of Poltava were discovered in a small wooden chocolate liqueur box, labelled by Nikolai as 'very important historical documents'.[6] That they were written at all is remarkable, for this is the same Theophan who was the Tsarina's confessor and the man responsible for introducing the imperial family to Rasputin. It was thus immediately obvious that these letters might contain vital clues to Chebotarev's true identity. Covering the decade from 1921 to 1931, the letters were written at a rate of about one every six weeks. Though Chebotarev's replies have not been found, it is possible to sketch the key features of the relationship from Theophan's side of the correspondence.

What is initially most striking is the form of address: 'Venerable Friend', a style appropriate only for a superior, used by an eminent middle-aged archbishop, a prince of the Church and one of its most prominent figures, to a young man who is still a teenager when the correspondence begins. Though this strongly suggests that Theophan was addressing someone of a higher social rank, which for an archbishop could only be a prince, nevertheless the indications are that he was not actually sure whether Chebotarev was the Tsarevich or not. The letters themselves make explicit mention of the rumours about Chebotarev's identity over a period from May 1925 to November 1927. In May 1925, for instance, Theophan suggests that Chebotarev may have to explain himself to Grand Duke Nikolai, 'but only if there is a real necessity to do so'.[7] In itself this is interesting, for Grand Duke Nikolai Nikolaevich, the commander-in-chief of the Russian armies at the start of the First World War, was the husband of Grand Duchess Militsa, Theophan's first patron. The priest's allegiances, therefore, appear to have remained largely unchanged from the conspiratorial early years of the century. Indeed, Theophan himself made his loyalties very plain on 8 March 1923 when he wrote to Chebotarev: 'Now it is no secret that in Russia there exists a powerful secret monarchist organization which in the near future will rise up in a revolution. The Grand Duke Nikolai Nikolaevich has already given his agreement but awaits the moment when he will have to stand at the head of that movement. He has been chosen by the Lord himself.'[8] In exile, Grand Duke Nikolai lived at the Château Santény near Paris. Many Russian émigrés regarded him, and not Nikolai II's cousin Grand Duke Cyril, as the real head of the Russians in exile.

Living in the Grand Duke's gate lodge at Santény was General Krasnov, the former Ataman of the Don Cossacks and close friend of Sister Valentina Chebotarev. Krasnov's wife had lived with the Chebotarevs in Tsarskoe Selo when the general was engaged in the war against the Bolsheviks, and Sister Chebotarev had gone to the Caucasus to organize nursing services there for the White armies, specifically at General Krasnov's request.[9] Krasnov had moved to Santény from Castle Seeon, the home of a Romanov relative, the Duke of Leuchtenberg, and incidentally also the home for a time of the Anastasia claimant, Anna Anderson. In 1924, when Chebotarev moved from Yugoslavia to France, Archbishop Theophan had proposed that he too should go and live at Santény, a suggestion the young man wisely declined.[10] According to a letter from Theophan in April 1926, one of the Krasnov family apparently believed the rumours – as, given the Krasnov family's connection to Sister Chebotarev, she was probably in a position to do – and her sister wanted to approach the Queen of Sweden about them. Queen Victoria of Sweden was the Kaiser's aunt and her daughter-in-law, the Crown Princess of Sweden, was Lady Louise Mountbatten, the Tsarina's niece and Alexei's cousin. 'I myself felt you should be put in the picture about this,' Theophan writes.[11] By 1926, therefore, the rumours had reached the very top echelons of royal society. Since the Swedish royal family was so closely connected with British royalty, the news is sure to have reached Buckingham Palace too.

Chebotarev appeared to think that Theophan himself was far from blameless in spreading the rumours. In his letters he wrote of a 'poisonous atmosphere'. Though the archbishop tried to exculpate himself, alleging that an O. V. Obukhova had been the first to broadcast them in May 1925 and saying they 'had been mixed with the usual female tittle tattle',[12] he apparently was still a party to them in the following year. In March 1926 he warned Chebotarev that the rumours had spread from Yugoslavia to Nice in France, and the Rakhleyev family, with whom Chebotarev was then staying, appeared to have heard of them. 'I only thought it my duty to forewarn you,' the archbishop writes rather piously, at the same time telling Chebotarev not to disclose that it was through him he had heard what the Krasnovs were saying.[13] On

11 November 1927 he added, 'You must not get distressed about the rumours. Now it is difficult to exist without unpleasantness. Everybody has his own unpleasantness.'

There is an indication in the Theophan letters that Chebotarev and his friends started an alternative rumour to divert attention away from these highly dangerous suggestions that he was Alexei. On 18 August 1926 Theophan advises Chebotarev not to 'get into difficulties over some kind of story about this'. It seems that the diversionary tactic was causing almost as many problems as the original. Some light was shed on the nature of the new story by Chebotarev's friend Mara Gorbadovsky, the grand-daughter of the émigré General Gorbadovski, who heard the alternative version from Baroness Hoyingen-Huene's daughter, Xenia. This had Chebotarev as the son of the Tsar and the Tsarina's sister, Grand Duchess Elizabeth. 'He visited Grand Duchess Elizabeth's grave in Jerusalem not as a tourist or pilgrim,' Mara Gorbadovsky said, 'but as a son.'[14] One glance at a studio photograph of Chebotarev taken in Paris in 1928 explains why the original rumours gained such currency: aged twenty-four, he bears a marked resemblance to a photograph of the Tsarina at the same age, taken in 1896 (see plates). But Grand Duchess Elizabeth was strikingly similar in appearance to the Tsarina, and this new spin on the original rumour was clearly intended to explain why Chebotarev looked so like the Empress. The trouble was that there needed to be a half-credible explanation as to how the Tsarina's sister had managed to keep a baby so quiet. This was where the alternative version got into the difficulties to which Theophan referred. In the Hoyingen-Huene version, Grand Duchess Elizabeth gave the baby to an Irish maid of honour, who then married an old man called Chebotarev who had been married twice before; after his death, she married a Prince Trubetskoye – a name identical with that of Colonel Joe Boyle's agent in the Caucasus. Allegedly, this Irish lady in waiting had another child who was later murdered, aged six, by the Bolsheviks because he would not tell 'where the jewels were hidden'.[15] Exhaustive searching in the *Almanack de Gotha* reveals, however, that Grand Duchess Elizabeth never had an Irish maid of honour. However, the Tsarina herself did have two Irish women on her staff: a Miss Eager, who was governess to the four Grand Duchesses before Alexei was born, and a Miss Downey, confirmed by Kathleen McCarthy to have been known by Nikolai Couriss as a member of the Tsarina's household.[16] This may have been the source of the presence of Irish women in the cover story.

A clearer picture emerged of the effects of the rumours after I spoke to Dame Elizabeth Hill and her friend Princess Sophie Wachnadze in 1995. Apparently Chebotarev had been asked to move on from Nice by the committee of White generals who supported the claims of Grand Duke Nikolai, because rumours that he was the Tsarevich were understandably attracting supporters to his cause.[17] In Nice, he had been staying with the Grabbes, the family of Count Grabbe who had been the commander of the Tsar's Cossack bodyguard, the Konvoy. Photographs of the Grabbe children dated 1925 are still in his album. This association – which no doubt itself fanned the rumours – continued throughout his life. In the late 1940s he stayed with the Grabbes again, this time on Long Island, New York. When Chebotarev moved to Paris, the rumours followed him there; according to Mara Gorbadovsky, he was asked not to appear at the Russian Orthodox Cathedral of St Alexander Nevsky on the rue Daru, the focal point of the Russian emigration, because his appearance caused too much of a stir.[18] Theophan's letter of 6 November 1929 specifically mentions his attendance at the rue Daru cathedral.[19]

Chebotarev's preoccupations, as disclosed through the letters, were those that would be expected of Alexei. In 1928, for instance, he questioned Theophan closely about the arrangements for the funeral of the Dowager Empress in Denmark. In 1923 Theophan reported on a projected uprising in Russia and in 1926 on a planned invasion, in minute detail down to the number of troops the various émigré communities in different European countries would supply. Both of these ventures failed. In 1929 the archbishop reported that Lord Glasgow, a well-known Fascist sympathizer in England, had offered to raise an anti-Bolshevik crusade.

In 1923 Grand Duke Cyril proclaimed himself 'curator of the Imperial throne', following this in 1924 with the assumption of the title Tsar-in-exile. Chebotarev had reacted angrily and outspokenly, in the way one would expect from the real Tsarevich; but this brought a warning from Theophan on 15 September 1924. 'I find it my duty to warn you. Be careful, take care with conversations to do with Grand Duke Cyril Vladimirovich. It is better at the moment not to say anything about him except for close people . . . it is necessary to be extra careful for you as they know of your friendship with me.' Kerensky, Prime Minister in the Provisional Government in summer 1917, relates how, on a visit to the imperial family at Tsarskoe Selo, the young Tsarevich had asked him if he were a lawyer, to which he replied in the affirmative. The Tsarevich then asked him, as a lawyer, if his father, the Tsar, had the right to abdicate on his behalf. Kerensky had to admit that under Russian law, he had not.[20] This vignette from those last days in the imperial palace is revealing of the tensions that lurked just below the surface within the imperial family itself, and hints at the understandable resentment which the son must have felt towards the father for depriving him of his rightful inheritance. If Chebotarev were Alexei, then Grand Duke Cyril's proclamation must have been hard to bear; and indeed, this assumption of the imperial role continued to rankle with him. Five years later, on 15 March 1929, he received from Theophan the following rather lame reply to a letter that must have concerned Metropolitan Anthony's endorsement of Grand Duke Cyril: 'It is very fair that Metropolitan Anthony accepted Grand Duke Cyril Vladimirovich as Emperor. Personally I regard it in the negative.'

And Theophan touched on the most sensitive subject of all – the survival of the imperial family. On 7 March 1927 he informed Chebotarev that the family were 'all truly alive with the exception of Grand Duchess Maria, who died of typhoid. This I know from a reliable source and, by the way, from the person who was an eye witness of the escape of the royal family from Ekaterinburg. They will probably stay in Russia for the next year.' This remarkable statement at such a late date could be dismissed as wishful thinking. Probably, it needs to be seen in the context of Theophan's continual probing about Chebotarev's past. In 1922 he was asking: 'I'd love to know your relatives . . . where you lived before the Revolution and where you were brought up.' In 1927 he wrote: 'Again, I have forgotten the name and patronymic of Baroness Huene. I ask you to write it in full for me.'[21] Chebotarev did not respond to this request. Nor, indeed, did he ever use a patronymic himself – an omission highly unusual in a Russian of this period. It seems that the curious archbishop, who knew all about the rumours, was getting to know very little about his 'venerable friend's' past. I was reminded of Stella Dalziel's comment that Chebotarev was 'very good at saying nothing'.[22]

Despite being the Tsarina's confessor, Theophan had not actually seen Alexei since 1910, when the Tsarevich was only six years old. In that year the prelate had broken with his former ally, Rasputin, and the *starets* had his former friend, now turned critic, promoted to the archbishopric of Poltava and Pereslavl in southern Russia, a thousand miles from St Petersburg, the springs of power and the imperial court. It amounted to internal exile. He might as well have been Bishop of Outer Space. Up to that point Theophan's career had been a glittering success. Born Basil Dmitrievich Bystrov in 1873, the son of a priest in the village of Podmosh in the St Petersburg diocese, he had been top of his class at theological seminary in 1892; in 1896 he completed his course at the prestigious St Petersburg Theological Academy, joining the staff in the same year. By 1901 he held the senior position of archimandrite, and in 1908, two years after completing his master's degree, he was appointed director of the Academy and titular Bishop of Yamburg, number four in the St Petersburg diocese.[23] Yet what really consolidated Theophan's position as one of the most powerful clerics in Russia was his office as confessor to the Empress and the Grand Duchesses Militsa and Stana. In 1910 he lost it all after presuming to warn the Empress about Rasputin's licentious conduct. 'I have shut his trap,' was Rasputin's comment on Theophan's transfer to Poltava.[24]

Theophan had originally turned on Rasputin following an internal dispute in an organization to which they both belonged: the right-wing, nationalist Union of True Russian Men, in which Theophan was deeply involved with his friend Bishop Hermogen. Rasputin's discovery of financial irregularities and fraud in this body, leading to two of Theophan and Hermogen's friends being convicted of embezzlement,[25] may well have sown the seeds of their hostility to their former protégé. Bishop Hermogen, like Theophan, suffered what amounted to internal exile. After the 1910 disaster, Theophan saw the Tsarina only once more – in 1911 when he travelled to Yalta, again to lobby against Rasputin. Alexandra Feodorovna heard him in silence and he was ushered out. In 1917 he repaid his sovereign for ruining his promising career by giving evidence against the Empress to Kerensky's 'truth commission', set up to investigate the 'dark forces' which had brought down imperial Russia.[26]

Viewed in the light of Militsa's and Stana's plotting in the past, their initial sponsorship of Rasputin, the rumours about Chebotarev's true identity and the candidacy of Grand Duke Nikolai for the vacant – if non-existent – throne, Theophan's solicitations could well have had an ulterior motive. Archbishop Theophan was unsure of Chebotarev's true identity; but he had proved himself a dangerous man in the past, and the correspondence probably represented considerable, if perhaps unavoid-able, danger for Chebotarev now. Once Theophan had moved to Paris in 1931, a fact he announced in a letter in February that year,[27] Chebotarev absented himself in Ireland with increasing frequency; and in that same year, according to the executors of Hilda Richardson's will, he officially gave up his right to work in France. Perhaps Theophan was too close for comfort.

It emerged in the course of my research that during the last year of his life, Chebotarev had tried to unburden himself of some great secret. He had tried to talk to several people, but no one would listen. Mara Gorbadovsky's response when he tried to speak to her in Paris in 1986, during that last summer of his life, was: 'I know what you are going to tell me. I don't want to hear.'[28] Alix Hill was too busy looking after her ailing mother to listen, though she does admit that he was agitated about it. He had told her on earlier occasions that he wanted to tell her something important but somehow, other things had always intervened. Staff in St David's Nursing Home in Common Lane, Sheringham in Norfolk, where he died, attest to his having tried to say something after his final stroke, but he could not make himself understood.[29] The Greek Orthodox priest who gave him the last offices of the Church, while saying that he could not divulge what anyone in that position said, admitted that in this case there was nothing to divulge because the dying man was 'beyond speech'.[30]

Chebotarev carried his secret to the grave with him. After his death, however, a few still remembered the rumours attached to his name in the 1920s, just a few years after the disappearance of the Romanovs, when memories were fresh. In places, I have encountered a strange deference to his name. When I spoke to Mother Seraphima at Walsingham Orthodox Convent in July 1994, she replied in hushed, even reverential tones when I asked her if she had ever met Chebotarev. 'I met him only once,' she said; and, pausing to think for just a moment, continued, 'It was in 1984. He was standing just where you are now.' I often wondered whether his true identity was a kind of open secret within the Russian Orthodox community; something they did not share with outsiders but which among themselves they all understood, or believed, might be so.

# ⌣ 14 ⌣

## The Company He Kept

If a man is judged by the company he keeps, then Nikolai Chebotarev was no ordinary Russian émigré. Not only did he move among the English country house set; the people with whom he mixed add a frisson of royal connection and far right-wing politics to an already intriguing picture. Taken overall, it is a heady concoction – but a social cocktail that would not be surprising in the milieu of a former Tsarevich.

Nikolai Chebotarev was never fully in charge of his own life. He did not choose his environment; it chose him. We have already seen how, soon after the young man bearing this name emerged from the chaos of the Russian Revolution in the company of the Dowager Empress, Sir Percy Loraine made his appearance to vouch for the apparently stateless teenager. In 1929, when he was appointed to one of the great pro-consular roles in the then British Empire as High Commissioner for Egypt and the Sudan, Sir Percy employed Nikolai as his private secretary. And it was Sir Percy again who in 1946 magnanimously obtained a post for Nikolai in the Language Translation Service of the fledgling United Nations, opening up a whole new phase in his life. Sir Percy's sister, Isaura, acted as guardian to Nikolai's niece in England after he brought her out of Yugoslavia in 1932.[1] All of this represents an interest in Nikolai Chebotarev's affairs far too consistent and long-term to be brushed off as mere general benevolence. Why, then, did so prominent an Establishment figure interest himself so closely and so persistently in the fate of one displaced Russian boy and his family?

A great landowner, with broad acres stretching across Northumberland and Suffolk and a London address in Wilton Crescent, the same street as Lord Mountbatten, Sir Percy moved in the highest aristocratic circles. In every sense a *grand seigneur*, he was a well-known figure on the Turf; two of his horses won Classics, the pinnacles of the British Flat racing season. He was also very well connected. His wife was the daughter of Lord Wharncliffe, and her relations included some of the greatest aristocratic families of the land – the Marquesses of London-

derry, the Earls of Antrim, the Earls of Sandwich and George VI's in-
laws the Earls of Harewood.[2] Sir Percy occupied a pivotal position in
British society. If one were looking for a minder for a displaced royal
relation living under a false identity, one could hardly do better.

Along with many other members of the upper reaches of British
society, Sir Percy's political inclinations were those of what might be
called the aristocratic far right. He was far from being alone in these sympathies; pro-German organizations had an ample supply of high-ranking
members between the wars. Many in the British upper classes believed
they saw the big picture better than those hampered by liberal sensibilities – and for them it was a picture of Europe divided between the
forces of left and right, between Bolshevism and Fascism. The choice, on
mainland Europe at least, was between these two; there was effectively
no middle ground. Ribbentrop, Hitler's ambassador in London, was
entertained by Lady Loraine's cousins, the Londonderrys,[3] at Mount-
stewart, their great house near Belfast, and also by Londonderry's
neighbour, Viscount Bangor. The Anglo-German Fellowship counted
among its titled members Lord Hamilton, an Ulster Unionist MP and
son of another Ulster peer, the Duke of Abercorn, as well as General
Sir Alfred Knox, the former commander of Britain's expeditionary force
against the Bolsheviks in Russia in 1917–19, whose family came from
Dungannon in Northern Ireland. The Duke of Westminster, an English
peer with large estates in Fermanagh, belonged to the far-right Anglo-
German Link, as did the Anglo-Irish Sir Barry Domvile, the former
head of naval intelligence. From even these few examples it is clear that
Northern Ireland's aristocracy, which wielded great power in the small
province, had pronounced far-right, pro-German sympathies. Other
Establishment figures of the same inclination were the Duke of Bedford;
the Duke of Wellington; the Marquess of Lothian, Britain's ambassador
in Washington; Lord Redesdale, father of the Mitford sisters, one of
whom, Unity, was close to Hitler; Sir Oswald Mosley, leader of the
British Union of Fascists, who married Unity's sister Diana; and Frank
Tiarks, Governor of the Bank of England, whose son was married to a
daughter of Couriss' friend the Marquess of Headfort.[4] Politically as well
as socially, Sir Percy Loraine was in distinguished company.

A significant feature of these far-right groups was their royal connections. The Earl of Airlie, Lord Chamberlain and head of the royal household, Viscount Bertie, another royal servant, and Lord Mount Temple,
grandfather of Edwina Mountbatten, were all in the Anglo-German

Fellowship. Sir Percy numbered among his Italian friends Mussolini's foreign minister and son-in-law Count Ciano, who had known King Edward VIII's future wife, Mrs Simpson, since 1923, when she was compelled by her then husband to frequent the brothels in Hong Kong and Shanghai. Mrs Simpson also had a clandestine relationship with Ribbentrop and was identified by British intelligence as the source of leaks from Cabinet discussions, reports of which the King received daily in his red boxes.[5] In 1936 this led directly to unprecedented action by Prime Minister Stanley Baldwin, who withheld state papers from the King.[6] In fact, the royal family had their own intermediary with the Nazis in the person of Baron Wilhelm de Ropp, who communicated through the Duke of Kent, husband of Nikolai Chebotarev's friend, Princess Marina.

Now that King Edward VIII's Fascist sympathies are more widely known and have been acknowledged as a possible major factor in his being forced to abdicate, all this is not as shocking as it once seemed. Even after the outbreak of hostilities, national loyalty did not automatically override political sympathies. Regarding Winston Churchill as a warmonger and a renegade, these far-right aristocrats would have liked nothing better in 1940–1 than to oust him from office and replace him with the pro-German Lord Halifax. As Britain's ambassador in Italy from 1938, Sir Percy was considered to be far too close to Mussolini and his Fascist government. Small wonder, then, that when he retired from this post in 1940, Churchill refused to give him any further official employment. As a former ambassador, Sir Percy might reasonably have expected to serve on some government committee or other; but instead he had to kick his heels, concentrating on breeding and training his racehorses – a pursuit which, incidentally, brought him frequently to Ireland.

As a young man Sir Percy Loraine had served for two years from 1905 in Britain's embassy in Constantinople. Here he worked alongside two other young diplomats, Sir Mark Sykes and Sir Ambrose Lloyd, later Lord Lloyd. Sykes was a member of a family with long-standing connections to royal circles: his uncle had been the closest friend of King Edward VII, the Tsar's uncle. According to his entry in Burke's *Peerage, Baronetage and Knightage*, Sykes was 'specially employed' – the official euphemism for intelligence work – in Russia from 1917 to 1919.[7] For his services he was awarded the Russian Order of St Stanislas and the Order of the Star of Romania, suggestive of links with Romania that may well have involved participation in activities with Colonel Joe Boyle. Sykes's son Christopher married Camilla Russell, the daughter of Russell Pasha, head of the Cairo police at the time when Loraine and Chebotarev were in Egypt. In 1928, Russell sold his home, Little Compton Manor, to Hilda Richardson's sister-in-law, Gertrude Leverton-Harris; and his photograph appeared in Moyallon. This photograph showed Russell standing alongside Olga Kerensky, wife of Alexander Kerensky, who had been secretary of the Russian Red Cross when the Tsarina was its president. Apparently, she had given the photograph with a book to May Friars, one of the Moyallon servants, as a memento of her stay at the house. It is hard to imagine what possible reason Kerensky's wife would have for visiting Hilda Richardson at Moyallon, in the depths of the Irish countryside, unless it were connected with the Russians staying there – Nikolai Chebotarev and the lady he said was his aunt, Baroness Lydia de Huene.

Sykes's daughter Angela married the Earl of Antrim,[8] and it was this connection, more than any other, that suggested to me that Sykes was part of a framework around Nikolai Chebotarev – a framework which also included Sir Percy Loraine. For Angela, Countess of Antrim was an associate of Nikolai Couriss and a regular visitor at Couriss' home at Collon, which Chebotarev also frequented. And it is here in Collon that Sir Percy Loraine's and Sir Mark Sykes's friend Sir Ambrose Lloyd enters the picture. Sir Ambrose was a first cousin of Britain's appeasement-era Prime Minister, Neville Chamberlain, as was Alizon Fox, the Quaker lady who brought Couriss to Ireland in the first place, set him up in Collon, visited him there and acted as his mentor and sponsor.[9] Chamberlain himself had a holiday home in Buncrana, County Donegal, right beside the Richardsons'; he had been a guest at Moyallon and had known Hilda Richardson since at least 1912, for it is then he appears in her visitors' book. Chamberlain's cousin, Sir Ambrose Lloyd, came from another noted family of royal 'fixers'.[10] Lloyd, a pilot and an honorary air commodore, held the Order of St Anne of Russia and had served in Russia during the First World War. He married well – a Lascelles, the family of the Earl of Harewood, which also provided a husband for King George V's only daughter Mary, the Princess Royal. And the Harewoods were also relatives of Lady Loraine. Lloyd's career was a glittering one, characterized by rapid promotion and many honours: a Knight Grand Cross of the Order of the Indian Empire in 1918, a governorship in 1918, a peerage in 1925. It was also a career which appeared to be shadowed by that of Sir Percy Loraine, for when Lloyd retired as High Commissioner of Egypt and the Sudan, Sir Percy replaced him – taking, as we have seen, Nikolai Chebotarev as his secretary. These three friends, the three knights – Loraine, Sykes and Lloyd – who as young men had worked together in Constantinople, seemed to be taking on the appearance of a protective group around the man rumoured at this time to be Alexei, Tsarevich of Russia.

In April 1995 I made two discoveries which seemed to reinforce this view. The first was an account of an interesting journey undertaken by Nikolai Couriss, recorded in a battered blue notebook (see plates). Headed 'Hotel des Dunes, Agadir', the page continued: 'visit Wendover from Baker Street (for Chequers)'. Underneath was written: 'Mon 24, 6.30 Mr Comatatos – Tangier – 12am Waterport Wharf – buses to Casablanca £1-10-0 – 11am–2.30 – Miramar – 100 pesetas – Bus goes to Marrakesh – Marrakesh to Agadir, 5.30–11.45, 7pm–1.30.'[11] The key to understanding this information lay in two apparently unrelated pieces of information. One I already possessed: this was the fact that Alizon Fox, Couriss' mentor, was a cousin of Neville Chamberlain, who in 1939 was the official occupant of Chequers, the country house left to the nation in 1919 which has been a retreat for Britain's Prime Ministers ever since. The second piece of information came from Natalie Cooke's daughter, Zoe, who told me that Baroness de Huene, Nikolai Chebotarev's aunt, had been living with her daughter, who was married to a French army officer, in Marrakesh when the war broke out in 1939. She gave me a mirror, framed in North African wood, which the Baroness had given her as a wedding present in 1946. A year later this information was confirmed in Paris by Mara Gorbadovsky, who named the Baroness' daughter as Olga and said she had married a member of the Toulouse-Lautrec family. Certainly the one photograph I had of Nikolai with the Baroness could well have been taken against a North African backdrop, with palm trees clearly in evidence (see plates).

Couriss' notes clearly show a journey beginning in Chequers, proceeding via Tangiers, Agadir and Casablanca, and ending in Marrakesh, with the return route marked out as well. The Moyallon visitors' book showed that the Baroness arrived at Moyallon on 8 July 1939; she remained in Ireland for the duration of the war. If the journey outlined took place in 1939, as I believe, then the words 'Mon 24' are a clue to the timing, for the twenty-fourth of the month fell on a Monday only in April, not in May or June. So Couriss' journey lasted from April to early July. Kathleen McCarthy confirmed that the Baroness had come to Collon in 1940 and again as late as 1948.

The journey raises some interesting questions. Why should it have been necessary to bring Baroness de Huene back from North Africa in the first place? Ireland, her destination, was hardly her home; and there was no sign that the Baroness' daughter came with her. And why should that enterprise have involved a visit to the British Prime Minister at Chequers? He would hardly have been involved in a straightforward mercy mission. But French North Africa would certainly have been a high-risk location for anyone the British government did not want to fall into Axis hands, for whatever reason; and the likeliest explanation is that the Baroness fell into this category.

'Baroness de Huene' is a French version of an essentially Baltic German name, correctly rendered as Baroness von Hoyingen-Huene. Given the situation in Europe, it is small wonder that the Baroness used a French adaptation of her name. Her title was Russian – in Germany, Baron would have been rendered Freiherr – and a Baron E. Th. Hoyingen-Huene had been a member of Nikolai II's Privy Council.[12] After the Revolution, the Hoyingen-Huene family had moved west and become integrated into Germany. Baron Oswald von Hoyingen-Huene joined the ranks of the German foreign ministry as a diplomat. By 1939 he was serving as German minister-resident in Portugal, and in 1940 he achieved momentary notoriety for his involvement in 'Operation Willi', the German plot to abduct the Duke of Windsor, willingly or otherwise, from Lisbon in neutral Portugal. Known for his Nazi links and sympathies, the former King was in open negotiations with the German government which were so far developed that Hitler had arranged to deposit fifty million Swiss francs for the Duke in Switzerland.[13] In outline, the German plan was that George VI would be deposed and Edward VIII would be restored to the throne, with Wallis Simpson at his side; Churchill would be deposed as Prime Minister and peace would be made with Germany. This was the agenda of the far right, in whose shadow Nikolai Chebotarev was obliged to move. Bearing a name like Hoyingen-Huene, the Baroness was bound to be of immediate interest to the Germans; in the event of an invasion of North Africa, she would have been deemed to be a German national and repatriated to Germany. Why, though, should Chamberlain and Couriss have involved themselves in the fate of an old German woman?

Perhaps a clue to the answer lies with Baron Oswald Hoyingen-Huene's employers. The German foreign ministry had certain policies which it had pursued ever since the days of the Kaiser and continued to pursue, regardless of the Nazi takeover in Berlin. One of these was the establishment of puppet regimes on the thrones of conquered territories, turning them into client states. The plan for the reinstatement of the Duke of Windsor as King was a case in point.[14] But there were other examples. In the summer of 1918 the Germans were discussing plans to marry Grand Duke Dmitri, Rasputin's murderer, to the Tsar's daughter Olga and make them sovereigns of the Ukraine under German protection.[15] According to her biographer James Blair Lovell, the Anastasia claimant, Anna Anderson, had been personally interviewed by Hitler.[16] Baroness de Huene's name coincided with that of the German minister in nearby Portugal; what else did he know about her? That minister was already involved with the implementation of the German foreign ministry's plan to restore fallen sovereigns under Nazi protection; and Baroness de Huene was called 'aunt' by the man who in the decade before this had been rumoured to be the Tsarevich Alexei.

Further questions are raised about the activities of the right-wingers around Chebotarev by a strange episode that occurred later during the Second World War, in June 1944. No one in her family could understand why Natalie Cooke, who liked her home comforts, suddenly agreed to submit herself to the discomforts of a small cottage with an outside toilet in Cushendall on the County Antrim coast, in the company of Baroness de Huene and Nikolai Chebotarev. The small property they rented, known as The Birdcage, comprised an old cottage with two former railway carriages in the garden that had been converted into art nouveau bedrooms. Mme Drinkwater, a local pianist of some renown, came to entertain them; they were also visited by the minister of Sinclair Seamen's Church in the shadow of the Belfast shipyard, for reasons which have remained obscure: Natalie Cooke was not known to frequent the company of clergy.[17] The garden of The Birdcage, beautifully kept with sub-tropical trees and carpet-soft lawns, ran right down to the sea. All the houses close by today have been built in the last twenty years or thereabouts; back in 1944 The Birdcage was in a particularly remote part of the village of Cushendall, just beyond the golf links. From it, there is an uninterrupted view of Garron Point, topped by Garron Tower, now a private school but then still owned by the local landowners, the Earls of Antrim. Angela, Countess of Antrim, Couriss' friend and Sykes's daughter, was the chatelaine of Glenarm, the nearby seat of a family which had ruled over the Glens of Antrim since the days of the Vikings.

The Birdcage had been owned by a Mrs Whan, who was a member of the Harland family of the Harland and Wolff shipyard in Belfast,[18] then engaged in wartime naval production. In her will Mrs Whan, an artist who owned and operated the local cinema, left the house to her gardener, Christopher McMullan. Surprisingly, when I tracked him down in 1995 he remembered the visit of this little party, even though it had been fifty-one years before and hundreds if not thousands of visitors from all over the world had stayed there since – for The Birdcage had always been let. He recalled the Russian playing golf on the green which peters out on to the beach and walking up and down the coastline incessantly. Today the sea looks peaceful, stretching out to Scotland only twelve miles away; but it was not so peaceful in 1944, for the North Channel was the principal approach to the Clyde estuary and the port of Glasgow, and was fertile hunting ground for German U-boats. Across the bay from The Birdcage is a flat-topped house which is still split from roof to foundations as a result of firing from a heavy machine gun mounted on the roof for action against these intruders.[19] Locals will still tell you how in 1916, in the First World War, the Germans had come ashore at nearby Ringfad, where the Spanish galleon the *Gerona* had met its watery fate some four hundred years earlier.

The recollections of one local, though, went further. James McCartney is a former police commander in the 'B Specials' and the respected retired local headmaster. According to him, Garron Point had been the site of German Kriegsmarine landings during the Second World War. Such was the confidence of the Germans that they drank in Hessie McNeill's pub on the waterfront in Cushendall. That confidence was well founded, for there was not a single military unit between Cushendall and Ballycastle on the north coast. Beyond Cushendall lay the glens of Antrim, stronghold of the Catholic Earls of Antrim and of the IRA, which had an active unit based there. Hessie McNeill's was a republican pub and no member of the security forces would have entered it. Only one Protestant drank there: a local Presbyterian minister, who was a romantic Irish nationalist, a hangover from the days of the Presbyterian radical tradition of the United Irishmen. And he had sorrows to drown, for his girlfriend, a Sunday-school teacher in Belfast, had been arrested and imprisoned by the RUC for printing *An Poblacht*, the banned newspaper of the IRA, in her home. Here, secure in the middle of a no-go area for crown forces, the Germans could slake their thirst and obtain fresh provisions, including sides of bacon.[20]

To the north of Cushendall lay the radar station at Torr Head, Glenarm. Its commander was Flight Lieutenant E. Lavington, who had stayed at Moyallon House when Nikolai Chebotarev was living there in 1940.[21] According to Zoe Cooke, who was in the WRNS and stationed at Glenarm, the effectiveness of the radar was limited because of the configuration of the Antrim coastline southwards to Belfast: U-boats hugging the shoreline could move up and down the coast with comparative ease. In the early days of the war the RDF radar at Glenarm could only detect surface craft in any case: PTI radar was installed only at Downhill on the north coast to defend the approaches to the port of Londonderry.[22] Thus Belfast was not only totally undefended against air attack, despite its major shipbuilding and air production facilities, but was poorly protected against maritime incursions as well. Red Bay near Cushendall was the mustering point for all escort ships for convoy duty, and cargo boats lay at anchor waiting for escorts there. It was a perfect location to spy on shipping and to relay messages to waiting submarines. Forewarned by Commander Kilgour of the coastguard, McCartney himself intercepted morse code signals passing between the shore and the sea, and was involved in the arrest of an IRA radio operator active in the area. McCartney also confirmed that he was watching the Countess of Antrim but couldn't touch her because of her high social standing.[23] If, as seems likely, communication was taking place between the Germans offshore and their sympathizers onshore, that communication need not have been restricted to shipping; in fact, it would be surprising if that was all they talked about.

Understandably, in the tradition of Irish republicanism the IRA saw Britain's difficulty as Ireland's opportunity. When the German spy Hermann Goertz parachuted into Ireland he was sheltered at Laragh in County Wicklow in the home of Iseult Stuart, the sister of Sean MacBride, chief of staff of the IRA. For a year and a half Goertz operated openly, even going to parties at the German ambassador's house.[24] The Stuarts had originally met Goertz when they were living in Germany, where Iseult's husband Francis was a lecturer at Berlin University.[25] Nor was co-operation with the Nazis solely a marriage of convenience. From January 1943, Francis Stuart broadcast anti-British propaganda to his fellow countrymen in his radio programme *Through Irish Eyes* from the same studio as the infamous Lord Haw-Haw – himself an Irishman, William Joyce.[26] Speaking in 1997, Francis Stuart still maintained that 'the Jew was always the worm that got into the rose and sickened it'.[27] In 1947, after Germany's defeat, Hermann Goertz committed suicide rather than face a war crimes trial at Nuremberg; Irish republicans formed a guard of honour around the swastika-draped coffin at his funeral.

Liaison between the Nazis and Irish republicans was overseen by Dr Edmund Weissenmeyer, Hitler's minister for nationalist movements – which included, of course, the IRA. Weissenmeyer ran a network of spies in Ireland which co-operated with the IRA. Contacts with the Nazis had been built up in the 1930s by Helmut Clissman, a German student in Dublin who married IRA activist Elizabeth Mulcahy, daughter of a Sinn Fein judge, and acted as the German military intelligence expert on the IRA during the war.[28] SS Major Henning Thomson, working from the German embassy at 58 Northumberland Road, Dublin, collated all useful information gathered by IRA volunteers on potential targets, bomb damage and civilian morale in Northern Ireland.[29] Jim O'Donovan was invited to Germany to cement relations between the Abwehr, German military intelligence run by Admiral Canaris, and the IRA. In 1942 Sean Russell, MacBride's successor as chief of staff of the IRA, died on board a submarine which was about to land him on the Dingle peninsula. Russell was returning from a meeting with Ribbentrop where he had signed an agreement to head up Operation Pigeon, in which the IRA, equipped with German arms and explosives, would have become the Nazis' fifth column in Northern Ireland. Roisin ni Meara Vinard, who worked for the Nazis in their Irish broadcasting service in the Rundfunkhaus in Berlin, was appointed by the Germans along with Francis Stuart to conduct an investigation into Russell's death. They found that no medical examination had been carried out on the body – there was no one on the submarine to conduct it – and that the body had been buried at sea. The Germans believed Russell had been poisoned; Roisin ni Meara Vinard ascribes the act to British intelligence.[30]

Thus a peculiar congruence of interest emerged between militant Irish republicanism and the pro-German upper reaches of the British aristocracy, otherwise linked only by the themes of extreme right-wing nationalism; and the man who lived in both worlds was Nikolai Couriss. Couriss himself was a close friend of Sean MacBride. Kathleen McCarthy remembers MacBride visiting the house,[31] but it was a friendship Couriss kept hidden from his Anglo-Irish, Protestant Ascendancy friends; Henry St George Smith was visibly shocked when he heard of it. We have already seen that the connections of Angela, Countess of

Antrim, included Sir Percy Loraine and his wife, and that she regularly visited Couriss in Collon; and Kathleen McCarthy told of the visits that Lord Londonderry made to Couriss in Collon, where he was simply known by his name, shorn of all titles: Charlie Stewart.[32] Collon today is a quiet, sleepy village; but it was not always so. As in all the territories near the Irish border, which in 1940 was less than twenty years old, the loss of the six counties of Ulster which became Northern Ireland was keenly felt. Republican sentiment was entirely understandable and patriotic. Two of the leaders of the 1916 Rising, still lionized as heroes in the South, were from Collon. As recently as 1956, according to Northern intelligence sources, it was the site of an IRA training camp where German ex-officers put IRA volunteers through their paces. It was here that Nikolai Couriss chose to live: in the Old Court House, well positioned in the centre of a staunch nationalist community.

Couriss had his own connections at a high level in Nazi Germany. He had spent a year in Germany in 1923–4, at the height of the right-wing Freikorps agitation, when Hitler led his beer-cellar putsch; and he was well acquainted with General Piotr Krasnov, one of many White Russian exiles who became embroiled in Nazi politics. General Krasnov, whose wife had lived with Sister Chebotarev when he was leading anti-Bolshevik forces in 1917, went further than most, becoming the commander of the Cossack division of the SS.[33] In 1946 Krasnov and his Cossack SS men were repatriated from an internment camp at Spittal in Austria to almost certain execution in Soviet Russia. In the 1920s General Krasnov had been a fervent supporter of the claim of Grand Duke Nikolai to the Russian throne; as noted in chapter 13, for a time he lived in the gate lodge of Nikolasha's castle in Santény in France.[34] For many dispossessed Russians like Krasnov, Hitler's Germany seemed to offer the best prospect for overthrowing the hated Communist yoke in their own country.

So what exactly was going on in Cushendall in June 1944? A cottage right by the sea, with an uninterrupted view of Garron Point where German landings were alleged to have taken place; a gardener, a glensman from that remote and splendidly picturesque area with active IRA sympathies, who remembers the people who rented a holiday cottage over half a century ago; an active IRA unit in the glens of Antrim; onshore communication with German U-boats; a Baroness with the same name as the German minister in Portugal who was part of a plot to kidnap the Duke of Windsor; a Countess with extreme right-wing connections and links to Couriss, himself known to be closely connected with the high-ranking members of both the IRA and the Nazis; what does it all add up to?

Enough, certainly, to ensure that Irish military intelligence, the 'G men', were keeping an eye on the inhabitants of the Old Court House. Prince Alexander Lieven, a Collon resident, was under surveillance as a student at Trinity College, Dublin. 'Prince Alexander Lieven, believed to be a Romanian is known to frequent Dublin docks in the early morning hours,' ran the report. 'Anything additional on this bird?' was the scrawled comment.[35] Whether he was in search of pleasure or on more serious business is never disclosed. Lieven went on to join the RAF after graduation. Couriss presents a similarly complex picture. An appeal had gone out for those able to speak Russian and English to come forward, and in 1943 Couriss volunteered to join the Red Army as an interpreter.[36] In the event, they turned him down because of a duodenal ulcer. Conversely, some locals believe Couriss was a Nazi and wanted Hitler to win. So which side was he on? The answer is probably both, and neither. For him, it was a case of survival. To a dispossessed émigré, ethics were a luxury; allegiance and action alike had to be tailored to circumstances and situations. Zoe Cooke believed Couriss was certainly a double agent, maybe even a triple agent. For their part, the IRA and the Germans may well have felt he was serving their cause. Conversely, the British may have used him to help control the IRA who, after all, did not have any military successes during the war. The British may have known exactly what supplies they had and what they were doing. We do well to recall Couriss' background as a gun-runner. And there is yet another take on Couriss: after the war, the American CIA saw Collon as another British security disaster, a hotbed of Russian espionage. The jury is still out on this.

The closest insight we are ever likely to get into Couriss' mind is that offered by his devoted housekeeper, Kathleen McCarthy. For Couriss, Kathleen had become a kind of replacement for his beloved son Ilya who had died so tragically of polio in 1934; in fact, Couriss thought so much of Kathleen that he wanted to leave his house to her. Kathleen knew his mind. She believes there was 'a big game going on'. 'Nick Couriss', she says, 'was leading them all a merry dance.'[37]

## ～ 15 ～

# The Irish Years

It was through Moyallon House that I had first been introduced to the
'Russian prince', and in Ireland that the roots of the mystery of my
parenthood lay. Naturally, then, I had a particular interest in what might
be termed the Irish phase of Nikolai Chebotarev's life, which lasted from
about 1929 until 1946. Though he came back on various occasions later,
it was during those years that his most intense association with Ireland
occurred. This association was dominated by two women, both of whom
had a major impact on his life but neither of whom was in any sense
romantically attached to him: Hilda Wakefield Richardson and Natalie
Karaulov Cooke. From 1929 he began to spend large parts of each year
in Hilda's manor house at Moyallon, and from 1939 to 1942 he lived
there entirely. After Hilda's death in 1942, he lived for the following four
years at Croft House in Holywood, the home of Natalie Cooke. Both
women have appeared at various points in the story so far. Now the time
has come to take a closer look at them and to understand what, if anything, they tell us about the man said to be the Tsarevich.

Hilda Wakefield Richardson was a wealthy Quaker widow whose
husband had either fallen off a balcony or committed suicide – no one
is sure which – in 1923. Following this tragedy Hilda, having no children, threw herself into Russian relief work in Paris. Precisely why and
how she came to do this remains a mystery. As with everything else
she undertook, this relief work had strong religious overtones: the home
she founded for Russian refugees in the French capital was known as
the 'Wakefield Maison de l'Evangile' and in 1936 she installed a resident
Welsh evangelist there, with the suitably sonorous name of Dewi Gyn-
fryn Lintern.[1] Yet how far her religious practice was a reflection of
genuine faith and how far a performance from a well-worn script is open
to doubt. Albert Uprichard, one of Chebotarev's riding companions at
Moyallon, was sure religion was an act for Hilda, a performance turned
on and off at will as from a tap. Those around her tolerated it because she
was a *grande dame*, a formidable personality it was best not to cross,

*Top left* Moyallon House today

*Top right* Chebotarev (left) at Moyallon with Stella Dalziel, Peggy Sinton and Hugh Richardson

*Centre* Chebotarev (right) with Stella Dalziel and Serge Aitov, 1937

*Right* Chebotarev (standing, second left), Moyallon, 1937. Hilda Richardson is seated, front right; Peggy Sinton is standing, left

Davos 2/ii 1938. KB1082

FRances and Tham
Laseo Bradley
A and Olga Knoop.

*Above* Chebotarev (second left) at Davos, February 1938

*Left* The inscription in Chebotarev's hand on the back of the photograph; he refers to himself as A

*Below* Chebotarev (left) riding with Serge Aitov, Moyallon, 1937

Chebotarev's effects (see p. 197): the Knight Commander's Cross of the Danish Order of the Dannebrog; a silk handkerchief in the imperial colours; a late nineteenth-century Russian gold wirework cross, which used to hang above his bed

*Above* Grand Duchess Ella, the Tsarina's sister; Chebotarev kept this photograph at his bedside all his life

*Right* Hilda Richardson

*Above* Chebotarev with the Baroness
Hoyingen-Huene. She lived with him in
Paris, Moyallon and Croft House

*Below* The page from Couriss'
notebook referring to his visit to
Chequers and North Africa
(see p. 172)

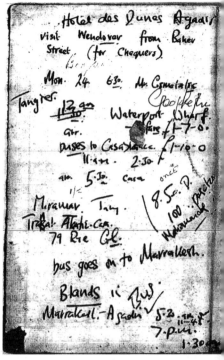

*Below* Croft House, Holywood, near Bangor,
home of Natalie Cooke. Demolished in 1996

The handbag pictures: *Above* Michael Gray as a baby with Countess Martha Apraxine and Prince Alexander Lieven  *Below* With Countess Apraxine  *Right* In front of a fountain believed to be at Clandeboye, home of Maureen Guinness

*Right* From the Gray album: the author with Beatrice McCutcheon, a Gray neighbour

*Above left* The building in Bangor that housed Dr Bowman's surgery, opposite Ward Park and the clinic

*Above right* The clinic today: 'I remembered a building whose walls sloped outwards'

*Left* Natalie Cooke's house from September 1948, Princeton Road, Bangor

*Below* The old forge building at Castlebellingham

*Above* Marina (left, in pushchair) and
Alexei (centre), Germany, 1910

*Above* The Tsar and Marina's
mother, Grand Duchess Helen,
Peterhof 1912

*Left* The Tsar and Marina's father,
Prince Nicholas of Greece, 1899

*Above* Chebotarev at Oyster Bay, 1947
*Top right* Marina's cousin Princess Xenia
Romanov; the inscription on the back
reads: 'To Kolya, the big boy now . . .'
*Right* Brooch found at Croft House. Note
the Kent coronet   *Below* Princess Marina
at Windsor Horse Show, July 1947; the
photograph identified by two of the Croft
House servants as 'Mme Velika'   *Bottom
right* Prince Edward of Kent (the present
Duke) as 'Bonny Socialist Baby', *Daily
Mail*, 2 February 1949

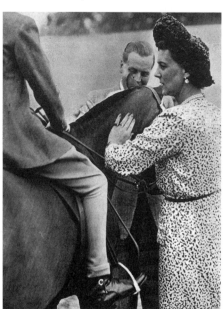

participation in the prescribed observances a necessary accompaniment to enjoyment of her largesse.[2] Attendance at the Sunday evening meet-ings in the garden room of Moyallon House was *de rigueur*, for Nikolai as for everyone else. Mrs Milburn-Fryar still recalls how, as Peggy Sinton, she giggled with him behind Hilda's back,[3] and Natalie Cooke's daughter Zoe remembers him, as Hilda preached from her bed, winking and whispering to her, 'I see the light of faith in your eyes.'[4] Hilda was without doubt a significant and forceful personality, and a consummate actress to boot. Zoe Cooke, who stayed at Moyallon in 1939 and 1940, said of Hilda, 'She was an embarrassing person to be around. In Brand's [a smart Belfast department store] she would announce: "I am a Richard-son, I do not pay."'[5] Iya Zmeova, Chebotarev's niece, who stayed at Moyallon in 1937, described how Hilda would throw sweets at bare-footed children from her chauffeur-driven car as they drove to visit her Airth Richardson relatives in Lisburn.

Hilda, with her sense of *noblesse oblige* and her conviction of the importance of her own status, offered Nikolai a taste of the life he had left behind in Russia. For ten years, winters meant Paris, summers meant Moyallon. Dinner was a black-tie affair, with a glistening samovar boil-ing in the corner of the opulent dining room. Walks were taken on mani-cured lawns; servants were on hand to attend to every need – there was even a chauffeur at Nikolai's disposal and Hilda's smart open-top white Alvis Silver Eagle to ride in. Bertie Mitchell still speaks dreamily of this powerful machine. And there was company. Anxious that Nikolai should not be bored, Hilda introduced him to the best available local girls – Peggy, daughter of her nearby landed neighbours, the Sintons, and the delightful Stella Dalziel, Peggy's friend from her exclusive school at St Leonards. Lazy summer days on the croquet lawn, picnics at Clogherhead on the coast near Couriss' home in County Louth, the splendid rolling County Down countryside to ride over, slipping out to a dance in Belfast in the Alvis after Hilda had retired to bed – life was idyllic. Locals saw the dinner guests in full evening attire walking down the great driveway of the house to take the air. Stella recalls Nikolai's skilful playing of the balalaika – a talent for which the Tsarevich Alexei was known – and how he would burst into song as he played.

For Hilda, Nikolai was the Prince; all the locals knew him as that. In 1933 Mrs Richardson hosted the wedding reception of the evangelist John W. Kingston at Moyallon House. In the account of his own wed-ding given by the Revd Kingston in his book *These Miracles Did Jesus in*

*Ireland*, the churchman makes particular mention among the guests of 'Prince Nicholas of Russia . . . who left nothing undone to make the happy occasion memorable'.[6] He was someone set apart, someone to be looked up to – and looked after. Maureen Hill, after all, had told me how, when Mrs Richardson delivered him to the Uprichards, on the neighbouring landed estate, for an afternoon's riding, she had cautioned them that on no account must Nikolai be allowed to sustain a fall. She gave the impression of someone entrusted with an important charge, his care a binding duty to be performed at all costs. Perhaps she thought she had a haemophiliac on her hands – certainly some of the locals and even members of the Richardson family believed this. Her guest was, after all, the man rumoured to be the Tsarevich.

Nikolai was not alone in the Russian coterie gathered about Hilda in being more than he seemed, certainly to the uncomprehending eyes of the locals. The Russians at Moyallon, and at the Couriss household in Collon, included members of the Romanov family – more than were immediately apparent from a glance at the names in the visitors' book. Among the other guests was Countess Natalie Kleinmichel, who stayed at Moyallon in July 1936 and again in July and August 1937, with her companion Catherine Takronzov, who also lived with her in Paris at 33 rue de la Tourelle, Boulogne-sur-Seine. Natalie or 'Tata' Kleinmichel had been born in 1890 and died, a centenarian, as recently as 1990.[7] Not only did she belong to a distinguished Russian family on its own account, she was in fact an illegitimate Romanov since her father, Count Constantine Kleinmichel, was the natural son of Tsar Nikolai I. Count Vladimir Kleinmichel, the executor of the will of the Tsar's sister Grand Duchess Xenia who died in London in 1960, was her cousin.[8] In her own will, Hilda Richardson bequeathed £500 to Countess Kleinmichel; she also left £1,000 to Nikolai Chebotarev, an amount she amended in a codicil dated later the same day, adding a further £1,000 to be invested for him. The date was 12 August 1942. It was the Tsarevich's thirty-eighth birthday.[9]

A closer look at Hilda's finances shows that her financial relationship with Nikolai Chebotarev may have been quite different from how it was perceived at the time. On the face of it, she seems to have been most generous to the young émigré. He first started coming to Moyallon in 1929 – that much we know from Maureen Hill, though he does not appear in the visitors' book until 1931. In a letter of 18 March 1943, at which point he was engaged in the humiliating experience of trying to squeeze money out of Hilda's executors, Nikolai asserted that 'he had given up his right to work in France from about 1932 and in consequence Mrs Richardson had allowed him £240 per annum'.[10] Two hundred and forty pounds would not come remotely close to sustaining Nikolai's lifestyle, even at 1932 values. Hilda left £42,000 in her will in property and bequests – a sum almost identical to that left to her by her husband in his 1916 will. As she brought no money into her marriage, this represents a triumph of prudence, especially in someone known for a lavish style of life. In 1936 Hilda received a letter from her bank manager telling her that she was overdrawn; since she passed her own capital on largely intact, this suggests that there had been an external source of funds which had suddenly dried up. Her first response, to tell the bank manager to liquidate capital, was patently unrealistic since the Richardson estate was an entailed trust, with beneficiaries having only a lifetime interest and no access to capital. So Hilda made – for someone in her position – drastic savings: the number of gardeners, for example, fell from nine to two.[11] What had happened?

December 1935 and January 1936 saw two deaths in rapid succession in the British royal family: first that of Princess Victoria, George V's sister, to whom he was particularly close; then that of the King himself. Both these individuals had close personal ties to the Romanovs, ties which their younger relatives simply could not have developed. Princess Victoria, or 'Toria' as she was known in the family, had been the Tsar's childhood sweetheart; George V was his cousin and friend, and the two were strikingly alike in appearance. Then, within a year of these deaths, the British monarchy underwent an unprecedented crisis and King George V's eldest son and successor, declining to relinquish his attachment to Wallis Simpson, was compelled to abdicate. This unforeseen event had a major impact on royal finances. As Prince of Wales, the future Edward VIII had accumulated a great deal of money from the Duchy of Cornwall estates; when he left the throne and the country, he took £800,000 abroad with him. George V had left each of his younger sons, including the new King, £50,000; but that did not resolve the issue of what was to happen to the private royal properties of Balmoral and Sandringham, indissolubly linked in the public mind with the monarchy but now owned by the man who had renounced it. In consequence, when George VI acceded to his brother's throne, he had to purchase the two residences from the new Duke of Windsor: this was effected under an arrangement by which the properties were valued and the interest on this capital sum paid as an annual income by the new King to the former monarch. Needless to say, this resulted in the new King being comparatively hard up for the first few years of his reign.[12]

If members of the Romanov family had survived, and if George V through the Trust of Kings had colluded in their departure from Russia, as suggested in chapter 11, then it would have been entirely logical for some of the Romanov funds abroad to be quietly transferred to the King, and for pensions to have been paid to the surviving Romanovs from these sums. George V was alive and had a legal identity, whereas the Romanovs, presumed to be dead, could hardly claim their own money – certainly not without breaking cover. The events of 1936, however, would have put an abrupt end to any such payments. For one thing, such discreet arrangements would hardly be mentioned in any royal will, even if unpublished. For another, King Edward VIII was unreliable at the best of times; he had no personal connection with or loyalty towards his Russian relatives, and when he lost his throne he became notoriously penny-pinching. He could hardly be expected to honour some private arrangement of the father he despised. And for a third, King George VI, saddled with a status he had never sought and the substantial expense of funding his errant brother, was desperate for cash and unlikely to be in a magnanimous mood. Indeed, any unattributed sums lying about unclaimed would no doubt have been gratefully sucked into the royal purse, any expendable pension payments seen as a useful area of economy.

The recovery of the British royal finances since 1936 has been truly remarkable and is hard to explain without recourse to some major outside source of capital. Even ignoring the outgoings on the Duke of Windsor's pension to offset the acquisition of Balmoral and Sandringham and assuming a rate of growth at 10 per cent each year, which far exceeds likely returns in the 1940s, and with no tax being paid following the terms of the 1916 agreement between George V and the government, the King's initial £50,000 would have grown to just £15.9 million by 1997. Allowing for an annual addition of £32,000, which were the average savings Edward VIII as Prince of Wales had been able to make between 1911 and 1936, the final sum would only be £26.08 million. Yet the present Queen's estimated personal fortune vastly exceeds this amount. Andrew Morton conservatively estimated the Queen's shareholding portfolio alone at £496 million in 1992, almost twenty times this figure.[13] By itself, that suggests the injection of capital from outside

King George VI's patrimony and likely savings. Where could such money have come from? Certainly not through marriage – Prince Philip was penniless.

In 1958 Anthony Sampson, then editor of the *Observer*, quizzed Baring's Bank about Romanov deposits in their keeping. He was informed that they amounted to £40 million in gold on deposit, and that any Romanov heir with proof of identity could claim this money.[14] This statement has never been denied or retracted; but when Baring's Bank crashed in 1996 £40 million was precisely the amount quoted as the Queen's holding. It may well have been the case that the Windsors took control of Romanov assets, and without touching the capital enriched themselves with the interest that accumulated over the years. In return, small pensions – bearing no relation to the scale of the wealth thus appropriated or accessed – may have been paid out to Romanov survivors who had lost their legal identity and were living incognito under British royal protection, if not necessarily in Britain all of the time.

As a guide to what is most likely to have happened, we may turn to the transactions between the House of Windsor and some known Romanov survivors: the Dowager Empress, the Tsar's mother – George V's beloved 'Aunt Minnie' – and her daughters Xenia and Olga. In 1924, in return for a modest (by royal standards) pension of £10,000 a year, paid not from his own resources but from parliamentary grant, King George V effectively made himself heir to the old Empress.[15] He did not have long to wait. In 1928, by which time he had paid out less than £40,000, his aunt died at the Villa Hvidore in Denmark. Seizing the opportunity, Sir Edward Peacock, Governor of the Bank of England, Sir Frederick Ponsonby, Keeper of the Privy Purse, and Sir Peter Bark, the Tsar's former finance minister, now managing director of the Anglo-International Bank and knighted by George V, presented themselves at the house and, before the hapless Olga realized what was happening, simply removed the box containing the late Empress' jewels from under her bed, and took it back to Buckingham Palace. Peacock himself estimated the value of the jewels at £350,000 – not a bad return on an outlay of less than £40,000 over a four-year period. William Clarke, the most recent expounder of the Windsor position, explains the difference between the £100,000 received by Grand Duchesses Xenia and Olga in 1929 and the £350,000 Ponsonby said they received as a lapse of memory on the part of the latter.[16] This is a rather large memory lapse for a Keeper of the Privy Purse to have made. Even stranger is the fact that Hennells, the jewellers who valued the items in the Empress' box, have no record of £100,000 ever having been paid out. (See Appendix, 'The Windsors and the Money'.)

Considering Chebotarev's position in the context of these known and surmised circumstances, it is entirely credible that he may have received a pension, albeit a small one by royal standards, paid for a time through Hilda Richardson; and that in the financial upheaval that followed upon the death of King George V, without the protection of a formal identity and a recorded arrangement, the influx of funds ceased. Of course, if he had been supported in this way by the British royal family, they at least must have been convinced of his true identity.

Chebotarev certainly did not behave like a man anxious about where his livelihood was to come from. Indeed, the Aitovs, friends in Paris, could not understand why he never felt the need to work.[17] In Helene Aitov's words a 'perfectly well educated man of the nineteenth century', he showed no sign of pursuing a career. After a year at the Sorbonne studying physics, chemistry and biology, he worked as a *préparateur* in a chemist's shop on the avenue Henri Martin (it is still there). He stayed for only three months. Yet in Moyallon servants spoke of his having a wardrobe stretching the entire length of a wall filled with the best of clothes from Paris. Hester Sterritt, who entered service in Moyallon as an eighteen-year-old maid in 1940, remembers having to clean his shoes – all thirty-two pairs of them. And Nikolai was always in the height of fashion. Albert Uprichard spoke of the Russian having the latest in riding gear, while Stella Dalziel recalled his monogrammed shirts and their evenings at the fashionable gypsy retaurants in London – 'and those places didn't come cheap,' she added. Chebotarev was clearly getting money from somewhere.[18]

Some time before Hilda's death in 1942 Nikolai and his 'aunt' Baroness de Huene had begun to spend increasing amounts of time at Croft House in Holywood, home of Natalie Cooke, and by August that year he was a more or less full-time resident there. Natalie's daughter Zoe believes that Nikolai and the Baroness became bored with Moyallon. The war had put an end to house parties, and the ageing Hilda was showing signs of dementia. Zoe recalled the surreal spectacle of Hilda descending the main staircase in Moyallon on a Thursday, her maid's day off, with only half her face made up. At dinner, instead of taking her place at table, Hilda sat on the floor, helping herself to the dog's food, and they had great difficulty in getting her up, while at the top of the stairs Mme Block whined for her semolina, the only food she would eat.[19] But there was more to Nikolai's departure than the degeneration of a formerly glittering household. Shortly after his arrival in Moyallon on 8 May 1939, an incident occurred which he seems to have taken as a warning that he was not entirely safe there.

In June 1939 Nikolai had a serious fall from his horse, as a result of which he was forced to wear a steel corset for a time and his back troubled him for the rest of his life. Alix Hill maintained that the only time she saw Nikolai Chebotarev speaking with venom, even hatred, in his voice was over this incident. He blamed it, she said, on 'a snake in the grass'.[20] He was speaking figuratively, of course, for there are no snakes in Ireland – a biological felicity attributed to St Patrick. Local people were told the horse had shied after a swan rose up out of the water of the canal near Moyallon: but Nikolai himself explicitly denied this.

Zoe Cooke was adamant that the fall did not happen at Moyallon, as locals said.[21] Nikolai had told her that it happened at Montalto, the estate of the 5th Earl of Clanwilliam in County Down. Where it did occur is important, and throws light on its possible causes. The Clanwilliams had a long, close and many-faceted association with the British royal family. Lord Clanwilliam's brother, Admiral Sir Herbert Meade-Featherstonhaugh, had been naval ADC to King George V and was first and foremost a royal servant, used to acting on the King's behalf. The Admiral's wife was the daughter of Bishop Carr-Glyn, a friend of George V, a royal chaplain and chaplain of the Venerable Order of St John of Jerusalem, and a relative of Thomas Preston, the British consul in Ekaterinburg in 1918.[22] One of the 5th Earl's sisters was lady in waiting to the Duchess of York, who by 1939 was the Queen, while another was married to Sir Stanley Colville, the uncle of the present Queen's private secretary from 1947 to 1949. It made perfect sense for Nikolai Chebotarev to be entertained by the Clanwilliams, since they had been regular guests at Small Downs, the home of Hilda's sister-in-law in the 1920s, along with Hilda herself and the Macnaghten sisters. But at Montalto, Nikolai was in the hands of people who owed their duty and loyalty exclusively to the British crown.

One individual who was probably at Montalto at the time of Chebotarev's fall had particular grounds in his own mind for animosity towards the Russian. This was Stephens Richardson, the heir to Moyallon, who had consolidated his position in the family by marrying

Wakefield's sister. He and Hilda hated each other. Servants recall them shouting at each other and fists being shaken.[23] Helene Aitov still laughs at the angry arguments between these 'two holy roller Quakers', as she calls them.[24] Zoe had an intense dislike of Stephens, whom she regarded as a lecher and as a fake evangelical who used his religion to cloak his activities with women. He certainly had a well-advertised affair with the village postmistress, Ellen Heathwood, to whom he left a substantial sum in his will.[25] Stephens Richardson disliked the Russians, whom he saw as squandering his wife's inheritance. As we have seen, he could not have been more wrong; Hilda left the bulk of her money intact, and bequeathed it to her own family. Nevertheless, Stephens Richardson perceived the Russians as parasites who threatened his future; and Chebotarev was one of them.

In June 1939 a religious group was holding a summer camp in the grounds of Montalto House. A photograph of the group which appeared in the *Belfast News Letter* did not include Stephens Richardson; but on 23 June 1939 Buckingham Palace replied to a telegram sent by him on behalf of the group. Signed by the King's private secretary, Alexander Hardinge, this message thanked Richardson for his loyal address on the King's return from Canada. So Stephens Richardson may well have been at Montalto at the time of Nikolai's fall. The telegram is disquieting; an odd missive from a religious group. Was the telegram a coded communication? And what exactly constituted the act of loyalty in the address?

But Richardson is not the only possible perpetrator of Nikolai's mishap. Other former subjects of Tsar Nikolai II had moved into the area. These included Jacob Shanik, a Jew from Minsk in Belorussia, and his partners the Blocks, who established a lace-making business in Portadown.[26] It appears a strange coincidence that two families called Block should settle at the same time in a small and very provincial town of only sixteen thousand people. The other Block – Carlotta – arrived for the duration of the war on the same day as Nikolai Chebotarev in 1939 and had been a frequent guest of Hilda Richardson in the 1930s.[27] We cannot establish whether or not there was a relationship between her and the lace-making Block family, since after nearly sixty years the files on aliens arriving in Northern Ireland at this period remain resolutely closed – not even in the Public Record Office but in the vaults of Stormont Castle.

Covering a time when the Soviet NKVD were using the massive movement of population occasioned by Hitler's terrorism in Europe as a cover for introducing 'sleepers' into Western countries, these files would provide interesting reading. After all, this was the period of Stalin's purges. Trotsky, who apart from his other perceived sins may have known in some detail about the departure of the Romanovs from Russia, was brutally done to death with an axe by Stalin's henchmen in Mexico City in 1940. Within Russia in 1938 the widow of Colonel Koblinsky, the sympathetic guard commander of the imperial family at Tobolsk, was closely questioned by the NKVD about all that had happened there and some missing Romanov jewels. Also in 1938 Yakovlev, the commissar who had conducted the Tsar to Ekaterinburg, was liquidated in a labour camp. A great many cases connected with the Romanovs were being terminally and definitively closed by the Russian secret police at this time.

Natalie Cooke, in whose home Nikolai and Baroness de Huene lived from 1942 to 1946, was a very different hostess from Hilda Richardson – indeed, it is difficult to imagine two people less like each other. Even the formidable Hilda herself held Natalie in some awe. Moyallon servants Hester and Netta Sterritt say that when Mrs Cooke came to visit everyone was on their best behaviour, and she was given the best bedroom in the house, with the four-poster bed.[28] Natalie was born Natalia Karaulov in 1897, the descendant of an old Tartar family tracing its roots to Prince Ivan Karagoul of the Golden Horde. Converting to Orthodoxy in 1505 and Russianizing his name, he became the progenitor of a line that produced an admiral for Catherine the Great and Natalie Karaulov herself.[29] Natalie's father, Mikhail Karaulov, was a friend of Kerensky and a minister in his government in 1917. He was also the Ataman of the Terek Cossacks, in which role his immediate predecessor was Prince Trubetskoye.[30] He was killed by his own men near Taganrog in southern Russia when returning from addressing a political meeting. The Princes Karakine, one of Russia's oldest boyar families, were Natalie's cousins. On her engagement to Northern Irish businessman Frank Cooke, Natalie's grandfather Jean Karaulov, the marshal of the nobility of Tver province and a friend of Kerensky, insisted that she get rid of the silver cigarette case she had bought her fiancé, Frank, and replaced it with one of Fabergé's best. It is still in the family. Rents from the Karaulov estate stopped abruptly in 1920. After that, Natalie swore to spend every penny her husband had.[31]

Natalie's marriage to an Ulsterman, which took place in 1915 in the British embassy in St Petersburg, was not so unusual a match as it may sound. Ulster linen merchants were attracted to Russia as a source of cheap flax. A Richardson cousin of Hilda's husband had married Baron von Gravenitz, one of the Baltic Germans who were so plentiful at the imperial court, in 1914 just before war had broken out.[32] Like every other occasion in her life, Natalie's wedding resounded with melodrama – the guest list, headed by Robert Bruce Lockhart himself, reads like a spies' convention. Cooke's best man, Natalie's cousin Freddie Hill, worked for Lockhart and ended up with him in the Lubianka.[33] Freddie was the brother of Dame Elizabeth Hill, the Cambridge professor who sent students to Couriss' language school at Collon. And Freddie and Elizabeth were the cousins of George Hill, Colonel Joe Boyle's deputy.

Natalie, a member of the decadent smart set of the monarchy's declining years, one of the sensation-seeking bright young things of pre-revolutionary St Petersburg high society, was an overstated extrovert, a woman so fundamentally out of control that nothing about her could ever be described as normal. Her first love, a sculptor who perished during the Revolution, was the adopted son of her great-uncle Prince Esper Ukhtomsky, the Tsar's adviser on Far Eastern affairs. Prince Ukhtomsky was also the notorious Dr Badmaev's sponsor, a connection which almost certainly produced the drug habit which persisted well into Natalie's middle age and probably beyond. According to her daughter Zoe, in the 1940s Natalie had organized her supplies through a tame doctor, Hector Northey, who obtained the drugs from his chemist brother in Belfast city centre. Zoe also said that during the Second World War Natalie had come close to being prosecuted for importing drugs.[34]

For so extravagant a character as Natalie, life in dour Ulster was hardly congenial; nor, after a while, was her marriage. In the early 1920s she frequented the louche night spots of London with her partner, the celebrated band leader Victor Silvester, and their friends, among them the scandalous Edwina Mountbatten and her lover, the black singer Hutch. Eventually separating from Frank, she took several flats in Paris – in rue Boucicault, rue de la Convention and rue de la Pompe. There her princely cousins, the Karakines, often came; her aunt, Princess Elizabeth Karakine, down on her luck and living in the 'cold water' district of Paris, visited for a bath once a week.[35] Summers were spent at the then fashionable French resort of La Palmyre. When war loomed in 1938, Natalie returned to Ulster, trailing in her wake the daughter she kept with her only for the sake of the generous allowance which her father gave her and which Natalie kept and spent on herself. Her cousin, Nina Berberova, later a professor at Princeton University, was left in charge of her flat while the Nazis ruled Paris. Frank was not overjoyed at Natalie's return to Ireland and promptly moved out to his club.

When Nikolai and the Baroness first arrived at Croft House, some time in early 1942, life still retained some semblance of normality. The household ran itself under the eagle eye of the spinster housekeeper Miss P. Herd, who harboured a secret passion for Frank. Frank, however, liked them younger and was seen with a string of young secretaries on his arm – to his daughter's considerable embarrassment when she met her father thus accompanied in Belfast's Grand Central Hotel. Bridie Gorman in the kitchen was capable, and people were regularly fed, but not in Natalie's presence. She refused to leave her room and ate in there, stealing other people's rations as a matter of course, and brewing up the most bizarre concoctions of food, all of which contained chocolate.

The *ménage* had its lighter moments. Mollie, the pretty maid, described as 'Marie Antoinette' by Nikolai, brought the house down below stairs when she tried on a pair of the Baroness's white pantaloon bloomers which had seen service in another age. As the war went on, it became hard to distinguish levity from black farce. Zoe, serving in the WRNS at Belfast Castle, from where she saw the German bombs rain down on the city, returned home on one occasion to discover all the inhabitants huddled in the air raid shelter with a goat tethered to the chain of the outside lavatory running wildly up and down, flushing the toilet each time. The Baroness had a particular horror of aerial bombing, which is not altogether surprising since a German parachute bomb actually landed in the garden of Croft House and nearby Bangor had part of its main street demolished. On one occasion the Baroness ran away, to be found, disorientated, at the railway station trying to escape.[36]

Disorder did not come to Natalie with war, however; her life had been full of it, quite apart from drugs. In Paris she kept a ballet-dancer lover who proposed marriage after Frank's death but vanished when he learned that there was no money coming with his bride-to-be. Her cat Hicks was named after a British officer in Paris with whom she had an affair. Zoe, with great frankness, told how Natalie had no fewer than three abortions while mother and daughter were living together in Paris, between 1928 and 1938. In the early war years Natalie repaired to Dublin which, as a neutral capital, was then free of all the restrictions and impedimenta of war and rationing. Her excuse was her daughter's recovery from an appendix operation; but Natalie's whim, as ever, was paramount. Zoe recounted how, while they were staying at the Gresham Hotel, her mother rose at noon and sent her hapless daughter, the supposed convalescent, out to the Kylemore cake shop near O'Connell Bridge to buy Natalie gelatine snowballs for breakfast. Every afternoon, Natalie vanished to an unknown destination: Zoe, glad to be rid of her incubus, did not follow but had her suspicions. In the very next breath she spoke of bumping into a German Kriegsmarine officer in full uniform in Grafton Street. It was very disquieting for a WRNS rating at war.

All of this background was interesting in delineating Natalie's character and placing her firmly in an imperial Russian and espionage milieu; but there was one thing about her past which, in terms of relevance to the identity of Nikolai Chebotarev, stands out above all others. Natalie Karaulov had served as a Red Cross nurse under Sister Chebotarev in the Tsarina's annexe of the military hospital in Tsarskoe Selo. A photograph exists of Natalie and her cousin Nina Berberova sitting in their nurses' uniforms at the feet of the Tsar and Tsarina (see plates). Typically of both women, they had pushed themselves into prime positions, right at the front. And there was evidence that Natalie's past was linked to Nikolai Chebotarev's. Soon after his arrival at Croft House, Zoe overheard her mother say in hushed tones to Nikolai Chebotarev, 'Imagine meeting again after all these years.'[37] Newly published imperial photograph albums from the Russian state archives show that the Tsarevich was often in that same military hospital with the nurses alongside whom his two elder sisters worked. For some hitherto inexplicable reason, the White émigrés had always denied that the Tsarevich had ever been in that hospital. Now, perhaps for the first time, light is being shed on precisely why that denial was made. Not only had the Tsarevich adopted the name of the sister in charge, but a nurse from that hospital was among his minders in the protracted exile from his country and his past that was to last for the remainder of his long life. Nor was Chebotarev the only house guest of Natalie Cooke's to come from that small imperial town of Tsarskoe Selo; there was another, the best friend of Sister Chebotarev's real son Grigori – Nikolai Couriss, with his wife Sana Bibikov.[38] How small a world it must have seemed. And they were all united by one man, once a boy born to rule all the Russias.

His own past, the persistent rumours, the people who surrounded him and their associations – with every step forward in my research it became increasingly clear that Nikolai Chebotarev was no ordinary émigré. Everywhere there was reinforcement of the proposition that he really was Alexei. But what of me? Was there anything about me and my past which linked me to him and suggested that I was anything more than what I appeared to be? In 1995 an answer to that question began to emerge.

# The Mysteries Combine

In 1995 the two people who had brought me up, but who I had long suspected were not my parents, died within six weeks of each other. It was this, more than any other occurrence, that opened up a sequence of events which was to link me personally with the mysterious Russian. I had already had hints of a possible connection; as the story of Nikolai Chebotarev had unfolded through my researches between 1993 and 1995, his friends – in particular Zoe Lytle, who as Zoe Cooke had lived in the same house as Chebotarev for nearly four years – kept telling me how much I shared his mannerisms.[1] Bill Phillips had made me aware within weeks of starting this quest of my own son's striking resemblance to the Tsarevich. These observations were interesting, even a little disturbing, but none of them constituted hard evidence. Mentally, I kept the quest for the truth about Nikolai Chebotarev's identity and the search for my own origins separate.

All this changed, however, when my supposed parents died in May and June 1995. In the first place, the possibility that they might tell me the truth was finally gone. They – he in particular – had come close on a couple of occasions; but the moment had passed, and the old and increasingly obvious untruths had reasserted themselves. Also, their deaths gave me the chance – indeed, the duty – to sift through their papers and possessions which had hitherto been closed to me. Any death entails a great deal of practical work for the surviving next of kin, not least the sorting out of the minutiae of papers, photographs and so on. The usual arrangements had, of course, to be made. An estate agent was brought in to handle the sale of the house and an auctioneer to deal with the larger items of furniture. My wife and son called down to the house on a day in late June with a view to clearing out any family possessions before the agents began to take prospective buyers around. My son had already proved to be extremely lucky in this regard, having found £100 in cash the week before, hidden behind a picture. His reward had been to share it with his sister as holiday money. On this occasion, though, he discovered something quite different. While rummaging in my late mother's bedroom, he uncovered three photographs in an old handbag in the bottom of a wardrobe. They were near none of the other photographs in the house, which were on the whole surprisingly well ordered. But these three were separate and clearly well hidden. When my wife brought them home she asked me, almost as an afterthought, who the people in the photographs were. One showed me as a baby of about six months with two people, a man and a woman, I did not recognize. Another showed me with the same woman in front of a tennis court. The third had me in the same baby carriage in front of an ornamental fountain. There was no doubt the child was me, as it matched one of the earliest photographs of me which existed. The people with me, however, were a mystery. I thought I had seen another photograph of the man, but recently, not long ago; and I couldn't place him. I could get no further; so, putting the photographs aside, I got on with the business of putting together the materials I would need for some interviews I hoped to conduct while on holiday.

About two days after this, we called on Kathleen McCarthy in Collon. I had wanted to ask her about some of Couriss' circle of friends to help me structure some of the interviews I was planning. Unknown to me, my wife had carried the three photographs in her handbag. Once again her magpie instincts were vindicated: Kathleen recognized the two adults straight away. It was like that with Kathleen – you got it straight. If she did not know the people you put before her, she said so, and right away. If she had doubts, she said so. But if she knew them, she did not hold back; and I already knew that she was very reliable. In this instance there was not an atom of doubt. They were, she said with certainty, Prince Alexander Lieven and Dr Martha Apraxine.[2]

It was one of those electric moments, a point in the train of events when you know something has irrevocably changed. All the strands of my enquiries seemed to have come together. I knew exactly what it meant: as a young child, I was linked to the Russians around Chebotarev. Alix Hill had told me that back in the 1940s, Lieven had been his best friend. Dr Apraxine, I already knew, was the daughter of the Tsarina's secretary. Collon was the thread that bound this mysterious story together. Kathleen McCarthy asked where we had found the photographs. When she heard, her response was a considered 'Well!' It was at that point that I recalled when and where I had seen the man in the picture. A year before, on 21 April 1994, when I had visited the headquarters of Irish military intelligence in Cathal Brugha Barracks in Dublin, Commandant Peter Young had allowed me to see, but not to photocopy, the files on the Russians at Collon. Lieven's file contained a tiny photograph of him. And yes, I now realized that the man in the photographs we had found in the wardrobe reminded me of the tiny photograph in that file: the same gaunt look – even the same suit, I thought.

Days later, we were in London and calling once again on Alix Hill in Edgware. It was a warm summer evening and Alix's husband Peter settled us into position on the covered veranda at the rear of the house. Easing rather uncomfortably into the suspended garden sofa, I showed Alix the photographs. She looked intently at them for a moment, then turned to confirm the identification of Lieven at once without the least prompting: she had, after all, worked with Lieven in the Ministry of Defence and was related to him. Apraxine she did not know or recognize. 'But who is the baby?' she puzzled. I replied that it was me; and I saw the effect my words had on her. Afterwards, she admitted to me that at that moment she knew for sure. She had seen her friend Nikolai Chebotarev in me in so many ways. Now, here was something tangible. Later revelations would all emanate from this moment, for now the conviction grew on her that I had the right to know. Up to that point she had been guarded – polite, but guarded. Having seen Lieven with me as a child, she opened up. All manner of revelations were to emerge from the woman who had been Nikolai Chebotarev's confidante in the last years of his life. A few months after this, just before Christmas 1995, I received a letter from her asking me to call. 'There are things', she said, 'I think you should know.'

It was New Year by the time I got there. Slowly, deliberately, she told me of something very important which Nikolai Chebotarev's sister had told her. It happened when she and her husband Peter had been looking after the old lady, whom everyone called 'Babushka', while her daughter and son-in-law took a holiday. Late one night, as they were all preparing to retire, Babushka had told her that Nikolai Chebotarev was the Tsar's son. Incredible as it seems, Peter hurried everyone off to bed and the opportunity to hear more was lost.[3] Alix went on to tell me that Fanny, Nikolai Chebotarev's companion in his later years, had despite all statements to the contrary not been his wife, and that Fanny had admitted this to her mother, the formidable Olga Hill, when questioned. Was she married, Olga asked? 'I couldn't do that, not after Victor [her late husband],' was Fanny's reply.

To mark these discoveries, Alix Hill gave me something Nikolai Chebotarev had given her in the year before he died, explaining that he always kept it with him and that it was therefore important to him. It was a small white enamelled cross: the Knight Commander's Cross of the Danish Order of the Dannebrog (see plates). The cypher 'C' denoted King Christian IX, the Tsarevich's great-grandfather who had attended Alexei's baptism in 1904. Both the Tsar and his mother, the daughter of King Christian, possessed such crosses, and at family ceremonies it was normal to exchange such decorations.

My discovery of those three photographs marked the point at which the two enquiries coalesced into one. For the first time there was hard evidence linking me to Chebotarev's Russian associates at Moyallon and Collon; and so, armed with the identifications of Lieven and Apraxine, both key members of Couriss' circle, I began to look at these photographs much more closely (see plates). Taken in high summer, they showed me about six months old, making nonsense of my supposed birth date of 5 August 1948 and suggesting that I had in fact been born towards the end of 1947 or early in 1948. I began to make enquiries about my records, such as they were. What I uncovered was a remarkable story of deceit and cover-up. To begin with I tackled the question of my birth certificate, since if I was six months old in midsummer it was clearly inaccurate. Both the Office of Population Censuses and Surveys and the local registrar in Birmingham, where I was supposed to have been born, made it clear to me that the responsibility for the information contained in the birth certificate rested with the informant and not with the registrar.[4] According-ing to them, the registrar simply recorded what he was told – no proof was required; no documentation from a doctor, midwife or hospital as to the actual event of the birth, its time and place, or who had witnessed it, was necessary. This remains the case today, just as it had been in 1948. As the birth certificate generated a medical number which brought with it the right to free medical treatment under Britain's National Health Service, this system seemed open to considerable abuse. It transpired that many fraudulent claims are indeed based on false birth declarations, with such 'ghost' children having subsequent entitlement to benefits and health care. It was, and is, an extraordinary loophole in the law.

Its immediate relevance to me, of course, was that my birth certificate might well have been falsified. If someone was determined to do this, there was no practical barrier in their way; and, as I have described in chapter 2, my earlier investigations into my medical record had already suggested that some interference with my documentation had taken place.

To clear the matter up, I decided to check my late mother's medical record to see if it could shed any light on the circumstances of my birth. Dr Martin, her general practitioner, was agreeable and helpful, but had already sent the relevant records to the Central Services Agency in Belfast, where they would be stored for five years before being destroyed. Frank Crummey, head of the Central Services Agency, was also very helpful and produced my late mother's medical record.[5] On the relevant section on the outside sleeve it showed a full list of medical practitioners stretching unbroken all the way from 1936 until her death in 1995. It was clear enough – from 1936 to 1940 her doctor had been Dr C. J. Boucher of Donaghcloney; from 1940 until 1949 it had been Dr Cocks of Church Square, Banbridge; and thereafter it was Dr J. W. B. Paton and his successor Dr Martin in Waringstown. All of them were in Northern Ireland; none was in England, yet my birth certificate has me born in Birmingham in England. It did not seem credible that at a time when any woman would require the services of a doctor, she had no English GP. Nor was it credible that an English part of her record had gone missing, for in the case of my own medical record, already the subject of much concern since I had first seen it in 1993, the record had been transferred from England and contained the names of doctors in both England and Northern Ireland.

Nor, even more oddly, did the record contain any evidence of her ever having had a child. This seemed, to put it mildly, a glaring omission. Her sister Anna had spoken of her having suppurating breasts after having given birth; a medical record would be expected to contain notes on such a condition, yet there was no mention of it. However, Anna never actually saw this symptom; indeed, none of the sisters actually ever saw my mother pregnant: she claimed to have gone to England before the birth, so that none of her family saw me until my supposed parents 'returned' to Northern Ireland with me.[6] Over the years my mother had given the duration of her stay in England as anything from six months to two and a half years. As the couple had initially lived with my father's mother on their presumed return, there was no way of checking this out – especially as their next-door neighbours were all killed in a car crash two months before my parents died. Experience had shown me that my mother's sisters were very close and loyal to each other, so I ceased to expect any enlightenment from them. By this stage I had the gravest of reasonably held doubts that the woman who had raised me could be my mother.

My father's brother and his wife were no better. At first they claimed that my parents had gone to England immediately after their wedding and returned again shortly, definitely in the same year. Yet this was not borne out by the records. They married on 15 January 1948 and returned only in August 1949, over a year and a half later. Then his brother changed his story. The couple had gone to Manchester, he claimed, not Birmingham. Yet this was patently incorrect, supported by neither my father's medical records nor my own birth certificate. If, as the photographs indicated, I had been born some six to eight months before summer 1948 – that is, between November 1947 and February 1948 – then I may already have been in existence at the time my supposed parents had been married. My father's medical record certainly had him in Birmingham – making it even less likely that my mother could have been there without its also being noted on her medical record – then returning to Northern Ireland.

My next clue to a way out of this morass of contradiction and obfuscation came with the name of a doctor. From 5 May 1948 in Birmingham my father had been on the list of Dr Isidore Jack Eppel. Born in 1908, Eppel was a Jew of German extraction who had qualified in Dublin in 1936, a member of a family that provided many noted physicians in the Irish capital. At first I questioned whether there could have been a link between Eppel and Dr Rudy Neumann, a doctor whom Kathleen McCarthy remembered being used by Couriss.[7] Neumann had qualified in Berlin in 1926, and like Eppel was a member of Dublin's small Jewish community. The two men lived in the same small neighbourhood of Rathmines, Eppel at 74 Grosvenor Road, and Neumann at Upper Rathmines Road, a few hundred yards away.[8] It seemed likely that they knew each other. My question was not fully answered for another two years – until 1997, when Couriss' friend Henry St George Smith told me casually in conversation that Eppel had been one of Couriss' doctors.[9] For my father to have Couriss' doctor as his general practitioner in Birmingham was a coincidence too far. It implied collusion.

The nature of Couriss' involvement in my early days began to emerge as I pondered on the photographs of me with his Collon friends, Prince Alexander Lieven and Dr Martha Apraxine. Recalling that my mother had told me as a child that my grandfather was a market gardener, I saw another piece of information I had come across in 1994 in a new light. In a letter Couriss had written in application for a job with the Ulster Flax Production Committee, he described himself as a market gardener.[10]

It seemed to suggest at least a possibility that if I had been handed over
to surrogate parents it might well have been through Nikolai Couriss,
and he might well have presented himself to the surrogates as the grandfather of the baby.

Though my supposed father's medical record has him registered with
Eppel from 5 May 1948, Eppel himself was not registered with Birmingham Health Authority until July;[11] so my father must have known
Eppel before the doctor was in Birmingham – or at least before he was
officially there. Also, the Birmingham Health Authority stamp on my
father's medical record is quite different from that on my own, despite
the fact that neither pre-dated the formation of the new National Health
Service on 5 July 1948 – his was dated September, mine 5 July.[12] Inevitably, the suspicion arises that Dr Isidore Eppel was involved in helping
to create a false identity for me – something which, as I now knew from
my investigation into how records of birth were made, would have presented few problems for a Birmingham GP.

For anyone with such fabrication in mind, the inception of the new
National Health Service on 5 July 1948 provided an opportunity. All
participating doctors had been issued with new medical record sleeves
for all their existing patients, pre-stamped with the health authority seal.
Naturally some of these had not been used, since some patients had died.
Where this happened, the cause of death should have been inserted in
the normal manner at the bottom of the sleeve and the word 'Cancelled'
stamped clearly across it, prior to its return to the health authority. The
system, however, was far from foolproof, and a sleeve that was not
returned could be put to other uses – such as creating a false identity for
an infant. Who better to have access to such an item than a participating
GP such as Dr Eppel? Believing as I now did that Couriss was involved
in creating the identity of 'Nikolai Chebotarev' for the Tsarevich back
in 1920, and knowing that he had six years' experience as a passport and
visa clerk in the British consulate in Salonika, I could see that the germ
of the idea may well have been his, with Eppel simply acting as his agent.
It also seemed likely, given that I was almost certainly born at or about
the time my surrogate parents were married, that their marriage, while
not necessarily undertaken to order, was at least in part designed to provide a home for me.

My surrogate mother had told me as recently as 1993 that 'a young
Dublin doctor' was involved at the time of my birth. I realized now that
this description fitted Martha Apraxine perfectly. Born in Simferopol,

the family estate in the Crimea, in 1913, she would have been just thirty-five in 1948.[13] Granted permission to reside in Ireland on 16 September 1931, Martha Apraxine had qualified as a doctor at University College, Dublin in 1942. Her medical practice was at 19 Fitzwilliam Place in Dublin, and later at Pembroke Lane. In addition, she was listed in the *Medical Directory* as assistant physician at the National Children's Hospital in Dublin from 1942 – excellent cover for moving a child.[14] Since Dr Martha Apraxine featured in two of the photographs I had found, it was possible that she had sent them to my surrogate mother before I was delivered to her.

Finding both my parents on the Birmingham electoral register for 1948 and 1949 did nothing to reassure me that they were actually there, since I knew that in Northern Ireland falsification of electoral rolls and personation is a way of life and would not have cost my father a second thought. He came from a Unionist community where this was nothing unusual. So widespread are these practices that they have now become the subject of a House of Commons investigation. (In 1996, to make the point, someone in Northern Ireland registered a cat which subsequently received a vote.[15]) As with birth certificates, no proof whatever was required to get on the electoral register. As evidence of my mother's whereabouts, her presence on the Birmingham electoral roll was far less persuasive than the absence of a doctor outside Northern Ireland on her medical record.

I could think of only one way to get closer to a conclusive answer to the question, and that was to talk to any surviving residents of the house at 387 Gillot Road in Edgbaston, where my parents had allegedly rented rooms, who had been there in 1948 and 1949. Two former residents were still alive, and both were willing to talk to me: Rosa Frost, and Audrey Nightingale, the daughter of the previous owner. I questioned them closely about all the residents of Number 387 in the post-war period. In both cases their memories were precise and quite clear. Rosa Frost, a bright and crisply spoken eighty-year-old, had no recollection of my parents' name, and she had lived in the house both before the war and afterwards, resuming her residence in 1945, after serving as a nurse in the conflict, and remaining there continuously until 1974. Nor was there any couple in residence; married couples were simply not allowed, she said, until much later – about 1970, in fact. She was equally certain that there had been no pregnant woman there and no baby. There was a shared kitchen and bathroom, she said; I would have remembered.[16]

Audrey Nightingale, who took over as landlady of the house when her mother died at the beginning of August 1948, also said that there was no couple, pregnant woman or baby there at that time. Her mother's death and her taking over the house were landmark occasions in her life, and she was likely to remember the circumstances. None of this accords with what my birth certificate says. It clearly gives the 387 Gillot Road address on the date the birth was registered – 9 August 1948.[17] Clearly, the birth certificate was provably inaccurate; and if it were wrong in that significant detail, why not in others? The indicators that some sort of fabrication had taken place were strong and getting stronger. My enquiries were certainly making progress, but far from resolving the events surrounding my birth, they were getting me into ever deeper waters.

I went back to the photographs found in the wardrobe. Was the baby really me? As I have said, it certainly looked like other photographs of me as an infant – for example, one which showed me taken with my parents' next-door neighbour, Beatrice McCutcheon. First I had local residents verify the identity of Beatrice McCutcheon in that photograph. As for my own identity, I sought expert help with the identification of the baby in the Lieven–Apraxine photographs from Dr Richard Neave, an expert on skull analysis at Manchester University. Asked to compare the photographs of the baby with Prince Alexander Lieven and Countess Martha Apraxine to the photograph of me with the neighbour, Dr Neave said, 'I can't be absolutely certain because the earlobe of the baby [in the wardrobe photograph] is covered with a bonnet, but my gut feeling is that this is the same baby.'[18]

The evidence of the concealed photographs with Prince Lieven and Dr Apraxine; the lack of an English doctor on my mother's medical record; no evidence in that record that she had ever given birth; no one who remembers her pregnant; Couriss' doctor, Eppel, being my father's doctor in Birmingham; the certainty of two former residents at Gillot Road that there was neither baby nor couple at that address in the crucial months; the ease with which birth certificates could be falsified – let alone what I had already discovered about my own medical record back in 1993: all this far outweighed the extremely dubious evidence of the electoral roll. By the end of the exercise I had become more, not less, convinced that I was not the son of the people who had brought me up, that I was definitely connected to the Russians at Collon – and that I was probably Nikolai Chebotarev's son.

My own early memories which, as I have described in chapter 2, had long troubled me intermittently, now began to fit into the emerging picture. Unusually for a child brought up by Protestants in the Northern Ireland of the 1950s, most of whom never crossed the border, I could recall frequent visits to the Irish Republic as a child. I put together all the images I could remember from these excursions, and found that they all pointed in one direction: to Collon. I had visited Monasterboice, a ruined Irish monastery with a round tower which is within three miles of Collon. I recalled visits to Ravensdale Forest, just to the north of Collon, and to nearby Omeath, a small coastal town. Travelling to Dublin on the N1 in 1996 I passed through the village of Castlebellingham, where I was surprised to recognize an old building with a curious horseshoe-shaped door next to a filling station where I remembered my father stopping to fill the car some time around 1957, when I was about nine years old. Castlebellingham is about eight miles from Collon.

Having got this far, it seemed sensible to show some photographs of myself as a child and of my surrogate parents to Kathleen McCarthy. It was 1997 when I finally did this; had I done so earlier, the connection with Couriss would have been corroborated much sooner. Kathleen recognized my supposed parents at once and said that they had come several times in the 1950s to see Nikolai Couriss, usually with me. She had been deputed to take me into the garden to play.[19] Kathleen said she did not care for my surrogate mother, whom she accurately described as 'bossy'; Couriss, she said, had 'kept them at a distance'. Looking at a photograph of me aged nine, she recalled seeing me as a boy in Ravensdale Forest on a picnic with Couriss. At the time, I felt I had been very remiss in not having shown these pictures to Kathleen earlier; but it had only slowly dawned on me that I should do this after my findings about Dr Eppel, in particular, and after finding the photographs of me with Lieven and Apraxine.

Still more information was locked up in those photographs. For instance, the one of me with the woman Kathleen identified as Dr Apraxine had been taken in front of a tennis court. Though that tennis court could in theory have been anywhere, it seemed logical to look somewhere I was known to have been as a child. My medical record had me in Bangor, County Down up to August 1949, so this seemed a sensible place to begin – especially as my surrogate mother would never go there and denied that I had ever been there. Directly adjacent to the doctor's surgery mentioned in my medical record – Dr Bowman's at 44 Hamilton Road – there was a park with tennis courts.[20] Enquiries revealed that they were no longer in their original position; but when I looked at the place where they had been in 1948, the photograph I had fitted the configuration of the house roof profile still there to this day, with a series of hipped-roof inter-war houses behind where the tennis courts would have been. Clearly, Dr Apraxine had been with me in this park in Bangor beside the doctor's surgery where I was registered as a patient.

Dr Bowman's surgery had been the subject of my investigations back in 1993 when I had found a building opposite I remembered from early childhood, the child clinic so memorable with its walls sloping outwards and upwards to the roof. In 1995 I looked at it again with renewed interest. With the knowledge I had gained since, I could see that this building had lodged in my memory so strongly because of my age when I left Bangor. My medical record showed that I had not been moved to Waringstown until August 1949; and if I had been born in the winter of 1947–8 – as the photographs indicated – by the new reckoning I would have been about one year nine months old when I left Bangor: quite old enough to remember the building.

A new reality was taking shape. This consisted of a birth some time in the period November 1947–February 1948, the selection of a couple to provide parents for the infant, the systematic creation of a false identity with appropriate documentation for the child, and the shepherding of that child until the point when he was finally handed over to the surrogate parents selected for the task of bringing him up in carefully protected anonymity. The extraordinary amount of trouble that had been taken in this concealment suggested that there must have been powerful and compelling reasons for it. No ordinary illegitimate birth would have required such a degree of planning. Nor would the child of just any parents, even noble parents, have needed such deep cover. And the hand behind this elaborate arrangement was that of Couriss, the ubiquitous Couriss, who had masterminded the creation of Chebotarev's new identity in 1920. Having achieved the disguise and reinvention of one fugitive Romanov, who else should arrange the disguise and disappearance of his son?

If, as now seemed to me almost beyond doubt, Chebotarev was the Tsarevich Alexei, it seemed also increasingly likely that he was my father. Assuming that these two startling conclusions were correct, they led inexorably to a further question: who was my mother?

## ⌣ 17 ⌣

## Marina

Before the revolution which swept away imperial Russia, the Tsarevich Alexei had been one of the best marriage prospects in Europe. There were, however, strict dynastic laws which governed whom he might marry. His bride would have to be a royal princess and preferably a member of the Orthodox Church. His own father, his grandfather, his great-grandfather and so on back to the early eighteenth century had married foreign princesses; but their brides had all had to convert to Orthodoxy for, as the national hymn 'God save the Tsar' proclaimed it, their husband would become 'the Orthodox Tsar'. In the normal course of events, the same requirement would have applied in the case of Alexei's marriage, for his father, Tsar Nikolai II, was essentially conservative on dynastic matters.

High on the shortlist of candidate brides had been Princess Marina of Greece. Indeed, Marina was not only a leading candidate; she was out in front of the field. Her dynastic credentials outstripped those of other Orthodox princesses like Princess Ileana of Romania. Not only was she royal – twice royal in fact, for she was a princess of both Greece and Denmark – but she was already Orthodox. Her mother, Grand Duchess Helen of Russia, was a Romanov and the Tsar's favourite cousin, despite belonging to the junior Vladimirovichi branch of the family which had given Nikolai II so much trouble. Indeed, an added advantage of the marriage would have been its contribution to healing the rift between these two wings of the divided family. Marina's father, Prince Nicholas of Greece, was himself the son of another Romanov, Queen Olga of Greece, formerly Grand Duchess Olga Constantinova of Russia, and was the Tsar's closest personal friend. Princess Marina was close to the Tsarevich in age: born in 1906, she was two years his junior, considered an ideal age difference.[1]

A marriage between the Greek princess and the Tsarevich would have had the added political benefit of extending Russian influence in the Balkans and eastern Mediterranean, where the abiding interest of imperial

foreign policy was the acquisition of Constantinople, the ancient capital
of the Greek Byzantine Empire and the seat of the Ecumenical Patriarch,
the head of world Orthodoxy. Marina's coronation as Alexei's Tsarina
would have been a tremendous symbolic act: for a Greek Tsarina had
been the basis of the title 'Tsar' in the first place when, in the fifteenth
century, the Grand Duke of Moscow had married Zoe, the daughter of
the last Byzantine Emperor Michael Palaeologus, inheriting through her
the claim to be the Emperor or Caesar – or, to use the Russian form of
the word, Czar. In a world still full of dress uniforms and medals, such
considerations continued to matter. And while those considerations may
have crashed out of public life when imperial Russia fell, the personal feelings and aspirations which lay behind them did not die with the empire.

In the 1920s Marina, like 'Nikolai Chebotarev' as the Tsarevich had
become, was unmarried, short of funds and living in Paris, in the small,
self-contained world of the 16th *arrondissement*. Across the Seine from the
powerful world of embassies, the gilt and marble of the Palais Bourbon
and the Quai d'Orsay, it exuded the atmosphere of the other Paris – a
vibrant, living place. In the 1920s the French capital was teeming with
Russian refugees. Initially, Nikolai lived with Baroness de Huene in a
ground floor flat on the rue de la Tour; Marina lived a hundred yards
away between the avenue Henri Martin, where in 1927 Nikolai worked
for a few months as a *préparateur* in a chemist's shop,[2] and the place du
Trocadero. Seven stops away on the number nine metro line, direction
Pont de Sèvres, Marina's father had his studio at Auteuil – right alongside the rue le Marois, Nikolai's later Paris address recorded in the Moyallon visitors' book. An accomplished artist, in great demand, Marina's
father sold paintings under the name 'Nicholas LePrince'.[3] Other relatives also lived in the 16th *arrondissement*: Prince Gavril Constantinovich
Romanov, for example, was nearby on the avenue Mozart. Mara Gorbadovsky told how his friend Nikolai Chebotarev would go round to write
his letters for him as Gavril never learned to write properly in French.[4]

Marina had not yet acquired the diet-induced figure for which she
was later to become famous. Zoe Cooke, who from 1928 lived with her
mother Natalie in her apartment at the rue de la Pompe, again just around
the corner, remembered sniggering with other girls behind the bus stop
as 'Princess Sausage', as they called Marina, left Mme Nesterovsky's ballet
school. 'So that's what you call a princess!' they hissed, as only spiteful
little girls can.[5] For Marina was on the plump side until 1934, when a
crash diet reduced her weight drastically in the year of her engagement

to the Duke of Kent. But in 1926 her unhappy marriage to the transvestite, bisexual duke was still eight years away. As children, Alexei and
Marina had played together in the gardens of Peterhof, Peter the Great's
palace on the shores of the Baltic;[6] now, according to many friends, they
danced together in Paris and on the Côte d'Azur. Dancing was certainly
a pursuit that Marina always loved; whether 'dancing' was also a polite
euphemism for a closer relationship it is impossible to know.

In 1927, after a year at Princess Metchersky's finishing school, Marina
went unchaperoned with her sister Elizabeth to French North Africa,
visiting Morocco, Tunis and Algiers.[7] French North Africa was a haunt
of both Nikolai Chebotarev and Baroness de Huene, whose daughter
was married to a French army officer and living in Marrakesh.[8] In that
same year Archbishop Theophan, with some attempt at subtlety, was
trying to talk Nikolai Chebotarev out of marriage. On 18 August he
wrote: 'There is nothing wrong with marital life, but would it help you
in your state of health?' Friends at the time attest to the fact that Nikolai
was perfectly healthy. The subject of marriage is rarely discussed in the
abstract. Inevitably, the question arises: who was the marriage partner,
prospective or actual? Judged by the imperatives of the past, a past which
at that stage was only ten years distant, Marina was an ideal choice for the
man who had been Alexei. Now, with both of them living as relatively
impoverished exiles in Paris and with no immediate prospect in either
case of a return to active royal status, marriage may have seemed a perfectly reasonable option to them. Both were at a suitable age: she was
twenty-one and he was twenty-three. There was no potential royal
match in sight for either of them in those circumstances and at that time:
Marina was not yet the very public person she was later to become, but
was just one more dispossessed princess, while Nikolai/Alexei was not
only dispossessed but in deep disguise.

If a form of marriage did take place as early as 1927 in North Africa,
it may well have been possible for others to persuade the couple that it
was irregular in some way. Certainly such a marriage would have been
mightily disapproved of by Marina's family; while Chebotarev was undoubtedly high-born, he was not, to the world at large, as eligible as
Alexei would have been – or as the Duke of Kent would be. And to
a young couple reared in an enclosed world dominated by protocol, a
marriage conducted without the usual Orthodox, or indeed royal, fan-
fare could have been portrayed as invalid without much difficulty by
those who cared about such things.

Nikolai's attachment to Marina appears to have been the greatest and most enduring of his life. Other girls – Stella Dalziel, Peggy Sinton, Moina Cowan – were important, particularly Stella; but Marina was set apart. Not only was he undoubtedly personally devoted to her, but he could never fully forget who he had been and what his dynastic duty was. Zoe Cooke said that Nikolai Chebotarev had acted as 'a kind of social secretary' to Princess Marina in the 1930s.[9] Her informant was Nikolai himself. She was equally certain that the two were 'related' in some way; and Marina was indeed the Tsarevich's second cousin. It remains possible they were a great deal more to each other than that. On 25 August 1942 the Duke of Kent was killed in an air crash in Scotland. Zoe recalled that she was the bearer of the tragic news to Croft House. Nikolai Chebotarev's reaction was immediate. 'He was', she said, 'unusually animated. He left the table at once. "I must send a telegram to Marina at Iver." That's what he called her,' Zoe went on, 'just "Marina".'[10] It seemed to Zoe that Nikolai was not entirely displeased at the news of the Duke's death.

Kent's untimely end amid the wreckage of his plane on a desolate Scottish hillside has been the subject of speculation for years. Alix Hill's husband Peter Thornton-Pett, a flight lieutenant at Lossiemouth at the time, heard that the crash was caused by drunkenness. Others see a more sinister explanation, especially in the light of the Duke of Kent's Nazi links and his closeness to his brother, the deposed King.[11] Whatever the cause of the crash, it left Marina a widow, no longer shackled in a loveless marriage. According to Thornton-Pett, whose mother had been one of the top society nurses of the period and consequently had got to hear everybody's secrets, Marina had sought release through divorce three times in the eight years she was married to the Duke of Kent.[12] Kent was a notorious bisexual, with a string of affairs with unsuitable women – and men – behind him, and indiscretions continued after his marriage. Noel Coward was numbered among his lovers. Robert Bruce Lockhart wrote that a large sum had to be paid to a young man in Paris in 1932 to recover love letters Kent had written to him, and on another occasion the Duke was arrested in a gay night-club.[13] He was also addicted to drugs, although his older brother David, later King Edward VIII and the Duke of Windsor, managed to wean him off this habit. Friends of Marina admitted to her most recent biographer, Sophia Watson, that the state of her marriage quite often reduced her to tears in private company, though never in public. Now her unsatisfactory husband was dead, and

Marina was free to renew her relationship with Nikolai Chebotarev. As far as the public image went, the Duke's death was followed by five years of dutiful widowhood; but by 1947 there were disquieting signs that Marina was seeking a new life out of the clutches of the House of Windsor. This, it transpired, was not to be allowed.

It emerged during 1997 that in the mid-1940s Princess Marina had stayed incognito at Natalie Cooke's homes at Croft House, Holywood and Princeton Road, Bangor. In 1995 Zoe Cooke had spoken of a 'Mme Velika' who had stayed at Croft House with Natalie in the post-war years.[14] Apparently, Natalie had made a great fuss over her. As Zoe had married in 1946 and was not frequently in her parents' home after that, she had never met this Mme Velika, and so could not give me any clues as to her real identity. In 1997, however, two of the Cooke servants came forward. Not only had they been there during the period of Mme Velika's visits, they had spoken with her. Bridie Gorman, who had been Natalie's cook and went on to found her own very successful home bakery business, and her younger sister, the housemaid Kitty Geddis, instantly and independently recognized a photograph taken of Princess Marina in 1947 as the Mme Velika who had stayed several times with their mistress.[15]

Marina's presence as a guest of Natalie was not surprising. The two women shared a past in 1920s Paris as well as some present friends: Lady Zia Wernher, for example, the morganatic daughter of Grand Duke Mikhail of Russia, the first cousin of Marina's mother, to whom it was planned that Zoe should be 'presented'.[16] The choice of pseudonym, 'Velika', was appropriate: it is the Russian for 'Grand' in the titles Grand Duke and Grand Duchess, and Marina's mother had been Grand Duchess Helen of Russia. Marina was no stranger to the use of aliases. As we have seen, her father, Prince Nicholas of Greece, sold his paintings in Paris as Nicholas LePrince. During the war Marina herself served as a nurse volunteer in Iver and Denham cottage hospital and in University College Hospital in London using the alias 'Nurse Kay' – a disguise that worked even when her husband, as president of the hospital, paid an official visit, though her cover was blown later by a dressmaker who recognized her.[17] It is interesting that she was able to get away with using an alias for so long at the centre of social and official life in London, where photographs of her were seen by many; how much easier, then, it must have been to go under an assumed name in Northern Ireland, in a house where the servants were Roman Catholic Irish nationalists who had little interest in British royalty.

The same two servants who recognized Mme Velika as Princess Marina also, and independently, remembered Nikolai Chebotarev staying at Croft House at the same time as her in September 1946 and 'running and laughing through the bedrooms together'. Kitty, more direct than Bridie, said, 'They were canoodling.' Outraged, the elderly housekeeper at the time, Miss Herd, said to the servants, 'That is Mr Nikolai's aunt, you know,' but no one believed her.[18] At the time of the events recounted by the servants, Marina had a twenty-two-day gap in her official engagements, from 5 September until 27 September,[19] shortly thereafter visiting the crash site where her late husband, the Duke of Kent, had been killed four years earlier. According to Kitty and Bridie, Mme Velika's last visit to Natalie Cooke was two years later, in September 1948. Just after Natalie and Frank returned from a Baltic cruise which took them, among other places, to Leningrad, Mme Velika had arrived completely unannounced at Natalie's new home in Princeton Road, Bangor, and had stayed for about two weeks.[20] Marina's official diary for 1948 has two large gaps in September, one of fourteen days between 6 September and 20 September, and one of ten days between 20 September and 30 September.[21] Once again, the servants' memories match the diary.

Early in 1947, from 1 February until 13 May, the entire royal family – the King, Queen, Princess Elizabeth and Princess Margaret – were safely absent on a prolonged state visit to South Africa, and Marina's official diary once again showed some significant gaps of unusually long duration. Between 8 February and 28 March 1947 Marina had no official engagements for a period of forty-eight days, save for reviewing a parade of Polish ex-servicemen on 4 March. All press releases from her office during this period were either formal announcements or the publication of messages, easily arranged beforehand.[22] Her only other visible engagement during these weeks was a private party at Lord Mountbatten's on 19 March. So we have a gap of twenty-four days from 8 February until 4 March, and another of fifteen days from 4 March until 19 March. Towards the end of this period, on 13–15 March, Marina sold paintings, silver, porcelain and furniture by auction at Christie's which raised a total of over £92,341, the equivalent of over £1.8 million today.[23] Two interpretations of this divestment offer themselves, one symbolic, one practical. First, many of these paintings and *objets d'art* had been collected by her art connoisseur husband; in selling them, as in travelling to the site of his death, it was again as if she was making a ritual break with the past. Secondly, the amount of money thus raised was far in excess of anything which could be required for an immediate need; certainly, it was more than enough to start the new life in America whispered of in the current rumours about Marina – rumours which were so prevalent at the time that they had to be officially denied by the British ambassador in Washington.[24]

Nikolai Chebotarev was already in America, having sent a postcard to Natalie Cooke from Long Island on 1 January 1947.[25] Here he was training at the UN establishment at Lake Success for the job found for him by Sir Percy Loraine. The useful Sir Percy had connections not only at the United Nations but also with Princess Marina: he was chairman of the Anglo-Hellenic League, of which Princess Marina was president.[26] He was thus ideally positioned to keep the couple in frequent contact. Marina herself had been involved with the United Nations right from its inception; a year earlier, on 10 February 1946, she had attended an evening party for UN delegates in London.[27] It is likely Nikolai was there as well. While Nikolai's job at the UN was undoubtedly found by Sir Percy, the idea of seeking employment for him there may have been Marina's own, part of a plan in which they would both move to America.

On Long Island, Nikolai lived at Mrs Malitsky's boarding house at Locust Grove in Sea Cliff – along with his old friends the Grabbes, with whom he had stayed in Nice back in 1924.[28] At Syosset, the next town to Sea Cliff, lived Princess Xenia of Russia, in 1947 newly married to her second husband, Hermann Jud. Xenia had been born in 1906, the same year as Marina, who was her first cousin: Xenia's mother, who had married Grand Duke George of Russia, had been the sister of Marina's father, Prince Nicholas of Greece.[29] Xenia, who had played with the Tsarevich as a child, obviously knew Nikolai Chebotarev very well, for on the back of a photograph of herself that Nikolai kept in his album she had written the suggestive message: 'To Kolya, the big boy now.'[30] What had he done to deserve this? Atlantic crossings in those days took only four days by sea – so Marina would have had ample time to travel out and back during those long absences from official engagements in February and March 1947.

Between 22 and 24 April 1947 Princess Marina made an official visit to Northern Ireland, a visit first announced on 27 March. Arriving in rough seas and freak weather conditions, heralded by local headlines referring to the 'Duchess of Kent's Stormy Crossing' and 'Ulster Weather at its Worst', Marina's ship HMS *Crispin*, an anti-submarine vessel captained by Commander J. Grant DSO, berthed at Pollock Dock number thirteen in Belfast harbour.[31] A fly-past of Mosquito aircraft had to be cancelled because of 55 m.p.h. winds. Ships were lost at sea and the Donaghadee lifeboat, near Bangor, had been called out. Still, thousands defied the rough weather to catch a glimpse of the Princess in a full programme of engagements. She launched an aircraft carrier, HMS *Centaur*, and, of more immediate relevance to this story, she visited two factories in Dungannon, County Tyrone, belonging to Major Robert Stevenson.[32] Not only was Stevenson the uncle of Peggy Sinton, one of Nikolai Chebotarev's friends at Moyallon, he had also acted as referee for Nikolai Couriss in his job application to the Ulster Flax Production Committee.[33] The figure of Couriss also hovered in the background of the one private visit Marina paid during the tour. This was to Mountstewart, the home of the Marquess and Marchioness of Londonderry;[34] Lord Londonderry, using his unadorned name Charles or Charlie Stewart, was a visitor to Couriss at Collon.[35] On 24 April, Princess Marina left Northern Ireland for Liverpool on board the HMS *Crispin* which, in its race to reach port, beat the record speed of the *Mauretania*. According to press reports, Marina left Lime Street Station, Liverpool for London at 5.25 p.m.[36]

So much for the public account of what happened on that trip; but it is far from the full story. Shortly after this, Prince Alexander Lieven called into the Ministry of Defence office on the outskirts of London where Alix Hill was working. He was in light-hearted mood, and bragged to Alix and her friend Vivian Jabez-Smith that he had been dispatched to apprehend Princess Marina at Belfast docks: she had been running away and had jewellery with her.[37] Lieven spoke of the atrocious weather conditions in which he had conducted his mission, a description which corresponds to the weather during Marina's visit to Northern Ireland. That Lieven was indeed working for British intelligence in the post-war period was confirmed by Henry St George Smith, whom Lieven himself had told over dinner in the Dolphin Hotel, Dublin,[38] and by Kathleen McCarthy, who added that Lieven's half-brother, Prince Leonid, worked for them as well.[39]

What had Marina been planning, and how had she been thwarted? Examination of the Belfast harbour master's Entry Books for Berthing Vessels and of the Port Traffic and Navigation Committee books opened up interesting possibilities. HMS *Crispin* appears in the logs as having docked on 22 April and departed for Liverpool on 24 April. Its pilot was Captain Robert Craig, the senior pilot of the port. Shortly after the

*Crispin* left on 24 April, two ships departed – both destined for a long journey. SS *Vasconia*, a Cunard-White Star ship registered in Liverpool and weighing 4,757 tons, arrived under the command of its master, G. D. Morris, on 27 April and departed on the same day at 4.55 p.m., bound for New York. On the same day, at 11.05 a.m., the SS *Lord O'Neill*, 5,687 tons, departed under its master R. A. Ferguson, bound for Montreal via Greenock in Scotland. It had two passengers aboard. The *Lord O'Neill* was the property of the shipping line of G. Heyn and Sons of Belfast.[40] The Heyns were personal friends of Natalie Cooke and her husband Frank; their children shared the same nanny.[41] Just as the *Lord O'Neill* was leaving, the duty pilot, A. Grace, had to board the vessel and detain it. According to the entry in the pilot's log, this was 'to JKS assist *Lord O'Neill* adjusting compass';[42] but this may well not have been the real purpose of the delay. Alexander Lieven may have been intercepting one of the two passengers. It would not have been beyond his capabilities simply to bundle the errant Princess off the ship under cover. The weather on 27 April was not very good; the wind was described by the pilot as fresh. Conditions remained little better than they had been during Marina's state visit – much as Lieven described them to Alix Hill and her friend.

If Marina was trying to escape from Belfast harbour, as Lieven said, it seems most likely that she intended to leave on one of the two ships sailing respectively for New York and Montreal three days after her scheduled departure for Liverpool on board the official warship. This could have been planned in two ways. First, Marina may well have left for Liverpool but never boarded the train for London at Lime Street Station. Her absence may not have been discovered, therefore, until she failed to arrive in London – at which point Lieven would have been sent to investigate and retrieve her. By the time he was on the trail, Marina could have been on her way back to Ireland. Between 24 and 27 April two ferries arrived in Belfast from Liverpool. They were the MV *Ulster Prince*, which arrived on 25 April, and the MV *Ulster Monarch*, which arrived on 27 April.[43] Both were overnight crossings; both left Liverpool after Marina's ship HMS *Crispin* docked and after she was supposed to board her train for London. Marina could easily have travelled to Liverpool on the warship, failed to get the train and returned to Belfast incognito on one of the two ferries – where Lieven apprehended her on 27 April, just before she sailed for America. Alternatively, Marina may not have left Belfast at all on 24 April but remained behind in Northern

Ireland waiting to board one of the two American-bound vessels. It would have been possible for her to board the Heyn-owned *Lord O'Neill* early, since it had been berthed in Pollock Dock number six in Belfast harbour since 28 March; or she could have stayed somewhere ashore during those three days. In the event, of course, whichever stratagem she did use failed her. There was to be no new life in America.

Despite what must have been a crushing disappointment, there is evidence that Nikolai and Marina continued their association after her abortive attempt to give the Windsors the slip. I found that in June 1947, for example, they were in Greece at the same time. Marina's visit is a matter of public record. She left for Athens on 28 May and extended her visit on 10 June, returning only on the twenty-third.[44] Nikolai Chebotarev's whereabouts at this time was not so widely known; but one man has particular cause to remember his presence there. Misha Viacheslav, who holidayed in a threesome with Nikolai Chebotarev and the Tsar's nephew Tikhon Kulikovsky, is an artist now living in Toronto. In 1995 he claimed that he owed his life to Nikolai, who apparently got him out of Greece when they were both in Athens in the early days of the Greek civil war, thus saving Viacheslav from what he regarded as certain call-up and almost equally certain death.[45] Nikolai was able to arrange for Viacheslav to leave Greece and go to live in France. Greece was certainly no holiday destination at this time; indeed, things were so dangerous that the King and Queen had to travel about in a tank.[46] It was, however, the perfect place for a discreet Orthodox wedding.

Princess Marina was known to be a firm believer in arranged marriages for the scions of royal houses. Unity Hall wrote that 'she was, in the manner of European royalty, a great believer in royalty marrying royalty. Keeping the family in the family, as it were. And she saw nothing wrong with arranged marriages.'[47] Certainly, she would not have married a man of lesser status than herself; and everyone would have known that. Her fixed views about the value of status, along with her sharp tongue, created a great deal of trouble for her within the royal family. She had scorned her sisters-in-law, the Duchess of York and Alice, Duchess of Gloucester, as 'those common little Scottish girls'.[48] Not an endearing remark at the best of times, it antagonized someone who could inflict real damage on her – for by the end of 1936 the Duchess of York was Queen; and Queen Elizabeth (now the Queen Mother) is well known for her capacity to bear grudges, most notoriously against the Duke and Duchess of Windsor.[49] Marina, according to Unity Hall, regarded the British royal family as only half-royal and was aware that her own children had the bluest blood of all of them.[50] Since everyone knew Marina's views on royal marriages, her own choice of husband would have come in for a great deal of public scrutiny. Such scrutiny would, inevitably, have blown Nikolai Chebotarev's cover. All the inconsistencies in his own meagre stories about his past would have been exposed in their weakness, and the rumours which had plagued him in the 1920s would inevitably have resurfaced. All this, at the height of Stalin's power, would have been unthinkable. Silence was the only possible option; but then, had he not lived with silence for the past thirty years? So Princess Marina was caught in a trap, unable to contemplate marriage with a non-royal partner, and unable publicly to acknowledge the entirely acceptable status of the partner she wished to marry.

The only possible option, then, to these two people in love – running through the bedrooms of Croft House together, or planning to decamp to America together, or arranging to meet up in Greece – was a secret marriage. Nikolai Chebotarev was a deeply religious man, and marriage for him would have been the only option. A hint that Nikolai Chebotarev did indeed contract a secret marriage is provided by the existence among his possessions of an icon of St Nikolai the Wonderworker, one of the personal saints of the imperial family. According to Alix Hill, this icon was given to him by one of the princely families 'on his marriage'. Fanny Tate herself insisted that her 'marriage' to Chebotarev was no such thing; so who was his bride?

Marina's views on marriage we have already examined; and after this time she refused all other offers. In 1955 the highly eligible King Olaf of Norway proposed, to be politely but firmly declined.[51] Marina's mother had always wanted royal marriages for her children and thrones for her daughters; Marina as Queen of Norway seemed like a perfect royal arrangement, one of which Marina herself would have thoroughly approved. Yet she turned him down – perhaps because she was married already. For Nikolai and Marina, however, marriage was not the end of the story.

In 1996 I travelled to Iver, in Buckinghamshire, where Marina lived in the 1940s and where, it emerged, Nikolai Chebotarev had visited her. Jim Barrett, who has lived in the village since the 1920s, recalls seeing him in 1947 in Swan Lane, which connected the back entrance of Marina's home, The Coppins, with the church end of Iver village.[52] Barrett, an active member of the Ramblers' Association, was single-handedly responsible for having Swan Lane opened to walkers – in the teeth of opposition from the royal residents of The Coppins and more particularly the royal servants in the nearby grace and favour houses, who would have preferred to keep the whole area a great, secluded and very private royal demesne. In honour of Jim Barrett, locals named the upper part of Swan Lane closest to The Coppins 'Jim's Lane', an honour of which he is very proud. It is quite easy to see why his royal neighbours were less than keen on his plans: the lane, which opens into the main Iver–Richings Park road at the Swan tavern, was the perfect way to come and go from The Coppins without being seen; and Nikolai Chebotarev was not the only clandestine visitor.

When I visited Jim Barrett in pursuit of information about comings and goings at Iver in the late 1940s, I took with me the photograph from Couriss' papers of the elderly Russian gentleman described by Kathleen McCarthy as 'Nikolai Alexandrovich'. I was interested in Jim's reaction because not only had he been in Iver since the 1920s, when he worked at the nearby great garden of Dromenagh, owned by Trevor Williams, he also had an exceptionally alert brain and acute powers of observation. He studied the photograph closely. 'I am certain', he began, 'that the gentleman in the photograph came to Dromenagh gardens. He came with Princess Victoria, the sister of King George V, and with Queen Mary. It was Baroness de Stoeckl who arranged the visits. The gentleman lived in her house.' He went on: 'The gentleman in the photograph bore such a striking resemblance to King George V that, on a couple of occasions, we thought the King had come. My workmates would say – was it the King? It looked like him – When you got close, though, you realized they were slightly different. One day, however, he came with the King. One king was bad enough. It was a bit overpowering to see what looked like two King George Vs at the same time!'[53]

'The gentleman,' he continued, 'was a Russian who lived on the royal property in the Coppins estate in both Princess Victoria's and Princess Marina's time. He was stockily built and about five feet seven tall. I am about five feet six, and he was just a little bit bigger than me. He had a quick walk and short steps. He smoked continuously at small cigars – cheroots – and cigarettes. He was always chumping at the cheroots. He would walk down Swan Lane and visit the village shop. It was a tobacconist's and newspaper shop and he bought his cheroots and cigarettes there. Usually he was accompanied by one of the people who lived on the royal property. On a very few occasions he was alone.'

Recollecting further, Jim added: 'When King George V was there with him, he sometimes wore a really posh suit and some medal ribbons – but not the actual medals. He seemed to be proud of them. They were dull in colour and blue, yellow or golden orange and white. One had stripes down it and one had a trim. He was like an army officer.'[54]

Naturally, this mass of detailed information made a deep impression on me. Jim Barrett's description of 'Nikolai Alexandrovich' conformed in every respect to what was known about the Tsar. His height, his military bearing, his interest in gardening, his chain-smoking – all were typical of Nikolai II and reminiscent of the visitor to Collon described by Kathleen McCarthy. Even the medal ribbons corresponded to the Russian Orders of St George and St Vladimir. There was the implication of his associations: 'Nikolai Alexandrovich's' appearances were almost invariably in royal company, as part of the royal party. Then there was the matter of his appearance, which was so strikingly similar to King George V that the gardeners, used to royal visits, could not tell them apart. (This resemblance is usually explained by the fact that their mothers were sisters. In 1994, however, a new factor emerged. It was alleged that George V's natural father was not King Edward VII but the Tsarevich Nikolai of Russia, the elder brother of Tsar Alexander III and uncle to Tsar Nikolai II. If this were the case, then King George V and Tsar Nikolai II were cousins twice over: their mothers were sisters and their fathers brothers.[55]) Everything that Jim Barrett had said, as with everything Kathleen McCarthy before him had said, strongly suggested that the man known as Nikolai Alexandrovich was none other than Tsar Nikolai II. And yet, exciting and disturbing though this lead was, I had to put it on one side; for my main quest remained the pursuit of the truth about Nikolai Chebotarev and Marina.

On 31 October 1947 The Coppins was broken into.[56] This was no ordinary burglary, for nothing was taken. If Marina and Nikolai had married that summer, then the royal family, anxious to avert any whiff of scandal, would have been keen to lay their hands on the documentation. And they may have been looking for evidence of something else, too: evidence of medication. For by this time there were rumours about Marina's health;[57] rumours that gained new strength when, soon after the break-in, on 19 November, at the pre-wedding ball of Princess Elizabeth and Marina's cousin Prince Philip, Princess Marina fainted.[58] One of the conditions with which fainting is associated, of course, is pregnancy. It may have been at this point that the royal family's suspicions about what had been going on became strong enough to prompt them to act. Immediately after the wedding of Princess Elizabeth, Marina was dispatched to Germany, accompanied by Queen Frederika of Greece, ostensibly to acquaint the German relations who had not been invited to the wedding with all the details of the great events.[59] This seems a less than convincing reason for the trip; the more so in the light of the rumours among locals at Iver at this time. Some said, according to Jim Barrett, that Marina had already given birth to a child; others that she was undergoing some unspecified treatment from Dr Hirschewitz, a medical practitioner from eastern Poland who later changed his name to Harding and moved his practice from Iver to nearby Richings Park.[60]

These rumours, with their leavening of detail that could not be known to outsiders, bore all the signs of leaked information. The press had been full of generalized rumours about Marina's health since August. In those days of relative royal privacy, concealment was a much easier option than today. Between August and November 1947, Marina had been absent from public duties for eighty-seven out of one hundred and five days. In the period from 27 December 1947 to 6 April 1948 she was similarly absent on ninety out of ninety-four days.[61] The pattern is consistent with a birth having taken place between November 1947 and February 1948. Within these months, two periods stand out: one of thirty-eight days between the end of December 1947 and early February 1948, and that of the trip abroad, ostensibly to Germany, between 24 and 28 November 1947, immediately after the fainting episode at Princess Elizabeth's wedding ball. Either is consistent with the estimated date range of my own birth.

In a bizarre postscript to these rumours, on 2 February 1949 the *Daily Mail* published a front-page story that caused some controversy. Under the headline, 'Baby Duke (1936) Now Bonny Socialist Baby', the story exposed an apparent gaffe by the Labour government in publishing a pamphlet promoting the success of the new National Health Service. The picture of a baby that had been used in the pamphlet, supplied by a picture library, turned out to be one of Princess Marina's sons (the present Duke of Kent), taken when he was a baby in 1936. This, clearly, was no National Health Service baby. As gaffes go it was minor in the extreme; yet it was judged to be worthy of a prime slot, on a day when there was no shortage of news to fill the front page. And the Labour party's General Secretary, Morgan Phillips, was forced to issue an apology, which suggests considerable sensitivity on the issue.

Labour party headquarters still has a copy of the original pamphlet. The text below the baby Duke's photograph runs: 'The prams of Britain are filled with the bonniest babies in living memory.' The pamphlet itself was entitled, 'What does this picture mean?' Both titles were highly suggestive. It could have been pure accident; or it could mean someone – either at the newspaper or in the Labour government – knew that Marina had given birth to a baby boy, not in 1936 but soon before 1949. Could the press story of 2 February have been a way of printing the unprintable, suggesting a hidden story by associating Marina with a baby boy?

Marina was one of those women who found concealing pregnancy comparatively easy. In a tantalizing hint from the diary of her friend, the inveterate gossip 'Chips' Channon, we learn that Marina had 'half-hid' her 1936 pregnancy 'in a trailing black velvet tea gown'. Photographs taken at the Royal Windsor Horse Show in July 1947 certainly suggest that she was carrying more weight than usual.

If I really were the child of Nikolai Chebotarev and Princess Marina, there were imperatives on both sides for my concealment. From his standpoint, the birth of a son was almost certainly in breach of any agreement reached over the release of the Romanovs back in 1918, and as a result would be highly likely to provoke punitive action against him and the child. Zoe Cooke's daughter Jenny, who was close to her grandmother Natalie, insisted that my concealment was for my own safety. From Marina's point of view, the birth of any child was compromising. There were her existing children to consider, the youngest of whom was still only five years old in 1947. More important in practice than her own family concerns would have been the intervention of the Windsors, who must have come to know of the pregnancy after the fainting episode; their interests would have been to avoid all scandal by total concealment. Though Marina was a widow and eligible to marry and have children, the family into which she had previously married was not about to relinquish its interest in her future connections. And, as we have seen, it was impossible that the true identity of her second husband should be made known.

Royal denials of major family events are far from uncommon. As recently as December 1997 it was revealed that the present Duchess of Kent had given birth in 1977 to a fourth child, Patrick, who died after just thirty-six hours, plunging his mother into a period of severe and acute depression.[62] Yet for years the royal family had maintained that the pregnancy had ended with a miscarriage in the fifth month. If the Palace was unwilling for the truth of this episode to become known, how much more unwilling would it have been to disclose the birth of a son to the previous Duchess of Kent and the former Tsarevich of Russia?

A secret birth, perhaps a royal marriage: it was inevitable that the child would have to be given a secret identity. What was to happen to me?

# The Chain of Custody

Since Prince Alexander Lieven and Dr Martha Apraxine appeared with me in the concealed baby photographs, it seemed logical to begin with them in my search for evidence linking me to Marina and Nikolai Chebotarev. With Lieven, I had quite a lot to go on. I knew from Alix Hill that he had been a close friend of Chebotarev and that Nikolai had visited him during his time at Trinity College, Dublin from 1938 to 1941.[1] I had also learned from Alix that he had told her and another colleague in the Ministry of Defence how he had brought Princess Marina back from Belfast harbour when she had been on the point of running away. And I knew from the surviving servants of Croft House, Bridie Gorman and Kitty Geddis, that Lieven, whose photograph they had recognized without hesitation, had visited Natalie Cooke both there and at Princeton Road in Bangor, as had his aunt Princess Sophie Lieven and Nikolai Couriss.[2] Lieven's social circle in Northern Ireland extended, however, well beyond Natalie Cooke.

At Irish military intelligence headquarters in Cathal Brugha barracks in Dublin I found a letter penned by Lieven, dated 10 August 1940, informing the Irish authorities where he was spending his holidays. It read: 'As an alien I would like to let you know that I am leaving for a holiday of a fortnight at the Manor House, Tollymore, Newcastle, County Down. I know it is unnecessary to notify of absences of less than one month but I thought you might find it useful to know of foreigners' whereabouts under present circumstances. Yours faithfully, Alexander Lieven.'[3] As it happened, he need not have been so punctilious in telling the authorities where he was going; they were already watching him.

In those days the Manor House at Tollymore was the residence of Elinor, Countess of Roden. Born Jessie Elinor Charlton-Parr, the daughter of Joseph Charlton-Parr of Grappenhall Hayes in Cheshire, she had married Robert, 8th Earl of Roden, in 1905.[4] It seemed strange to be uncovering a vital piece of information about a member of Northern Ireland's Unionist Establishment on a dusty desk in a military barracks in

Dublin under a portrait of Michael Collins, the great IRA war leader and first head of the Free State army. But these connections, unlikely as they seemed on the surface, were to prove crucial in tracing the threads of my story. Lady Roden's brother had married Lord Roden's sister, and in 1914 her own sister, Margaret Alicia, had also made an Irish marriage, the third in the family.[5] Her husband was Major Holt Waring of Waringstown in County Down, scion of a family which had owned that manor since 1660; the Charlton-Parr marriage brought money into the troubled Waring estate that was to sustain it for a further sixty years. Alicia Waring was very close to her sister Elinor and they frequently visited each other; in her will she left the bulk of her fortune – the fortune she had brought into the Waring family in 1914 – to her nephew, the 9th Earl of Roden. Just four years after their wedding, Major Holt Waring was dead, killed in a gas attack shortly before the end of the First World War. His widow lived on in the great Jacobean house as lady of the manor of Waringstown until her death fifty-five years later, in 1973. Waringstown was the village where I had grown up.

Alicia Waring's connections to this story went further. Not only did her circle include Alexander Lieven, but she was also related to Martha Apraxine: Mrs Waring's aunt proved to be the great-niece of Prince Bariatinsky, Dr Apraxine's grandfather.[6] This was no distant, exotic connection: these people were still alive when Alicia Waring was a girl. Kathleen McCarthy remembered Martha Apraxine's Bariatinsky cousins visiting at Collon; she also remembered Mrs Waring coming to visit Couriss, and being particularly friendly with Martha. Mrs Waring had more recent Russian connections, too. Edmund Waring, her late husband's cousin, had married a Russian girl, Anna Pavlovna Filina, daughter of a Captain Paul Filina of the imperial Russian army.[7] I also knew that Alicia Waring had links with my surrogate father's family going back to the 1920s, when she had personally taken his sister, then dying of tuberculosis, for treatment at an expensive Harley Street clinic. Such concern suggested a close connection.

Alicia Waring, then, was connected to both of the people in the baby photograph with me, to the village where I had grown up, and to my surrogate parents. And her social standing put her in an ideal position to arrange the secret placing of a baby with a new family. For Mrs Waring was a formidable Unionist grandee who, in the effective one-party state that Northern Ireland was in those days, considered herself beyond the law. Living in the great house with its own private path to the ancient parish church where she sat in the massive black oak Waring pew with its ornately carved coat of arms – a pew which no one else was allowed to enter – she ran her village along semi-feudal lines. Concealing a baby with villagers of her choice is unlikely to have presented serious difficulties for her, and she was easily capable of the resolute action necessary. Her family motto, in an age when such things still counted, was *Faire sans dire* – do without saying. The village's name still meant what it said: in Waringstown, Mrs Waring was all-powerful. John Paton, the local doctor, who had stamped over Dr Bowman of Bangor's stamp in my medical record, almost obliterating it in the process, was, as villagers put it, 'under Mrs Waring's thumb'.[8] If, as seems likely, he was a party to this deception, it would have been under the great lady's orders. Paton and Bowman would also have known each other, and must have attended some classes together, since lectures in those days at the Queen's University medical school, where both doctors qualified, were organized so that students from different years mixed with one another.

Alicia Waring initially chose as her heir the son of Samuel Barbour Combe, the nephew of her late husband. Waring Combe changed his name to Combe Waring in anticipation of his inheritance, but broke his neck in a riding accident before he had a chance to enjoy it. Samuel Barbour Combe, his father, was a close friend of Natalie and Frank Cooke and a frequent guest in Croft House. The circle, it seemed, was beginning to close: for not only had Natalie Cooke harboured Nikolai Chebotarev during the latter half of the Second World War but he was a frequent visitor at her home in the post-war years as well, and I had the testimony of the Croft House servants Bridie Gorman and Kitty Geddis that he had been accompanied there in 1946 by Princess Marina, in the guise of Mme Velika. A chain of custody was beginning to form, linking Natalie Cooke, Martha Apraxine and Prince Alexander Lieven through Alicia Waring to my surrogate parents and Dr Paton; and the more I found out about this group, the more echoes resounded from my own disjointed early memories.

Mrs Waring was a quintessential Establishment figure. Dominating the local Unionist hierarchy, she had been an MP in the 1930s and by the 1950s ran the local hospitals authority. Her mother's cousin, Commander Russell Lister-Kaye, was gentleman usher to King George VI. He was the same age as Mrs Waring herself. Another cousin was married to yet another courtier family, the Ponsonbys, and was a relative of Lady Antrim. Mrs Waring herself was a striking figure with her severe blue serge suit and large hobnailed boots. I can still recall being fixated on those boots and her – as it seemed to me – gigantic feet when I alone, out of the entire primary school, was brought up and presented to her on the one occasion I ever remember her visiting the school. I did not imagine then that she might actually have come to see me.

Mrs Waring travelled in a navy-blue chauffeur-driven Citroën, very unusual for Northern Ireland in those days, with yellow, opaque windows. I discovered that it matches, in every respect, the car in that early memory of a rainy night and the voices of several men and one woman saying, 'He's tired, get him home quickly.' It had the same rear-view mirror mounted on the dashboard and the windscreen wipers operating from the top, not the bottom of the window. I can still smell the leather of the seats.

Generations of village families had served the Warings, nearly all of them descendants of the English planters her husband's ancestors had brought from his native Lancashire. Mrs Waring herself was spoken of locally in hushed, even reverential, tones. Always the same story was told: of the young bride carried into the village in 1914 to the adulation of the tenantry massed with their oil lamps to greet her, of the distraught wife in 1918, widowed by a fatal gas attack in the closing days of the Great War, and of her subsequent life as a widow in that gloomy mansion. Her land agent, James Hampton, lived with her in the big house, leaving his own wife and family in their tied cottage on the estate. No one dared even to snigger behind their hands at this arrangement. Hampton's wife Margaret was the closest friend of my surrogate father's mother: both had turned to religion in an extreme form – Plymouth Brethrenism – one because she was a widow, the other because she might as well have been. Every time Margaret Hampton visited my surrogate grandmother she presented me with a string of black liquorice produced from her dirty coat pocket. I never ate it.

Waring connections to the Russians in Ireland do not end with Alexander Lieven and Martha Apraxine. The Warings were twice married into another Irish county family, the McClintocks of County Louth, who were particularly close friends of Nikolai Couriss. Both the aunt and great-aunt of Holt Waring, Mrs Waring's late husband, were McClintocks.[9] Margaret Elizabeth McClintock had married his Uncle Holt, after whom he was named, and Alexander McClintock had married his great-aunt Jane. The McClintocks were also related to the Grubbs, close relatives of the Richardson family: Hilda Richardson's father-in-law had been John

Grubb Richardson. The Waring estate in Waringstown was only eight miles distant from Moyallon, and it is easy to see how these connections could have reactivated and strengthened Mrs Waring's ties to the Collon set. In a social world of landed families circulating between grand country houses, the links of birth and descent, deepened and widened by generation after generation of intermarriage, were all-important in creating the networks within which family business was conducted – in secrecy and with discretion.

Just as the complexity of the Waring connections unravelled, so other parts of the jigsaw began to fall into place. Bangor had still more secrets to disgorge. Every year my surrogate grandmother would travel there, basing her summer holiday around an annual missionary convention held in the town. That convention was held in the Plymouth Brethren Hall, which was situated in Central Avenue. Central Avenue joins Princeton Road, where Natalie Cooke lived from September 1948, with Hamilton Road, where Dr Bowman's surgery, the child health clinic I remembered, and the park with the tennis courts in which one of my baby photographs with Dr Martha Apraxine was taken were all situated. At Number 29 Central Avenue lived Muriel Todd, herself a member of the Brethren, in a house sandwiched between the Brethren Hall on one side and the Quaker meeting house on the other, as if physically expressing the link between the Richardson Quakers and my surrogate father. Muriel Todd would have considered the convention my surrogate grandmother attended as a key occasion in the religious calendar, not to be missed. My surrogate grandmother also knew Stephens Richardson, Hilda's successor at Moyallon, whom I recall seeing on a couple of occasions when I was a young child.

Muriel Todd visited Moyallon twice in 1940 with Natalie Cooke.[10] To describe the extravagant Russian émigré aristocrat and the strait-laced member of the Brethren as an unlikely pair of travelling companions, let alone house-guests, is a considerable understatement. Quite how they found each other is anybody's guess; but they did, and the occasion is documented in the Moyallon visitors' book. Zoe Cooke also remembered it – she drove the car. Muriel Todd was a children's nurse; matron of a maternity home in Malone Place, Belfast, close to the city hospital, and with her own home in Bangor, ideally placed to look after a baby. Dr John Bowman was not Natalie's doctor, but the Croft House servants recall that he had something to do with the Cookes, though they cannot remember exactly what. Bowman's surgery is less than half a mile from

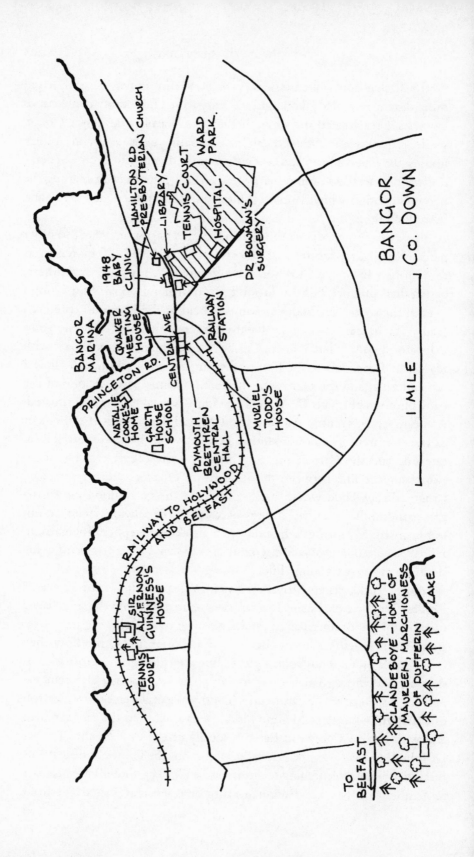

BANGOR
Co. DOWN

1 MILE

BANGOR MARINA

QUAKER MEETING HOUSE

PRINCETON RD.

NATALIE COOKE'S HOME

GARTH HOUSE SCHOOL

CENTRAL AVE.

1948 BABY CLINIC

HAMILTON RD PRESBYTERIAN CHURCH

LIBRARY

TENNIS COURT

WARD PARK.

HOSPITAL

DR BOWMAN'S SURGERY

RAILWAY STATION

PLYMOUTH BRETHREN CENTRAL HALL

MURIEL TODD'S HOUSE

RAILWAY TO HOLYWOOD AND BELFAST

SIR ALGERNON GUINNESS'S HOUSE

TENNIS COURT

TO BELFAST

CLANDEBOYE - HOME OF MAUREEN, MARCHIONESS OF DUFFERIN

LAKE

Natalie's house and Muriel Todd's home is exactly half way between them. Someone must have looked after me on a day-to-day basis in 1948–9, and, based so strategically in the town where, according to my medical record, I was being kept at that time, Muriel Todd has to be a strong candidate.

Bangor held yet more surprises. According to Zoe Cooke, Nikolai Chebotarev had taught French during the war to Sheridan, the young son of the Marchioness of Dufferin and Ava, at Garth House, a preparatory school on Maxwell Road in Bangor.[11] The Marchioness, who before her marriage had been one of the 'golden Guinness girls' of 1920s London society, lived in the sprawling mansion of Clandeboye House on the outskirts of Bangor;[12] and here, it seems, I was an unwitting infant visitor. My source for this startling piece of information was Billy McDonald. A trained engineer and one of the foremost piano restorers and tuners in Ireland – the only man in the country permitted by Steinway to recondition their pianos outside their own workshops – McDonald is a very precise man, a man for whom detail and accuracy matter. Now in his sixties, as a young man he spent time on the Clandeboye estate where his Uncle William was head joiner. Billy McDonald is adamant that the ornamental fountain in one of the concealed photographs of me as a baby used to be at Clandeboye House. It has since been removed.[13]

Other associations linked the people at Clandeboye to the Cooke–Couriss Russian set. Lady Dufferin's uncle was Lord Moyne, the British minister in Cairo who was killed by Jewish terrorists in Palestine in 1944, and Moyne had provided a home in Dublin for a member of the city's diplomatic set, Lydia Prescott.[14] Her surname, that of her Irish civil servant husband George Prescott, disguised her origins; Lydia Stepanova Prescott was originally from Kiev, and her circle of friends included Natalie Cooke, Martha Apraxine, Nikolai and Sana Couriss, Hilda Richardson and the Princes Paul and Alexander Lieven. Too many of these people were involved in my own early life and in Nikolai Chebotarev's story for Lydia Prescott to be ignored. Kathleen McCarthy has a photograph in which Mrs Prescott appears on the arm of old Prince Paul Lieven. Describing her Dublin home, known as Bettyglen, as beautiful, with a delightful garden and full of the cats which were her passion, Kathleen added that in Collon they called her 'the vamp'.[15] Zoe Cooke recalls her frequent visits to Natalie's homes at Croft House and Princeton Road; Natalie called her 'Dumpy' Prescott. Both Lydia and her husband feature in the Moyallon visitors' book, along with Natalie Cooke, in 1940. Lydia Prescott was Martha Apraxine's closest friend and, according to Kathleen McCarthy, the two regularly visited Northern Ireland together. In view of these connections, it made perfect sense that Martha Apraxine would visit Clandeboye.

Maureen Guinness, Lady Dufferin, was also a friend of Princess Marina – *The Times* of 18 July 1949 records that they dined 'privately' together – as was her niece, Lady Honor Guinness, and Lady Honor's husband Sir Henry 'Chips' Channon; the Channons had been neighbours of the Princess in the late 1930s when she had lived in Belgrave Square. The more closely I looked, the denser became the network of interrelationships; and every thread led inexorably back to Lieven, Apraxine, Couriss and Cooke.

Nor did the Guinness connections end here. The first of Maureen Guinness' three husbands – and, according to her, 'the best' – was a war hero. Coming from a very distinguished Ulster family, Basil Sheridan Hamilton-Temple-Blackwood, 4th Marquess of Dufferin and Ava, had volunteered during the Second World War for 'special duties' behind enemy lines in Burma, having previously served on the staff of the Supreme Allied Commander, South-East Asia, Louis Mountbatten; he was killed in action on 25 March 1945.[16] From 1937 to 1940 he had served in government as Under-Secretary of State for the Colonies, in which capacity one of his closest colleagues was Viscount Caldecote, Secretary of State for Dominion Affairs; and Caldecote's brother, Sir John Inskip, was Hilda Richardson's solicitor. Here was another thread in the network. There were royal links – Dufferin was also a lord in waiting to King George VI, and his wife was a lifelong friend of George VI's consort, now the Queen Mother – and there were Russian links: Lord Dufferin's grandfather, the 1st Marquess, had been British ambassador in St Petersburg from 1879 to 1881, the year in which Tsar Alexander II was assassinated. Since the 1880s he and his wife, who had died as recently as 1936, had been friends of Baroness Agnes de Stoeckl, a close friend of Princess Victoria, George V's sister, who lived in The Coppins at the back entrance of Victoria's home at Iver – the home she bequeathed to Princess Marina in 1935.[17] Maureen Dufferin herself may also have had Russian connections of a sort. In 1960 her niece, Lady Elizabeth Maria Guinness, married David Hugh Lavallin Nugent of Ross Castle, Mount Nugent, County Cavan. His grandfather, Major-General Nugent of Mount Nugent, had been the Commanding Officer of the Royal Scots

Dragoon Guards when Tsar Nikolai II had been their colonel-in-chief – a regimental link so strong that a contingent of Royal Scots attended the funeral of the Ekaterinburg bones in July 1998.

Another officer who, like the Marquess of Dufferin, had served on Lord Mountbatten's staff during the war was Gerry Lytle, who in 1946 married Natalie Cooke's daughter. Zoe explained that Gerry was the first serviceman repatriated by Mountbatten from south-east Asia by special dispensation under a section 8 order. Mountbatten's interest in Gerry did not end there: he went on to find Lytle a job in the British Army's small arms training centre at Bisley.[18] In the context of the Romanovs' affairs, any connection with Mountbatten has to be viewed with suspicion. Gerry Lytle, in fact, worked in intelligence; and when he died, Zoe learned with horror that the man she had been married to for decades was known in intelligence circles as 'Paddy' and that his death was viewed with suspicion by the police. Lytle also had personal connections with the Dufferins; when the Clandeboye estate manager, Agar, moved to England, Zoe and Gerry looked after his son Ian for six months. And it may not be pure coincidence that Gerry Lytle was the first cousin of David Andrews, chairman of Isaac Andrews Flour Mills, the firm for which my surrogate father worked for over twenty years from the late 1950s.[19] Wherever I looked there were ties linking Clandeboye to those close and overlapping circles of Russians and intelligence operatives in which my early life had become deeply involved.

Further probing of the Cooke–Mountbatten connection produced some interesting findings. As mentioned in chapter 17, Natalie Cooke had apparently planned to 'present' her daughter Zoe to Lady Zia Wernher. Not only was Lady Zia the morganatic daughter of Grand Duke Mikhail of Russia and a friend of Princess Marina, she was also the sister of Nada Mountbatten, Marchioness of Milford Haven and sister-in-law to Louis Mountbatten. No doubt this was the network Natalie had accessed to ease her prospective son-in-law Gerry Lytle's speedy repatriation by Mountbatten. Such transactions usually entail a price, and the price Natalie paid was almost certainly information on the fast-developing relationship between Nikolai Chebotarev and Princess Marina, alias 'Mme Velika', taking place under her own roof at Croft House during 1946. Mountbatten's sister-in-law Nada was the person most responsible for bringing up Prince Philip, who had been abandoned to schools in England when his own parents had drifted off to lead their separate lives. Prince Philip also came under the wing of his older cousin, Princess Marina, who, as Duchess of Kent after 1934, eased his introduction into the British royal family – possibly more deftly than his uncle Lord Mountbatten, who was a little too obvious in this regard – and helped out by providing a secluded location for his courting of Princess Elizabeth at her home in Iver, Buckinghamshire, so conveniently close to London, yet so much more private.[20] Her interest in her young relative, however, went much further back, to Paris in the 1920s, where she had often looked out for him. Nikolai Chebotarev, of course, had been part of the same circle; indeed, his niece Iya told me that he had known Prince Philip when the latter had been a boy in Paris.[21]

One more piece in the puzzle was slotted in by Zoe Cooke, who told me of an unusual visitor in 1946: a Father Barnabas from Paris, who came to Croft House for a time, after which he went on to stay with a fellow clergyman in Belfast.[22] This is most likely to have been Hieromonk Barnabas, the priest who buried Archbishop Theophan in 1940. In Nikolai Chebotarev's papers are the records of a train journey he took from the Gare d'Austerlitz in Paris to Tours and thence to Amboise, which lies just across the River Loire from Limeray. There, on a bluff just above the town and overlooking the river, is the cemetery containing Theophan's remains. Since Nikolai was in Ireland from May 1939 and Theophan only moved to Limeray in September that year, this journey must have taken place after the war, probably during a visit Nikolai made to Paris with Natalie Cooke and Baroness de Huene in 1945 or 1946. Natalie and Nikolai came back fairly quickly, according to Zoe; Natalie did not find the privations of post-war Paris to her taste. Nikolai probably brought Father Barnabas back with him; but why? This was in 1946 – the year when he and Marina were 'canoodling' in the bedrooms of Croft House, to use Kitty Geddis's phrase. It is at least possible that Barnabas may have been there to conduct a wedding – or a baptism, as he is known to have remained in Ireland for some time.

All the links in the chain of custody leading from Princess Marina and Nikolai Chebotarev, through Prince Alexander Lieven, Dr Martha Apraxine, Alicia Waring, Natalie Cooke and Nikolai Couriss to me and my surrogate parents were now in place. Sent by the intelligence services to bring her back from Belfast, Lieven was already on Marina's case in April 1947; his presence in the photograph with me taken in the summer of 1948 indicates that he was still on it some fifteen months later, and that the authorities who had ordered her interception the previous year were taking a close interest in what happened to me. Lieven's link to Alicia

Waring through her sister may have cemented a relationship already based on kinship with Dr Apraxine. Alicia Waring could easily have procured the prospective parents for the unwanted child – unwanted, that is, by the house of Windsor though probably not by Princess Marina. The marriage of the chosen surrogate parents in January 1948 suggests that the plan to place me with them must have been afoot about the time of my birth.

It was clear, however, that there were tensions within the apparently seamless web of contacts and alliances within which this arrangement was being made, tensions no doubt associated with the irreconcilable division between Natalie Cooke's deep and abiding hatred of the house of Windsor, so strongly apparent in the post-war years, and the equally deep and abiding loyalty to the British ruling family of the reactionary Unionist, Alicia Waring. While Mrs Waring would unquestioningly and unwaveringly follow the line laid down by the British crown, Natalie would have had little sympathy with Windsor priorities and sensitivities. Marina's last, hasty and unannounced visit to Natalie's new home in Princeton Road, Bangor, in September 1948 may have been a desperate attempt to forestall the action that by then was already determined; for Couriss, through his links to Dr Eppel outlined in chapter 16, probably organized the creation of my new identity that August. Zoe Cooke knew that some kind of Russian summit had been held in Croft House during 1948 which she believed involved Lieven. If that summit had been called to decide – or more likely to announce – my fate, as Zoe Cooke believed, then its decisions may have been resisted by the people who were least consulted in all of this: my parents, Nikolai and Marina. Natalie Cooke may have shared their distaste for the outcome, and for the way in which Martha Apraxine and Alexander Lieven were acting as agents for British royal interests.

At this point, with the whole affair in crisis, in August 1948 Natalie went for a cruise. This was odd on several counts. First, she went with Frank, despite the fact that they had now been living apart for some years, and had a profound aversion to each other's company, which they avoided whenever possible. Second, this was a Baltic cruise, aboard the *Polar Star*, a ship of the Stella Polaris line, including among its ports of call Leningrad and Tallinn, both firmly inside the USSR. Natalie said that she would not get off the ship in Leningrad as she was afraid they might detain her. Third, this was a time of confusion as the Cookes were moving house; they returned from the trip to their new home at

Princeton Road in Bangor. It is at least arguable that one motive for the trip was to avoid the chaos of a house move, but this is not a sufficient explanation. Why visit somewhere where you cannot disembark? Why go with a husband you detest? Natalie's visit to Leningrad may well have been represented as a threat; she had, after all, saleable information. Certainly, it appeared suspicious. Lieven may well have used it as the reason to move me to a new location, ostensibly for my own safety, to a place the whereabouts of which Marina and Nikolai did not know and were not told. This could have prompted Marina's desperate unannounced visit as 'Mme Velika' to Princeton Road, Bangor in September 1948. Ironically, I may well still have been very close by, still in the same town, but no longer in the hiding place Marina and Natalie knew about; that is, at Maureen Dufferin's home at Clandeboye. Prince Alexander Lieven, operating for British intelligence, knew; Dr Martha Apraxine knew; and the blame for the move was put on Natalie and her suspect trip to Leningrad. But she was almost certainly effectively excluded from detailed information on my whereabouts. Natalie felt thereafter that she should be vindicated, and to this end, she placed relevant papers and documentation in a black safe deposit box which she lodged in a bank. I have been given the key for this box. Towards the end of her life, Zoe and her relatives tried to locate the box, without success.[23]

The trouble facing unhappy members of the royal family like Princess Marina – as Diana, Princess of Wales was to discover half a century later – is the difficulty of knowing whom to trust. Virtually everyone Marina knew was intimately connected with the royal house; and if she had confided in any of them she would have been putting their loyalty under enormous strain. This constraint had the effect of isolating her. Maureen Guinness was a case in point. A friend of Marina she may have been; but one of her oldest friends was Queen Elizabeth, now the Queen Mother. Late in 1997 we sought an interview with Maureen Guinness, but the normally loquacious Marchioness declined. In the business of her attachment to Nikolai Chebotarev and the birth of a child, Marina would have been out on a limb. In the eyes of senior royalty this would have been viewed as an act of rebellion within the family with possibly serious ramifications. Separated from the policies and protection of senior royal figures, people like Marina are very vulnerable. Northern Ireland was a place of unquestioning loyalty to the crown. Its Governor, Earl Granville, was married to Queen Elizabeth's sister, and Lady Granville was the head of Ulster society. Her influence extended everywhere; Stephens Richardson's wife, for instance, was her friend.

Powerful, cynical and resolute forces were at work here to protect royal interests and prevent scandal. Determined to provide a solution to a difficult situation, the agents of the Windsors passed me along this chain of custody to my ultimate keepers. The terms in which this solution was represented depended on one's viewpoint. For the Windsors it was the provision of deep cover for an embarrassment which had the potential not merely to fracture the public image the royal family wished to present to the country but also to unearth arrangements made with and for the Romanovs thirty years previously. For those closer to the situation in the Russian–Irish network, it was probably explained away as a means of providing protection for a baby who, according to whatever arrangements had been made with the Bolsheviks in 1918, should never have been born in the first place. In this hidden spider's web linking Lieven, Couriss and Apraxine with Cooke, Prescott and Waring, and all of them with Nikolai Chebotarev and Princess Marina, lay both the solution to the immediate problem and the means of my deep concealment. Operating out of Natalie Cooke's homes in Bangor and Croft House and Couriss' home in Collon, this network of secret and secretive people had the means to dispose of a child and effectively brush over the traces of what they had done.

Without knowing how these people all related to one another, through connections many of which were obscure or invisible from outside, it would be impossible to penetrate the network which carried out this concealment. For as long as the deception worked, and the connections were never revealed, royalty could keep their distance from this unexploded bomb. After the death of all the leading parties it must have seemed that it would lie hidden for ever – Marina and Martha Apraxine had died in 1968, Alicia Waring in 1973, Couriss in 1977, Nikolai in 1987, Alexander Lieven in 1988. Yet in 1993 the cover slipped. Questions were raised, with the results described so far in this book – and so was royal interest.

# Royal Reaction

Bill Phillips, the museum curator whose approach had led me to begin this quest back in April 1993, announced in September 1994 that he had himself been approached by someone called Timothy Rearden. Phillips claimed that Rearden had been directed to his house having turned up at a filling station opposite asking questions about a local family – the Blackers of Carrickblacker, near Moyallon. This interest soon evaporated, Phillips said, into direct questioning about the Russians.

From the very outset Rearden made no secret of his royal and Russian connections. Prince Michael of Greece, he said, had just been his house-guest in his home in the grounds of Huntingdon Castle in Clonegal in County Wicklow. Prince Michael of Greece was the first cousin of Princess Marina, the son of Prince Christopher of Greece, younger brother of Marina's father. Two years earlier, Prince Michael had been working in the newly opened Russian state archives to gather material for his photographic book, *Nicholas and Alexandra, the Family Albums*. He was among the first Westerners allowed to do so. It seemed reasonable to wonder whether his interest in the Romanovs extended beyond the photographic record. Rearden also claimed to have known Lord Louis Mountbatten who, he said, when asked why he could not recognize Anastasia, had replied mysteriously, cutting him off, 'Well, there wasn't any money.' His friend Lady Maria Levinge knew Prince Lvov and Prince Yusupov. He claimed to have had connections with ex-King Milo of Montenegro, another exile who had lived in Ireland – at Roundstone in Connemara – and that his grandmother Lady Sybil Gaunt had seen the Tsarina hyperventilating at the Bolshoi Theatre.

Mention of his own family cast some light on Rearden's background, but raised just as many questions as it answered. Lady Sybil Gaunt, the widow of W. O. Joseph of Cairo, was the second wife of Admiral Sir Guy Reginald Archer Gaunt and lived at Oxshott in Surrey; she had one daughter. Though Rearden claimed his mother was a member of the Durdin-Robertson family and that one of his homes was located in the grounds of their family seat, there was no mention of anyone answering his mother's description in Burke's *Irish Family Records*, which contains a full genealogy of that family.[1] Rearden also claimed to have been brought up by the Hohenzollerns – not the Kaiser's branch, as he later explained to me on the one occasion when we spoke, in October 1995, but the Hohenzollern-Sigmaringens, who were the royal family of Romania. He went on to say they had a Belgian connection. Queen Marie of Romania's husband, King Ferdinand, had a brother, Prince Karl Anton of Hohenzollern-Sigmaringen, who married Princess Josephine of Belgium. Their son, Prince Albrecht of Hohenzollern-Sigmaringen, was born in 1898 and he and his wife Ilse Margot von Friedburg fit the description of Rearden's 'adoptive' parents.[2] They are related to the self-styled Grand Duchess Maria Romanov and her young son, George, claimants to the Russian throne. Such a connection might suggest who had set Rearden's enquiries in train. But the answer may lie closer to home.

According to Phillips, Rearden's father had been in military intelligence and had been killed in the Second World War. Apparently, he had returned home for visits through Portugal, where he had ambassadorial friends – Baron Oswald von Hoyingen-Huene had been German ambassador there at that time, and Rearden appeared to have some knowledge of the Hoyingen-Huene family. Yet later, when Phillips was quizzed about Rearden's age, he gave it as forty-one in 1995, a figure borne out by the age of Rearden's closest friend Nicholas, Earl of Caledon, with whom he stayed regularly. Caledon, like Rearden an old boy of Gordonstoun, Prince Philip's school, was born on 6 May 1955.[3] If Phillips was right and the two men were of an age, Rearden's father could not have been killed in the war. Yet it was only later – well into 1995, after my suspicions of Rearden and his relationship with Phillips were aroused – that I began to pore over my notebooks and notice these inconsistencies. The Earl of Caledon was Her Majesty's Lord Lieutenant for County Armagh – a role which goes much further than the public image of the flunkey in semi-military uniform who appears on royal visits. In each county of the Union, the Lord Lieutenant is the Queen's eyes and ears, and supervises a whole system of vice-lieutenants and deputy lieutenants, below whom are the justices of the peace. The responsibility of training the Lords Lieutenant falls to Prince Philip, who has for many years entrusted the task to the Rt Revd Michael Mann, the Dean of Windsor.

Rearden told Phillips that he was a friend of lawyer Helen Cleveland, whose great-aunt, Joan Blacker, had been at Moyallon with Nikolai Chebotarev. Another of her relatives had been at Eton with Voislav Misitch and her husband, Bill Powell, was the grandson of Flight Lieutenant Lavington, who had been billeted over the Post Office at Moyallon, visited Moyallon House and commanded the radar station at Torr Head in the Second World War. Phillips also confirmed to me that when Rearden spoke of the Russian at Moyallon, he did not even ask for his name. He appeared to know it already.

Either Rearden was a name-dropper of truly titanic proportions, or he really was at the heart of a web of royal and Russian connections. And if he knew so much already, why did he need to talk to anyone? It appeared that there might be a royal agenda in all of this. Within five weeks of Rearden's first appearance on 28 August he was offering, through Phillips, to send questions 'up the line' to the British royal family. The offer, made on 3 October, was relayed to me by Phillips in the plainest of terms: 'Write down the questions and I will get you the answers.' Rearden had already spoken of having been to Russia recently to look at paintings, accompanied by 'a fat woman' from the CIA. This was immediately before the Queen's much-trumpeted visit to Russia, which began on 17 October 1994, and Phillips suggested that Rearden had been preparing her way. Others whom I told about Rearden associated him with Princess Anne, possibly as her press secretary at one stage. Zoe Cooke's daughter Jenny, who admitted knowing Rearden, ran out of the room in a panic, leaving her bag and purse behind, when Zoe started to ask questions about him. At one point soon after this, someone answering Rearden's description turned up on Zoe Cooke's doorstep, purporting to conduct a population survey. He was driving a make of car which matched Rearden's – 'a clapped-out white Ford', to use Phillips' phrase.

Rearden explained to Phillips that these questions 'up the line' were to be transmitted through his friend 'Maddy Dillon', who he said was Princess Anne's lady in waiting. Prince Michael of Greece, who according to Rearden had recently stayed with him, was the cousin of Princess Anne's father, Prince Philip, as well as of Princess Marina. At the time, I checked out Maddy Dillon and found her to be Hon. Madeline Mary Dillon, Princess Anne's deputy private secretary. She was the daughter of the 20th Viscount Dillon who, according to Zoe Cooke, had holidayed with Natalie Cooke at the Grand Hotel, Malahide, on the coast near Dublin, in 1929, in the days before he inherited his peerage.[4] Lord

'Mick' Dillon, as his friends called him, and Lady Dillon, who still lives in Drogheda, near Collon, had been friends of Couriss, Tolstoy and Lady Antrim. Their ancestral home, Rath House, was at Termonfeckin near Collon. The Dillons, like the Antrims, were Roman Catholics. Their family had been 'wild geese', supporters of the deposed King James II who had fled to France after his defeat at the Battle of the Boyne in 1690 and, as a consequence, they possessed a French title – Count Dillon – in addition to their Irish one. 'Mick' Dillon carried this affiliation one stage further. He was president of the Royal Stuart Society, which maintained in a very supine and discreet way the principle that the exiled Stuarts were the rightful British royal family. No practical implications whatsoever should be drawn from this, however, as this society has no active aspirations to supplant the present British royals.

Satisfied that Rearden really did represent a direct link into the royal family, I wondered at the time if it constituted some kind of approach by the Windsors, not directly but discreetly and deniably through the medium of royal servants. It certainly bore all the hallmarks. In the year and a half since I had started to make enquiries, I had uncovered a great deal – perhaps too much for some people's comfort.

Shortly after Rearden's request had been relayed to me, I framed two questions for the royal family. They were designed to hint at what I suspected without actually saying it, and were framed in such a way that it would be difficult to answer in the negative. First, I enquired whether they knew all of Princess Marina's Russian connections. Secondly, I asked whether they would like to know more about Romanov survivors. Phillips later told our researcher that on Friday 20 October Madeline Dillon had flown to Dublin airport specifically to collect the questions and take them to a meeting of the newly formed royal 'Way Ahead' group at Balmoral that same weekend. Within a week, like clockwork, an answer came back.

The response came in the form of a note to Phillips scrawled by Rearden. After I asked to see a copy, Phillips faxed it to me on Saturday 29 October 1994. It read, in that clipped shorthand so typical of courtiers: 'I never got a chance to come Nth but will ring soon. Dep here am Sun for Scotland then home. I of M [Isle of Man] intermittently till Xmas. Maddie [Madeline Dillon] answered me that her boss [Princess Anne] wd most def not be interested in Anything at all about the R's – But P M of K [Prince Michael of Kent] wd! Will spk. Timothy.' Though Phillips was anxious that I should respond to this invitation, I hesitated. At that stage, in October 1994, I felt that I needed to know more before I spoke to anyone. If what I now believed about Nikolai Chebotarev and Princess Marina were true, it was little wonder that Prince Michael of Kent was showing an interest.

It was some months after this, in mid-1995, after Zoe Cooke had warned me of her intense suspicions of Phillips, that I gained access to his office telephone bills through a local alderman who was on the governing board of the museum. These told me that Phillips had been in touch with Rearden's circle much earlier than he had led me to believe. Phillips had dated Rearden's first appearance at 28 August 1994, but the itemized account showed that he had been speaking to Rearden's friends as early as 9 March 1994. He may even have been in contact before that, since the telephone bills prior to this date were not itemized. This discovery raised considerable doubts in my mind about the nature and extent of Phillips' connection to Rearden. Had it been Rearden who had activated Phillips in the first place? While he may well have called out of the blue at Phillips' home, this may have happened not in August 1994, which is what Phillips led me to believe, but much earlier – before that first approach to me at the end of April 1993.

I could see why Phillips would have seemed a good person to use for such an approach. Not only was he local, so that it would not be surprising that he knew something of the goings-on at Moyallon House, but he was peripherally connected to me through work, having been an education officer in the local education authority while I was a college principal. And he might have surprising connections. He had, for instance, spoken to me about his extensive travels behind the Iron Curtain in the Communist era, to places I thought were off limits at that time. One of his stories, I recalled, included his near-arrest in a Soviet drinking den. Now I wondered what Phillips had been doing inside Russia, what kind of people he had been mixed up with and if they had some form of control over him. In 1992 Rory Peck, the brother-in-law of Rearden's friend the Earl of Caledon, had been killed entering the Ostankino Television Headquarters in Moscow with Communist insurgents during the anti-Yeltsin coup.[5] The Pecks, of Prehen House in Londonderry, had been Orthodox members of Nikolai Couriss' flock when he became a priest after Sana's death in 1967. There was sufficient connection here to suggest that the people behind Phillips were active within Russia itself and knew something of what Couriss had been doing. Phillips himself may have been chosen

to approach me not only because of his local credentials, but because
he was already known to them. If, as seems likely from the dates,
Rearden had activated Phillips, the only real question remaining was:
who had activated Rearden?

It seemed clear to me that Rearden's note to Phillips outlining the
royal response to my two questions was designed to lead me into direct
contact with Prince Michael of Kent – Princess Marina's son and the
Queen's adviser on all things Russian. Prince Michael also possessed an
intelligence background, having been recruited into military intelligence
in 1967. Speaking the language, the grandson of a Russian Grand Duchess, and apparently doing his best to look like the last Tsar, Nikolai II,
he appeared to be the official voice of Britain's royalty on Russian questions. But was he? Or was he, in this matter at any rate, following an
agenda of his own? Enough is known about the affairs of Prince Michael
and of his private secretary, John Kennedy/Gvozdenovic, as discussed in
detail in chapter 6, to make this at least a plausible proposition. Could
the revelations threatened by Kennedy – revelations which, he claimed,
could 'bring down the whole bloody lot of them' – have concerned pretensions to Russian royal status on the part of his employer? For a junior
member of a troubled royal house who receives no money from the
public purse, Russia – even a little piece of Russia – could be a glittering
prize.

Why, then – if this were true – had I been invited to present questions
to be referred to the royal family? The official umbrella of a reigning
royal house could offer not only access to intelligence networks and
influence, enabling minor members of the royal family to pursue their
own private interests, but also protection, witting or unwitting, against
unwanted intrusion into their affairs, without involving the wider or
more senior royal family. If the initial approaches through Rearden and
Phillips were contained within the Kent connection alone, could the
invitation to pose specific questions have been aimed at bringing about
the involvement of more senior levels of the royal family, individuals
with greater power to block any unwelcome investigations than, for
example, Prince Michael of Kent himself? Prince Philip in particular,
known for his hostility to the claims of 'Anna Anderson' to be Anastasia
and to investigations which might involve his own background and lineage, was in a position to have provided the weight of influence to bring
a halt to my activities which the Kents, on their own, lacked. Whether
or not he was involved remains a matter of conjecture.

Some digging in the family connections of Rearden and Dillon revealed that both had potential access to the Chebotarev story. Rearden's friend Nicholas, Earl of Caledon, could have known of Nikolai Chebotarev through his mother, who before her marriage had been Anne Marie de Gravenitz, daughter of the Russian baron who in 1914 married Daphne Airth Richardson, a cousin of Hilda Wakefield Richardson's husband.[6] Madeline Dillon's family were friends of Couriss and could have got to hear of Nikolai Chebotarev's real identity in those quarters. They could even have learned of the identity of his child through Couriss, especially if I had been brought down to Collon to be inspected by him. 'Mick' Dillon's sister was married to the Earl of Onslow,[7] a cousin of Marina's close friend Lady Honor Guinness, wife of 'Chips' Channon; it might well have been possible to learn of the Marina part of the equation from this quarter, especially as Channon was such an inveterate gossip. Between them, Rearden and his friends Lord Caledon and Madeline Dillon had many potential points of access to the facts about Nikolai Chebotarev and Princess Marina; but, as royal servants, it is highly unlikely that they would have raised the matter on their own account without a nod from some royal source. In view of the direction in which I was being nudged, the question had to be: was that royal source Prince Michael of Kent?

On reflection, I was wise not to take the bait and become further entangled, but instead to go on intermittently with my own enquiries. However, it seemed that this outside interest in my enquiries, once aroused, would not simply go away and leave me alone. Nothing could have prepared me for what was to happen next. By the end of 1994 my career was ruined, my reputation in tatters, and the life I had known at an end.

At the same time as the Russian affair started in 1993, my situation at work began to deteriorate. I had been principal of a college for the past five years. In June 1993, just two months after Phillips approached me, a decision was announced to amalgamate the Northern Ireland colleges; mine was to be combined with two others to form a new institute. Much of the pressure of work to which I have referred in various chapters of this book arose out of the great debates taking place in and around those issues – and the job applications I was forced to make, since all existing principals were declared redundant in December 1993. My own employment situation did not settle down until May 1994, when I was appointed deputy director of the new institute.

Winding up the affairs of my college at this point, I realized that I had overlooked the payment of telephone charge card bills, something which I set about clearing up in June 1994, just before going on holiday to France. I paid the bursar immediately for what I could see at a glance were personal calls, and agreed with him to sort the rest out when we had time after I returned from holiday. When I got back in August I found a letter from the education authority enquiring into the matter. Believing I had done nothing wrong, I fully co-operated. As I pointed out, I was the only principal in the area to have itemized billing, something I was not likely to have arranged had I intended not to pay for personal calls. Only the amounts for payment ever came to my desk; the itemized bills themselves went straight to the bursar. I had made payments to cover the calls on any bills I could find, though, strangely, some had gone missing and could not be found. As far as I could see the only mistake I had made was to fail to put in place a foolproof system, and the existing system had let me down.

On 31 August 1994 I ceased to be a principal, with the protection of my own board of governors, and on the following day took up my new post as deputy director of the institute into which my college had been incorporated. It was then that action against me started, at first in the form of disciplinary proceedings. And it was at the time of these first rumblings that Rearden appeared on the scene. Immediately after a visit in October 1994 by the education minister, Michael Ancram MP, officially to open the new institute, the action against me was stepped up to dismissal proceedings. At the same time, Rearden took the questions I had been invited to ask 'up the line'. It was as if the two processes were running in parallel.

My case was heard in December 1994, by which time I had made it plain to Phillips that I was not going to respond to Rearden's note by arranging to meet Prince Michael of Kent. The ten-hour hearing, before a disciplinary committee appointed by the governors, felt like a show trial. There was a lot of shouting. Suddenly my word was doubted. The chairman of the panel, who I knew by his own avowal to have been a friend of Count Tolstoy at Collon, kept plying me with questions about my 'Russian research'. The first decision was not to dismiss me; it was reversed in a second, hastily convened meeting of which no minute was kept and confirmed by the governors, with many absentees, by the narrowest possible majority on 14 December, just in time for Christmas. The aim, it seemed, was not just dismissal but also demoralization. I received notification of the final decision on 16 December – my daughter's twelfth birthday.

By then, I had already arranged to travel to Canada and the United States in the new year to interview Bill Pinkney, the friend of Grand Duchess Olga, and to meet Olga Kulikovsky and Princess Vera Romanov. Despite the uncertainty into which our lives had just been thrown, my wife and I decided I should go ahead. While I was away, she was telephoned by local journalists asking if the Russian at Moyallon had left an heir and if he was in the country at the moment. Phillips admitted being the source of this leak and, after strong words on the telephone, he agreed to silence the press to whom he had promised a story.

On my return from New York I was received with the news that the education authority had referred my case to the police. I was interviewed two days later by apologetic policemen who were obviously acting reluctantly under orders. My appeal, heard in February 1995, was dismissed, after the chairman of the board of governors refused to have me back – a condition of any appeal going forward – and my salary was stopped that day.

The proceedings were characterized throughout by scant regard for the proprieties. That second, unminuted meeting which reversed the first decision was highly irregular. A 165-page dossier on me had been prepared without my knowledge. The Labour Relations Agency refused to give me reasons why they upheld the dismissal, taking four weeks to produce a one-line reply to my request. Puzzled friends tried to find out what was going on; former governors of my old college appealed as a body on my behalf, but were ignored. This wall of silence could only mean that the orders were coming from a very high level indeed.

This treatment, for failure to pay telephone bills on time, seemed excessive by any standard; not only to me, but to many others, including my lawyer. I planned to sue, but abandoned the idea when I found that the amount I could recover would be little more than the costs of bringing the action, since I did not have a fixed-term contract and therefore could not sue for the balance of salary owed me. My lawyer, too, had been privately advised against pursuing the case by an appeal judge. On the very same afternoon as I dropped my case, the Director of Public Prosecutions announced that the Crown Prosecution Service would be taking no action against me. This juxtaposition of events was not lost on my lawyer, who remarked that he had never seen anything like it.

In the midst of all this, my surrogate father telephoned my wife to encourage her to leave me and take the children with her. Angry and shocked, she did not tell me at the time, fearing the impact the news would have on me. Knowing what I do now about his gambling habit, I suspect that he had been paid by someone to make the call. So intense was all this action that I have little doubt it was meant to silence me. At the time, the full horror of how much this had cost my family turned life into a surreal nightmare. Even now, over three years after these events, it is very painful to write about them.

It was at this point that the intelligence services made themselves known to me. In March 1995 an approach was made to one of the governors supporting me by a local councillor and businessman, offering assistance in taking my employment case further. Naturally, I welcomed the overture, having been abandoned by almost everybody, including many who owed their entire careers to me. However, it soon became clear that this approach was less straightforward than had at first been suggested, and that my would-be benefactor's real interest was in my 'Russian research'. Admitting that he was an intelligence operative, he referred what had happened to me to a member of the Joint Intelligence Committee, who, in turn, put it under the watchful eye of the top MI5 agent in Northern Ireland, a leading public figure.[8] Speaking of the whole operation against me, my first contact said it had the 'handiwork of Prince Philip written all over it', and suggested that I was correct in assuming Princess Marina was my mother.[9] The second contact added: 'This may have to wait until Prince Philip is no longer with us.'[10] This remark was never explained. When I asked if he could find out in London what was going on in relation to me and my researches, he responded on his return with one word: 'solidification'.[11] By that I understood that a wall of silence was descending; 'they' were closing ranks. Now they were all in it together. On the royal family, my contact offered the further comment: 'I think they're scared.'

At the same time as all this action against me was being taken, new things were happening in my 'Russian research'. I am certain that not merely the content but the sheer pace of my discoveries contributed directly to what happened to me. At the end of June 1994, immediately before I went on holiday, Willi Korte had arranged for Charles Ginther, who had carried out the tests on Princess Sophie's blood, to conduct tests on samples of my own blood that I was to send him. Arrangements were well advanced. The wording for the blood sample on the shipping documents to clear customs was chosen ('Blood sample for scientific purposes (research) only'), the shipping agent (Federal Express) was chosen, the cost ($25.30) was established, Ginther was to send the blood sample kit. Everything was prepared; then everything went wrong. Bill Maples told me on 27 June that he had never seen Willi Korte so angry. It was remarkable that Ginther's departure from Berkeley should happen at the very time that my blood sample was on the verge of being sent for DNA testing in a laboratory which had tooth and bone samples from the Ekaterinburg bones. Could that work in any way have upset Gill's analysis of my blood, carried out in January 1994? Bill Maples was already saying that Berkeley did not agree with Gill on the Tsar identification. Meanwhile, Gill's laboratory was using Prince Philip's blood to discredit the claims of the long-dead Anna Anderson to be the Tsar's daughter Anastasia.[12] The news media carried the story on 2 October 1994. It seemed to matter an inordinate amount to Sir Brian McGrath, Prince Philip's former private secretary, that Anna Anderson should be seen to be a fake. Why was he so concerned? She was, after all, dead, and had no heirs. There had to be an undisclosed motivation.

It was in the same summer of 1994 that Nikolai Chebotarev's niece Iya gave me the Archbishop Theophan letters – letters which spoke of marriage in 1927, of the imperial family being alive in 1928, and of the rumours about Nikolai Chebotarev's identity. At the same time my enquiries into Marina's movements in 1946–9 were hotting up; notes on them dominate the first part of volume nine of my notebooks, dated August 1994. My researches were progressing and gathering pace, touching on areas which were annoying to those people who wanted the bones buried, and the story of the Romanovs with them. I believe that when the approach from Prince Michael came in October 1994 I was expected to see him, or his secretary, and thereby run obligingly into the alleyway they would have prepared for me. I would be told that if I kept quiet I might be allowed to hang on to my job, where I would continue working all the hours that God sent and as a result my 'research' would grind to a convenient halt. As solutions go, it was cost-effective, for it would not have cost them a penny. But I did not reply; and so the questions I had asked, because I was invited to do so, may have been seen as a threat, a kind of blackmail – which they most certainly were not. My failure to respond in October 1994 sealed my fate, and made my dismissal certain.

Publicly humiliated, apparently deprived of the resources to continue the research, isolated, with my mail regularly opened and my telephone

Princess Marina in 1934,
aged twenty-eight

Michael Gray at eighteen

Alexei, Tsarskoe Selo, April 1917

Chebotarev at Bela Cirkva, 1923

*Above left* Alexei, 1914
*Above right* The author's son aged seven, 1993

*Below left* Chebotarev aged twenty-four, Paris, 1928
*Below right* The Tsarina aged twenty-four, 1896

*Above left* Alexei with Father Vassiliev, his Russian tutor   *Above right* The
author's son, with his sister and the author

*Below left* Alexei, 1913   *Below right* Michael Gray, aged about forty-seven

*Above left* King Constantine II of Greece, aged twenty-eight
*Above right* The author, aged about twenty-eight

*Above left* Chebotarev in England, 1986   *Above right* The head of
Tsar Nikolai I from a banknote

*Top* Grand Duchess Maria (third from left), showing the injury to her right ring finger caused by a train door in 1910

*Right* Chebotarev with 'Lydia', the woman he called his sister, Yugoslavia, 1933. Note her right ring finger

*Above* 'Lydia' (standing, second from right) working in a Yugoslavian soup kitchen, late 1920s   *Below left* 'Lydia' in later life   *Below right* The Grand Duchesses, 1914. Compare the stance of Maria (left) with that of 'Lydia' in the photograph above

The man (left) known as 'Nikolai Alexandrovich', Collon, 1948

Nikolai Chebotarev

tapped, I felt the force of royal displeasure in a supposedly free society. On one occasion at this time I was speaking to Willi Korte in Germany by telephone.[13] When he asked me whose I thought the Ekaterinburg bones really were, our conversation was suddenly and rudely interrupted with a woman's voice announcing 'hold the line': then I was cut off. For the rest of the day I could not reach Korte; when I eventually got through, at eleven that evening, he announced: 'The trouble was at your end.' I suspected that only GCHQ would have this capability. My second intelligence contact in those early months of 1995 said it wasn't them, by which he meant MI5. If I believe that, and on balance I do, that leaves only one option in the British intelligence pantheon. Our home was entered several times; on one occasion the intrusion was so obvious that a document I had filed away in my office was left sitting beside the kitchen telephone. Whether such clumsy action would ever have received official sanction remains a moot point. I refused to be tempted into litigation over my employment case, which would have used up time and money; I had always run my research on a shoestring and continued to do so. Even so, eventually we would simply run out of money. I would have to find some other job – though all attempts to do this inexplicably failed – and would be unlikely to have time to continue my enquiries.

Rescue came from an unlikely quarter with the deaths, in quick succession, of my two surrogate parents in May and June 1995. By this time we had already been living on money inherited from my mother-in-law. My surrogate father died first, cutting me out of his will and naming my surrogate mother's nephew as his executor. I could not bring myself to go to his funeral, so great was my sense of betrayal by a man to whom I had only ever shown kindness. When the next month my surrogate mother died suddenly, soon after her admission to Craigavon Hospital, I was out of the country and found out only later. But her death resulted in our inheriting their house and money, which enabled us to go on. It was an outcome my opponents could not have anticipated.

# Solutions

Fifty years after they happened, it has at last become possible to piece together the jigsaw of events which took place in the late 1940s to complete the story of Nikolai Chebotarev. It is a story both shocking and heartwarming, revealing much that is dark and cynical in human motivation and behaviour, yet also the resilience and resourcefulness of two individuals pitted against the power of a pervasive authority. As the evidence chipped away the layers of denial and obfuscation embedding, even burying, this story, so a whole secret history came to light – a history hitherto hidden but, once exposed, entirely understandable and clear. That history can now be told.

By 1946 the relationship between Princess Marina and Nikolai Chebotarev, a relationship which had been founded in the 1920s in Paris and renewed after the death of the Duke of Kent in 1942, had developed so far that the couple were running and laughing through the bedrooms of Croft House together, to the amusement of the servants. At the end of September that year, after staying incognito as 'Mme Velika' with Nikolai in Croft House, Marina paid a visit to the remote Scottish hillside where her late husband's plane had crashed just over four years earlier. It was a ritual leave-taking before she embarked on a new phase of her life, abandoning dutiful widowhood to marry and make a new beginning. Rumours so persistent that they had to be officially denied in 1947 by the British ambassador in Washington placed that new life in America, where Nikolai had been waiting for her since the beginning of the year. Marina had organized Nikolai's job in the United Nations through Sir Percy Loraine, the chairman of the Anglo-Hellenic League of which Marina was president, and a man whose links to Nikolai went back as far as 1920 and the issue of his Nansen passport. Marina planned to provide for that new life by selling off most of the collection of paintings and porcelain she had amassed with her late husband, the Duke of Kent. At Christie's on 13–15 March 1947 she raised over £92,000 in this way – the equivalent of £1.8 million today and more than enough for her purpose. That fresh start in New York was only four days away by sea. Six weeks after that sale, while two ships bound for transatlantic destinations, New York and Montreal, lay in Belfast harbour, one of them belonging to friends of the Cookes, Marina was apprehended at the end of an official visit to Northern Ireland by British intelligence agent Prince Alexander Lieven and brought back to London. Lieven stayed on her case from that moment.

Marina had been driven to these lengths by the intolerable burden of royal duty and the constrictions of royal life, which in her case meant a lonely widowhood, eked out with meagre financial support from the Windsors, after a loveless marriage to the transvestite Duke of Kent during which she had sought divorce three times in eight years. In this situation, the imperative for the Windsors was threefold: avoid even a whiff of scandal; provide for the three existing Kent children; and prevent Marina making off with money they considered to be theirs, since the original purchases of the paintings and *objets d'art* which were sold in March 1947 had been funded out of money the late Duke of Kent inherited from his father and aunt. Marina, after all, had brought nothing much into her marriage but undoubted royal status. Queen Elizabeth (the present Queen Mother), who wielded the real power in the royal family, had already shown she knew how to bear grudges in the affair of the Duke of Windsor; she was unlikely to forgive that most royally descended of princesses, Marina, who had called her a 'common little Scottish girl'.

Running away to a new life in America when the King's and Queen's backs were turned, away on an official tour of South Africa, was one thing. Pregnancy, and the birth of a child, was quite another. Though Marina's effort to join Nikolai Chebotarev in America was frustrated in April, by June they had both managed to slip away together again – this time to Greece. By then they must have known a baby was on the way and, if the position had not already been regularized by marriage in 1946, when a ceremony could have been conducted by Hieromonk Barnabas who had buried Archbishop Theophan, it was certainly done so quietly now. Greece was a perfect setting for the private Orthodox wedding which both Nikolai and Marina would have wanted; indeed, no form of wedding other than marriage in an Orthodox church was legal in Greece until 1974. Greece, in the throes of civil war, was not a healthy place to be in 1947; yet on 10 June Marina extended her stay by a fortnight.

Royal suspicions had already been aroused. Rumours about Marina's health were rife. On 31 October her home at The Coppins in Iver, where Nikolai slipped in and out quietly by the back entrance in Swan Lane, was burgled. Tellingly, nothing was taken; the intruders must have been on a covert intelligence operation, looking for documentation of a marriage or evidence of medication that would indicate pregnancy. On 19 November 1947 their questions were to all intents and purposes answered when Marina fainted at the pre-wedding ball of Princess Elizabeth and Prince Philip of Greece. From that point the situation, as far as the royals were concerned, was one to be managed.

On 21 November, the day after the wedding, Marina was sent abroad for four days with Queen Frederika of Greece. Birth may well have been induced during this time, on or about 25 November 1947, or have occurred between then and February 1948. After this date Marina's official diary was characterized by large gaps. For ninety out of ninety-four days in the first four months of 1948, Princess Marina was missing from official duties. Three photographs of myself as a baby, concealed so well they were not uncovered until after my surrogate mother's death nearly fifty years later, are consistent with a birth date at the end of 1947 or beginning of 1948. And they show me with Prince Alexander Lieven, who was still on Marina's case – Prince Alexander Lieven, intelligence agent and friend of Nikolai Chebotarev. They show me with Lieven and Dr Apraxine. They show me with Dr Apraxine in Bangor, which agrees with my medical record. And they show me beside a fountain in Clandeboye, the home of Maureen Guinness, Marchioness of Dufferin, Marina's friend – but also the Queen's.

Now an alternative reality had to be crafted into which the child could be silently transferred. Surrogate parents were found through Alicia Waring. Lieven knew Alicia Waring through her sister Lady Roden and through Mrs Waring's relative, Dr Martha Apraxine. With her Unionist background and with relatives among the courtiers, she could be relied on as a willing participant in a royal cover-up. She chose the surrogate parents from a family she had known since the 1920s, a family she knew she could rely on. The selected couple were quietly married on 15 January 1948 and went through the pretence of going to live in England. In fact my surrogate mother never went there; nor, for that matter, did she ever give birth. Residents at their English address have no memory of them or of a baby; indeed, there was a house policy against married couples and babies.

Prime mover in the creation of my identity, as he had been in the creation of Nikolai Chebotarev's new identity back in April 1920 in Constantinople, was Nikolai Couriss. Couriss had almost certainly been recruited by British intelligence in the period 1926–32 when he worked as a passport clerk in the British consulate in Salonika – the same town where George Hill had been taken on – though there is a possibility that he was picked out even earlier, when in 1919 he served as an interpreter on board British warships for Admiral Fremantle in the Black Sea fleet. Couriss certainly worked for the British – but by no means certainly exclusively for the British. Through his doctor, Isidore Jack Eppel, who had also been the doctor of my surrogate father since May 1948, Couriss arranged the fabrication of a phantom identity for the non-existent baby of the chosen surrogate parents. Eppel moved to Birmingham in July 1948, enabling him to procure one of the medical record sleeves issued by the newly founded National Health Service, stamped on 5 July 1948 with the Birmingham health authority stamp. This was an unused sleeve marked 'Cancelled', denoting that it had been issued but not used, probably because one of the patients on Eppel's panel had died. Falsifying a birth certificate presented no problem – responsibility for the information it contains rests with the informant, not the registrar. A false declaration of birth was duly made on 9 August 1948 with an address at which my surrogate parents were definitely not living. The birth certificate generated a medical number which was inserted on the false medical record sleeve. After the name of a nearby English doctor was handwritten on the sleeve, it was sent to Dr John Bowman in Bangor who duly stamped it. His name was in turn obliterated by the stamp of Dr John Paton, the GP in Mrs Waring's village of Waringstown.

Each stage in this process distanced me still further from my point of origin. The scheme was brilliant in its conception and bold in its execution, creating a complete alternative reality. Such elaborate precautions and such deep cover would never have been sought for an ordinary illegitimate child. Only the discovery of well-concealed evidence and links between the principal players unravelled this carefully crafted illusion – half a century later.

Using Natalie Cooke's visit to Leningrad in August 1948 as an excuse, alleging that it posed a threat to my safety, Lieven and Apraxine spirited me away from Natalie Cooke's and Marina's control. This caused a rupture in relations between Natalie Cooke and the Apraxines. It also confirmed Natalie in her lifelong enmity for the house of Windsor. As for my infant self, though out of the direct control of Natalie Cooke, I was still in or near Bangor for part of the time at least – most likely at Clandeboye, the home of Maureen Guinness, Marchioness of Dufferin. Dr Apraxine's consultancy at Dublin's children's hospital must have been a useful cover at this time. I remained in Bangor and Collon for almost a year after Marina's last visit in September 1948, leaving only in August 1949. It is no wonder I could recall buildings near Dr Bowman's in Bangor. This one-year gap suggests that there was a transitional phase, possibly involving the occasional visit to my surrogate parents for acclimatization. They were still not in Waringstown, so I could have visited them for a day at a time without the neighbours among whom I grew up guessing at the truth. Though, according to my medical record, I was clearly in Bangor, their medical records place them both somewhere else – she in Banbridge and he in Birmingham. The final handover must have been traumatic, for I can still recall it – the car, the smell of leather upholstery, the rain, the people, and the words: 'He's tired, get him home quickly.'

My surrogate parents later brought me to Collon at regular intervals to be seen by Couriss who, among others, must have been reporting on me to Marina, who herself continued to visit Collon incognito during the 1950s. Kathleen McCarthy remembers all my visits, and I clearly recall places near Collon such as Monasterboice, Castlebellingham and Ravensdale Forest. There are indications that Nikolai Chebotarev, too, had some idea of where I was. In a small box he left behind marked 'very important historical documents', along with mementoes of his imperial past – ninety-nine letters from Archbishop Theophan; a silk handkerchief bearing the imperial crest in the imperial colours, and a medal ribbon in the Russian national colours; several pictures of St Seraphim of Sarov, the saint canonized on the Tsarina's personal orders to give thanks for the birth of the Tsarevich – was a postcard of Dan Winter's cottage near Portadown, where the Orange Order was founded. This was only three miles from where I grew up, in a house opposite an Orange hall. Alix Hill still remarks how, when they went for walks, he would stop and ask her wistfully, as if his mind were somewhere else, what age she thought children playing nearby were. And when he spoke of Marina, Alix said, 'a far-away look came into his eyes'. His child was far away indeed.

All these arrangements may have been very convenient for the power-brokers at the time, but they were high-handed in the extreme. They could, of course, be justified from several points of view. For the royal family it was an efficient way to deal with a series of incipient scandals. If the immediate one – a connection between Marina and Nikolai, probably involving marriage, and a child – had come out, others stood to come out as well: Romanov survivals, Romanov money, King George V's parentage – where would it stop? For Marina, there was the need to return to duty, welcome or not. She could easily be made to feel she had a responsibility to her other children. Couriss could congratulate himself on another job well done, whether for his current British or for his former Romanov masters. As for Nikolai Chebotarev, he was hardly in a position to do anything – non-people rarely are. He would just have to fall into line with whatever was decided. He could console himself that it was for the best, for my protection. These were, after all, the early and perilous years of the Cold War, of the Iron Curtain and the Berlin airlift. Russia and half of Europe were ruled by Stalin.

The right to identity, though, is a fundamental human right and has been defined as such by the European Convention on Human Rights. All of the arrangements made in 1947–9 in relation to my future ignored the one person in the equation whose rights were being violated. And that, of course, was me. Pleading circumstances is an evasion of responsibility, because circumstances are ultimately created by people. Someone, some-where, rightly or wrongly, for good or bad reasons, determined that I be ripped away from my own past and background and transplanted in an alien environment among people I knew instinctively were not my own. And they left it too late: by the time I moved I was already old enough to remember, albeit inchoately, an earlier life. What they did, however understandable, was wrong. To me these people – the Tsarevich, Princess Marina, the Tsar, the Tsarina – are not a series of titles. They are pri-marily people, my people, my own flesh and blood. As such they interest me as human beings with likes, dislikes, fears, attitudes. I am interested in knowing why they acted as they did. I look at my own son, in whom so many people see a remarkable resemblance to the Tsarevich, and wonder in how many ways he resembles his grandfather. I have been denied the right to know my own father as I know my son, to know my mother as I know my daughter. To me, meeting Nikolai Chebotarev's friends has been of interest primarily not for what key piece of evidence they could supply but for what they could tell me about my own father. Despite the undoubted excitement of the quest – and at times it has been very exciting – it is seared with pain.

Enormous barriers have been erected to prevent the truth coming out.

Some of these are obvious. When you think about it, no rational person could really believe in a shamanistic holy man healing a sick boy by a mixture of hypnosis and 'special powers', down a telegraph wire when necessary. Yet that is essentially what we have been asked to accept about Rasputin for the last eighty years. Other barriers are a less obvious but no less formidable a part of the fabric of deception which has surrounded the Romanovs since 1918. By proclaiming the entire imperial family saints and martyrs in 1982, the Russian Orthodox Church Abroad effectively silenced all talk of survivors among the faithful. The official Orthodox Church within Russia is aware of this, and has so far avoided getting itself into the same predicament – notably by declining to subscribe to the authenticity of the Ekaterinburg bones. Within the Russian exile community, even to raise the possibility that members of the imperial family survived became tantamount to questioning the authority of the Church-in-exile. In a Church which accords great weight to episcopal authority, this forces many older Russians into silence. Many of them know something – not everything but something, some little piece of information, some snippet of the truth. Yet how could they come forward with any such information and, in so doing, effectively destroy the authority of a Church which has been one of the key points of cohesion in a beleaguered, dwindling exile community cut off from its roots? Some came close, then retreated. A friend of Nikolai Chebotarev who had been lined up to meet me in Paris by Mara Gorbadovsky ran away to the South of France to avoid meeting me. Some, though not many, defended themselves with aggression from the outset. Some took refuge behind irrefutable religious assertions: Olga Kulikovsky claimed that she had prayed to Alexei when she was fourteen and he had answered her prayer.

Many of these old exiles were initially quite open, but when the questioning became too difficult, or more usually when someone from the Church brought pressure to bear on them, they grew reticent, withdrew what they had said, or parroted the Church's official position – that we must not disturb the peace of the blessed 'Tsar-Saint-Martyr' and his family. When you hear these words you know the person you are talking to has been got at by the Church-in-exile. In this way, two whole generations of émigrés have been effectively silenced. Many old Russians end up in the care of the Tolstoy Institute, in whose nursing homes they are carefully looked after and access by strangers can be easily monitored. Conventional excuses are rolled out. They must not be troubled. Talking would tire them too much. On one occasion the phone rang when I was speaking to Princess Vera Constantinova Romanov in her cottage within the Tolstoy Institute at Nyack, Redland County in New York State. I had been admitted after simply giving my name at the door, and, though I had been told that she never gave interviews – at least, she had not done so for about ten years – she received me enthusiastically, propped up in her bed. Our ensuing conversation was perfectly calm, friendly, cheerful and completely non-threatening. It was interrupted by a telephone call. The caller, Princess Irina Sergeevna Bagration-Mukhransky, harangued me down the line, calling me 'a false Tsarevich'. This was in early 1995, when I was making no claim to be Alexei's son; I was just asking a few straightforward questions about Nikolai Chebotarev. The violence of the attack was certainly food for thought. Yet after the interruption, Princess Vera held on to my hand for over five minutes and gave me her blessing before I left, asking me to return next day with photographs of my children.

Others do not perform as expected. Misha Viacheslav was brought along to meet me in 1995 in Bill Pinkney's grand house in Hamilton, Ontario by Tikhon Kulikovsky's widow, Olga. I believe he was expected to debunk Nikolai Chebotarev. Instead, he genuflected when he met me at the door. He said Nikolai had gone on holiday with him and Tikhon in the days before Kulikovsky married Olga, who was his third and final wife. And, as related in chapter 17, to cap it all he said that he owed his life to Nikolai Chebotarev, who had got him out of Greece in 1947 just as the civil war was starting. After his wife found out about this last comment, he tried to withdraw it; but it was heard by two witnesses. Obviously they knew the import of Nikolai Chebotarev being in Greece in the summer of 1947 at the same time as Princess Marina.

Allowed to speak freely, many of these older generation Russian exiles, while not knowing the whole story, could pass on details which might be vital links and clues in piecing together that story. Some of these pieces of information are immediately intelligible; others make hitherto unseen connections. For example, Nikolai Chebotarev had a favourite saying, which he often repeated: 'Just because you are born in a stable, it doesn't make you a horse.' When I uttered this at Bill Pinkney's, Olga Kulikovsky, who had been talking incessantly, suddenly went silent. 'My husband used to say that,' she said, reflectively. Then, recollecting herself, she continued, 'But everyone says that.' They don't, of course. I have been told that it is some kind of royal code, a means of recognition.

The tragedy is that so many of these older people are slipping away.

Even during the period of my investigations, death has claimed Dame Elizabeth Hill in 1996, Prince Leonid Lieven in 1997, Zoe Cooke and Maureen, Marchioness of Dufferin in 1998. I have been working against time.

I have, of course, thought about the import of Nikolai Chebotarev being both the Tsarevich Alexei and my father. The conclusions I have reached are clear. I have no pretensions whatever to titles or status. People whose primary interest is in what title they might claim are essentially irrelevant to Russia, which with all its difficulties has no need of any additional burdens. Political and constitutional systems should be generated by the country itself in a natural way and should reflect what Russia itself feels it wants or needs. Alexei, despite his difficult life, remained a Russian patriot until the end of his days. It is an attitude, now that we are aware of our family heritage, that both my son and I share. East European and Balkan royals jockeying for their former thrones present a very unedifying spectacle. I cannot imagine such machinations are driven by anything other than self-interest: pious talk about the stability and constitutional enlightenment monarchy can bring belongs firmly in the humbug category. To want my father's and my grandfather's name, however, is surely both reasonable and right.

In the end, the quest which has taken me so far and led to my meeting so many people has brought me right back to myself. I believe the case that has emerged through these investigations for Nikolai Chebotarev being the Tsarevich, for his having married Princess Marina and for my being their son is a persuasive one. Both as a detective story and as a human tragedy, it is a compelling tale. If I am not their son, then who on earth am I?

APPENDIX

# The Windsors and the Money

During the latter two years of the First World War Joe Boyle was backed to the tune of £10 million from the British government and 100 million francs from the French.[1] Questions were asked by the Treasury about Boyle's failure to account properly for how he spent these massive sums, and these problems bedevilled him as late as the autumn of 1921. Quite simply, it was not credible that Queen Marie of Romania, out of her own resources, could have funded Boyle's large-scale bribery of the Bolsheviks to obtain the release of the fifty Romanian hostages in March 1918 – or, for that matter, of the Romanovs. If British agents (Boyle himself, George Hill, Richard Meinertzhagen) were used on the ground to effect the departure of the Romanovs from Russia – and only they had the flexibility and autonomy to act quickly in the fast-changing situation in Russia in 1918 – it is equally likely that British money was used.

Of course, the question of what constituted British money or Russian money was a vexed one. The British had experienced considerable financial difficulties in the prosecution of the war. For the most part, these had been associated with the level of the Bank of England's gold reserves which ultimately underwrote the currency. Of the three allies – Britain, France and Russia – Russia had by far the largest gold reserves. In 1914 these exceeded 1,700 million roubles, the largest reserve in the world, whereas France in comparison had the equivalent of only 1,500 million and Britain a paltry 800 million.[2] By 1915, arms purchases from the United States had caused Britain's reserves of gold to drop below safety levels, and the government had to ask France and Russia to help by transferring gold to London. The Russian finance minister Bark, however, needed to maintain Russian gold stocks at an adequate level to support the rouble. To do this while responding to the British request, he resorted to a legal fiction. British Treasury bonds issued against the gold were made repayable in gold; thus on a balance sheet Bark could technically show these instruments as gold held abroad. It bore little relation to reality, but it kept the books right.[3] During the war Russia transferred £68 million in gold to London – the equivalent of £2,750 million today. Only £48 million worth of redeemable bonds were issued against this, leaving the final consignment of gold – some £20 million (the equivalent of some £800 million today) transferred in March 1917 – unpaid for.⁴ The Bank of England avoided this since bond payment fell due in November 1917 after the Bolsheviks had toppled the Kerensky government. Precisely how much of this gold was set against munitions purchases is unclear, but it is small wonder that the Tsarina told Lili Dehn that they had massive deposits of gold in the Bank of England. Exactly whose gold this was is a matter of doubt: Nikolai II owned the gold mines in the Atlai mountains which produced the bulk of these reserves, though it could be argued he did so only as head of state and not in a personal capacity. Whatever the formal ownership of the reserves, the British and French underwriting of Joe Boyle's anti-German activities should be seen in the context of the massive wartime transfers to London from Russia.

There remains the matter of private Romanov wealth. Precedents for what is likely to have happened to this exist in known dealings between the Windsors and other Romanovs outside the Tsar's immediate family. Both the Tsar's cousin, Grand Duke Mikhail, who was already living in England with his morganatic wife, and the Tsar's mother, the Dowager Empress Maria Feodorovna, entered into financial arrangements with King George V. Grand Duke Mikhail received an advance of £10,000. Though no security was required or formal documents drawn up, the King's Keeper of the Privy Purse, Sir Frederick Ponsonby, mentioned that the jewels belonging to Grand Duke Mikhail's wife and lodged at the bank might be regarded as 'nominal security'. They were worth £40,000.⁵

In the case of the Dowager Empress, initially an agreement was reached by which King George V, Queen Alexandra, Queen Mary and Princess Victoria would jointly provide her with an income of £10,000 a year. Within months, however, the King had managed to transform this private commitment into a provision of the whole sum out of the Privy Purse.⁶ The Privy Purse existed to top up the money the King received from parliamentary grant – the Civil List – with income from lands owned by the Duchy of Lancaster: fifty thousand acres in Yorkshire, Lancashire, Cheshire and Staffordshire. These lands and estates have been in crown hands since 1265 and are in no way private resources of the royal family but are permanently linked to the occupant of the throne.[7] So King George V was paying the Dowager Empress of Russia, his 'Aunt Minnie', out of what were essentially British public funds – it was not costing him personally one penny. This was characteristic of the King's canny approach to money management, at which he was quietly adept. In 1916, for instance, he privately arranged with the government to stop paying any tax on his various incomes. If this had become public at the time, it would have been construed as a less than patriotic act during wartime and would have caused as much political fall-out as the alleged German sympathies which led to his much-publicized change of family name.

It is likely that the contents of the Dowager Empress' jewel box were understood to be security for the annual payment of £10,000. (There was, of course, nothing in writing.) Before the Dowager Empress could even open this box, she had to have two keys. One of these was held by her dresser, the other by Captain Andrup, the Danish naval officer appointed by Ponsonby to look after the Dowager Empress' finances once she had left England to settle in Denmark, where she spent the remainder of her life. Ponsonby thus ensured that his 'nominal security' was in no way depleted. In the time-honoured fashion of exiles and in a reflection of the financial competence of a woman who had never handled money before, she kept the box under her bed. According to Grand Duchess Olga, George V had tried to talk the Empress into sending the box to London where he would himself see to arrangements for the sale of its contents.[8] But his aunt would not let it out of her sight.

In 1928, when the old lady died, Buckingham Palace acted with an alacrity which was barely decent and which indicated the existence of an understanding that the jewels were security for advances to the Empress. Through Sir Frederick Ponsonby, King George V sent Sir Peter Bark, the Tsar's former finance minister and now managing director of the Anglo-International Bank, a subsidiary of the Bank of England, to Copenhagen with instructions to get his hands on the jewel box and send it back to Buckingham Palace. Taken from the Empress' room and sealed in the British legation at Copenhagen, the box was sent by royal messenger to England and placed in the safe at Buckingham Palace.[9] The King was informed the moment the jewels arrived in London. Such feverish activity implies a very definite arrangement. King George was looking for a return on his investment; and possession, we are told, is nine parts of the law. According to Ponsonby, the Dowager Empress' two daughters, Grand Duchesses Xenia and Olga, were consulted about the removal of the jewels; but Olga told her biographer, Ian Vorres, quite clearly in 1959 that this was untrue. At no time was she consulted.[10] Only her sister Xenia appeared to know anything, but she was a favourite of King George.

What happened then has been the subject of controversy and confusion ever since. Ponsonby believed the jewels were worth £350,000;[11] Bark had put the figure as high as £500,000.[12] According to Sir Edward Peacock, Grand Duchesses Xenia and Olga were apparently advanced £100,000 between them immediately by Hennells, the jewellers, on account.[13] No further money was received. Peacock was strategically placed to be in possession of the facts – as an executor of the Dowager Empress, the trustee for the two Grand Duchesses, the Governor of the Bank of England and a Director of Baring's, a bank used by the Tsar.

In 1985 the author Suzy Menkes alleged that Queen Mary had held on to the jewels without paying for them until 1933 when, claiming that the slump had depressed jewel prices, she paid only £60,000 instead of £100,000.[14] Menkes said the Queen settled the debt in 1968. Subsequent investigations by William Clarke, who had access to the royal archives at Windsor and to the newly discovered Hennells records – or what remains of them – appeared to have debunked this story in 1994. The initial valuation of £144,000 was increased by Hennells to £159,000 and the total sum raised by selling the items in the difficult market conditions over the four years of the depression was £136,000.[15] Clarke, in fact, exonerated Queen Mary, who by his account paid full market value for the jewels and over the lower post-slump values for some items. In addition, Hennells have no record of an advance of £100,000 ever having been paid out.[16]

These are the facts as revealed by the papers extant on the subject. Yet it remains unlikely that men with the financial experience and expertise of Ponsonby and Peacock could have got it so wrong. Peacock as an executor must have known what he advanced to Grand Duchesses Xenia and Olga in 1929. He was quite specific about it and told Olga's biographer, Ian Vorres, that Xenia got about £60,000 and Olga £40,000.[17] Yet Hennells' accounts have no record of any advance being paid. Rather, they show money coming in slowly over a four-year period, set against a master-list of seventy-six items of jewellery.[18]

If any advance was paid – as indeed it must have been, if Peacock said it was – then it was not from Hennells and cannot have related to the seventy-six items on their list. As for where it did come from, the answer

may also explain half of the enormous discrepancy between the figure of
£350,000 mentioned by Ponsonby and the £159,000 valuation of Hennells. Peacock's explanation – that Ponsonby's memory had failed him
– is simply not credible with such a large amount of money: £200,000
is, after all, the equivalent of £3.6 million today. That £100,000 advance
verified by Peacock must have referred to items outside the list. Seventy-
six items does, after all, appear a little conservative for the jewellery
collection of the former Empress of Russia. Some of the most expensive pieces in the British royal collection today are former Russian royal
jewels. One brooch formerly owned by the Dowager Empress is worth
£294,000, and another Russian brooch bought by Queen Mary is worth
£118,000.[19] In her heyday, Tsarina Maria Feodorovna thought nothing
of giving quantities of jewels to her poorer sister, Queen Alexandra. Precious stones – diamonds, rubies, emeralds – were freely mined in Russia,
which has massive reserves. One tiara given by the Dowager Empress to
Queen Alexandra is currently valued at £530,000. Another pearl neck-
lace given by 'Minnie' to 'Alex' has a current value of £206,000.[20] The
items famously missing after Queen Alexandra's death, which apparently
occasioned Queen Mary's inventory of royal jewels after her mother-in-
law died in 1925, are said to consist for the most part of precious stones
– mostly rubies, pearls and sapphires from Siberia – given to Alexandra
by the Dowager Empress.

The real answer to what happened to the Dowager Empress' jewels
lies in the months between 14 October 1928, when they were taken by
Sir Peter Bark from the dead Empress' bedroom, and 22 May 1929, when
the box was opened at Windsor in the presence of King George V,
Queen Mary and Grand Duchess Xenia. It must have been represented
to Grand Duchess Xenia and Olga that the 1929 advance was made
against the trickle of sales by Hennells, whereas in fact it was made against
the value of items not covered by the Hennells valuation. As Hennells
sold various items between 1929 and 1933, they made the cheques for
the proceeds payable to King George V.[21] Clarke states that this money
was passed on by the King to Sir Peter Bark to put in the trust set up for
Grand Duchesses Xenia and Olga, but he offers no evidence for this. If
George V had paid the £100,000 advance to his cousins, is it not more
likely that he simply kept the money Hennells passed on against this sum?
The important point is that the original £100,000 was paid by the King,
but set against the value of the £200,000 discrepancy pointed to by
Ponsonby.

Of course, the King may have had other secret Romanov commit-
ments to meet, such as the upkeep of survivors not known to the public:
payments to be made which could hardly appear on a balance sheet.
He may, therefore, have had very good reason for holding on to that
£200,000, and for wanting to recoup the outlay against the Dowager
Empress' estate. In all, between 1925 and 1928 when the arrangement
lapsed with her death, George V must have paid out in the region of
£40,000 to the Dowager Empress. Presumably, he simply kept this
£200,000, and thus the portion of that money that had originally been
set against the pension paid by the Duchy of Lancaster would have
become private royal money. Then, he was content to recoup his
advance to Xenia and Olga as the money trickled in from Hennells.
After all, if he had gained so much, he could probably afford to do this.
Having made an initial investment of £40,000 spread over four years and
a one-off payout of £100,000 to his cousins, he could pocket the balance
of the £350,000, a total of £210,000 over an eight-year period. This
represents a return of 50 per cent per annum in a prevailing investment
climate where 3–4 per cent was the norm; but there were risks involved.
Disposal of such material would have been quietly done, and unlikely
to raise the full market price; some of the items may never have been
disposed of but have been held in raw, unmounted form. There would
have been no written contract of the deal for William Clarke to turn
up in the archives at Windsor. The jewels, like Grand Duke Mikhail's,
would remain 'nominal security'. And the King would still have to meet
the hidden costs of maintaining any secret survivors, though they probably did not cost more than a pittance and were hardly in a position to
protest.

Successful investors try to repeat their successes – whatever they
believe has worked for them in the past – and in the matter of profiting
from the Dowager Empress' jewels Buckingham Palace may have been
attempting a repeat of arrangements made back in 1917–18 concerning
the Tsar's fortune abroad. It could be that the real cause of the delay in
getting the Tsar out of revolutionary Russia was the time taken to work
out the detail of what it would cost and how the British would be repaid.
King George V may have put up the hard cash in Russia in 1918 to pay
for the Romanovs' departure, probably on a one-by-one basis for each
member of the family. To be more precise, he may have facilitated the
use of British money in much the same way as he facilitated the payment
of the Dowager Empress' pension from Privy Purse funds. In Russia in

1918 this may have taken the form of the disbursement of British tax-payers' money held by Colonel Joe Boyle and never properly accounted for – but, as Boyle said, 'put to good use'.

The King had a well-established network of the co-operative relation-ships needed to effect such a deal. He had a cosy relationship with the British government, which since 1916 had accepted his non-payment of tax – payments which Queen Victoria and Edward VII had been willing to make without question. He also appears to have had a cosy relation-ship with Colonel Joe Boyle. The King's repayment for services rendered to the Tsar would have involved, as with the Tsar's mother six years later, the signing-over of Romanov deposits and assets abroad. And George V had yet another cosy relationship with Sir Edward Peacock, Governor of the Bank of England and a director of Baring's, where the Tsar banked, and another with Sir Peter Bark, the Tsar's finance minister – who was knighted in Britain for some service rendered. Nevertheless, despite all these supportive elements, problems may have arisen from such a trans-fer. The King may have had to rely on the word of the Tsar in the first instance, for his cousin might have been allegedly dead when the actual signing-over of assets took place. Accounts may simply have been coded or numbered and so the possession of that information may have been sufficient to access them. And the mercenary and cynical nature of such a transaction, had it become public, would have irretrievably damaged the King's reputation.

Despite assertions to the contrary, it is not the case that no Romanov money existed abroad after the Tsar repatriated all his foreign deposits on the outbreak of the First World War. No doubt some imperial invest-ments overseas were repatriated in 1914–15 as a patriotic measure; but this is far from the whole story. Writing on 29 August 1915, for instance, the Tsarina specifically spoke of the British ambassador Sir George Buchanan bringing over £100,000 from England – long after the sup-posed repatriation of all money from abroad.[22] In 1914 Sir Peter Bark did transfer some of the state funds from Berlin to St Petersburg, but not all: some were transferred to Paris.[23] Again, with the amount of imperial Russian gold being transferred to London, which was after all an allied capital, it is unlikely that all funds were repatriated, since it would have been counterproductive to move gold in two directions at once. And there were the Tsar's daughters to be considered; if, as was highly likely, they made foreign marriages, they would need money abroad since they would then have no further claim on the imperial funds.

Count Benckendorff, the minister of the imperial court, went on record as saying that at the time of the Revolution each of the Tsar's children possessed a private fortune amounting to several million roubles 'abroad and in the state bank'.[24] Even William Clarke, who speaks for the Windsors having clean hands in this business and was given unprecedented access to the royal archives at Windsor, admits to finding a bank in Switzerland which owned up to having Romanov deposits. Clarke does not name the bank in his work *The Lost Fortune of the Tsars*, though he tells us that Swiss banking became centred in Berne and Zurich only after the Swiss Banking Act of 1934, and that banks which would have been used by pre-revolutionary Russians were situated around Lac Leman, in Geneva and Lausanne, where many of the Russians had property.[25]

Baring's Bank, which crashed in 1995, admitted in 1959 to Anthony Sampson, the then editor of the *Observer*, to holding a £40 million deposit belonging to the Tsar.[26] This figure is suspiciously close to the amount of money the Queen is alleged to have lost in the fall of Baring's. These claims, Anthony Sampson says, were never refuted by Baring's or the Romanov family at the time. More recently, William Clarke has dismissed these 'Baring balances' as the residue of clearing deposits held by various British banks against the transferred Russian gold. Of these banks, only Baring's resisted attempts by the British Cabinet to come to an accommodation over these balances with the new regime in Moscow. Ultimately Clarke argues that the special account at Baring's was in the name of the Chancellerie de Crédit in Petrograd and the imperial Russian embassy in London. In all, the balance of this account, dated May 1918, the details of which were only released to the public in 1993, stood at just under £4 million. Clarke argues that this account, which stood at an end figure of about £46 million, eventually came to an end after the 1986 agreement on Anglo-Soviet debt between the two governments. As for Romanov family money, he says, on the authority of Nicholas Baring, that there was none.[27]

Clarke goes on to dismiss claims that the Tsar had deposits in the Bank of England on the same basis. Any money there, apart from a paltry sum of about £5,000 which lay in an account the Tsar had apparently forgotten about after 1895, was state funds, not the personal money of the Tsar and his family. The transfers of Russian gold bullion mentioned earlier were earmarked for munitions purchases. Other money had been dissipated in the ultimately doomed effort to support the value of the rouble – a total of over £26 million between April 1916 and February 1917.[28]

Thus Clarke systematically dispenses with the main claim advanced by supporters of Anna Anderson's cause: that there was money in London, in either the Bank of England or Baring's – or both – that could be claimed by Romanov heirs. To paraphrase Lord Mountbatten's comment to Bill Phillip's associate Timothy Rearden: 'There was no money.'

Clarke's work appeared to be reasonably conclusive and authoritative. Only his failure to account for the exact spending on munitions on behalf of the Russian imperial government during the First World War seemed to leave any room for doubt. In the absence of that figure, the opportunity still existed for asserting that debts which had in fact never been incurred in the first place were still owing. This would have provided the basis of a claim for holding on to Tsarist gold. It was a matter of record, for instance, as noted above, that the last £20 million shipment of gold was never paid for in British government bonds. This casuistry in relation to a massive sum of money leaves a slight doubt about the probity of all Britain's financial dealings with the Russian government. Similarly, the demand by the British that Russian gold be shipped to London to cover the British, who were perilously low in their gold reserves, also suggests that all of this money may not have been for Russian munitions as opposed to allied munitions. Such doubts would concern only the British government's handling of Russian Tsarist government deposits, rather than whether or not the money belonged to the Tsar. There is, however, one other aspect of British dealings with Russian imperial money which shifts these doubts on to a different plane.

William Clarke appeared to demolish another central Romanov myth, namely the accusation gradually devised by Anna Anderson's adviser, Edward Fallowes, and finally formulated by her biographer Peter Kurth into an outright claim, that Sir Peter Bark had financed the flotation of the Anglo-International Bank from tsarist deposits in the Bank of England. Much of what they alleged was based on the fact that Bark, the Tsar's former finance minister, was appointed managing director of the new Anglo-International Bank and knighted by King George V. Clarke pointed out first that the Anglo-International was financed by a joint-stock flotation and the combined assets of two former Bank of England subsidiaries, the British Trade Corporation and the Anglo-Austrian Bank, and second that all of this occurred in 1926 – nine years after the Revolution and six years after the last vestiges of non-Bolshevik power

had collapsed in Russia – and deduced from this that no underhand business would have been possible.[29] His analysis appeared, on first sight, to
be sound. Further probing, however, revealed a different picture – a
picture perhaps more consistent with Fallowes' and Kurth's suspicions.

In 1921 when Montagu Norman, Governor of the Bank of England,
and Benjamin Strong, chairman of the US Federal Reserve, decided to
use an existing bank – the Anglo-Austrian Bank – as a vehicle for regen-
erating the post-war east European economies, Norman chose Bark as its
managing director. This was only a matter of months after the last White
Russian troops evacuated the Crimea and only three years after the disappearance of the imperial family in Ekaterinburg – considerably closer
to those events than the 1926 date mentioned by Clarke. If Bark was in
such close contact with the Bank of England at such an early date, the
question arises as to where the money to operate the Anglo-Austrian
Bank was obtained. It is so close to the collapse of imperial Russia as to
suggest that Russian funds might have been used. If it is accepted that the
funding of the Anglo-International Bank nine years after the collapse of
the Tsar's regime means that the two events cannot be linked, then it
must surely also be accepted that the establishment of Anglo-Austrian
Bank under Bark so soon after the demise of imperial Russia raises the
suspicion that its funds may have been tsarist in origin. As Clarke himself
said,

> Every subsequent investigator could not ignore the fact that Bark,
> as the Tsar's last Finance Minister, had been close to both the
> British and Russian royal families, had been a prime player in the
> wartime financial negotiations, knew all about the Russian gold
> shipments, had later been appointed to a senior post at the Bank of
> England, had become an adviser to King George V and a trustee of
> both Grand Duchesses Xenia and Olga and, above all, had even
> successfully removed the former Empress Marie's jewel box from
> Copenhagen to Buckingham Palace immediately after her death.[30]

This sleight of hand in dealing with the very early date on which
Bark became involved with the Bank of England subsidiary is repeated
in Clarke's method of dealing with the gold bullion. Though the movements of the gold are detailed carefully and the fact that the last transfer
of £20 million in March 1918 was never paid for is admitted, the
question of precisely what war *matériel* was paid for with the bullion
transfers is never addressed and the main discussion is siphoned off into

an investigation of the vexed question of the missing gold deposits in the imperial state bank depositories in Moscow, St Petersburg, Samara and Kazan. This is itself an interesting question, but it leaves unanswered the question of what exactly happened to tsarist funds transferred to England.

At the core of this question was the urgent request made in 1915 by the British government to its wartime allies France and Russia that gold deposits be transferred to London. This request was made, as noted above, because Britain had insufficient gold left to support its currency because of payments to the United States for arms. Bark was paid for the transfer with British government exchequer bonds redeemable in gold at three- to five-year intervals.[31] If these were redeemable they were, by definition, not spent – on war *matériel* or anything else. All bullion transfers after the finance ministers' meeting at the Crillon Hotel in Paris in 1915, attended by Lloyd George for Britain, M. Ribot for France and Peter Bark for Russia, were made on this understanding. That covered the transfer of £10 million in December 1915, £10 million in June 1916, £20 million in December 1916 and £20 million in March 1917 – £60 million in all, or the equivalent of nearly £2,300 million in today's values. Some of this was undoubtedly eaten up in paying for war *matériel* and in supporting the rouble in 1916–17, but not all. None of the Treasury bonds issued against this gold have ever been redeemed.

Equally, it has to be asked how the Tsarina could have been transferring funds from the Bank of England to pay for her Red Cross hospitals in Russia if there was no money to draw on. As mentioned above, in August 1915 she transferred £100,000 through the British ambassador Buchanan.[32] Clarke makes much of the failure of the Tsarina to grasp that this gold in the Bank of England was Russia's and not hers personally. There was a blurring in her mind, he argues, between what were state and what were private funds. That blurring could have worked in two directions, though. She is, after all, known to have used private funds for what amounted to state purposes – the funding of war hospitals. That money may well have been set against part of the state gold transfers made from the Russian government to the Bank of England's depositories.

On the matter of Romanov deposits in Baring's Bank, new information which substantially contradicts the conclusions of William Clarke came to light within Russia in 1997. Clarke represents the agreement made in 1986 between the Soviet government of Mikhail Gorbachev and the British government of Margaret Thatcher as the definitive solution to the historical controversy over Romanov gold held in Baring's Bank. Successive British governments had been trying to lay their hands on this money since the early 1920s. Winston Churchill, as Chancellor of the Exchequer, had set up a Cabinet committee to consider the matter; but, despite considerable pressure to release the money, Baring's had always resisted, pointing out that the government had no right to these balances. If that was the case in 1927, it is difficult to see that it could have changed by 1986. Clarke claims the Cabinet assessed the value of these deposits at £5 million in 1927; with the accumulation of interest payments, by 1986 the balances had risen to £46 million – a figure agreed by the two governments. The 1986 accord between the British and Soviet governments was used to pay claims, not against the Tsar personally, but for economic disruption and losses caused to companies and individuals by the Russian Revolution and the refusal of the Soviet regime to honour Russian government bonds issued in the days of the Tsar. Clarke represents these balances as consisting wholly of Russian state money derived from imperial Russian embassy deposits used for munitions purchases, currency support and secret service work. These conclusions are flatly contradicted by V. I. Sirotkin in *Russia's Gold and Real Estate Abroad and International Relations*, published in Russia in 1997. Sirotkin's statistics included all the state-owned gold mentioned earlier but they included something more – and something very significant at that. According to Sirotkin, in January 1917 the Tsarina deposited 5,500 kilogrammes – some five and a half tons – of gold in Baring Brothers' Bank, the personal bank of the Romanov family in London. Sirotkin states clearly that this gold was the personal property of the Tsar's family.[33] According to Sirotkin, the 1986 accord between Gorbachev, his foreign minister Edvard Shevardnadze and the British Prime Minister Margaret Thatcher resulted in about £40 million of this gold being used as compensation for 'the Tsar's debts' in England. Only in that does Sirotkin agree with Clarke. The remaining £60 million of the account was, Sirotkin says, 'written off in England's favour'.[34] Contemporary gold valuation would put the value of the five and a half tons deposited by the Tsarina at about £92 million. Payments of £46 million from this would leave a balance of £46 million – a figure, as noted before, suspiciously close to the amount of money the Queen is said to have lost in Baring's crash.

If this gold was private property, however, then Gorbachev and Thatcher had no right to touch it, and what they did amounts to state-sponsored theft. It is hard to accept Clarke's conclusion that this gold deposit attracted any interest – gold on deposit at any bank retains its inherent intrinsic value as an anti-inflationary hedge but it does not earn interest since it cannot be touched. Clarke makes much of members of the Baring family denying having any money of the Tsar. That may be an exercise in semantics, however, for the money was in the Tsarina's name.

For the Tsar's government to deposit such a large amount in Baring's when it had already deposited some £68 million in gold at the Bank of England would have been both inappropriate and counter to its normal practice. To purchase armaments and *matériel* the Tsar's government used the copious credits it had at the Bank of England. Sirotkin brings to light another deposit of gold bars and coins to the contemporary value of 4.8 million gold roubles in October 1917 by the Kerensky Provisional Government. Equivalent to about £6.3 million today, this was placed in the Swedish Riksbank.[35] Like the Bank of England, this was a state bank and the money was used for precisely the same purpose – 'the purchase of cannons, missiles, armoured cars and motor cycles'. Similarly, 70 million gold yen was transferred for the same purpose to Japan in September 1916.[36] Since, unlike these banks, Baring's was a private bank, it appears much more likely that the Baring deposits were private funds belonging to the Tsarina and no part of state arrangements.

The time at which the Tsarina transferred the five and a half tons of gold – January 1917 – is equally interesting. It suggests that the Tsarina may have felt qualms about the risk of disorder breaking out within Russia itself. Taken in conjunction with the 'Hessenreise' – the secret visit of her brother Grand Duke Ernst of Hesse to Tsarskoe Selo in December 1916 – and the fact that the Tsarina was transferring money to her relatives in Germany through her stockbroker Rubinstein without her husband's knowledge,[37] it could indicate that her own brother, if not the German government, was warning her that her husband's position was not necessarily impregnable. Such a conclusion could also imply that the Germans were involved in fomenting the internal insurrection which led to a general strike, general public disorder and the collapse of the Tsar's regime – a regime the German military had conspicuously failed to defeat on the battlefield after three years of war. By January 1917 Rasputin was dead; the Tsarina, deprived of her trusted counsellor, beset by doubts and a mother's anxiety for the personal well-being of her family, may have been acting for once with commendable prudence.

This private deposit was consistent with what the Tsarina told her friend Lili Dehn. 'At least', she said, 'we will not want. We have millions deposited in gold in a bank in England.'[38] Lili Dehn imparted this information to Anna Anderson, who claimed to be Anastasia, and she in turn told Grand Duchess Olga, the Tsar's sister, who visited her in the Dalldorf clinic in Delmenhorst in 1924. From this exchange stemmed Anna Anderson's claim to the gold, which her advocate Fallowes represented as gold in the Bank of England rather than what the Tsarina had actually said, which was a bank in England. When, at the same time, Anderson raised the spectre of the visit to Tsarskoe Seloe by Grand Duke Ernst of Hesse, alarm bells must have started to ring. It is generally assumed that it was this that led to Grand Duke Ernst's virulent opposition to Anderson, because he did not want the potentially treasonous visit to be revealed; but this cannot be so – by the time Anderson's claims were being advanced, the Kaiser's government was long gone. Likewise, the content of the meeting between the Grand Duke and the Tsar has always been assumed to have been the offer of a separate peace to the Tsar by Germany. This may well be so; but it may not have been the sole purpose of the visit. 'Ernie', as he was known in the family, may have been telling his sister of the German plans to destabilize her husband, in consequence of which the Tsarina moved the gold. No one now seriously disputes that the visit took place, since it has been independently verified by Prince Dmitri Galitsyn and Vladimir von Meck, Grand Duchess Ella's secretary.[39] From the revelation about the Baring's gold deposits stemmed the rejection of Anna Anderson by most of the imperial family and the beginnings of both British and Soviet interest in what exactly Baring's had. Naturally, Baring's, which had served as the imperial banking house for well over a century, may have possessed more than one Romanov gold deposit. When Clarke refers to the 'Baring balances' he may well be – indeed, almost certainly is – referring to gold other than that deposited by the Tsarina in January 1917.

Nor did Romanov private wealth end with the Tsarina's gold in Baring's. Extensive property holdings – thirty-seven pieces of real estate in all – spread through seven countries as far apart as the United States, France, Switzerland, Greece, Italy, Jordan and Israel include a castle on the shores of Lake Geneva, a house in San Francisco, several cathedrals and Mount Athos on the Halkidiki peninsula. Most controversial of these was the Sergei Palace, described by Sirotkin as 'a plot of land and the Sergei Townhouse building bought with the personal means of Grand Duke Sergei Alexandrovich',[40] the Tsar's uncle and the Tsarina's brother-in-law. Situated on a prime redevelopment site in East Jerusalem, this plot of land is worth in excess of £60 million, and has been controversially claimed by Prince Philip.[41] The Tsar also owned twelve other properties in East Jerusalem and the Mount of Olives.

Sirotkin calculates that since October 1917 two-thirds of the gold reserves of the former Russian Empire, amounting to a sum of 2,503 million gold roubles, have remained in England, France, Japan and Sweden. In 1917 that was the equivalent of £179 million; today, of £3,315 million. It is small wonder, then, that the Russian State Duma or parliament has set up a Committee on the Repatriation of Russian Funds Abroad. The existence of such Russian wealth and who has rights to it is a hot political issue. It is shocking to think that the country which today struggles for IMF loans may well have been defrauded out of billions of pounds. The accord between Thatcher and Gorbachev – to whom the British Prime Minister famously referred as a man she could 'do business with' – may be illegal on two counts. First, the two premiers clearly had no right to tamper with private gold deposits. Second, the Soviet system could be represented as an illegal regime; and in any event, the Tsarina who made the deposit was no subject of that government.

Another aspect of the ownership of this private wealth is the question of who are its legal heirs. The burial of the Ekaterinburg bones may be an attempt to declare the owners of that gold legally dead, so that others may become its legal, if peripheral, heirs.

In the final analysis it is difficult intellectually to accept that the Tsar, arguably in his day the richest man in the world, left nothing behind but the £5,000 deposit Clarke refers to in the Bank of England, dated 1896 – surely no more than the small change for his visit that year to his wife's 'darling grandmama', Queen Victoria.

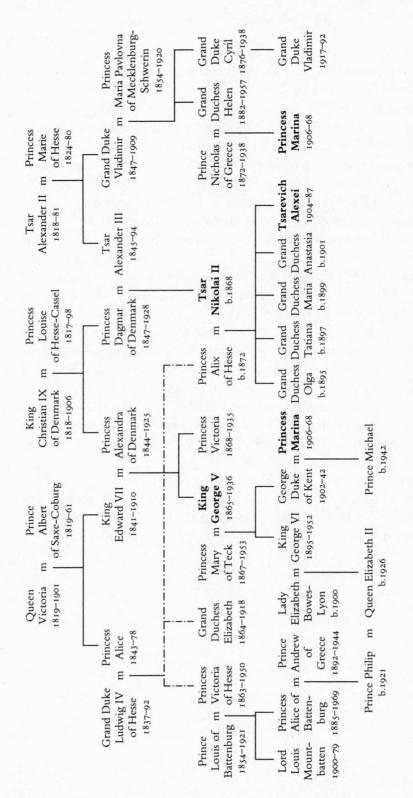

*Family tree, showing the relationships between the Tsarevich Alexei and Princess Marina, King George V and Tsar Nikolai II, the Tsarina Alexandra and Prince Philip, and the Russian imperial family and the British royal family*

# Notes

## Chapter 1: *The Fuse is Lit*

1 Now the property of Mr Hugh Richardson, Moyallon House, copied by Phillips on 10 May 1993.

2 Produced by Bill Phillips on 14 May 1993. One photograph of Mme Kerensky showed her with Sir Thomas Russell, 'Russell Pasha': the head of the Cairo police and a relative of the Duke of Bedford. Another photograph of her had been taken by Francis Streath in London on 6 October 1925.

3 Small Downs House visitors' book, now the property of Mr Hugh Richardson, Moyallon, copied by Phillips on 14 May 1993. Lady Louise Mountbatten was the sister of Lord Louis Mountbatten; their mother was born Princess Victoria of Hesse-Darmstadt and was the sister of the Tsarina. Lady Louise visited Small Downs on 4 November 1923, the day of her marriage to the Crown Prince of Sweden, the future King Gustav Adolf: 'Last visitors of the day HRH the Crown Prince of Sweden with his new Crown Princess', written in Arthur Leverton-Harris's hand. Princess Marie-Louise was present on 31 August 1920. A group photograph was inserted including Lady Beauchamp (mother-in-law of Prince Zevelode Ioannivich Romanov), Princess Marie-Louise, Gertrude Leverton-Harris (*née* Richardson), Frederick Leverton-Harris, Lord Frederick Hamilton and Lady Marjoribanks.

4 George Hill was present on 17–20 February 1919.

5 Richard Pipes, *The Russian Revolution 1899–1919*, London 1990, p. 767: 'There was indeed in the area [Ekaterinburg] a Serbian officer and member of the Serbian military mission to Russia, Major Jarko Constantinovich Micic [Misitch] who had aroused suspicion by asking to see Nicholas [the Tsar]. It is also known that Micic travelled to the Urals to locate and rescue the Serbian Princess Helen Petrovna, the wife of Grand Duke Ioann Constantinovich, interned at Alapaevsk. But it can be established from the recollections of Micic's travelling companion Smirnov that the two men arrived in Ekaterinburg on July 4.' Pipes' sources are Serge Smirnov, *Autour de l'assassinat des grands-ducs*, Paris, 1928, and P. M. Bykov, 'Poslednie dni poslednego tsaria', in N. I. Nikolaiev, *Rabochaia revoliustiia na Urale*, Ekaterinburg, 1921, pp. 909–10. See also Viktor Alexandrov, *The End of the Romanovs*, London, 1966, p. 223, where the author refers to 'an important Serbian group commanded by Major Michich, NCO Bogetchich and one Smirnov, former steward to the Serbian Princess married to Grand Duke Ioann Constantinovich'. Voislav Misitch first appears in the Small Downs visitors' book on Whitsunday 1919, along with Sir Douglas Brownrigg, chief naval censor to the Admiralty, and Lady Brownrigg. Thereafter Misitch appears

regularly: 28 March–1 April 1920, 4–18 April 1921 and 24 June–7 July 1921 with
Eton schoolfriend Dudley Bushby; Easter 1922 and 8 July 1922 with Hilda
Richardson's sister-in-law Anne W. Richardson, Vice-Principal of Westfield
College, University of London; and in August 1922, 23–25 September 1922, 1
October–4 November 1922 and 4–10 June 1924.

6 Captain R. J. Mitchell, former Unionist MP for North Armagh in the Stormont
Parliament (1968–72), Chairman of the Parliamentary Home Affairs Committee
(1970–2).

7 Captain R. J. Mitchell in conversation with the author, 20 May and 4 June 1993.

## Chapter 2: *Questions of Upbringing*

1 The author in conversation with Mrs J. Pearson, Office of Population Censuses
and Surveys, Smedley Hydro, Southport, and Miss Ferris, Birmingham Family
Health, Aston Cross, Birmingham (the successor authority to Birmingham Executive Council), both 4 January 1994.

2 The author in conversation with Dr P. D. Hutchinson, 7 September 1993. Dr
Hutchinson gave me a photocopy of the sleeve in the first instance, and later the
sleeve itself.

3 The author in conversation with Frank Crummey, Head of the Central Services
Agency, 13 April 1994.

4 Natalie Cooke appears in the Moyallon visitors' book on three occasions: in
August 1940 with her daughter Zoe, in November 1940 with Lydia and George
Prescott, and again on 7–14 January 1941.

## Chapter 3: *Searching for the Key*

1 John Bidlake in conversation with the author, 8 June 1993.

2 Phillips supplied me with a copy of this by fax from London. Details on the death
certificate were: Registration District, North Walsham, sub-district of Erping-
ham, County of Norfolk. Date of death 2 January 1987 at St David's Nursing
Home, 52 Common Lane, Sheringham. The deceased's name was given as
Nicholas Tchebotareff. His date of birth was given as 9 February 1903, Russia.
He was described as an International Civil Servant, retired. The informant was
John Hulbert (husband of Chebotarev's niece Iya), who was stated as 'causing
the body to be buried'. Mr Hulbert's address was given as 29 Cromer Road,
Holt. Cause of death was given as cerebral thrombosis, generalized athero-
sclerosis and coronary ischemia. Death was certified by Dr John Barnett.

3 Albert Uprichard in conversation with the author, 24 June 1993.

4 Maureen Hill, *née* Uprichard, in conversation with the author, 24, 25 June 1993,
23 July 1993, 27 August 1993.

5 Iya Zmeova in conversation with the author, 27 June 1993.

6 Iya Zmeova in conversation with the author, 1 July 1993.

7 Natalie Basilievsky, *née* Wrangel, in conversation with the author, 3 August 1993.

8 The author in conversation with Alexandra Kishkovski, 3 and 4 August 1993;

with Fr Viacheslav, Church of the Transfiguration, Brooklyn, 5 August 1993; with Fr Alexander Garclough, Holy Trinity Sea Cliff, 5 August and 5 October 1993; with Bishop Hilarion, Holy Trinity Monastery Jordanville, 5 and 12 August 1993.

9 Stella Dalziel and Peggy Sinton in conversation with the author, 15 July 1993.
10 Stella Dalziel in conversation with the author, 15 January 1994.
11 *Rossiya*, 5 January 1968.
12 Harax was the location of the Dowager Empress' Crimean dacha. The Tsar's, rebuilt by Nikolai II as an Italianate palace, was at Livadia; the Yalta conference at the end of the Second World War was held there. There were other Romanov dachas in the Crimea at Ai-Todor and Oreanda. See Ian Vorres, *The Last Grand Duchess*, London, 1960, pp. 161, 165; *Imperial Russian Journal*, vol. 1, no. 2, Spring 1994, p. 49.
13 Jonas Lied, *Return to Happiness*, London, 1943, pp. 159, 187.
14 Alix Hill in conversation with the author, 9 June 1993.

## Chapter 4: *A Court in Exile*

1 Marianne Cross in conversation with the author, 1 August 1993.
2 Alumni records, Trinity College, Dublin. Prince Alexander Lieven, born Rostock 13 September 1919, was admitted as a student on 3 October 1938, having paid his fees on 10 July 1938. He had been educated at the French School in Brussels. He obtained a first class degree in modern literature and was awarded the gold medal for the leading scholar of his year.
3 Roy Bradford in conversation with the author, 6 August 1993; Douglas Gageby in conversation with the author, 6 August 1993.
4 Conor Cruise O'Brien in conversation with the author, 7 August 1993.
5 Henry St George Smith in conversation with the author, 14 August 1993.
6 Burke's *Landed Gentry of Great Britain*, London, 1972, pp. 906–11.
7 Marquis de Ruvigny, *Titled Nobility of Europe*, London, 1914, pp. 257, 299.
8 Irish military intelligence files G2/3786, grant of resident status to Dr Martha Apraxine: 'Marthe [*sic*] Apraxine born 23 March 1913 Simferopol, Russia. Russian by birth and parentage. Arrived in Ireland from GB 2.9.1930. Last address 191 Rue de la Sainte Gilles, Brussels. Granted permission to reside in Ireland 16.9.1931.'
9 See Richard Pipes, *The Russian Revolution 1899–1919*, London, 1990, pp. 179, 410–12, 421; Dmitri Volkogonov, *Lenin: Life and Legacy*, London, 1995, pp. 120–5.
10 Prince Leonid Lieven in conversation with the author, 18 August 1993.
11 Public Records Office of Northern Ireland (PRONI) 160/142, no. 519, dated 12 August 1942.
12 Jacques Ferrand, *Descendances naturelles des souverains et grands-ducs de Russie de 1762 à 1910*, Paris, 1995, pp. 111, 112, 119.
13 Ibid., p. 147.
14 Kathleen McCarthy in conversation with the author, 30 October 1993.
15 Alexander Bokhanov et al., *The Romanovs: Love, Power, Tragedy*, London, 1993,

pp. 30–2; Colin Wilson, *Rasputin and the Fall of the Romanovs*, London, 1977, p. 136; Maria Rasputin, *Rasputin: The Man Behind the Myth*, London, 1977, pp. 107, 151.

16  Ferrand, *Descendances naturelles*, p. 329; Burke's *Royal Families of the World*, vol. 2, London, 1977, pp. 475–6.

17  Michael Occleshaw, *The Romanov Conspiracies*, London, 1993, pp. 139–44, 151, 179, 185.

18  Burke's *Peerage, Baronetage and Knightage*, London, 1959, pp. 1836–7.

19  George Blake, *No Other Choice*, London, 1990.

20  Alix Hill in conversation with the author, 18 August 1993.

21  Kathleen McCarthy in conversation with the author, 21 December 1993.

22  Ferrand, *Descendances naturelles*, p. 121.

23  *Irish Times*, 25 February 1982: 'Previously secret government papers to be released in Sweden today claim that a Russian Count who lived in Ireland for 30 years up to his death 18 months ago was a Soviet spy – and that this was known to the Irish authorities. The documents written in 1955 say that Count Michael Koutouzoff Tolstoy, who lived in Delgany, Co. Wicklow [he moved there after leaving Collon], worked as a Soviet agent in Budapest at the end of the Second World War and that he passed on intelligence to the Soviets which led to the arrest of the Swedish diplomat, Raoul Wallenberg . . . a note among the Swedish documents written in 1960 said that the Irish authorities believed Count Tolstoy to be a Soviet agent . . . the documents from the Swedish Foreign Office show that Count Tolstoy worked with the Swedish Red Cross in Budapest. The Swedes believe he was also employed as a Russian agent . . . In 1955 when a full investigation into Wallenberg's disappearance by the Swedish Government was in progress, Tolstoy approached the Swedish authorities and told them that while he was working in Budapest in 1945 Wallenberg was killed in an accident. It was two years before the Russians declared that Wallenberg had died in one of their prisons. The Swedish Foreign Ministry believe that the Count was one of a number of Soviet agents intent on blocking or leading the investigation astray. They believe that even in the mid-1950s while he was living in Ireland Tolstoy had Communist sympathies and they were suspicious of visits he made to the continent. The papers released today are part of 42 volumes comprising 13,000 pages.'

## Chapter 5: *The Throne of Blood*

1  Greg King, *The Last Empress*, London, 1994, p. 123. For family reaction see Andrei Maylaunas and Sergei Mironenko, *A Lifelong Passion: Nicholas and Alexandra, Their Own Story*, London, 1996, p. 206. See also Marfa Mouchankow, *My Empress*, New York, 1918, p. 91.

2  Ian Vorres, *The Last Grand Duchess*, London, 1960, p. 80.

3  *Letters of Tsar Nicholas and Empress Marie*, ed. Edward J. Bing, London, 1937, p. 139.

4  Count A. A. Mosolov, *At the Court of the Last Tsar*, London, 1935, p. 72: 'Under a statute of the Imperial family each Grand Duke was entitled to an annual

allowance of 280,000 roubles [£500,000 today] . . . the great-grandsons of an Emperor, simple princes of the blood, had the right only to a single lump sum payment, fixed once and for all, of a million roubles [£1.8 million today] . . . it was only natural that the distant relatives of the Tsar should be aggrieved.'

5  Vorres, *The Last Grand Duchess*, p. 72.
6  King, *The Last Empress*, p. 178. Princess Catherine Radziwill did her best to spread this rumour. Edvard Radzinsky in *The Last Tsar* (London, 1992, p. 89) discusses the Tsarina's relationship with Major-General Orlov. The Tsarina denied to both Anna Vyrubova and Lili Dehn that there was anything improper in her relationship with Orlov.
7  Robert Massie, *Nicholas and Alexandra*, London, 1968, p. 371.
8  Burke's *Royal Families of the World*, vol. 1, London, 1977, p. 235.
9  Declaration of Nicholas Romanov, Prince of Russia, Rome, October 1995, in *Royalty* magazine, vol. 14, no. 3, January 1996: 'Sixteen Princes of the house of Romanov are now living and in full possession of their rights of inheritance to the Imperial throne of Russia and the passage of such rights into the female line is baseless.'
10  Robert Massie, *The Romanovs: The Final Chapter*, London, 1995, p. 265.
11  Grand Duke Alexander Mikhailovich, *Once a Grand Duke*, New York, 1932, pp. 66–7.
12  Burke's *Royal Families of the World*, vol. 1, pp. 414–5. For Militsa's and Stana's ambitions, see Mosolov, *At the Court of the Last Tsar*, p. 91.
13  King, *The Last Empress*, p. 38.
14  Prince Felix Yusupov, *Rasputin*, London, 1927, p. 19; Mosolov, *At the Court of the Last Tsar*, p. 50. Philippe was far from a mere 'butcher's boy': along with his mentor and predecessor in the favour of Militsa and Stana, Papus, he is reported to have founded a Rosicrucian Cathar lodge in St Petersburg. It was in opposition to the Rosicrucians' activities that the Tsarina's sister Grand Duchess Elizabeth used her protégé Nilus to produce the 'Protocols of the Elders of Zion' in 1903 ('Zion' referred to the Cathar organization known as the Priory of Sion); it was only after the document was taken up by the Okhrana that it was adapted to be used against the Jews. See also N. Cohn, *The Protocols of the Elders of Zion: Warrant for Genocide*, London, 1988.
15  Yusupov, *Rasputin*, pp. 120–1.
16  Edvard Radzinsky, *The Last Tsar*, London, 1992, p. 57.
17  Richard Betts, 'Holy Hierarch: Theophan of Poltava', *Orthodox Word*, Amsterdam, 1988, pp. 59–69. See also St Herman's Brotherhood, *Great Orthodox Hierarchs of the Nineteenth and Twentieth Centuries*, New York, 1988, pp. 191–225.
18  John Snelling, *Buddhism in Russia*, London, 1993, pp. 85–9, 47–9.
19  Ibid., pp. 47–50, 79.
20  Ibid., pp. 72, 84, 85, 131.
21  Mosolov, *At the Court of the Last Tsar*, p. 90.
22  Radzinsky, *The Last Tsar*, p. 62, citing the pre-revolutionary socialite Vera Leonidovna Yurevna.
23  Ibid., p. 132.
24  Willi Korte first told me of the existence of these documents early in 1994. He had obtained them from the palace at Tsarskoe Selo. Though I asked for copies,

he only gave them to me late in 1995 after I told him what had been written about him in John Klier and Helen Mingay's book, *The Quest for Anastasia* (London, 1995). We are currently searching for more of the records.

25  The record is handwritten and signed by Dr Hirsch and Professor Otti. According to Mosolov, *At the Court of the Last Tsar*, p. 33, Hirsch treated Nicholas II for typhoid at Livadia in 1900. Hirsch was the uncle of Catherine Schneider, the Tsarina's lectrice or reader, who had originally taught her Russian. Schneider had originally worked for Grand Duchess Elizabeth. Ibid., p. 60.

26  Maylaunas and Mironenko, *A Lifelong Passion*, pp. 217–19. Mironenko is director of the Russian State Archive.

27  Burke's *Royal Families of the World*, vol. 1, pp. 414, 215.


## Chapter 6: *Bones and Blood*

1   'Tsar's Bones Hoax', *Sunday Express*, 24 January 1993, p. 11.

2   Olga N. Kulikovsky-Romanov, untitled article in *Imperial Russian Journal*, vol. 2, no. 4, Autumn 1995; Robert Massie, *The Romanovs: The Final Chapter*, London, 1995, pp. 27–32.

3   John Klier and Helen Mingay, *The Quest for Anastasia*, London, 1995, p. 187, 181.

4   Leonid Bolotin, quoted in 'Tsar's Bones Hoax', *Sunday Express*, 24 January 1993, p. 11.

5   Home Office news release, 'Tsar Nicholas II – Family Remains', 9 July 1993; Forensic Science Service Research Results, 9 July 1993; Peter Gill et al., 'Identification of the Remains of the Romanov Family by DNA Analysis', *Nature Genetics*, vol. 6, February 1994, pp. 130–5.

6   Gill et al., 'Identification of the Remains of the Romanov Family', p. 132.

7   Massie, *The Romanovs*, p. 96.

8   *New Yorker*, 19 February 1996, p. 96; *Toronto Star*, 7 December 1995; 'Tests Delay Burial of Tsar', *Daily Mail*, 25 February 1996; *Daily Telegraph*, 9 February 1996.

9   Massie, *The Romanovs*, p. 96; Dr William Maples in conversation with the author, 7 February 1994.

10  Massie, *The Romanovs*, p. 103.

11  Anthony Summers and Tom Mangold, *The File on the Tsar*, London, 1976, pp. 143–56; Edvard Radzinsky, *The Last Tsar*, London, 1992.

12  William Maples in conversation with the author, 7 February 1994.

13  William Maples in conversation with the author, 12 August 1994.

14  William Maples in conversation with the author, 7 February 1994.

15  William Maples in conversation with the author, 11 November 1994.

16  V. L. Popov in conversation with the author, 2, 3 April 1998; V. L. Popov, *Identification of the Remains of the Tsar and Romanov Family Members: Forensic, Stomatological and Ballistic Study* (in Russian), St Petersburg, 1994, pp. 44–50. Professor Popov was the ballistics expert and forensic scientist who originally worked with Dr William Maples in Ekaterinburg. He is Professor at the Military-Medical Institute in St Petersburg.

17 Willi Korte is one of the world's foremost investigators in the area of tracing stolen works of art. On 28 June 1998 he featured in a Channel 4 television documentary *Making a Killing* about tracing Jewish-owned art looted by the Nazis.

18 Willi Korte in conversation with the author, 24 March 1994.

19 Alexander Murzin, 'Don't Rush to Bury Us', *Komsomolskaya pravda*, 27 January 1998; BBC Television news, 15 September 1992; Massie, *The Romanovs*, p. 82; Klier and Mingay, *The Quest for Anastasia*, p. 197.

20 'Tsar's Bones Hoax', *Sunday Express*, 24 January 1993.

21 Decision of the Holy Synod of the Russian Orthodox Church, 26 February 1998, reported in *Moscow Times*.

22 William Maples in conversation with the author, 7 February 1994.

23 Willi Korte in conversation with the author, 19 October 1994; see also Massie, *The Romanovs*, pp. 109–10.

24 Willi Korte in conversation with the author, 8 May 1995.

25 William Maples in conversation with the author, 21 November 1995.

26 Willi Korte in conversation with the author, 26 June 1994.

27 Massie, *The Romanovs*, pp. 102–10.

28 William Maples in conversation with the author, 21 November 1995.

29 William M. Shields, State University of New York, Syracuse, 'The Future of Forensic DNA Testing', paper presented to the American Association for the Advancement of Science (AAAS), 17 February 1998, reported in *Irish Times* and *Guardian*, 18 February 1998.

30 William Shields, reported in *Guardian*, 18 February 1998.

31 William Maples in conversation with the author, 27 June 1994.

32 Jonathan Koehler, 'The Future of Forensic DNA Testing: When Are Jurors Impressed by DNA Match Probabilities', paper presented to the AAAS, 17 February 1998, reported in *Irish Times*, 18 February 1998.

33 *The Times*, 31 May 1994.

34 Editorial, *Nature Genetics*, vol. 8, no. 3, November 1994, pp. 205–6.

35 Vladislav Plaksin, *The Times* magazine, 10 August 1996, p. 11; *Daily Telegraph*, 25 February 1996.

36 Sir Brian McGrath, quoted in Massie, *The Romanovs*, p. 242.

37 Massie, *The Romanovs*, p. 240. See also Dr Mark Stoneking et al., 'Establishing the Identity of Anna Anderson Manahan', *Nature Genetics*, vol. 9, January 1995, p. 9.

38 This subject is fully discussed in Anthony Lambton, *The Mountbattens*, London, 1989, pp. 110–24.

39 Andrew Morton, *Inside Buckingham Palace*, London, 1992, p. 24.

40 The second occasion was on 6–13 July 1994. See Robert Massie, 'The Last Romanov Mystery', *New Yorker*, 21 August 1995, p. 93. The television film was made by Granite Productions for Granada Television. It was presented by Prince Michael of Kent and directed by Amorer Wason.

41 Olga Kulikovsky-Romanov, untitled article in *Imperial Russian Journal*, vol. 2, no. 4, Autumn 1995, p. 134.

42 Massie, 'The Last Romanov Mystery', p. 93. See also Murzin, 'Don't Rush to Bury Us'.

43 Paul G. Debenham, 'Heteroplasmy and the Tsar', *Nature*, vol. 380, 11 April 1996, p. 484.

44 Davis Leppard and Adrian Levy, 'Prince Michael Aide Claims he is Victim of MI5 Smear', *Sunday Times*, 29 January 1995. Another article in the same edition was entitled 'Why Was Prince's Aide Tailed for Two Years by MI5 Agents?' See also *The Times*, 28 January 1995; *Majesty* magazine, vol. 16, no. 3, March 1995, p. 10; *Royalty* magazine, vol. 14, no. 2, December 1995, pp. 50–3.

45 David Leppard and Tim Kelsey, 'Prince Charming's Chequered Career', *Sunday Times*, Focus, 26 May 1996. See also 'Serbs Give Tories £100,000', *Sunday Times*, 19 May 1996; David Leigh and Jonathan Calvert, 'Rifkind Put Paid to Inquiry into Milosevic', *Observer*, 18 May 1997.

46 David Leppard, Tim Kelsey and Jason Burke, 'Prince Pays Off Fixer with £100,000', *Sunday Times*, Insight, 15 December 1996.

47 *The Times*, 28 January 1995.

48 'New Cash Crisis for Prince Michael', *Sunday Times*, 19 October 1997. See also *The Times*, *Guardian*, 20 October 1997.

49 *Sunday Times*, 26 May 1996.

50 Burke's *Royal Families of the World*, vol. 1, London, 1977, pp. 474, 475, 326.

51 *Daily Express*, 6 September 1996.

52 *The Times*, 14 October 1995, 27 March 1997; *Royalty* magazine, vol. 14, no. 6, December 1996.

53 Donald Foreman, 'A King for Poland', *The Times*, 2 November 1996. See also 'The Uncrowned Head of Poland', *The Times* magazine, 19 October 1996.

54 For possibilities of restorations, see *The Times*, 26 May 1996 (Bulgaria), *The Times*, 1 June 1996 (Italy), *Daily Telegraph*, 9 January 1997 (Yugoslavia), *The Times*, 21 April 1997 (Albania).

55 *The Times*, 17 July 1998, p. 16.

Chapter 7: *Burying the Evidence*

1 V. L. Popov in conversation with the author, 3 April 1998.

2 John Klier and Helen Mingay, *The Quest for Anastasia*, London, 1995, pp. 175–86. Speaking to a public session of the Duma on 21 May 1998, Professor Popov demonstrated that the skulls of skeletons 5 and 6 could not have been found in the positions at the north-east corner of the burial site opened in 1979 by Ryabov and Avdonin, but should have been at the opposite end of the pit, over six feet away. Neither Ryabov nor Avdonin had been able to answer the State Prosecutor on this point.

3 Alexander Bokhanov, 'A Quest for Truth', *Royalty* magazine, April 1993, pp. 66–74.

4 V. L. Popov in conversation with the author, 3 April 1998.

5 Olga Kulikovsky-Romanov, untitled article in *Imperial Russian Journal*, vol. 2, no. 4, Autumn 1995, p. 132.

6 Olga Kulikovsky-Romanov, *Submission to the State Commission on the Ekaterinburg Bones* (in Russian), Moscow, 1995.

7 Edvard Radzinsky, *The Last Tsar*, London, 1992, pp. 381–2.

8  Lubov Millar, *Grand Duchess Elizabeth of Russia*, Frankfurt-am-Main, 1991, p. 220. See also *Novoe russkoe slovo*, New York, 11 August 1984.

9  Millar, *Grand Duchess Elizabeth of Russia*, p. 218.

10  Richard Pipes, *The Russian Revolution 1899–1919*, London, 1990, p. 750.

11  Radzinsky, *The Last Tsar*, p. 393.

12  Klier and Mingay, *The Quest for Anastasia*, p. 185.

13  Alexander Murzin, 'Don't Rush to Bury Us', *Komsomolskaya pravda*, 25 January 1998.

14  This dissenting report was addressed to B. E. Nemtsov, Deputy Prime Minister of the Government of the Russian Federation, and signed by S. A. Belaiev, Senior Scientific Research Fellow, V. V. Alexiev, Russian Academy of Sciences, and Metropolitan Yuvenali of Krutiski and Kolomna. It was dated 12 November 1997. Issues raised included: (1) Were the bones all buried at the one time? (2) Why was the scar of the Otsu mark missing from the alleged Tsar skull? (3) Why were ten volumes of KGB evidence, which spoke of a family like the Tsar's in appearance being killed in Ekaterinburg in 1918, ignored? (4) Why were the alleged imperial family remains not compared with items of clothing known to belong to the individuals in Pavlovsk, Tsarskoe Selo and Moscow? (5) Why had the commission taken contradictory positions at different times on the two missing bodies? These issues were then taken up by journalist Alexander Murzin in *Komsomolskaya pravda* on 25 November 1997.

15  William Maples in conversation with the author, 19 February 1994; V. L. Popov in conversation with the author, 3 April 1998.

16  V. L. Popov in conversation with the author, 3 April 1998.

17  V. L. Popov, *St Petersburg Times*, 11 February 1998.

18  Robert Massie, 'The Last Romanov Mystery', *New Yorker*, 21 August 1995, p. 90.

19  V. L. Popov in conversation with the author, 3 April 1998.

20  Vladimir Malevianny, 'The British Lead in the Romanov Affair', *Nezavisimaya gazeta*, 28 November 1997 (in Russian).

21  Ibid.

22  William Maples in conversation with the author, 9 May 1994. Robert Massie, *The Romanovs: The Final Chapter*, London, 1995, p. 63.

23  V. L. Popov in conversation with the author, 3 April 1998. See also V. L. Popov, *Identification of the Remains of the Tsar and Romanov Family Members: Forensic, Stomatological and Ballistic Study* (in Russian), St Petersburg, 1994, pp. 42–5.

24  William Potts in conversation with the author, 12, 13 October 1995. D. M. and W. T. W. Potts, *Queen Victoria's Gene*, London, 1995.

25  Seamus Martin, 'Tsar Wars', *Irish Times*, 21 February 1998, citing as sources Fr Nikolai Semyonov and Prince Alexei Scherbatov.

26  Ian Vorres, *The Last Grand Duchess*, London, 1960, p. 171.

27  William Maples in conversation with the author, 7 February 1994; see also Massie, *The Romanovs*, p. 62.

28  Millar, *Grand Duchess Elizabeth of Russia*, pp. 224–48.

29  Sergei Mikhailovich was not only the same age as the Tsar (he was born in 1869, the Tsar in 1868), but bore a physical resemblance to him.

30  Tatiana Pavlova and Vladimir Khrustalyov, 'Tsar for a Day', *Royalty* magazine, 1994, pp. 74–81.

31  James Blair Lovell, *Anastasia: The Lost Princess*, London, 1992, p. 347.

32  Alix Hill in conversation with the author, 17 January 1998.

33  V. L. Popov in conversation with the author, 3 April 1998.

34  Alix Hill in conversation with the author, 17 January 1998.

35  William Maples in conversation with the author, 24 March, 8 May, 6 October 1994.

36  Letter dated 1 November 1994.

37  Letter dated 10 November 1994.

38  William Maples in conversation with the author, 9 May 1994. See also Popov, *Identification of the Remains of the Tsar and Romanov Family Members*, pp. 42–5. Professor Popov stated that the elongated skull was present in only 10% of the population, the horseshoe-shaped jaw and crowded teeth in 10%, and A+ blood group in 15%. There is consequently a probability of approximately 0.15% of all three features appearing in one individual by chance.

39  Professor Popov calculated that there was only a 1.5% chance of this close correlation occurring randomly. Another way to put this was that there was a 98.5% chance I was related to the bones. While not amounting to absolute certainty, this was precisely the same degree of probability that Dr Gill claimed for his identification of the bones as those of the imperial family.

Chapter 8: *The Inheritance of Blood*

1  Ian Vorres, *The Last Grand Duchess*, London, 1960, p. 143.

2  Andrei Maylaunas and Sergei Mironenko, *A Lifelong Passion: Nicholas and Alexandra, Their Own Story*, London, 1996, p. 351: diary of Grand Duchess Xenia, the Tsar's sister, 10 March 1912.

3  Robert Massie, *Nicholas and Alexandra*, London, 1968, pp. 190–3.

4  Robert and Suzanne Massie, *Journey*, London, 1975.

5  Prince Felix Yusupov, *Rasputin*, London, 1927, pp. 121–3; Viktor Alexandrov, *The End of the Romanovs*, London, 1966, p. 118.

6  John Snelling, *Buddhism in Russia*, London, 1993, pp. 46–52, 53, 66, 85, 96, 116, 130, 131, 203–4.

7  Zoe Cooke in conversation with the author, 23 July 1994; deposition by Zoe Cooke, 23 December 1996.

8  Snelling, *Buddhism in Russia*, p. 88.

9  Count Kokovstev, *Out of My Past*, Stanford, 1933, pp. 478–9; Alexandrov, *The End of the Romanovs*, p. 116; Richard Pipes, *The Russian Revolution 1899–1919*, London, 1990, p. 239.

10  Alexandrov, *The End of the Romanovs*, pp. 116–17.

11  O. A. Tucker, *Henbane*, Grolier Electronic Publishing, 1993.

12  Snelling, *Buddhism in Russia*, pp. 138–9.

13  William Le Queux, *Rasputin, the Rascal Monk*, London, 1917, pp. 48–50.

14  Massie, *Nicholas and Alexandra*, pp. 199–202; R. J. Minney, *Rasputin*, London, 1972, p. 107; Colin Wilson, *Rasputin and the Fall of the Romanovs*, London, 1977, pp. 148–51.

15  Maylaunas and Mironenko, *A Lifelong Passion*, p. 351.

16 Medical Report on the Tsarevich's Condition, Spala, 20 October 1912, signed by Count Mosolov, Head of the Imperial Chancery.

17 Massie, *Nicholas and Alexandra*, p. 177.

18 Ibid., p. 173.

19 Medical Report on the Tsarevich's Condition, Spala, 20 October 1912.

20 Massie, *Nicholas and Alexandra*, p. 176.

21 Wilson, *Rasputin and the Fall of the Romanovs*, p. 177. For the police report on the incident, see Edvard Radzinsky, *The Last Tsar*, London, 1992, pp. 97–8.

22 Wilson, *Rasputin and the Fall of the Romanovs*, p.178. See also Radzinsky, *The Last Tsar*, p. 131.

23 *The Fall of the Romanovs* by 'A Russian', London, 1918; repr. London, 1992, p. 32; Massie, *Nicholas and Alexandra*, p. 219. Grand Duke Ernst was speaking to Foreign Minister Sazonov.

24 Maylaunas and Mironenko, *A Lifelong Passion*, p. 435: letter from the Tsarina to the Tsar, 24 August 1915.

25 Radzinsky, *The Last Tsar*, pp. 135–9.

26 Wilson, *Rasputin and the Fall of the Romanovs*, p. 186, gives the cause as the Tsarevich hurting his nose on the window when the train jolted. Maylaunas and Mironenko, *A Lifelong Passion*, p. 443 (extract from the Tsar's diary, 3 December 1915) give the cause as sneezing.

27 *The Fall of the Romanovs* by 'A Russian', pp. 32–3.

28 Massie, *Nicholas and Alexandra*, p. 362. See also Marc Ferro, *Nicholas II: The Last of the Tsars*, London, 1991, p. 179.

29 Pipes, *The Russian Revolution*, p. 266.

30 Yusupov, *Rasputin*, pp. 56–7.

31 Greg King, *The Last Empress*, London, 1995, p. 266.

32 Gregory P. Tschebotarioff, *Russia, My Native Land*, New York, 1964, p. 61: from the diary of Sister Valentina Ivanovna Chebotarev, 5/18 February 1917, p. 120.

33 William A. Pinkney in conversation with the author, 9 December 1994.

34 Scottish historian Dr Michail McDonald, *Sunday People*, 24 June 1979, quoting as source a bank clerk at Coutts, the royal bankers, stated that payments of £250 a quarter were made by King Edward VII to a Louisa Brown in Paris. Allegedly she was born in Switzerland in 1866. Kathleen McCarthy recounts how she interrupted a conversation between Nicholas Couriss, his wife Sana and Prince Paul Lieven. Sana Couriss was speaking of Queen Victoria having two illegitimate children by Brown. Kathleen was sent away on a pretext. Louisa Brown, as it happens, was the name of Hilda Richardson's mother.

35 Massie, *Nicholas and Alexandra*, p. 106.

36 Maylaunas and Mironenko, *A Lifelong Passion*, p. 399: from Pierre Gilliard's memoirs, 5 August 1914.

37 Carolo Townend, *Royal Russia*, London, 1995, p. 51.

38 Maylaunas and Mironenko, *A Lifelong Passion*, p. 378, Pierre Gilliard memoirs.

39 Ibid., p. 379, letter from Anna Vyrubova to Rasputin, June 1913.

40 Edvard Radzinsky, quoted in *The Times*, 28 November 1996.

41 Maria Rasputin, *Rasputin: The Man Behind the Myth*, London, 1977, p. 230.

42 Pipes, *The Russian Revolution*, pp. 266, 266n. Alix Hill's mother, Olga von Berg,

was one of the bright young things of pre-Revolution St Petersburg society and was present at the party in Yusupov's home, the Moika Palace, on the night Rasputin was murdered; she left at 2 a.m. She was in love with Paul Stepanov, who participated in Rasputin's murder. He disappeared shortly after this. Maria Rasputin, the *starets'* daughter, mentions Stepanov in her book *Rasputin: The Man Behind the Myth*, which accords with what Alix Hill knew; but none of the other books, including that of Greg King, *The Murder of Rasputin*, London 1996, mentions him.

43 Brian Moynahan *Rasputin*, New York, 1997, London, 1998.
44 King, *The Murder of Rasputin*.
45 Snelling, *Buddhism in Russia*, p. 204.
46 'Aspirin', *Encyclopaedia Britannica*, 6th edn, vol. 28, pp. 542–3; Grolier Electronic Publishing, 1996.
47 'Blood', *Encyclopaedia Britannica*, 6th edn, vol. 15, p. 1152.
48 *Quinidine*, Grolier Electronic Publishing, 1996.
49 *Ergot*, Grolier Electronic Publishing, 1996.

## Chapter 9: *'This disease is not in our family'*

1 D. M. and W. T. W. Potts, *Queen Victoria's Gene*, London, 1995, pp. 25, 32, 42–4, 132, 134–8. For relationships see Burke's *Royal Families of the World*, vol. 1, London, 1977, pp. 215, 476, 142.
2 These include Factor VIII deficiency haemophilia, the most common variety, affecting 85% of haemophiliacs; Factor IX deficiency or 'Christmas Disease'; PTA Factor XI deficiency; Factor V deficiency; prothrombin deficiency; and von Willebrand's disease.
3 Malcolm Potts in conversation with the author, 30 September 1995.
4 M. M. Wintrobe, 'Clinical Haematology', *Encyclopaedia Britannica*, 6th edn, London, 1967.
5 Brian Roberts, *Cecil Rhodes and the Princess*, London, 1969, p. 138; Princess Catherine Radziwill (alias Count Paul Vassili), *Behind the Veil at the Russian Court*, London, 1913, p. 394.
6 Lili Dehn, *The Real Tsaritsa*, London, 1922, p. 81.
7 William Potts in conversation with the author, 12, 13 October 1995; William Wheeler in conversation with the author, 12 October 1996; John Röhl, Martin Warren and David Hunt, *Purple Secret: Genes, Madness and the Royal House of Windsor*, London, 1998.
8 V. A. McCusick, 'The Royal Haemophilia', *Scientific American*, 1965, pp. 2, 88–95, 213.
9 Potts, *Queen Victoria's Gene*, pp. 120–33; Burke's *Royal Families of the World*, vol. 1, pp. 214–15, 308, 501–2.
10 The family relationships may be found in Burke's *Royal Families of the World*, vol. 1, pp. 138–42, 304–6, 528–34.
11 Potts, *Queen Victoria's Gene*, p. 40, quoting Queen Victoria's journal, 14 January 1875.
12 Wintrobe, 'Clinical Haematology'.

13 For the kidney bleeding, see Andrei Maylaunas and Sergei Mironenko *A Lifelong Passion: Nicholas and Alexandra, Their Own Story*, London, 1996, p. 351, Grand Duchess Xenia's diary for 10 March 1912; for the Spala incident, see Medical Report on the Tsarevich's Condition, 20 October 1912, signed by Count A. A. Mosolov, and Robert Massie, *Nicholas and Alexandra*, London, 1969, p. 175; for the nosebleed of 1915, see Maylaunas and Mironenko, *A Lifelong Passion*, pp. 443–5, Massie, *Nicholas and Alexandra*, pp. 289–90, and Colin Wilson, *Rasputin and the Fall of the Romanovs*, London, 1977, p. 186.

14 Ian Vorres, *The Last Grand Duchess*, London, 1960, p. 124.

15 Rosemary Biggs MD, A. S. Douglas MD, R. G. Macfarlane MD, J. V. Dacie and W. R. Pitney, 'Christmas Disease: A Condition Previously Mistaken for Haemophilia', *British Medical Journal*, 27 December 1952, pp. 1378–82.

16 Wilson, *Rasputin and the Fall of the Romanovs*, p. 187.

17 Alix Hill in conversation with the author, 3 April 1998.

18 Alix Hill in conversation with the author, 25 September 1996.

19 Letter from Dr J. R. O'Donnell, Consultant Haematologist, Beaumont Hospital, Dublin, to Dr Michael Farrell, Consultant Neuropathologist, Beaumont Hospital, Dublin, 1 May 1998.

20 Massie, *Nicholas and Alexandra*, p. 39.

21 'The Life of Grand Duke George Alexandrovich', *Imperial Russian Journal*, vol. 2, no. 1, Winter 1995, p. 25; Vorres, *The Last Grand Duchess*, pp. 63–4.

22 Massie, *Nicholas and Alexandra*, p. 153.

23 Potts, *Queen Victoria's Gene*, pp. 70–2.

24 Ibid., p. 6.

25 John Röhl, Martin Warren and David Hunt, *Purple Secret: Genes, Madness and the Royal House of Windsor*, London, 1998, p. 202.

26 Massie, *Nicholas and Alexandra*, pp. 152–3.

27 Edvard Radzinsky, *The Last Tsar*, London, 1992, p. 125; Greg King, *The Last Empress*, London, 1994, p. 177.

28 King, *The Last Empress*, p. 92.

29 Princess Marie-Louise, *My Memories of Six Reigns*, London, 1956, p. 63.

30 Meriel Buchanan, *Dissolution of an Empire*, London, 1932, pp. 36–7; King, *The Last Empress*, p. 92.

31 Potts, *Queen Victoria's Gene*, p. 57.

32 Louis Levine, *Genetic Diseases: Autosomal Dominant and Recessive Genes*, Grolier Electronic Publishing, 1993.

33 S. B. Vardy, *The Bathory Family*, Grolier Electronic Publishing, 1993.

34 Letter from Dr J. R. O'Donnell, Consultant Haematologist, Beaumont Hospital, Dublin, to Dr Michael Farrell, Consultant Neuropathologist, Beaumont Hospital, Dublin, 1 May 1998; Thomas Stuttaford, *The Times*, 26 March 1996.

35 Stuttaford, *The Times*, 26 March 1996.

36 Maylaunas and Mironenko, *A Lifelong Passion*, p. 379, Tsar Nicholas II's diary, 16 July 1913, Peterhof.

37 W. A. Pinkney in conversation with the author, 9 December 1994.

Chapter 10: *Windows of Opportunity*

1  Richard Pipes, *The Russian Revolution 1899–1919*, London, 1990, pp. 595–6: 'By virtue of Brest Germany tripled in size.' A total of 750,000 sq km was handed over by Lenin's government to the Germans, an area nearly twice the size of the German empire.

2  Envoys Hautschild, Riezler, Mirbach and Helfferich all raised the issue of the Romanovs with the Bolshevik government: Pipes, *The Russian Revolution*, p. 783. See also Anthony Summers and Tom Mangold, *The File on the Tsar*, London, 1976, pp. 361–5; Michael Occleshaw, *The Romanov Conspiracies*, London, 1993, pp. 60–4.

3  Summers and Mangold *The File on the Tsar*, pp. 292, 364.

4  Pipes, *The Russian Revolution*, p. 783.

5  Hannah Pakula, *Queen of Roumania*, London, 1989, p. 271.

6  Summers and Mangold, *The File on the Tsar*, p. 361.

7  Greg King, *The Last Empress*, London, 1994, p. 49; Queen Victoria, *Advice to a Granddaughter*, London, 1975, p. 111.

8  Viktor Alexandrov, *The End of the Romanovs*, London, 1966, p. 170–1.

9  Public Records Office of Northern Ireland (PRONI) D 1943, 1–3.

10 William Rodney, *Joe Boyle: King of the Klondike*, Toronto, 1974; Leonard W. Taylor, *The Sourdough and the Queen*, London, 1983; George A. Hill, *Go Spy the Land*, London, 1932.

11 Summers and Mangold, *The File on the Tsar*, p. 102.

12 Robert Bruce Lockhart, *Memories of a British Agent*, London, 1932, pp. 262, 280, 323.

13 Zoe Cooke in conversation with the author, 9 March 1994.

14 Kathleen McCarthy in conversation with the author, 15 February 1996; Dame Elizabeth Hill in conversation with the author, 11 February 1996.

15 Alix Hill in conversation with the author, 21 July 1994.

16 Hill, *Go Spy the Land*, p. 59.

17 Letter from Mrs M. McClenaghan, Ministry of Defence, Ref. 91/39194/CS ® 2b/6, 7 October 1991, to Dr Una Kroll, daughter of Brigadier George Hill, containing the service record of Brigadier George Hill DSO MC MBE P/80722.

18 Hill, *Go Spy the Land*, p. 89.

19 Una Kroll in conversation with the author, 12 February 1996.

20 Hill, *Go Spy the Land*, pp. 88–9.

21 On 20 June 1994 James ('Jimmy') Boyle gave me details of Col. Joe Boyle's visits to Upper Buckna, and told me how he placed the Colonel's papers in the Public Records Office of Northern Ireland.

22 Rodney, *Joe Boyle*, p. 206; PRONI D 1943/1/1, letter from Joe Boyle to Queen Marie telling her he had intercepted Crown Prince Carol and Zizi Lambrino in Odessa on 2 September 1918. They had married on 31 August.

23 Burke's *Royal Families of the World*, vol. 1, London, 1977, pp. 271, 307, 475.

24 Prince Michael of Greece, *Nicholas and Alexandra: The Family Albums*, London, 1992, p. 186.

25 Rodney, *Joe Boyle*, pp. 188–9.

26 Ibid., pp. 178–87; Taylor, *The Sourdough and the Queen*, pp. 243–59.

27 Richard Pipes, *Russia under the Bolshevik Regime 1919–24*, London, 1994, p. 442.

28 Ibid., pp. 410–12; Dmitri Volkogonov, *Lenin: Life and Legacy*, London, 1995, pp. 123, 126.

29 Public Record Office, Kew (PRO) FO 371/3296, Moscow, 3 April 1918. See also Rodney, *Joe Boyle*, p. 189; Taylor, *The Sourdough and the Queen*, p. 282, letter from Prime Minister to Duke of Devonshire, Governor General of Canada.

30 Taylor, *The Sourdough and the Queen*, pp. 208–9. Boyle met Lenin, Dzerzhinsky, Karahan, Joffe and Antonov-Ovsenko.

31 Rodney, *Joe Boyle*, pp. 166, 211.

32 PRONI D 1943/1/3/10 N6, Kishinev, 28 May 1918, D 1843/1/3/10 N20, 9/22 July 1918.

33 PRONI D 1943/1/3/10, 31 July 1918.

34 PRONI D 1943/1/3/10 N3, expense account for July 1918.

35 Rodney, *Joe Boyle*, pp. 194–6.

36 Marquis de Ruvigny, *Titled Nobility of Europe*, London, 1914, pp. 1471–2.

37 PRO FO 371/3350; Occleshaw, *The Romanov Conspiracies*, p. 96; John Bradley, *Civil War in Russia 1917–1920*, London, 1975, p. 71.

38 Taylor, *The Queen and the Sourdough*, p. 299.

39 Summers and Mangold, *The File on the Tsar*, pp. 87–8.

40 Ibid. p. 86; PRO FO 371/3977, Sir Charles Eliot to A. Balfour, 5 October 1918.

41 Summers and Mangold, *The File on the Tsar*, pp. 70, 131, 89. See also Marc Ferro, *Nicholas II: The Last of the Tsars*, London, 1991, p. 259; *New York Tribune*, 5 September 1920.

42 Summers and Mangold, *The File on the Tsar*, pp. 88–9.

43 Ibid., pp. 102–3.

44 Occleshaw, *The Romanov Conspiracies*, p. 98.

45 Ibid., p. 99. R. Meinertzhagen, Diary, Rhodes House Library, Oxford, vol. 20, pp. 169–70. See also Mark Cocker, *Richard Meinertzhagen: Soldier, Scientist, Spy*, London, 1989, pp. 200–3, pl. 5.

46 Cocker, *Richard Meinertzhagen*, pp. 210–29.

47 Occleshaw, *The Romanov Conspiracies*, p. 98; Meinertzhagen, Diary, vol. 20, pp. 169–70.

48 Moyallon House visitors' book.

49 Melvyn Fairclough, *The Ripper and the Royals*, London, 1994, pp. 17, 75.

50 Meinertzhagen, Diary, vol. 20, pp. 169–70; Occleshaw, *The Romanov Conspiracies*, pp. 98–9, 143–7; Cocker, *Richard Meinertzhagen*, p. 202. For operations of the Dvina River column, see Robert Jackson, *At War with the Bolsheviks*, London, 1972, pp. 67–77, 81–8, 152–60, 163–70. In times and circumstances where personal connections could count for a great deal, it is instructive to note who inhabited this small world of British diplomatic, military and intelligence activity in Russia. The financial adviser to General Poole's mission turned out to be the brother of Mary Spring-Rice, who was married to Margaret Meinertzhagen's brother-in-law. The founder of the Scottish Aeroplane Syndicate, which produced the more advanced de Havilland DH9s which were available from March 1918, was the Hon. Alan Boyle, a son of the Earl of Glasgow and the brother of the late Hon. James Boyle, first husband of Lady Trenchard (Burke's *Peerage, Baronetage and Knightage*, London, 1959, pp. 1586, 2248, 937,

938, 251, 1461). Alan Boyle's sister, Viscountess Caldecote, was the sister-in-law of Sir John Inskip, Hilda Richardson's solicitor and executor who served as a lieutenant in the Royal Flying Corps from 1915 and later had dealings with Chebotarev over Hilda's will (PRONI D 1252/1A/155, Letter Books of Carleton Atkinson and Sloan, Solicitors, Portadown). This firm was deputed by Hilda Richardson's executor Sir John Inskip to act for him in Northern Ireland; Northern Ireland has a separate legal system from England and Sir John, as an English solicitor, was not qualified to act there. For Inskip see Burke's *Peerage, Baronetage and Knightage*, London, 1959, p. 1939; *Dictionary of National Biography*, London, vol. 2, p. 1549.

51 Bill Phillips gave me this detail on 29 October 1994. His source was Arthur Chapman, a leading Quaker and former Headmaster of Friends' School, Lisburn.

52 J. M. Bruce, *De Havilland Aircraft of World War One*, London, 1991, pp. 22–39.

53 These included the DH9, capable of carrying a load of over 1,100 pounds: ibid., pp. 94–5.

54 'The Tsarevich asked Kerensky, "Well then, can you tell me whether my father had the legal right to abdicate the throne in my name?" Kerensky's answer was, "From a strictly legal point of view such an abdication was not exactly legal." Alexei's reply was, "Thank you. That is all I wished to know."' From *The Fall of the Romanovs* by 'A Russian', London, 1918, p.139; repr. Cambridge, 1992, ed. Alan Wood.

55 Willi Korte in conversation with the author, 7 April 1994.

56 Jackson, *At War with the Bolsheviks*, p. 189.

57 Pipes, *Russia under the Bolshevik Regime*, pp. 427–33.


Chapter 11: *The Glory is Departed*

1 Letter to Anthony Summers from R. Bruce Lockhart, 6 November 1974: Romanov papers, in the collection of Anthony Summers, hereafter referred to as Summers Collection.

2 George A. Hill, *Go Spy the Land*, London, 1932, pp. 219–22, 228, 255–8.

3 Letters to Anthony Summers from Beatrice Alley, dated 22 July 1974; dated 28 February 1975; Summers Collection.

4 Letter from Commander Michael Peer-Groves, dated 24 January 1972, Summers Collection.

5 Transcript and tapes of an interview with Commander Michael Peer-Groves, Romanov File II, Roll One, A/2, Summers Collection.

6 Marc Ferro, *Nicholas II: The Last of the Tsars*, London, 1991, p. 267.

7 Burke's *Royal Families of the World*, vol. 1, London, 1977, p. 215.

8 Ferro, *Nicholas II*, p. 267; Burke's *Royal Families of the World*, vol. 1, p. 215.

9 R. Pipes, *The Russian Revolution 1899–1919*, London, 1990, p. 694.

10 Burke's *Royal Families of the World*, vol. 1, p. 184. See also Marquis de Ruvigny, *Titled Nobility of Europe*, London, 1914, pp. 553–4.

11 Ferro, *Nicholas II*, p. 242.

12 John Bradley, *Civil War in Russia 1917–1920*, London, 1975, p. 181.

13 Edvard Radzinsky, *The Last Tsar*, London, 1992, p. 256.
14 Ibid., pp. 256–9.
15 Ibid., p. 257.
16 Ibid., p. 258.
17 Viktor Alexandrov, *The End of the Romanovs*, London, 1966 pp. 206, 211, 212.
18 Ibid p. 212.
19 PRONI D 1943/1/3, 12 April 1918.
20 Leonard W. Taylor, *The Sourdough and the Queen*, London, 1983, p. 276 and plates.
21 Alexandrov, *The End of the Romanovs*, pp. 79–81.
22 Ibid p. 222.
23 Alexander Bokhanov et al., *The Romanovs: Love, Power, Tragedy*, London, 1993, p. 298.
24 Mark D. Steinberg and Vladimir Krustalev, *The Fall of the Romanovs*, New Haven, 1995, p. 215.
25 Charlotte Zeepvat, 'Helen of Serbia', *Royalty* magazine, June 1995, p. 61. When Princess Helen and Grand Duchess Elizabeth (Ella) arrived in Ekaterinburg they were told by Mrs Atamanov, with whom they lodged, that the Tsar, Tsarina and one daughter were there. They were also told Dr Derevenko was there practising medicine.
26 John F. O'Conor, *The Sokolov Investigation*, New York, 1971, p. 247.
27 Princess Eugénie de Grèce, *Le Tsarevich Enfant Martyr*, Paris, 1990, pp. 236–7.
28 Vladimir Kozlov and Vladimir Krustalev, ed. Robert Massie, *The Last Diary of the Tsaritsa Alexandra*, New Haven, 1997, p. 105.
29 Ibid., pp. 1–198.
30 Vladimir Kozlov and Vladimir M. Krustalev, *The Last Diary of Tsaritsa Alexandra*, ed. R. K. Massie, London, 1997, pp. 5, 8, 9, 200.
31 Lili Dehn, *The Real Tsaritsa*, London, 1922, pp. 136–7.
32 Alexandrov, *The End of the Romanovs*, pl. 39.
33 Radzinsky, *The Last Tsar*, p. 293; his source was the Chekist Rodzinsky.
34 O'Conor, *The Sokolov Investigation*, pp. 246–7.
35 Ibid., pp. 249–50.
36 Zeepvat, 'Helen of Serbia', p. 61.
37 Alexandrov, *The End of the Romanovs*, p. 80.
38 Pipes, *The Russian Revolution*, p. 767.
39 Eton School Lists, 1921, Upper Remove.
40 Small Downs House visitors' book.
41 Burke's *Peerage, Baronetage and Knightage*, London, 1959, p. 176; Burke's *Royal Families of the World*, vol. 1, p. 470.
42 Taylor, *The Sourdough and the Queen*, p. 181. Taylor mentions reports that Boyle met with the Tsar at this time.
43 Alix Hill in conversation with the author, 3 April 1998.
44 Andrei Maylaunas and Sergei Mironenko, *A Lifelong Passion: Nicholas and Alexandra, Their Own Story*, London, 1996, p. 558, Tsar's diary, 9 March 1917; p. 576, Pierre Gilliard's memoirs.
45 Alix Hill in conversation with the author, 3 April 1998.
46 Steinberg and Krustalev, *The Fall of the Romanovs*, p. 163.

47  Ibid., p. 168.

48  William Rodney, *Joe Boyle: King of the Klondike*, Toronto, 1974, pp. 212–14.

49  Zoe Cooke in conversation with the author, 9 March 1994.

50  PRONI D 1943/1/10 (D9a).

51  PRONI D 1943/1/10; the bill, dated 27 February 1919, was for a four-day stay.

52  Rodney, *Joe Boyle*, pp. 237, 239, diary of Queen Marie of Roumania, III/116, 12 March 1919, III/117, 29 March 1919.

53  Taylor, *The Sourdough and the Queen*, pp. 306–7.

54  PRONI D 1943/1/1, [September] 1918.

55  Taylor, *The Sourdough and the Queen*, p. 299.

56  Dehn, *The Real Tsaritsa*, p. 198.

57  Surviving handwritten manuscript for Nicholas Couriss' book on his service with the Volunteer Army, now in the author's possession. Given by Kathleen McCarthy.

58  Kathleen McCarthy in conversation with the author, 6 December 1997.

59  Radzinsky, *The Last Tsar*, p. 350.

60  Gregory P. Tschebotarioff, *Russia, My Native Land*, New York, 1964, p. 34; Dehn, *The Real Tsaritsa*, p. 89; Kathleen McCarthy in conversation with the author, 29 October 1997; Henry St George Smith in conversation with the author, 14 November 1997.

61  Jacques Ferrand, *Descendances naturelles des souverains et grands-ducs de Russie de 1769 à 1910*, Paris, 1995, p. 121.

62  Henry St George Smith in conversation with the author, 6 December 1997.

63  Kathleen McCarthy in conversation with the author, 15 April 1996.

64  Henry St George Smith in conversation with the author, 6 December 1997.

65  Ruvigny, *Titled Nobility of Europe*, pp. 1448–9; Ferrand, *Descendances naturelles*, p. 147.

66  Grand Duchess Marie of Russia, *Things I Remember*, London, 1930, p. 376.

67  Robert Ingham, *What Happened to the Empress*, Malta, 1949, pp. 53, 66.

68  Burke's *Landed Gentry of Great Britain*, London, 1972, pp. 906–11.

69  Guy Richards, *The Hunt for the Tsar*, London, 1972, pls 10, 11.

70  Kathleen McCarthy in conversation with the author, 15 April 1996.

71  Letter from Mrs McClenaghan, Ministry of Defence 91/39194/CS® 2b/6, 7 October 1991, to Dr Una Kroll, containing the service record of her father, Brigadier George Hill, DSO MC MBE P/80722.

72  Letter from Nicholas Couriss to S. Clarke, Secretary, Flax Production Committee, 19 February 1941, Irish military intelligence files G2/1882.

73  'Prince Paul Lieven, father, Latvian b. 24.9.1875, Russian, Engineer, 16 Avenue Emile Dermot, Brussels, Latvian Passport No. 003996K 20/6/38, Collon, 19/9/40, Collon', Irish military intelligence files G2/2611.

74  Radzinsky, *The Last Tsar*, pp. 304, 312, 322, 334–6, 349–50.

75  Pipes, *The Russian Revolution*, pp. 661–2.

76  Prince Leonid Pavlovich Lieven in conversation with the author, 18 August 1993.

77  The Tsarina actually wrote this in her diary on 16/29 April 1918. See Kozlov and Krustalev, *The Last Diary of the Tsaritsa Alexandra*, p. 116: 'The Omsk Sovdep wld not let us pass Omsk as feared one wished to take us to Japan.'

78  Pipes, *The Russian Revolution*, p. 370.
79  Obituary of Prince Alexander Lieven, *The Times*, 1 April 1988.
80  Kathleen McCarthy in conversation with the author, 15 April 1996.
81  Alexander Bokhanov et al., *The Romanovs*, pp. 28–9. This teenage love affair – Nikolai was only fifteen – is well documented. He confided to his diary, 'I am in love with Toria.' She never married.
82  Maylaunas and Mironenko, *A Lifelong Passion*, pp. 585–6, Lord Stamfordham to A. J. Balfour, 24 March 1918.
83  Summers and Mangold, *The File on the Tsar*, p. 251.
84  Small Downs visitors' book.
85  Obituary of Arthur Leverton-Harris, *The Times*, 18 November 1926.
86  Mervyn Fairclough, *The Ripper and the Royals*, London, 1994, pp. 190–2.
87  Alix Hill in conversation with the author, 2 January 1996.
88  James Blair Lovell wrongly attributes this scar to Anastasia in his book *Anastasia, the Lost Princess*, London, 1992, p. 93. The accident is described by Grand Duchess Olga, the Tsar's sister, in Ian Vorres' biography, *The Last Grand Duchess*, London, 1960, p. 178: 'It was Marie . . . who got her hand hurt rather badly and it did not happen in a carriage but on board the imperial train.' See also John Klier and Helen Mingay, *The Quest for Anastasia*, London, 1995, p. 157.
89  Alix Hill in conversation with the author, 2 January 1996.
90  Count A. A. Mosolov, *At the Court of the Last Tsar*, London, 1935, p. 164; Bokhanov et al., *The Romanovs: Love, Power, Tragedy*, London, 1993, p. 127.
91  Bokhanov et al., *The Romanovs*, pp. 127–9.
92  Alix Hill in conversation with the author, 2 January 1996.
93  Kathleen McCarthy in conversation with the author, 25 June 1996.
94  Ibid.
95  Zoe Cooke in conversation with the author, 15 April 1996.
96  Bridie Gorman and Kitty Geddis in conversation with the author, 24 November 1997.
97  Maylaunas and Mironenko, *A Lifelong Passion*, p. 458, letter from the Tsarina to the Tsar: 'I daily have my face electrified for a quarter of an hour – the pains are rare, only such a stiff feeling in the jaw – am sure is gouty.'

Chapter 12: *The Shoemaker*

1  Mara Gorbadovsky in conversation with the author, 4 April 1996.
2  Robert Ingham, *What Happened to the Empress*, Malta, 1949, p. 13.
3  Kenneth Rose, *King George V*, London, 1983, pp. 82–7; James Pope-Hennessy, *Queen Mary*, London, 1959, pp. 428–9.
4  Small Downs visitors' book.
5  Countess Ekaterina Petrovna Kleinmichel, 'The Departure of an Empress', in Misha Glenny and Norman Stone, eds, *The Other Russia*, London, 1990, pp. 160–6.
6  Letter from Nicholas Couriss to S. Clarke, Secretary, Flax Production Committee, 19 February 1941, Irish military intelligence files G2/1882; Gregory P. Tschebotarioff, *Russia, My Native Land*, New York, 1964, pp. 21–2, 279.

7  Tschebotarioff, *Russia, My Native Land*, pp. 279-80.
8  Zoe Cooke in conversation with the author, 9 March 1994.
9  Count A. A. Mosolov, *At the Court of the Last Tsar*, London, 1935, p. 51.
10  Tschebotarioff, *Russia, My Native Land*, p. 62.
11  Ibid., p. 57.
12  Ibid. pp. 190–8 and fig. 27. The Tsarina sent Sister Chebotarev a ham for Easter 1918.
13  Ibid., pp. 191, 201.
14  Ibid., p. 201.
15  Sonya Bill Robertson in conversation with the author, 12 November 1996.
16  Tschebotarioff, *Russia, My Native Land*, pp. 244–5, 3.
17  John F. O'Conor, *The Sokolov Investigation*, London, 1972, p. 246.
18  Vladimir A. Kozlov and Vladimir Krustalev, ed. Robert Massie, *The Last Diary of Tsaritsa Alexandra*, New Haven, 1997, p. 198, from the Tsarina's diary of 3/16 July 1918.
19  Anthony Summers and Tom Mangold, *The File on the Tsar*, London, 1976, p. 312.
20  Ingham, *What Happened to the Empress*, p. 61.
21  Ibid., pp. 66–7, Appendix B.
22  Alix Hill in conversation with the author, 11 November 1996.
23  Ibid.
24  Burke's *Peerage, Baronetage and Knightage*, London, 1959, p. 1406.
25  Marc Ferro, *Nicholas II: The Last of the Tsars*, London, 1991, p. 272.
26  *Thom's Directories*, London, for 1918, 1920, 1921; *Who Was Who*, vol. 4.
27  Guy Richards, *The Hunt for the Tsar*, London, 1972, p. 149.

## Chapter 13: *Rumours*

1  Iya Zmeova in conversation with the author, 28 June 1993.
2  Alexander Bokhanov et al., *The Romanovs: Love, Power, Tragedy*, London, 1993, p. 274.
3  Dame Elizabeth Hill in conversation with the author, 9 February 1996.
4  Tatiana Torporkov in conversation with Clare Selerie, April 1997.
5  W. A. Pinkney in conversation with the author, Hamilton, Ontario, 4 January 1995; Alix Hill in conversation with the author, 28 March 1996.
6  With the letters were: a silk handkerchief with the imperial crest in the imperial colours; a medal ribbon in the Russian national colours; two icon cards, one of which was of St Seraphim of Sarov; and a photograph of Dan Winter's cottage, where the Orange Order was founded, and which is a few miles from where the author grew up.
7  Letters from Archbishop Theophan to Nikolai Chebotarev, 22 May 1925, 6, 15 November 1925, 30 December 1925, 14 March 1926, 9 April 1926, 18 August 1926, 11 November 1927.
8  Letter from Archbishop Theophan to Nikolai Chebotarev, 8 March 1923.
9  Gregory P. Tschebotarioff, *Russia, My Native Land*, New York, 1964, pp. 191, 201.

10 Peter Kurth, *Anastasia*, London, 1983, pp. 213–68, 499; letters from Archbishop Theophan to Nikolai Chebotarev, 3 May 1924 (Krasnov's move to France) and 25 May 1924 (Krasnov invites Nikolai Chebotarev to France).

11 Letter from Archbishop Theophan to Nikolai Chebotarev, 9 April 1926.

12 Letter from Archbishop Theophan to Nikolai Chebotarev, 22 May 1925.

13 Letter from Archbishop Theophan to Nikolai Chebotarev, 14 March 1926.

14 Mara Gorbadovsky in conversation with the author, 1 April 1996; deposition, 4 April 1996.

15 Ibid.

16 Miss M. Eager, *Six Years at the Russian Court*, London, 1906, repr. Toronto, 1997; Kathleen McCarthy in conversation with the author, 15 April 1996.

17 Dame Elizabeth Hill and Princess Sophie Wachnadze in conversation with the author, 30 March 1996.

18 Mara Gorbadovsky in conversation with the author, 2 April 1996.

19 Letter from Archbishop Theophan to Nikolai Chebotarev, 6 November 1929.

20 *The Fall of the Romanovs* by 'A Russian', London, 1918, p. 139; repr. Cambridge, 1992, ed. Alan Wood.

21 Letters from Archbishop Theophan to Nikolai Chebotarev, 11/14 July 1922, 11 December 1927.

22 Stella Dalziel in conversation with the author, 15 January 1994.

23 T. R. Betts, 'Archbishop Theophan of Poltava 1873–1940', *Great Orthodox Hierarchs of the Nineteenth and Twentieth Centuries*, St George's Orthodox Information Service, London, 1995 (supplied by Andrew Bond), p. 191.

24 Greg King, *The Last Empress*, London, 1994, p. 185; Anna Vyrubova, *Memoirs of the Russian Court*, New York, 1923.

25 Maria Rasputin, *Rasputin: The Man Behind the Myth*, London, 1977, p. 151.

26 Nun Nectaria McLees, *A Gathered Radiance: The Life of Alexandra Romanov*, Chico, California, Valaam Society of America, 1992, p. 91.

27 Letter from Archbishop Theophan to Nikolai Chebotarev, 6/19 February 1931.

28 Mara Gorbadovsky in conversation with the author, 4 April 1996.

29 The author in conversation with staff at St David's Nursing Home, Sheringham, Norfolk, 1 July 1993.

30 The Orthodox priest who administered the last rites was Fr Patrick Hodgson of Dereham, Norfolk.

Chapter 14: *The Company He Kept*

1 Iya Zmeova in conversation with the author, 27 June 1993.

2 Burke's *Peerage, Baronetage and Knightage*, London, 1959, pp. 1406–7, 2365–6, 1396–8, 2005–6, 1065–8, 77–9; Gordon Waterfield, *Sir Percy Loraine: Professional Diplomat*, London, 1967.

3 Gwynne Thomas, *King Pawn or Black Knight*, Edinburgh, 1995, p. 74. Also Lady Mairi Bury, Lord Londonderry's daughter, and the present occupant of Mount-stewart, speaking on BBC2, *The Aristocracy 1919–45*, broadcast (rpt) on 3 August 1998.

4 A full list of aristocratic members of the Anglo-German Fellowship and the

Anglo-German Link is published in Nigel West, *MI5*, London, 1981, pp. 134–5.

5 Thomas, *King Pawn or Black Knight*, pp. 37, 40–1, 55–6.

6 *The Traitor King*, Hart/Ryan Productions for Channel Four Television, directed by David Hart and Nick Read. Historical advisers John Costello and Len Deighton. Broadcast 16 November 1995.

7 Burke's *Peerage, Baronetage and Knightage*, pp. 1406–7, 2191, 1391.

8 Ibid., pp. 77–9.

9 Burke's *Landed Gentry of Great Britain*, London, 1972, pp. 906–11.

10 Melvyn Fairclough, *The Ripper and the Royals*, London, 1994, pp. 78, 106, 115.

11 Nicholas Couriss papers in the possession of the author, given by Kathleen McCarthy.

12 *Almanack de Gotha*, London, 1914, p. 1121.

13 Thomas, *King Pawn or Black Knight*, pp. 12, 201, 203, 206; see also Michael Bloch, *Operation Willi*, London, 1984.

14 Thomas, *King Pawn or Black Knight*, pp. 114, 205, 206.

15 Marc Ferro, *Nicholas II: The Last of the Tsars*, London, 1991, p. 270. The proposals were discussed with the former Tsarist Foreign Minister Milyukov.

16 James Blair Lovell, *Anastasia, the Lost Princess*, London, 1992, pp. 198–9.

17 Zoe Cooke in conversation with the author, 21 April 1995.

18 Ibid.

19 Christopher McMullan in conversation with the author, 22 April 1995.

20 James McCartney in conversation with the author, 22 April 1995.

21 Zoe Cooke in conversation with the author, 21 April 1995.

22 Ibid.

23 James McCartney in conversation with the author, 22 April 1995. Further investigations revealed that Fergus McAuley, an associate of James McCartney, had met (in Auckland, New Zealand) the captain of the U-boat whose crew had come ashore. He was living in Australia. Apparently, German aristocrats (from Brandenburg) had attended a nearby boarding school and the whole area had been mapped out from the time of the German landings at Ringfad in the First World War. McCartney apparently had a confrontation with the Countess of Antrim. She refused him permission to play the national anthem, saying, 'We own Glenarm and we want no trouble.'

24 Lt-Col. John P. Duggan, Irish Army, RTE, *The Emergency*, directed by Justin McCarthy, Dublin, May 1996.

25 David O'Donohue, *Hitler's Irish Voices*, Belfast, 1998, pp. 44, 61, 106; Roisin ni Meare Vinard, interviewed on RTE, *The Emergency*, May 1996.

26 O'Donohue, *Hitler's Irish Voices*, pp. 40–4, 80–1, 99–104.

27 Sebastian Sebag Montefiore, *A Great Hatred*, Channel Four Television, 1998.

28 O'Donohue, *Hitler's Irish Voices*, pp. 22, 48, 140, 145–6, 149–52, 153–5, 166.

29 Ibid., p. 23. Also Roisin ni Meare Vinard, *The Emergency*.

30 Roisin ni Meara Vinard, *The Emergency*.

31 Kathleen McCarthy in conversation with the author, 15 April 1996.

32 Ibid.

33 Gregory P. Tschebotarioff, *Russia, My Native Land*, New York, 1964, pp. 301–8.

34 Letter from Archbishop Theophan to Nikolai Chebotarev, 25 May 1924; Tschebotarioff, *Russia, My Native Land*, p. 303.

35 Irish military intelligence files G2/2611 (2).
36 Ibid., G2/1882.
37 Kathleen McCarthy in conversation with the author, 15 April 1996.


Chapter 15: *The Irish Years*

1 Moyallon House visitors' book, 8 July 1936.
2 Albert Uprichard in conversation with the author, 24 June 1993.
3 Peggy Sinton in conversation with the author, 15 July 1993.
4 Zoe Cooke in conversation with the author, and deposition, 23 December 1996.
5 Zoe Cooke in conversation with the author, 21 April 1995.
6 John W. Kingston, *These Miracles Did Jesus in Ireland*, London, 1934, p. 96.
7 Moyallon House visitors' book, 3 July–6 September 1937. See also Jacques Ferrand, *Descendances naturelles des souverains et grands-ducs de Russie de 1762 à 1910*, Paris, 1995, pp. 112, 119.
8 Ferrand, *Descendances naturelles*, p. 118. See also James Blair Lovell, *Anastasia, the Lost Princess*, London, 1992, Appendix 1.
9 PRONI, Last Will and Testament of Hilda Sophie Richardson, 12 August 1942.
10 PRONI D 1252/1A/155, Letter Books of Carleton, Atkinson and Sloan, Solicitors, Portadown.
11 Hester and Netta Sterritt in conversation with the author, 10 June 1993.
12 Andrew Morton, *The Wealth of the Windsors*, London, 1993, pp. 73–6.
13 Ibid., pp. 88–90, 85.
14 Peter Kurth, *Anastasia*, London, 1983, p. 306.
15 William Clarke, *The Lost Fortune of the Romanovs*, London, 1994, pp. 111–12.
16 Ibid., pp. 165, 169.
17 Helene Aitov in conversation with the author, 1 April 1996.
18 Hester and Netta Sterritt in conversation with the author, 10 June 1993; Albert Uprichard in conversation with the author, 24 June 1993; Stella Dalziel in conversation with the author, 15 July 1993.
19 Zoe Cooke in conversation with the author, 9 March 1994.
20 Alix Hill in conversation with the author, 28 March 1996.
21 Zoe Cooke in conversation with the author, 21 April 1995.
22 Burke's *Peerage, Baronetage and Knightage*, London, 1959, pp. 466–8.
23 Hester and Netta Sterritt in conversation with the author, 10 June 1993.
24 Helene Aitov in conversation with the author, 1 April 1996.
25 PRONI, Last Will and Testament of Stephens Richardson, 1 July 1957. He left an estate valued at £36,255 (1957 values).
26 Information from Bill Phillips, 20 June 1993.
27 Hester and Netta Steritt in conversation with the author, 10 June 1993; Captain R. J. Mitchell in conversation with the author, 4 June 1993; Moyallon House visitors' book, 25 July–1 October 1934, 11 July 1935, 18 April–17 September 1935, 22 May–23 September 1937, January–30 August 1938, 4 May 1939. Died there 1943.
28 Hester and Netta Steritt in conversation with the author, 10 June 1993.

29 Zoe Cooke in conversation with the author, 21 April 1996. Cooke family papers, 'Origins of the Karauloff Family', by Natalie Cooke.
30 Count Kokovstev, *Out of My Past*, Stanford, 1933, Appendix.
31 Zoe Cooke in conversation with the author, 21 April 1995.
32 Burke's *Landed Gentry of Great Britain*, 1972, p. 592.
33 Zoe Cooke in conversation with the author, 21 April 1995; Robert Bruce Lockhart, *Memories of a British Agent*, London, 1932, pp. 262, 280, 323.
34 Zoe Cooke in conversation with the author, 21 April 1995.
35 Ibid.
36 Ibid.
37 Ibid.
38 Bridie Gorman and Kitty Geddis in conversation with the author, 24 November 1997.


Chapter 16: *The Mysteries Combine*

1 Zoe Cooke in conversation with the author, 21 April 1995.
2 Kathleen McCarthy in conversation with the author, 2 July 1995.
3 Alix Hill in conversation with the author, 2 January 1996.
4 The author in conversation with Mrs J. Pearson, Office of Population Censuses and Surveys, 21 January 1995, and with Birmingham Family Health, 12 April 1994.
5 The meeting with Frank Crummey took place on 8 August 1995; he provided me with certified copies of my late surrogate father's and mother's medical records.
6 The author's late surrogate father's brother and sister-in-law in conversation with the author, 21 June 1995.
7 Kathleen McCarthy in conversation with the author, 15 April 1996.
8 Medical Register, General Medical Council, London.
9 Henry St George Smith in conversation with the author, 29 October 1997. For the Eppel family, see Dermot Keogh, *Jews in Twentieth Century Ireland*, Cork, 1998, pp. 81, 212–16, 238, 241.
10 Irish military intelligence files G2/1882, 19 February 1941.
11 General Practitioners Register and List, Birmingham Family Health, Birmingham.
12 Certified copy of the medical record of the author's surrogate father, obtained from Central Services Agency, Belfast, 8 August 1995.
13 Irish military intelligence files G2/X/0797, Aliens List – Russians, marked 'Secret'.
14 The Royal College of Physicians in Ireland, The Royal College of Surgeons, Dublin.
15 Reported on the front page of the *Belfast News Letter*, 15 May 1997. Chester the cat from Killinchy, County Down, received a vote, much to the annoyance of Pat Bradley, the Chief Electoral Officer. 'He would be conservative by nature,' said his owner.
16 Rosa Frost in conversation with the author, 1 April 1997.

17 General Registry, London.
18 Letter from Dr Neave to Clare Selerie, research for present work, 20 March 1997.
19 Kathleen McCarthy in conversation with the author, 29 October 1997.
20 Ward Park, Bangor, County Down.


Chapter 17: *Marina*

1 The family relationships may be traced in Burke's *Royal Families of the World*, vol. 1, 1977, pp. 472–6, 325–8.
2 Helene Aitov in conversation with the author, 31 August 1993.
3 Sophia Watson, *Marina*, London, 1994, p. 51.
4 Mara Gorbadovsky in conversation with the author, 2 April 1996.
5 Zoe Cooke in conversation with the author, 23 July 1994.
6 Watson, *Marina*, p. 30.
7 Ibid., p. 62.
8 Zoe Cooke in conversation with the author, 23 July 1994.
9 Zoe Cooke in conversation with the author, 14 May 1994, deposition 23 December 1996.
10 Zoe Cooke in conversation with the author, 14 March 1994.
11 The Duke of Kent was the main intermediary between Baron Wilhelm de Ropp, the Nazi representative, and the British royal family. See Gwynne Thomas, *King Pawn or Black Knight*, Edinburgh, 1995, pp. 25–6.
12 Peter Thornton-Pett in conversation with the author, 23 March 1996.
13 Watson, *Marina*, pp. 87–8; Christopher Warwick, *George and Marina*, London, 1988, pp. 70–1.
14 Zoe Cooke in conversation with the author, 23 July 1994.
15 Bridie Gorman and Kitty Geddis in conversation with the author, 24 November, 9 December 1997.
16 Zoe Cooke in conversation with the author, 12 August 1994, deposition 23 December 1996.
17 Watson, *Marina*, pp. 51, 167–8.
18 Bridie Gorman in conversation with the author, 24 November 1997; Bridie Gorman and Kitty Geddis in conversation with the author, 9 December 1997.
19 *The Times*, Court and Personal, Princess Marina's official engagements, September 1946.
20 Bridie Gorman and Kitty Geddis in conversation with the author, 24 November, 9 December 1997.
21 *The Times*, Court and Personal, Princess Marina's official engagements, September 1946.
22 *The Times*, Court and Personal, Princess Marina's official engagements January–April 1947.
23 Watson, *Marina*, p. 192.
24 Ibid., p. 192.
25 Now in the author's possession, given by Zoe Cooke, 18 March 1994.
26 Burke's *Peerage, Baronetage and Knightage*, London, 1959, pp. 1406–7.

27 *The Times*, Court and Personal, 10 February 1946.
28 Mrs Natalie Basilievsky in conversation with the author, 3 August 1993.
29 Burke's *Royal Families of the World*, vol. 1, pp. 475-6, 325-7.
30 Nikolai Chebotarev's photograph album.
31 *Belfast Telegraph*, 21 April 1947; PRONI HAR/1G/7/2/28, Harbour Master's Entry Books for Berthing Vessels, Port of Belfast, 1947.
32 *Belfast Telegraph*, 22 April 1947.
33 Irish military intelligence files G2/1882, 19 February 1941.
34 At 4 p.m.: *Belfast Telegraph*, 22 April 1947.
35 Kathleen McCarthy in conversation with the author, 15 April 1996.
36 *Belfast Telegraph*, 24 April 1947.
37 Alix Hill in conversation with the author, 1, 2 September 1997.
38 Henry St George Smith in conversation with the author, 29 October 1997.
39 Kathleen McCarthy in conversation with the author, 15 April 1996.
40 PRONI HAR/1G/7/2/28, Harbour Master's Entry Book for Berthing Vessels; HAR/1F/2, Pilot's Log Books; HAR/1F/1. The Traffic and Navigation Committee. Books are missing for the period 1946-50 – the only ones missing in the entire history of the Port Authority.
41 Zoe Cooke, deposition 23 December 1996.
42 PRONI HAR/1F/2, Pilot's Log Books.
43 PRONI HAR/1F/2/28, Harbour Master's Entry Book for Berthing Vessels, and HAR/1F/2, Pilot's Log Books.
44 *The Times*, Court and Personal, Princess Marina's public engagements, May–June 1947.
45 Misha Viacheslav in conversation with the author, W. A. Pinkney and David Keough, 11 January 1995.
46 Prince Michael of Greece and Alan Palmer, *The Royal House of Greece*, London, 1990, pp. 89-91.
47 Watson, *Marina*, p. 219.
48 Ibid., p. 125; also Warwick, *George and Marina*, p. 136.
49 Michael Bloch, *The Duchess of Windsor*, London, 1996, pp. 209, 111.
50 Watson, *Marina*, p. 219; Sarah Bradford, *Elizabeth*, London, 1996, p. 291.
51 See Warwick, *George and Marina*, p. 156; Watson, *Marina*, pp. 224-5.
52 James Barrett in conversation with the author, 3 July 1996.
53 James Barrett in conversation with the author, 2, 3 July 1996.
54 Ibid.
55 See Melvyn Fairclough, *The Ripper and the Royals*, London, 1994, p. 207. It is alleged that the Tsarevich Nikolai Alexandrovich fathered King George V during an affair in Denmark in September 1864 with Queen Alexandra, wife of Edward VII. Burke's *Royal Families of the World*, vol. 1, p. 474, gives the date of the Tsarevich Nikolai's death as 24 April 1863. If this were so he could not have fathered George V, who was born on 3 June 1865. However, Jacques Ferrand, in *Romanov: un album de famille*, Paris, 1990, p. 25, gives the date of the Tsarevich Nikolai's death as 24 April 1865. If this were so, then he could be George V's father. Ferrand goes on to give details of the Tsarevich's movements in 1863-5, which included a visit to Denmark in September 1864.
56 *The Times*, 1 November 1947.

57 *The Times*, 25 October 1947.
58 Tim Heald, *The Duke: A Portrait of Prince Philip*, London, 1991: 'The wedding took place on 20 November 1947 preceded by two glittering parties at the Palace during which the Duchess of Kent fainted and the Duke of Devonshire was molested by a drunken Maharajah.'
59 Watson, *Marina*, p. 200.
60 James Barrett in conversation with the author, 4 July 1997.
61 *The Times*, Court and Personal, Princess Marina's public engagements, August 1947–April 1948.
62 *Daily Mirror*, 23 December 1997; *Daily Telegraph*, 22 December 1997.

## Chapter 18: *The Chain of Custody*

1 Alix Hill in conversation with the author, 21 July 1993.
2 Bridie Gorman and Kitty Geddis in conversation with the author, 9 December 1997.
3 Irish military intelligence files G2/2611.
4 Burke's *Peerage, Baronetage and Knightage*, London, 1959, pp. 1924–6.
5 Burke's *Landed Gentry of Great Britain*, London, 1972, p. 703.
6 Ibid. See also Burke's *Peerage, Baronetage and Knightage*, pp. 747, 2050.
7 Burke's *Landed Gentry of Great Britain*, p. 703.
8 Thomas and Mary Clarke, Waringstown, in conversation with the author, 11 November 1996.
9 Burke's *Irish Family Records*, London, 1982, pp. 748–55.
10 Moyallon House visitors' book, 9 May 1940.
11 Zoe Cooke in conversation with the author, 18 May 1995.
12 Burke's *Peerage, Baronetage and Knightage*, p. 720.
13 William McDonald in conversation with the author, 2 July 1995.
14 Zoe Cooke in conversation with the author, 21 April 1995.
15 Kathleen McCarthy in conversation with the author, 2 July 1995.
16 Obituary of Maureen, Marchioness of Dufferin, *The Times*, 4 May 1998; Burke's *Peerage, Baronetage and Knightage*, pp. 719–20.
17 Baroness Agnes de Stoeckl, *My Dear Marquis*, London, 1952, p. 49.
18 Zoe Cooke in conversation with the author, 21 April 1995.
19 Zoe Cooke in conversation with the author, 23 December 1995.
20 Chips Channon noted this in his diary in 1947. See Sophia Watson, *Marina*, London, 1994, pp. 199–200.
21 Iya Zmeova in conversation with the author, 28 June 1993.
22 Zoe Cooke in conversation with the author, 21 April 1995. The clergyman with whom he stayed was Canon L'Estrange, St John's Malone, Belfast.
23 Zoe Cooke began the search for this box. In Natalie's bank in Bangor, County Down, she was told that it was not there, and that someone else had been searching for it six months earlier – someone not from the family. The bank would tell her no more.

## Chapter 19: *Royal Reaction*

1  Burke's *Irish Family Records*, London, 1982, p. 988.
2  Burke's *Royal Families of the World*, vol. 1, London, 1977, pp. 457–8.
3  Burke's *Peerage, Baronetage and Knightage*, London, 1959, pp. 376–7.
4  Ibid., pp. 681–5; Zoe Cooke in conversation with the author, 23 December 1996.
5  *Belfast Telegraph*, 5 October 1993, 'Secret Life of the Hero shot Dead in Moscow'.
6  Burke's *Peerage, Baronetage and Knightage*, p. 376; Burke's *Landed Gentry of Ireland*, London, 1980, p. 592.
7  Burke's *Peerage, Baronetage and Knightage*, pp. 681–5.
8  This occurred on 4 June 1995. Meetings with the two operatives then followed between 4 June and 4 November 1995.
9  Conversation on 14 August 1995.
10 At a meeting on 15 August 1995.
11 Conversations with author, 14, 20 September 1995.
12 Press conference, 5 October 1994. See John Klier and Helen Mingay, *The Quest for Anastasia*, London, 1995, p. 227; Robert Massie, *The Romanovs: The Final Chapter*, London, 1995, p. 239.
13 The telephone call took place on 23 September 1995.


## Appendix: *The Windsors and the Money*

1  W. Rodney, *Joe Boyle: King of the Klondike*, Toronto, 1974, pp. 192–3. See also George A. Brinkley, *The Volunteer Army and Allied Intervention in South Russia 1917–1921*, Notre Dame, 1966, p. 29; Public Record Office, Kew, PRO FO 371/3283.
2  William Clarke, *The Lost Fortune of the Tsars*, London, 1994, p. 179.
3  Ibid., pp. 179–80.
4  Ibid., p. 180. See also V. I. Sirotkin, *Russia's Gold and Real Estate Abroad and International Relations*, Moscow, 1997, p. 259.
5  Clarke, *The Lost Fortune of the Tsars*, p. 109.
6  Ibid., p. 111.
7  Andrew Morton, *The Wealth of the Windsors*, London, 1997, p. 177.
8  Ian Vorres, *The Last Grand Duchess*, London, 1960, p. 181.
9  Clarke, *The Lost Fortune of the Tsars*, p. 1623.
10 Vorres, *The Last Grand Duchess*, pp. 182–3.
11 Clarke, *The Lost Fortune of the Tsars*, pp. 164–5, citing Sir Frederick Ponsonby, *Recollections of Three Reigns*, London, 1951.
12 Clarke, *The Lost Fortune of the Tsars*, p. 164.
13 Ibid., p. 165. See also Vorres, *The Last Grand Duchess*, p. 183.
14 Clarke, *The Lost Fortune of the Tsars*, pp. 166–7.
15 Ibid., p. 168.
16 Ibid.
17 Vorres, *The Last Grand Duchess*, p. 183.

18  Clarke, *The Lost Fortune of the Tsars*, pp. 168–9.

19  Morton, *The Wealth of the Windsors*, pp. 172–5.

20  Ibid.

21  Clarke, *The Lost Fortune of the Tsars*, p. 168.

22  Ibid., p. 220, citing *Letters of the Tsaritsa to the Tsar 1914–17*, London, 1923.

23  Clarke, *The Lost Fortune of the Tsars*, p. 225.

24  Ibid., pp. 264–7.

25  Ibid., pp. 222–4.

26  Peter Kurth, *Anastasia*, London, 1983, p. 306.

27  Clarke, *The Lost Fortune of the Tsars*, p. 257.

28  Ibid., p. 254.

29  Ibd., pp. 207–8.

30  Ibid., p. 200.

31  Ibd., p. 179.

32  Ibid., p. 220.

33  Sirotkin, *Russia's Gold*, p. 260.

34  Ibid., p. 260.

35  Ibid., p. 261.

36  Ibid., p. 260.

37  Edward Radzinsky, *The Last Tsar*, London, 1992, p. 139.

38  Kurth, *Anastasia*, p. 308; Clarke, *The Lost Fortune of the Tsars*, p.181; sworn statement of Lili Dehn, 23 September 1955, Hamburg.

39  Kurth, *Anastasia*, pp. 434–5.

40  Sirotkin, *Russia's Gold*, pp. 273–4.

41  The *Sunday Times* reported on 24 September 1995 that Prince Philip had claimed to be the 'legal heir' to the Sergei Palace in West Jerusalem. Situated in 'one of the city's most desirable districts', the newspaper said, its 'value for commercial redevelopment' was 'as high as £50 million'. This claim by Prince Philip was, according to the *Sunday Times*, directly in opposition to the Russian government, which also claimed the building.

## PHOTOGRAPHIC CREDITS

The majority of the photographs in this book come from the author's collection; of these most came from Nikolai Chebotarev's own album. Photographs from the imperial archive, which are assumed to be out of copyright, are sourced from the following volumes: *Nicholas and Alexandra: the Family Albums*, ed. Prince Michael of Greece; *The Romanovs: Love, Power and Tragedy*, by Alexander Bokhanov et al.; *Royal Russia: Private Albums of the Russian Imperial Family*, ed. Carol Townend; *Romanoff: un album de famille* by Jacques Ferrand; *Descendances naturelles des souverains et grands-ducs de Russie de 1762 à 1910* by Jacques Ferrand. Other photographs came from: *Joe Boyle: King of the Klondike* by W. Rodney; *The Sourdough and the Queen: the Many Lives of Klondike Joe Boyle* by Leonard W. Taylor; *The Duchess of Kent: an Intimate Portrait* by Jennifer Ellis; *Go Spy the Land: Being the Adventures of I.K.8 of the British Secret Service* by Capt. G. A. Hill; *Richard Meinertzhagen, Soldier, Scientist and Spy* by Mark Cocker; *Russia, My Native Land* by Gregory P. Tschebotarioff; *What Happened to the Empress?* by R. Ingham. The photographs of Bangor, Castlebellingham, Moyallon and Kathleen McCarthy were taken by Mike Petty; that of Alix Hill by the author's son Simon. If any copyrights have inadvertently been infringed the copyright holders should contact the publisher in the first instance.

# Index